DEEP

COMMUNITY

ADVENTURES IN THE
MODERN FOLK underground

"As a source book, it's a prize."

"Writers who are comfortable with the genre of folk are few and valuable.
Alarik's sensitivity to the folk community and his ability to present their voices in
literate and heartfelt terms are most welcome."
Noel Paul Stookey (of Peter, Paul & Mary) – THE BOSTON GLOBE

. . . .

"An essential primer to the continuing folk revival."

"Highly recommended to anyone remotely interested in American music, folk, and the music industry."
Dave Szatmary – THE LIBRARY JOURNAL

. . . .

"If someone approached me wanting to know more about
this music that I love so dearly, I would buy that friend
a copy of Deep Community."

"…the scores of Robert Corwin's black and white photos are worth the price of admission."
Rich Warren – SING OUT! THE FOLK MUSIC MAGAZINE

. . . .

"An impressive—no, make that essential—collection of
writing from one of America's most astute music critics
and chroniclers."

**Earle Hitchner, music columnist for the IRISH ECHO and contributing
music writer to THE WALL STREET JOURNAL**

. . . .

"I'm treating it like a box of superb chocolates."

"I read one or two segments a night as a treat, hoping to make it last longer…
I recommend it without reservation."
Music fan **Jack Murray**

DEEPCOMMUNITY

ADVENTURES IN THE
MODERN FOLK underground

SCOTT ALARIK

WITH PHOTOGRAPHS BY ROBERT CORWIN

BLACK WOLF PRESS

ACKNOWLEDGEMENTS

No art is created in isolation. This is why arts awards shows always go on too long. So, while I have at least as many people to thank as are included in this book, I will do that on my own time, not yours.

There are a few folks who must be acknowledged here, beginning with Black Wolf Press, Ralph Jaccodine, Lisa Fehl-Parrette, John MacNeil, and Ellis Paul, without whose support this book would not have been possible. Of course, I must thank *The Boston Globe* for having the vision to see this music as a permanent part of New England's cultural landscape, and allowing me the privilege of covering it for so many years. I especially want to acknowledge those who first brought me into the *Globe,* and taught me how to do this job: Jeff McLaughlin, who all but created the folk beat for the *Globe,* Jan Shepherd, Steve Morse, and Ellen Clegg.

Sing Out! deserves all folk lovers' gratitude for being there so long, mine for the pleasure of writing for it. My thanks to Marc Schechtman, Ted Gartland, Dar Williams, and Pete Seeger for their special help on this project; to David Perry for the smart design that makes this book feel just the way the modern folk world does. And of course, to Robert Corwin for his photographs —my words could not be in better company.

—Scott Alarik

Deep Community: Adventures in the modern folk underground.

©2003 Scott Alarik

Black Wolf Press
PO Box 381982
Cambridge MA 02239
(617) 441-3808
contact: Ralph Jaccodine

www.blackwolfpress.com

Design:
David Perry for Sing/Song Books
64 Plains Road
New Paltz, NY 12561

www.singsongbooks.com

ISBN 0-9720270-1-7
BWP 00002

TABLE OF CONTENTS

TABLE OF CONTENTS

TABLE OF CONTENTS

TABLE OF CONTENTS

TABLE OF CONTENTS

TABLE OF CONTENTS

TABLE OF CONTENTS

TABLE OF CONTENTS

AUTHOR'S INTRODUCTION

At a time when the mainstream music industry is in historic decline, the small, substream world of folk music is thriving as never before. Why? This book attempts to answer that question by looking across the vast, rich landscape that is folk music today.

Though a few folk stars and records occasionally nose above the radar of mainstream music, this is not a genre driven by, or dependent upon, prevailing trends. Folk music today is a sturdy, grassroots world of career performers, community venues, independent record labels, radio shows, shops, and businesses run by people who are, first and foremost, fans.

I don't think there has ever been a book quite like this, one that views the modern folk world the same way its fans do. Typically, folk books come in two types: anthropological or historical studies of specific genres, such as bluegrass, blues, Celtic; or biographies of stars that examine particular eras (usually the '60s) through their lives.

This is not a book about bygone days. It presents a vitally modern, forward-looking music form that is thriving precisely because it remains in a constant state of reinvention. Folk is a music with a history, to be sure, but hardly a music of the past.

The stories here are primarily drawn from articles of mine published over the past 10 years in *The Boston Globe* and *Sing Out! The Folk Music Magazine*. The book travels as folk fans do, darting from Celtic bands to folk-pop songwriters, bluegrass divas to folk-rock pioneers, old-time fiddlers to cutting-edge radical troubadours; from sprawling festival to cozy coffeehouse, grand concert hall to Irish pub.

Today's hottest stars are here, including Alison Krauss, Ani DiFranco, Dar Williams, Ellis Paul, Solas, Chris Thomas King, Kate Rusby, Altan, Eliza Carthy, Vance Gilbert, Nickel Creek, the Waifs, Eileen Ivers, Richard Shindell, Guy Davis, Lori McKenna, and Eddie from Ohio. Many of folk's most enduring stars are also profiled: Pete Seeger, Joan Baez, Emmylou Harris, Judy Collins, Utah Phillips, Shawn Colvin, Nanci Griffith, Chris Smither, Greg Brown, Suzanne Vega, Ewan MacColl, Lead Belly Ledbetter, Dave Alvin, Mary Black, Martin Carthy, Maddy Prior, Holly Near, Ronnie Gilbert, the Klezmer Conservatory Band, Gordon Bok, and Bill Morrissey.

But it would not tell the whole story of folk music today, and how it survives in a commercially-driven culture that all but ignores it, without also focusing on the behind-the-scenes people who keep the music's fires banked through good times and bad, revivals and droughts. There are profiles of savvy, devoted activists who tend the business of folk music day to day, year to year, and era to era: concertmakers and independent record labels, coffeehouse volunteers and high-tech professionals who use the latest information technology to allow folk performers to bypass the heedless superhighways of the mainstream music industry, and build stable, permanent careers.

This book should not be taken as a "best of" compilation. While many of folk's biggest stars are profiled, my work has been inevitably informed by the serendipity of a daily newspaper. Some artists and folk businesses who deserve to be included in any encyclopedia of the music are not here, simply because I've not yet had the opportunity to write about them.

But Boston is a vital center for the music today, some would say its most vital center, and it offers a fine opportunity to show how this genre really exists. The stories here were selected with that in mind. All of them, I think, have some lasting tale to tell beyond the allure of the stars, or the fun of peeking behind the stage curtains.

The stories are presented essentially as they were originally published. Specific concert information was deleted, but they have not been otherwise updated. The idea is to capture moments as they happened, just as Robert Corwin does so wonderfully in his photographs. Place names are in Massachusetts, unless otherwise noted.

One reason people have trouble grappling with the idea of folk music today is that the term refers to two distinct, though overlapping, things. One is the music itself, tracing back into tradition, and including all the music that was passed orally from generation to generation by the common folk who gave the form its name. Folk was the label given to all the music made by ordinary people as they worked, played, worshipped, marked the passing years, lived and loved: the self-made soundtrack to their daily lives.

But today, the term folk music also refers to a modern performance and recording genre. It evolved in response to the arrival of radio and records in the first half of the 20th century. This new, mass technology made it possible for ordinary people—the folk—to have their own professionally made music, and to create their own music stars. The term popular music actually once meant the same thing as folk music, the music of the people. It was adapted in the early 1900s to describe this new form of professionally-made music aimed at ordinary people, and its name soon shortened from popular to pop.

Around that same time, the term folk music began to be used to describe a genre of professional performing and recording artists who emerged from, or adhered to, that older form of musical expression. As it exists today, that genre remains rooted in the older form, whether by artists who continue to play in traditional styles, or by modern songwriters who seek to write about authentic life experiences in more honest, closely observed, and intimate ways than mainstream pop usually does.

As a professional folk singer, I was ambivalent about the precision of these definitions. When I became a journalist specializing in covering folk music, I no longer had that luxury. I had to use words my readers understood. I came to rely on both definitions of folk music as they are understood by people both within the folk world and outside it. In writing about the old, orally transmitted music, I tend to substitute the word "traditional" whenever possible, or to simply call it traditional folk music.

But I think we are basically stuck with folk music as the label for the contemporary genre that grew from that older traditional form. Like it or not —and many folk people today do not—it is the term by which the majority of people today correctly identify what connects the modern songwriter to the blues singer, the Celtic group to the salsa band.

It is the only term I know that includes everything that should be included. Roots music tends to leave out too many contemporary—and international—folk forms. Acoustic music leaves out too many electrified forms, such as zydeco and Chicago blues. Vernacular music leaves out too many urban and modern folk hybrids, such as progressive bluegrass and the contemporary songwriter. That is not to say those terms are not helpful in describing the music that fits within their boundaries. But folk music is also the only term that gives us room to describe those vibrant, important artists who cross all boundaries, who mix old and new, urban and rural, electric and acoustic, traditional and original, international and domestic; and yet remain tied, in some way, to the best aesthetics and instincts of tradition.

Folk music is simply the most useful term I have found to describe the entire genre as it exists today; it is almost universally understood as a description of the kind of music presented in this book, and found on the stages of coffeehouses and folk festivals throughout the world.

No modern music form has suffered more than folk from the fickle, careless, often bullying whims of our increasingly corporatized pop culture, and yet no form has prospered more by finding new, adventurous, and profoundly human ways to grow through the cracks of that culture. This book looks deep into those cracks, down the avenues where folk intersects with the fast, dangerous streets of the pop industry; and down the smaller, surer backroads where this real-life, human-sized music has always thrived, where it continues to plant the deep roots of community—and to sing the songs of that community.

Scott Alarik
Cambridge, Massachusetts, 2003

'Sometimes reporters will ask me if I think this is a viable career, and that always gets me mad. I'll say, `Viable? How many rock bands can you name from the '70s that are still working?' —Garnet Rogers

How is a modern folk star measured?
Garnet Rogers, Greg Brown, Nerissa and Katryna Nields

How is a modern folk star measured? If the standard music-industry yardsticks are used—hits, commercial radio airplay, presence on a major record label—folk music would seem a puny, almost extinct genre. But the scores of vibrant folk venues that dot the New England landscape as never before, even during the height of the '60s revival, suggest that is hardly the case.

In such a substream, grass-rootsy, stubbornly non-commercial world, success is charted differently; and by those yardsticks, Canadian songwriter Garnet Rogers is among the most significant folk stars working today.

So how does he measure success?

"Sometimes reporters will ask me if I think this is a viable career, and that always gets me mad," he says. "I'll say, `Viable? How many rock bands can you name from the '70s that are still working? The '80s, the '90s? I've been doing this full time, making a good living, supporting a family, for over 25 years. How many rock stars can say that?"

Rogers has never been on a major label; in fact, he regularly turns down offers from Canadian majors, and has released all nine of his solo CDs on his own Snow Goose Records. He does 100 to 125 dates a year, and his management company, Fleming Tamulevich & Associates, estimates that more than 75 percent of them are return appearances at venues he has played regularly for years.

Rogers's favorite business axiom is from legendary raconteur Utah Phillips: "There are no career moves in folk music."

"The way I take that is not as a self-deprecating crack that you can't have a career in folk music," he says, "but that this is not a career-driven field in the same way commercial music is. You're part of a community, and playing music just happens to be your job in that community."

Rhode Island folk-popsters Nerissa and Katryna Nields have enjoyed success in both rock and folk, but recently pared their band down to a coffeehouse-friendly duo. Katryna Nields said they love the energy of a good rock club such as the Paradise, but that what the folk world offered ultimately meant more to them.

"Nerissa and I always felt very comfortable in the folk world," she says. "It's a wonderful community, a wonderful circuit of nice places to play. We played places with the band where we were going on at 11:30 at night on a Tuesday, in the kinds of clubs where there's no door on the bathroom. That just got very bleak for me; it wasn't how I wanted to spend my life.

"The folk world allows a person to be a professional musician without dealing with the mainstream music industry. That doesn't mean that everyone decides to go that path, but the opportunity is there if you want it. So I get to have a sane, ordinary life, with a family and a garden and friends and neighbors; and at the same time, I get to make my living singing. I can't think of anything luckier than that."

Iowa songwriter Greg Brown is, like Rogers, a lifer on the circuit, with more than 20 years as one of the country's most popular folk headliners. In fact, his recent struggle has been to cut down the number of shows he does, from Rogers's level to about 40 shows a year. He is just ending a yearlong sabbatical from performing, and says it never occurred to him to worry that such a long absence could adversely affect his career.

"The thing about this little folk world is that I have relationships with a lot of my promoters," he says. "They've become friends over the years, so I knew they'd give me a shot when I came back. That's the nice thing about folk music; if you stick with it, and you're lucky, and you love what you're doing, you can make your living doing this as long as you want to."

The mature contentment of a secure artist shimmers through every note of Rogers's gorgeous new CD, "Firefly." Unlike so many artfully brooding songwriters today, he sings about the quiet joys of a settled-down life. Most of his new songs take place on the Ontario farm he shares with his wife of 21 years, Gail Rogers; and he displays a rare gift for writing passionately about the pleasures of such lasting love.

He says he hotly resents those who regard the folk world as a throughway to some other stardom. "If you see the folk clubs as a stepping stone to somewhere else, you don't belong in them. This has been my community my whole life; why would I want to lose that? If I moved on to larger halls, I'd lose that sense of walking into a roomful of friends and neighbors, sharing a night out with them in that kind of community setting.

"Folk music is about real life; that's its form and function. I don't have to write hits, don't have to worry about things like that. My audiences have proven to me over the years—and this is still extraordinary to me—that they will allow me to do whatever I want. I wrote a song on my last album for a friend's wedding, and I've had over 50 people come up to me and say they sang it at their wedding or a friend's wedding. That's what you look for, a song that people take into their own lives, shape for their own use. That's a hit in this world."

—January 25, 2002

Why the pop music industry is ignoring folk music— and why that may be good news

Emmylou Harris, Gillian Welch, Joan Osborne, Emily Saliers of Indigo Girls, Patty Larkin, John Schoenberger of Radio & Records magazine

Is the mainstream music industry making itself irrelevant? On the surface, it seems an absurd question about an industry that, last year alone, earned more than $10.4 billion, according to the National Association of Recording Merchandisers. But if, as the music world likes to say, today's fringe is tomorrow's mainstream, there are signs of trouble on the horizon.

For a growing number of commercially successful stars, the machinery of mainstream music, especially commercial radio, has grown largely irrelevant, both artistically and professionally.

Emmylou Harris, for example, is among country music's most durable and respected stars. She proudly calls herself "the poster child for life after radio," and did not even bother to send her critically acclaimed new Nonesuch CD, "Red Dirt Girl," to commercial country radio for consideration.

"More people are putting records out on their own and doing very well," she said. "They're building careers that don't require the record-company machinery. It's like the commercials where people are interviewing big banks and turning down offers, because they can pick and choose banks on the Internet. Artists are increasingly saying to labels, 'Well, what can you give us? With digital recording now, we can record in our house, sell records on the Internet, and we don't really need you.'"

Even as record sales have remained strong, overall radio listenership has declined 15 percent in the past seven years, according to the Arbitron national ratings.

Last year, Edison Media Research did an extensive survey for the Country Radio Seminar on why that format is suffering an even more severe decline. Country record sales are down 11 million since 1994, and radio listenership during that period dropped 28 percent. What they found should disturb not just country-music moguls, but anyone in mainstream music.

The number of listeners is declining, and the sameness of the music is seen as a major reason; the number of songs that made the Top 15 in the Contemporary Hit Radio format dropped from 137 in 1990 to 117 in 1999. The number of artists on CHR's Top 15 in that same period dropped from 91 to 51. When it comes to country radio, the numbers were more startling: 146 songs on the Top 15 in 1990, 94 in 1999, with the number of artists dropping from 64 to 47.

Harris cited hot country-folk duo Gillian Welch and David Rawlings as artists whose music she loves (she recorded Welch's "Orphan Girl") but for whom she believes a major-label career would be a big mistake. She was delighted when she heard they had turned down several major-label offers, choosing instead to start their own label, Acony, on which Welch has released a wonderfully raw, earthy CD called "Time (the Revelator)."

"I didn't start a label because I had any burning desire to get more involved in the industry," Welch explained, "but I am interested in making records. There's a lot of stuff going on at the major labels right now that makes it harder to do that. For one thing, they keep getting bought and sold and conglomerated, and every time that happens, artists get shifted around, and you pretty much lose a year, at least. So strangely, the world of the major labels looks less stable now than the indie world."

Joan Osborne could tell Welch a thing or two about losing career time while labels reconfigure and conglomerate. In 1997, she was the darling of Mercury Records, coming off her multiplatinum CD "Relish" and its gargantuan worldwide hit single "One of Us." Then Mercury was bought by the Universal Music Group, and she found herself starting all over again.

"When I was first at Mercury, it was a great spot to be," she said. "But it was a very different culture when I brought them what was to be my second record. I guess they just didn't hear something they thought they could make a quarterly report to their stockholders about. But why they let me go is something I still don't completely understand. I was just faced with a situation and had to circumvent it to keep doing what I do."

Osborne landed on her feet, signing with Interscope last year and releasing the blues-laced "Righteous Love." During the nearly three years the label change took out of her then-sizzling career, she started her own online magazine, Heroine (heroinemag.com), and produced an Alligator CD for R&B legends the Holmes Brothers. Discussing the lowered expectations her new CD met, she sounded positively relieved.

I was aiming for a Tom Waits sort of cult career," she said, "connecting with enough people that the record companies would keep putting my music out, but not selling so much that there would be somebody standing over you telling you how to do it next time. That seemed the perfect balance; hopefully it will happen during this post-hit-single phase I seem to be in now."

In other words, the mistake Osborne made was to become a big moneymaker for her label. She congratulated artists such as Aimee Mann and Welch for starting their own labels, and is clearly reassured to know that option is open to her. She also mentioned the Indigo Girls, still with Epic after 13 years, as proof of what a hard thing major-label success is to maintain.

Does Emily Saliers of the Indigo Girls think they would get a major-label contract today?

"No way," she said. "We're not even a blip on Epic's radar screen anymore. There's really no loyalty in the record business today. Jobs are shifting; there's so much pressure to just get hit makers out there, and there's no such thing as building or nurturing a band's career anymore. Most of the people I know who have major-label record contracts are pretty beleaguered by the bleak landscape, particularly of radio."

Radio & Records magazine is the radio industry's primary trade paper. John Schoenberger, the magazine's editor for the Adult Album Alternative format, sees the industry creating a double-edged sword through radio's narrowing playlists and the big labels' shrinking talent rosters.

One blade is the growing number of big stars leaving major labels for the indie world, such as Mann and Dolly Parton, who is happily making bluegrass records for indie Sugar Hill. The other blade cuts even deeper at the industry's prestige, with more and more acts, such as Dave Matthews and Train, building hugely successful careers on their own, then signing independent deals with major labels who have invested nothing in those careers and to whom the artists owe nothing.

He said if the trend continues, he thinks the mainstream music industry may go the way of the Hollywood studio system.

More and more, the major film houses have become manufacturing and distribution centers," he said. "They forge deals with the entrepreneurs actually making the films, who use them only for distribution and marketing. I think you're going to see that more and more, with the big five labels letting artists develop on their own, then forging deals with them for production and distribution. They're not going to be the talent brokers; they're going to let artists develop on their own."

For genres like folk, this double-edged sword is a double blessing. The migration of major stars to the indies adds enormously to those labels' visibility, respectability, and cash flow. As more artists achieve stardom on their own, that once-crucial major-label cachet becomes less important.

Finally, as commercial radio loses listeners, more people are finding other ways to satisfy their musical tastes. Edison Research found that fewer than 50 percent of consumers today cite radio as the place they find out about CDs they purchase.

Of all Edison's statistics, the most revealing—and encouraging—may be the tally of what kind of music is purchased most by the key demographic of those between 25 and 34 years old. Rock came in only second, with 16 percent; country and alternative tied for third at 12 percent. And number one? The segment labeled "Other"—meaning 19 percent of purchasers listening to folk, world, jazz, classical, and other nonmainstream musics.

"My theory is that everything that is happening outside the mainstream is good," said Patty Larkin, a Vanguard recording star and longtime New England folk fave. "Everything the majors and commercial radio do now is so business-driven, and all that music is aimed at people who are 10 and 11 years old. They're creating this teenage monster baby that is less and less appealing to people who really love music.

What I'm finding is that people of all ages are seeking out alternatives to mainstream music. And you don't have to work very hard to get off the beaten track before you find out how much great music there really is out there. I don't think the industry is going to be able to control every single aspect of success anymore."

—July 29, 2001

Dar Williams: *Her battle cry of kindness*

Dar Williams is growing up. That thought will cross most listeners' minds at some point during the New England songwriter's long-awaited new CD, "The Green World," her first solo work since 1997's breakthrough "End of the Summer." In between, she formed the hugely successful songwriter ensemble Cry Cry Cry with Richard Shindell and Lucy Kaplansky; moved from Northampton to a house she bought in New York's Hudson Valley; and changed management from Young/Hunter, who handle Shindell and Chris Smither, to AGF, the New York firm that launched the careers of Suzanne Vega and Shawn Colvin.

"The Green World" (Razor & Tie) is a typically sharp-minded, tenderhearted masterpiece from Williams, 33, who may be the finest folk songwriter of her generation. As her fans know, she has been growing up on her previous three discs: part of her appeal is the uncompromising honesty with which she lets us glimpse, through her, all the painful, joyful, graceful, and bumbling inner journeys of growing up a woman in modern America. But "The Green World," more than ever before, finds her coming to terms with coming of age.

There is a recurring theme of accepting the world as it is, not as we would like it to be; but that acceptance is presented as a call to arms, never a surrender. With the ebullient strut of the opening cut, "Playing to the Firmament," she warns against the dangers of growing up too much to savor the wild innocence of the green world around us: "What's the rush? Dip your brush into this twilight / There are leaves upon the skylight / Trace your hand, trace your hand."

Even in the toughest, most searingly intimate ballads, moments of anguish and deep depression find quiet resolution through a simple acceptance of our imperfect selves and of the imperfect world swirling around us.

"I think in my 20s, I thought that religion and spiritual practice meant doing things right," she says. "Now I think it's about realizing you can't do everything right, and figuring out how you're going to live with the fact that you're going to fall short. That's where you find grace and unconditional love; not because you did all these perfect actions to deserve it, but because you are. That kind of understanding of being a flawed person looking at religion, not a person running to catch up with her better self, reawakened a lot of the spiritual texts I had read while studying religion in college."

Williams majored in religion and theater at Wesleyan University in Middletown, Conn., and the two wrestled for her attention until she discovered the subterranean folk scene while living in Boston in the mid-1980s. Through it, she found a way to honor both muses as a dramatically potent, spiritually incisive songwriter.

The CD title is a theater term describing one of the two worlds in William Shakespeare's plays. There is the court world, where most of his historical dramas and tragedies are set. Then there is the green world, the wild, fey forests of "A Midsummer Night's Dream" and "As You Like It." She takes that magic place—which seems anarchic to outsiders, but has its own rules and hierarchies—and uses it as imagery for what she calls "the chaotic spaces of our own lives, where we learn things we had no desire to learn but that are incredibly valuable."

"'End of the Summer' was titled," she explains, "because its central theme was about people coming into authority and deciding what to do about it, facing power and the abuse of power and figuring out what to do about the plagues of an ordered world. 'The Green World' is about people who go inside and find their own authority, then come back and have to deal with that in the ordered, closed world around them."

Musically, "The Green World" falls nicely between the stark folkiness of "Mortal City" and the thicker folk-rock of "End of the Summer." Producer Stewart Lerman built arrangements around each song's mood, bringing in resonant instruments like a Dylanesque Hammond organ to create lush but never busy soundscapes for Williams's sparely eloquent guitar and sure, pretty vocals. Her voice has never sounded so rich, at once conversationally close and operatically soaring.

This is also her most impressionistic album, sticking less to narrative paths than capturing moments of quiet revelation. In the brilliant meditation "After All," she harrowingly describes chronic depression: "It felt like a winter machine that you go through and then/ You catch your breath and winter starts again / And everyone else is spring bound." By song's end her head is poking through the gray: "The sun rose with so many colors it nearly broke my heart / It worked me over like a work of art / And I was a part of all that."

Perhaps because this is her most impressionistic recording, it can sometimes be a bit too obscure. In the musically gorgeous "We Learned the Sea," the listener

I think in my 20s, I thought that religion and spiritual practice meant doing things right. Now I think it's about realizing you can't do everything right, and figuring out how you're going to live with the fact that you're going to fall short. That's where you find grace and unconditional love; not because you did all these perfect actions to deserve it, but because you are. —Dar Williams

is given too little to know what reality is moving behind the imagery, why we are supposed to feel the way the sad, sweeping melody suggests. And in the wonderfully titled "I Won't Be Your Yoko Ono," Williams seems to break one of her own cardinal rules, basking in the cleverness of the concept at the expense of being clear about just what she is trying to say.

But even these songs contain wonderful moods and moments. All the songs have little songs tucked within them, sparkling nuggets of wit and insight that shine all on their own. In "Spring Street," for example, she contemplates a fresh start in New York City before realizing that new beginnings must begin within us. Within her musing, she fires this fierce broadside at Manhattan pretensions: "I can find a small apartment where a struggling artist died / And pretend because I pay the rent I know the pain inside." The next verse begins with a beautifully sculpted freestanding couplet: "This year April had a blizzard, just to show she did not care/ And the new dead leaves made the trees look like children with gray hair."

In her hands, kindness becomes as powerful a tool of radical insight as rage is in the hands of political songwriters such as Ani DiFranco. For her kindness, like DiFranco's fury, has the courage to break the rules. Amid the youthful desolation of "After All," she dares to thank her parents for battling their inner demons enough to not pass them on to her, thus giving her a fighting chance to master her own. In the stunningly effective "Happens Every Day," she empathizes with the mundane torments of youth, watching college students at a coffeehouse: "You would think they're carefree, I have seen their trials/ Frowning into Shakespeare and practicing their smiles."

In the anthemic "Another Mystery," she surgically debunks "the cult of beautiful pain," the black-lipsticked poseurs who mask their fear of life with a studied diffidence she calls "an inscrutable pout." "I don't want to be another mystery" she shouts, concluding, "I wanna be the one to feel the sun / So if you want to see the world with me, let's go."

It is this healing courage, most of all, that makes Williams such an important songwriting voice. She never wraps herself in the alluring veil of her angst, wearing her scars like fashion statements. She shows us growing up as the painful thing it truly is, offering her insight and experience as signposts to the green world waiting for us just outside our darker selves.

"In all these songs," she says, "there is an acceptance of the beauty and grace of the things that you're not going to figure out or that are not going to come to you through the conventional channels. We're so good at thinking we know all the answers, but if you go into a wild space, if you just stare at a tree for long enough, you learn things that a very economy-driven, faux-moralistic society like ours cannot teach you. Accepting that these truths are going to be subtle is probably the biggest theme of the record, because the green world doesn't have rubber-stamp answers, which is probably the best thing the green world has going for it. And maybe that's the best thing being alive has going for it."

—*August 20, 2000*

Young stars stick to their roots
Nickel Creek, Kate Rusby, the Waifs

Since the staggering success of the soundtrack to *O Brother, Where Art Thou?* the pop music industry and mainstream media seem suddenly aware of this thing currently being called roots music, and variously known as old-time, traditional, vernacular, or just plain folk music. But is *O Brother* really the whole story, the whole iceberg, or just the tip of a larger, more profound phenomenon sweeping our culture?

Three disparate young folk acts with sizzling-hot careers strongly suggest the latter. British folk singer Kate Rusby, Australian folk-popsters the Waifs, and bluegrass whiz kids Nickel Creek perform very different styles of music but have uncannily similar tales to tell about how they came to their music, the artistic passions that stoke their muses, and the grass-roots groundswells that are making them stars.

The most striking similarity is that all three acts literally grew up around the music they perform, giving them an innate, almost preternatural understanding of the ancient aesthetics that still drive and define folk music.

Rusby's parents were professional folk singers at the height of the '60s folk revival in England and later became sound engineers at summer festivals. She said her lifelong familiarity with the ancient British folk ballads she sings, which inspire her own timeless songs, helped give her the confidence to sing utterly in her own voice instead of in the faux-traditional style so many '60s singers affected. It was hearing her sing old ballads in an entrancing, whispery mezzo—and in the full glory of her working-class Yorkshire accent—that first won attention and droves of young fans.

"Most of my friends in school," she says, "if they sung a song, they would do it in kind of a mid-Atlantic accent. I always thought it was strange to hear people sing differently than they talked. It made the whole thing seem false. I think that's another way I've been brought up, being very grounded and from a working-class background. There's no airs and graces in our family; everybody's just who they are all the time, whether you're on stage or sipping tea with your brother or sister."

These young folk artists are steeped in the traditions they perform, yet they are all driven by a passion for personal authenticity. The Waifs sing bracingly modern songs set to a buoyant, folk-pop pulse and freewheeling, chatty melodies: tart in-love songs, breakup songs written as personal declarations of independence, and scathing indictments of the falseness, meanness, and vanity of modern pop culture.

Donna and Vikki Simpson, who with guitarist Josh Cunningham make up the Waifs, were the children of an Australian salmon fisherman who took them to fishing work camps for four months every year. They cut their musical teeth at late-night campfires where old folk songs were sung and everyone pitched in. Their sound may be bitingly modern, but they were profoundly influenced by the best instincts of the folk troubadour: to tell the truth as they see it, uncompromisingly and without consideration of market tastes.

"I think there's a sense of honesty and realism about what we're doing, and a lot of other folk artists are doing today," Donna Simpson says. "Even if it's not strictly folk, our music is acoustic and it's real. I mean, there's so much bull out there, all about image and attitude. We're not sending out any messages; we're just singing about what *is* in our lives."

That marks another crucial characteristic all these artists share, a disdain bordering on contempt for most modern pop.

The members of Nickel Creek got their first taste of bluegrass hearing a local band at a pizza joint in Carlsbad, Calif. By the time Chris Thile was 5, he was taking lessons from the band's mandolinist. Sean and Sara Watkins were also taking lessons from the band and called Thile to ask if he'd like to start a kiddy bluegrass band. Chris and Sara were 6, Sean 10—and they have been a band ever since.

"When you start playing that young, I think you develop in a way that the music just becomes part of you," Thile says. "I didn't know any better than to think it was normal to play bluegrass. Contemporary bluegrass combines classical control and jazz spontaneity in a unique way, and I really want to score off that. But to do that, you have to have a firm foundation; you've got to be standing on something before you can jump."

That masterful mix of the classic and the playful has become Nickel Creek's trademark. Their own songs can be as brooding and sophisticated as any coming from the urban songwriter scene, but when they decide to do an old standard they display an awesome command of tradition and a grand instinct for where the rules can be bent and new sounds added to the mix.

While these artists have always attracted hard-core folk fans, they are all seeing a terrific upsurge in young fans coming to their shows over the last couple of years—and particularly of people just discovering folk in all its sundry forms.

"I get a sense that our younger fans are looking for something that's a bit more real than the pop they're being exposed to right now," says Thile. "They're not

Contemporary bluegrass combines classical control and jazz spontaneity in a unique way, and I really want to score off that. But to do that, you have to have a firm foundation; you've got to be standing on something before you can jump.
—Chris Thile

as stupid as major labels think they are, and they're sick of being marketed at: 'You're in this demographic, so you're supposed to like this and this and this.' I think people relate to this music because it's very basic. Even though we like to think what we play is fairly complex, we're just playing our instruments, singing, trying to tell good stories and communicate real feelings. That's really all we've got to show people.

Rusby said that even in England, *O Brother* has cracked the window open a bit wider into the folk subculture that, judging by attendance at her concerts and summer folk festivals, is thriving as it has not since the '60s.

"People ask me all the time now, do you want folk music to become bigger?" she says. "Half of me does, because I would love more people to hear it. But half of me really likes that it's a small scene, a little secret gem that not many people know about. Part of me wants to safeguard that, but you can't, because the songs have to move along as they always have, getting passed on and taken up by new generations. It will keep having surges whenever the media pops back in, but even if there's only five people in every town who like it, the music will always carry on. I've learned that much."

—April 7, 2002

No more awards! Pete Seeger

"Too many awards," Pete Seeger said a little glumly. "After this, if somebody wants to give out awards, they can give them to somebody else. If they want me to come and sing for them, I'll come sing."

The legendary American folk singer has always been a most iconoclastic icon, and the awards heaped on him recently are heady fare indeed: the National Medal of Arts from the National Endowment for the Arts, the Kennedy Center Lifetime Achievement Honor, the Rock and Roll Hall of Fame.

As uncomfortable as he is with this kind of attention, he was genuinely pleased and honored when asked to accept the second Harvard Arts Medal (Jack Lemmon received the first in 1995): "My wife, Toshi, and I decided years ago that I would refuse any honorary degrees, since I'm not really part of academia, but that we would make an exception if Harvard asked."

An arts award seems to sit better with the 76-year-old Seeger than an honorary degree, since he spent less than two years at Harvard, dropping out in 1938.

"Well, I guess I did take Fine Arts 1-A," he said cheerfully, as if trying to help bolster Harvard's case for the award. "Learned that the name for the curve on a Greek pillar is entasis. Gives a sense of weight, they said. Fine Arts 1-A."

After this, if somebody wants to give out awards, they can give them to somebody else. If they want me to come and sing for them, I'll come sing. —Pete Seeger

His brief Harvard career actually revealed much of the man he would become. He recalled attending classes with what is perhaps best described as a defining sense of independence, spending much more time working with the student union than with his studies, starting an underground paper called *The Harvard Progressive*, and becoming furious with a professor who always used the biggest, densest words possible; what Seeger has ever since called "scholar-gawk."

Musically, he was not admitted to the jazz band because he couldn't sight-read quickly enough ("I've been strictly an ear musician all my life"). He did join the Banjo Club, but its policy of learning just one tune at a time, practicing it exclusively until it was performed—and wearing tuxedos while performing—greatly abbreviated their association.

This month, Seeger is also celebrating a new printing of his wonderfuly vivid, anecdote-rich and properly song-filled memoir "Where Have All the Flowers Gone?" (Sing Out), and his first studio recording in 17 years: the deliciously Seeger-esque "Pete" on Paul Winter's Living Music label. He said the project was Winter's idea, since many of his more recent songs had not been recorded. Seeger's fame as crowd-pleasing folksinger, human rights advocate and environmental activist often eclipses his songwriting. He has penned some of the most memorable tunes in the American songbag: "Where Have All the Flowers Gone?," "If I Had a Hammer" (with fellow Weaver Lee Hays), "Turn, Turn, Turn" (lyrics from Ecclesiastes).

His voice has suffered from what he calls "a wobble" for some years, but sounds great here, rich in texture and personality. Pete-purists may find it a bit overproduced, laced with Winter's sax, Joanie Madden's tin whistle and three separate vocal choruses. But it feels like a Seeger show, with lovely choral work and Pete joyfully urging the singing along.

Many of his best-loved anthems are here: "Well May the World Go," "My Rainbow Race" and "All Mixed Up," along with standards such as "Water Is Wide," "Kisses Sweeter Than Wine" and "How Can I Keep from Singing?" It is always pretty and, though sometimes heavy on the choral arranging, all the more quintessentially Seeger for including so many voices.

"My main purpose in life is not to put songs in people's ears but to put them on their lips," he said. "I think singing together is important, whether it's a mother singing to a child or a family singing together or a choir. Because it's a way people can relate to each other besides talking. Now, talking is good, but it has its limitations. My father called it the lingo-centric predicament. The world is full of people who say, `Aw, you can't talk to them, they don't make any sense.' Or, `The only language they understand is guns.'

"I think we're less human beings when we don't participate, and this nation is being turned into a nation of spectators. For years I've joked about it, that people don't bother participating in sports, they just watch a professional athlete. They don't tell jokes to each other, they just watch a professional jokester. I've been on a campaign recently to get the papers to pay more attention to participation sports. They're part of the problem, not the solution, if all they talk about are stars. And the supreme stupidity is a husband and wife sitting there watching a professional lover pretend to kiss a professional lover on TV. Is that what living is all about? No, you want to do something in this world, not just watch other people doing things. And singing, well, singing can lead to other things."

—April 26, 1996

The quintessential Boston songwriter finds his roots in Woody Guthrie
Ellis Paul

Believe it or not, there is actually a species of musician called "the Boston songwriter." The moniker is more likely to be applied outside the Boston beltway than here and refers to the introspective, literate breed of singer-songwriter so prevalent in the modern folk-music landscape.

The term does not always refer to Boston musicians; such national artists as Shawn Colvin, John Gorka, and Susan Werner are often labeled "Boston" or "Boston-style" songwriters because of their confessional tone. But whenever examples of the form are cited, local songwriter and emerging national folk star Ellis Paul is sure to head the list. He has seen "quintessential Boston songwriter" by his name so many times, the 32-year-old Paul must wonder if it appears on his birth certificate.

His irresistibly catchy, yet movingly intimate new CD, "Translucent Soul" (Philo), is not likely to help him escape the moniker. His fourth CD is his best, the most personal and yet accessible, and it is already getting significant national airplay, not only on public radio folk shows but commercial AAA formats.

"People are always throwing that tag on me, and I do think there is such a thing as a Boston songwriter," he said. "Certainly people like me, Dar Williams, Bill Morrissey, and Patty Larkin fall into that category. We tend to be a little more word-heavy and personal. It's more about the lyric than the melody, and it's intimate, thoughtful, but also relevant. There are a lot of songs about social issues."

So who is the role model for this quintessential Boston songwriter? Who does Paul claim as his chief influence? He was quick to credit Morrissey and Larkin as "guideposts" for his generation of songwriters, saying he and Williams—along with Jonatha Brooke, Jennifer Kimball, Vance Gilbert, and Jim Infantino —went to their shows and took notes about their songwriting style and warm, witty stagecraft.

But his main guru and guidepost, the troubadour whose face he wears proudly tattooed on his arm, might surprise people, especially those who criticize contemporary songwriters for their introspection and lack of traditional roots.

"To me, Woody Guthrie is ground zero," he said, "the prototype in a long line of people I'm a huge fan of. He was the real thing; he was authentic. His image was the only thing I could put on my body that would be like a badge of who I am."

When Paul listens to Guthrie, who wrote such American folk anthems as "This Land Is Your Land" and "Pastures of Plenty," he does not hear someone writing quaintly about bygone days. He hears an urgent populist who carved modern ballads from the musical fabric of his own life and times. Just as Guthrie pulled melodies from the rural folk songs and blues he heard as a boy in his birthplace, Okemah, Okla., Paul builds his catchy folk-pop sound from the music he grew up with, the Beatles and Bob Dylan.

What is important to Paul, what he pulls from Guthrie's legacy, is the honesty, the uncompromising commitment to tell the truth in every song, however hard, radical, or unpopular.

In "She Loves a Girl," he paints a deeply troubling portrait of a family torn apart by the revelation that one of its members is gay. In "Translucent Soul," he ponders the never-ending blight of racism in American society—not from the perspective of a victim, but as himself, painfully watching a dear friend wrestle with fears and crises that he, as a white man, never has to confront. It is precisely because he addresses these social problems from his own experience that the songs carry such power and that they are the most Guthrie-esque.

"He wasn't somebody from Connecticut pretending he was from the rural South," he said. "He was writing authentically about where he came from, and that's what I feel I'm doing. Even when I write about other places, I'm always a Boston person visiting those places. I'm always clear about who I am and where I'm from. That's what Woody was doing and why his songs have lasted so long. It's not that he was writing about the Dust Bowl era, it's that he was writing from his own experience."

Paul usually sings Guthrie songs in his shows and has been taken under the family's wing, especially by daughter Nora, who asked him to sing at the celebration when Guthrie was inducted into the Rock and Roll Hall of Fame in 1996. Last month, Paul was made an honorary citizen of Okemah for his efforts to keep the late troubadour's legacy alive.

He would like more of his fellow Boston songwriters, wherever they call home, to see how much can be learned from Guthrie, not just about sticking to principles but the craft of songwriting.

"You can borrow a lot about the fabric of how songs are built from Woody," Paul said, "how to suggest things you want to emphasize. In his song `Hard Travelin','' for example, he uses the word `hard' in every verse to hammer his point home. It becomes almost invisible, but you end up knowing the song is not really about traveling; it's about hard, how hard life is.

"That's why he was such a brilliant songwriter. There was so much going on beneath the surface, things you barely notice but that affect the way the song makes you feel. He's shown me the story is in the details, not in dictating the meanings to people. Not preaching, but allowing them to witness the songs and come to their own conclusions."

—December 4, 1998

King of the hip-hop blues Chris Thomas King

Controversy is mother's milk to Chris Thomas King, so he is having the time of his life right now. His bold fusions of blues with rap, hip-hop, and modern R & B have earned him fans all over the world but also kept him in a hot cultural crossfire: He's too bluesy for straight-up hip-hop, too hip-hoppy for blues purists.

Since his charismatic role as 1920s bluesman Tommy Johnson in the Coen brothers film *O Brother, Where Art Thou?*, he now has a whole new set of problems.

"Most people who follow the blues genre know who I am and have followed my career," said King. "I've been using a DJ instead of a drummer since 1990, so when they hear me doing sampling, scratching, and stuff, they know that's my signature. But millions of people heard me through *O Brother, Where Art Thou?*, so I have a whole new audience that has not heard my discography. For them, it's a little bit of a shock; they didn't realize anyone was doing hip-hop, rap, and blues."

That shock has been exacerbated with his "All Over Blues" tour with the Muddy Waters Tribute Band, featuring older bluesmen Luther "Guitar Junior" Johnson, Calvin "Fuzz" Jones, Willie "Big Eyes" Smith, Jerry Portnoy, and Bob Margolin. Planned before *O Brother* was released, it was intended to display the proud past and promising future of the blues. The band pays homage to Waters, the Delta blues giant who all but invented the electric blues when he moved to Chicago in the 1940s, then follows those selections with King's radically modern fusions.

But after *O Brother*, many assumed the show would be entirely roots-oriented, with King performing as he did in the film. He cheerfully reported negative reactions from some hard-core blues fans, including jeers and heckling, amid the largely enthusiastic responses his shows have always received.

My music is just confrontational, and there's some audience members that will get confrontational right back. You need positive and negative energy to create light, you know? —Chris Thomas King

"My music is just confrontational," he said, "and there's some audience members that will get confrontational right back. You need positive and negative energy to create light, you know? For me as an artist, the highest compliment is to paint a picture and have two people stand there and debate about it."

Perhaps King feels so comfortable innovating within the blues form because he was absolutely dipped in the music as a child. His father owned Tabby's Blues Box in Baton Rouge, La., a renowned showcase club, and at the age of 9 King was already jamming with legends such as Buddy Guy and Guitar Kelly. It was from them, and from his keen understanding of how the blues evolved, that he was inspired to fuse his music to modern forms.

"None of the blues guys I knew were trying to be retro," he said. "They were all very much of the moment in the way they dressed, spoke, and made music. So now to have a whole lot of blues guys coming up in the 21st century trying to emulate these past sounds, and the only amplifier they're going to play is one made back in 1944—I just don't understand all that stuff."

King believes this rigid purism, this devotion to the blues only as it existed in the past, is a barrier keeping more young black people from embracing the music. And when he says these things, there is real anger.

"People claim they're presenting authentic blues, that they're saving a genre of music. The blues don't need saving. What these high-minded arts preservers need to do, instead of being so quick to put something in a museum, is to not dictate to people about how they're supposed to be playing their music. Obviously, black kids are going to rebel against that; anybody would. If you came up to white kids and said, 'Oh no, Elvis didn't sing like that,' or, 'This is the way Jerry Lee Lewis played it, and you have to sound like that if you want to play rock 'n' roll'—they'd rebel, too. Nobody says what Radiohead plays isn't rock because it doesn't sound like what Elvis did. I don't have to reference Tommy Johnson to play my music, any more than Metallica has to reference Elvis to play rock 'n' roll."

For all the controversy it engenders, King's blues is alluringly soft-spoken, personal, and insightful. Whether rapping bitterly about ghetto life, whispering a sexy ballad, or tearing off vintage blues classics, he displays an easy mastery that's hard to resist. It is also palpably clear that he is bringing his music up from deep, real places in his heart, that he believes every word he sings and every note he plays.

"It's not that I'm trying to change the world or anything," he said. "I just come from a hip-hop background. I wouldn't be honest as an artist if I pretended that I didn't hear the music around me, any more than I would be if I put down my guitar and did straight-up hip-hop. When I hear Tommy Johnson or any blues artist

I respect from another era, I learn a lot about the social conditions of that day—the culture and where we were as Americans at that particular time. Those artists weren't recording songs in 1950 trying to sound like 1890, you know what I'm saying? If you really want to be like Johnson or Muddy Waters, I think you have to live in your time and be true to your experience. Because that's what they did."

—*November 16, 2001*

Irish music gets younger and older at the same time
Sharon Shannon, Karan Casey, Niamh Parsons

Irish music has never been so visible on the world stage. Both the Celtic and world music revivals of the past 20 years have launched a tidal wave of young, hip traditional Irish bands and solo artists to stardom—Altan, Solas, button accordionist Sharon Shannon, and singer Niamh Parsons, to name a few.

"The music seems to be getting stronger and stronger all the time, and there's lots of really amazing young players coming up," said Shannon. "There's more musicians out there playing the music for a living than there ever were before, more new albums coming out, and lots of new ideas and new music for young people to be excited about."

Casey is a brilliant young singer from County Waterford. She left the American-based supergroup Solas in 1999 for a solo career. Her new CD, "The Winds Begin to Sing" (Shanachie), is beautifully austere, her willowy soprano hauntingly spacious and emotional.

To her, the most exciting part of the revival is how hands-on it is, more a social than a commercial movement.

"There seems to be a newfound pride in the music, thanks to the economic boom," she said. "It has inspired a confidence in people, a desire to look into their own culture. Parents are now encouraging their children to learn the music, dance, and the Irish language. When I was growing up it wasn't seen as very hip or cool to be into things Irish. Now it is."

The new face of Irish music is not only younger; it is also much less likely to be whiskered than 20 years ago. Powerful new female stars such as Shannon, Casey, and Parsons are providing vibrant role models for young Irish women. But all three stressed the past male domination in Irish music affected only its public face, the one outsiders saw at pubs, concerts, and dance halls. When music was played in the home, women always played a prominent role.

Shannon was inspired to play the accordion in part by her grandmother's concertina playing. Casey said one need only look at the bold, independent

When I was growing up it wasn't seen as very hip or cool to be into things Irish. Now it is. —Karan Casey

women portrayed in the old songs to know what a vital part of Irish music they were.

Parsons' last two CDs, the gorgeous and very traditional "Blackbirds and Thrushes" and "In My Prime," both on Green Linnet Records, have reinvigorated her career after it floundered in the folk-rock band Loose Connections.

She said the male domination of Irish music is actually a recent phenomenon. In the 1930s, ceilidhs, or dance parties, were banned from homes, where they had been held for centuries, by pressure from the Catholic church and the powerful Gaelic Athletic Association. It was feared that private dance parties led to licentiousness, so they were moved into the prim confines of community halls. It wasn't deemed respectable for women to be seen as part of the large ceilidh bands who performed for these public dances.

"From my knowledge and memory," Parson said, "it was always women as well as men singing the songs. It was just that women stayed in the home more back then, not just in Ireland but all over the world. So perhaps those passing by, just looking in on the music, might conclude it was only the men, because they were out in public more. But those who really knew what the story was would know that Mrs. So-and-So was a great player."

When Shannon burst on the Irish music scene in the early 1990s, she brought a charismatic sense of fun to the old music, which had sometimes suffered from the dour seriousness of preservationists and purists. Her latest CD, "The Diamond Mountain Sessions" (Compass), is a fond, swashbuckling romp through Irish and American song, with such un-Celtic guest stars as Steve Earle, Jackson Browne, and John Prine. While she is known for her modern sensibilities and playfulness, when it comes to the old music itself, Shannon is the same wonder-struck Galway girl she was at 7, when she first picked up a tin whistle and trotted off to the village ceilidh.

"The way I look at my music," she said, "is that if you take away all the other instruments that play along—the drums and bass and jazz solos—what I'm doing is really rooted and traditional. Maybe I bring a bit of a fresh attitude to the music, having a bit of fun and not getting too serious about it. But if you listen to my accordion, it's usually just the tune I'm playing. That's like the trunk of the tree; everything else is just like decorations on the branches. But if that trunk is not really strong, then it's all just decoration, and that, to my mind, doesn't work. It's the tradition, the tune that's the center of the music; that's what's so important to keep alive."

—*March 16, 2001*

Did they get it right when they called it Celtic music?
Johnny Cunningham, Kevin Burke

In Ireland or Scotland, if you ask where there's some nice Celtic music, you're likely to get a bewildered look and directions to the nearest ancient circle of stones. But nearly any folk music fan hereabouts will know just what you mean: the traditional music of Ireland, Scotland, Wales, Brittany. The term particularly refers to the music of the great folk revival in those lands during the 1970s, energized by tradition-steeped but pop-savvy bands such as Scotland's Silly Wizard, Ireland's Bothy Band and Brittany's Kornog.

The fiddlers from those three seminal Celtic revival bands occasionally tour and record as the Celtic Fiddle Festival. Silly Wizard founder Johnny Cunningham is joined by Bothy Band's Kevin Burke, among the most virtuosic, inventive and respected of Irish fiddlers, and Kornog's Christian Lemaitre, who has done much to restore the fiddle to its long-lost place in the heart of Breton folk music. The concerts celebrate their musical heritage and seek the common Celtic threads that bind them.

The Celtic folk revival, as such, is waning, its energies diluted by the world music craze, the dissolution of many of the bands that fueled it, and its increasing infusion into the pop mainstream. Cunningham, for example, may no longer be a Silly Wizard, but his fiddle wowed the rock world during his tenure with the Rain Dogs, and he is currently in the popular Windham Hill band Nightnoise, as well as a busy local record producer and session player. His brother Phil, also a Silly Wizard founder, is a prolific producer and composer whose music was heard recently on the soundtrack to "Last of the Mohicans."

Cunningham is delighted to see the energies of the revival he helped shape influencing so much of the popular music landscape, but surprisingly sad to see the term Celtic music fall into disuse. Known for his teasing, often scathing stage wit, a sassy response to such a marketing-tool moniker might be expected.

"You can be easily sarcastic about the term," Cunningham said, clearly tempted at the prospect, "because I think it's just another sign of how the music industry and media need to label things. But this time around, I think they've come up with the right label—through no fault of their own."

He said he never heard the term applied to music until the early 1970s, when many young people in Scotland tired of the pervasiveness of American music.

"I don't think it was a backlash really, but there was this wealth of music coming out of America being played all over our country. It was like, do we not have anything? It's an amazing thing, these countries so culturally rich in language and art and music for so long, and in this century, except in pockets, they were really ignoring a large part of their own culture."

What can go wrong with using Celtic as a title is that people's image of the Celtic world—that kind of Celtic mists, airy-fairy thing—can be romanticized into something that's no longer moving or living or breathing or struggling to survive rather than music that's actually managed to survive and grow over centuries. —Johnny Cunningham

When these hot new bands began to come to these shores, a marketing dilemma was indeed encountered. The problem was targeting the huge folk audience that existed for Scottish, Irish, Breton and Welsh folk music, not to mention British, without offending any one group. The first of the groups to tour extensively here immediately begged the question. Boys of the Lough were comprised of Scottish, Irish and English players. There is a widely held theory that the term Celtic was coined by early promoters to deal with describing them, even though most of England is not Celtic.

The fact that, after years of Scotland being described as a British culture, the English must now fuss with a moniker they find ill-fitting, is okay by Cunningham. "It kinda cheers me up," he said with customary sass.

Irish native Kevin Burke never heard the term applied to his music until he came to America.

"Irish music is very different from Scottish music," he said. "But when you're over here, thousands of miles away, you can see why people regard it as similar. I don't think about it much, because it's other people's idea. It's true that what I do is from one of the Celtic countries, but I would always refer to it as Irish music, unless I was specifically trying to broaden the spectrum, if I was talking about bands from Scotland, Ireland and Brittany.

"I see them more as individuals than as a family, though intellectually I know there's a link between all those places and the word for describing that link is Celtic."

Cunningham said, "What can go wrong with using Celtic as a title is that people's image of the Celtic world—that kind of Celtic mists, airy-fairy thing—can be romanticized into something that's no longer moving or living or breathing or struggling to survive rather than music that's actually managed to survive and grow over centuries."

What excites Cunningham is the way the term reminds Celtic cultures around the world that they have a common bond.

"The term takes on a world view rather than a more closed one. You're forced to acknowledge the similarities between cultures rather than the differences. It brings a lot of warring factions together and reminds them of a bond that really does exist between their cultures. Because for years, you know, the powers that be have been trying to split us up. As a force, we're pretty powerful culturally.

"In my travels throughout the world, finding pockets of what's called Celtic culture, the people are very similar in their attitude toward life, work and death. And that's not just where pockets of Scots and Irish are around the world. I'm talking about going to Golithia in Spain, the Isle of Man, down into Cornwall and Brittany, even parts of India. You get the same feeling from the people.

"There's great store set by the oral tradition, by humor and a different way of

...in these small rooms, each audience is unique, as opposed to big pop concerts, where the whole point is to do the same show night after night. —Greg Greenway

dealing with life. It's almost like a different set of values; people tend to really appreciate what they've got. It's not an incredibly materialistic culture. Maybe it's because it's the culture I most understand and feel most comfortable with. But I can always be assured of good company, great hospitality, a good laugh, a good story, and great music."

—November 5, 1992

The community coffeehouse: Quiet heart of the folk circuit
Greg Greenway, the Shaw Brothers, *A New Song Coffeehouse* director Jerry Christen

Nestled in the suburbs outside Boston is a quiet phenomenon called the community coffeehouse. Ask scholars or music pundits why Boston is the nation's premier hotbed for folk music, and they will likely wax about the '60s revival, urban hives such as Club 47, from which the era's big folk stars emerged, including Joan Baez and Tom Rush.

Ask a modern folk performer, however, and they will tell you it's because there is more work for them here than anywhere else. And the hub of that circuit is not Boston, but the wide wheel of suburban coffeehouses that surrounds it.

These venues are not better known outside the folk world because they each serve small core audiences who savor the neighborly charms their local coffeehouse offers.

That obscurity is beginning to change, thanks to Jerry Christen, founding director of A New Song Coffeehouse at Bedford's First Church of Christ Congregational. After retiring in 1999 as director of the Massachussetts Council for Quality, he began reaching out to other suburban coffeehouses. Last year, they founded the Boston Area Coffeehouse Association (BACHA), and named Christen director. As chairs were set up for a show, he talked about the new organization.

"BACHA is a coalition of nonprofit coffeehouse directors and other volunteers who decided to get together and figure out how we could help each other, work better with each other, find ways to cooperate. We also want to explore ways we can work together to expand the total marketplace for folk music, the overall awareness of what all these coffeehouses offer."

"As I began to talk to other coffeehouse people, it seemed like we're all little islands out there, all trying to run the whole show by ourselves. If we got together in a cooperative way, we could ease everybody's burdens, and see each other as colleagues more than competitors."

He said the biggest ongoing challenge suburban coffeehouses face is simply convincing their neighbors to give them a chance. Because many of them are held in churches, some fear they are religious shows, which they are not. Others have sour stereotypes about folk music clubs, and imagine dank evenings hearing sullen troubadours whine about their troubles.

In fact, nearly all suburban coffeehouses are informal but first-rate music venues, run by local volunteers, featuring nationally touring headliners skilled at the uniquely personal stagecraft of the modern coffeehouse.

About 110 people came to see this night's headliners, the Shaw Brothers, an average crowd for A New Song. As they sang sweet old folk standards, many popularized by the Shaws' first group, the Brandywine Singers, the crowd responded warmly. From the kitchen, a variety of coffees, teas, and organic soft drinks were available, along with fresh pumpkin, pecan, blueberry, and chocolate cream pies, all home-baked by the volunteers. The crowd was casually dressed, ranging from teens to seniors, but predominantly people in their 30s and 40s.

Bedford couple Bill Deen and Meredith Clark have been A New Song devotees since the coffeehouse began in 1985, and attend most of the monthly shows that run from October- May.

"It's incredible to be able to drive 10 minutes from home and hear great performers in a comfortable setting like this," said Deen. **"It's show business on a personal level. Most of the performers sing about things in their real lives, things that have personally touched them, and there's a power to that."**

Clark said, "I like the size very much, the intimacy. You can talk to the performers during the break if you want to. Sometimes I'll ask about the stories behind songs that particularly moved me. I've never seen anyone here without great stage presence, a real ability to connect with their audience."

Greg Greenway is a quintessential coffeehouse act who has performed many times at A New Song. He's never had a hit record, never been on MTV, but makes a good living singing his fiery populist songs and warm romantic ballads in these small clubs.

"People who play these places have to be entertainers," he said. "They know that a good half of their audience may have no idea who they're coming to see; they just want to be at their community coffeehouse. So the performers who do well are funny and personable, and really know how to invite listeners into their songs; to incorporate the energy of that night into a show that's just for that audience. Because in these small rooms, each audience is unique, as opposed to big pop concerts, where the whole point is to do the same show night after night."

The Shaw Brothers have been folk stars for more than 40 years. As they prepared to perform, they said these small suburban venues offer crucial exposure, let them connect with their natural audience more than they do at the higher-paying cruise-ship concerts and tourist clubs they perform all over the world.

"We love playing places like this," Ron Shaw said. "It's a chance to play for a real listening crowd. And it's so intimate; it's almost like playing in someone's living room."

Rick Shaw said that if clubs like A New Song had existed in the '60s, the folk revival might not have collapsed as completely as it did. Most venues then were commercially driven, and vulnerable to changing music tastes.

"These coffeehouses stay open through their own efforts more than how well-known the stars are or how popular the music is at any one time," he said. "The commercial market may never recognize the viability of this music the way it did in the '60s, but when you see what's happening in these clubs, it shows that folk music is quite successful on its own terms."

Christen hopes BACHA will help all the coffeehouses in the area attract more fans. It has a brochure listing all 17 member coffeehouses, which is available to fans at each venue. There is also a new BACHA Web site (www.bostoncoffeeho uses.org) offering links to each coffeehouse's site, along with general information on what the venues offer.

But he said he knows these coffeehouses will always remain small, independent, community-based clubs. It taps something deep in New England's self-determined, town-hall culture. "When people see something worthwhile here," he said, "it's just natural for them to say, 'Hey, I'll bet we could do that in our town.'"

He recalled when Bill Schaeppe first talked to him about wanting to found the Joyful Noise Coffeehouse, at the First Baptist Church in Lexington.

"I said, 'Why don't you just come join us?' But he wanted to do something for his community, his church, the same way I did when we started A New Song. I think a lot of people feel that way. When they get to love this music, they want to bring it into their own communities."

Coffeehouse fan Deen said, "Bedford is still governed by an open town meeting, so there's a long tradition of people in the community creating things for themselves, whether it's what Jerry's done organizing this coffeehouse, or the park that's being created where the old Bedford train depot was. That's also a grass-roots community effort. People around here are a little more inclined to organize among their friends to get what they want, rather than waiting for someone else to tell them what kind of park or entertainment they ought to have."

—November 11, 2001

Folk's family feud: traditionalists vs. songwriters
Eric Andersen, Christine Lavin, Eddie from Ohio's Robbie Schaefer, Tony Barrand, Steve Tilston, music manager David Tamulevich

The popular mythology says that the folk wars began at the Newport Folk Festival in 1965. Singer-songwriter Bob Dylan appeared with an electric guitar, singing obscure, introspective songs, and was booed off the stage by hordes of intolerant traditional purists. Since then, songwriters and traditional folk musicians have been a-feudin' and a-fussin'.

Like most enduring myths, it is not entirely true. Dylan played all the songs he had intended to that August night and was, for the most part, enthusiastically received. In fact, he was brought back for two encores.

But also like most enduring myths, it endures because it is built upon a bedrock of truth. The worlds of traditional folk music and the acoustic singer-songwriter have not quite been armed camps, but a very cold war has raged between them since the dawn of the 1960s folk revival.

"I think there was always a gulf between songwriters and traditional folk people," said Eric Andersen, who rose to stardom with the first wave of '60s songwriters, which included Dylan, Tom Paxton, and Phil Ochs. "For a songwriter, it was tough at first, because nobody took you seriously. The first people who played at Club 47 in Cambridge, for instance, they all tried to play just like [Southern traditional musicians] Doc Watson or Clarence Ashley. I mean, imitating them was like a stamp of authenticity, and songwriters were looked on as weird, upstart-type people."

John Roberts and Tony Barrand are among the most respected singers of traditional British folk songs in this country. Barrand, who grew up in England, also teaches folklore and psychology at Boston University, and said he believes most of the animosity, at least originally, came from traditionalists.

"The singer-songwriter thing was seen as a rejection of this amazing traditional material, this heritage," he said. "I remember being at folk clubs in England in the '60s, and the purists—these people who were just then intensely discovering the old songs—saw it almost as a travesty to create songs when there were so many great traditional singers to listen to and imitate, and all these amazing old songs to learn."

As the folk revival gained commercial viability, however, the traditional artists got left by the wayside. At coffeehouses like Club 47 and major festivals like Newport, the constant, seductive hum of what Joni Mitchell called "the starmaker machinery" could be heard. But then as now, pop wanted its stars young, hip, attractive—and singing contemporary songs.

Steve Tilston, who sings both traditional and original songs, came of age in the waning days of the British folk revival and remembers how hardened attitudes had become by the early '70s.

"I still remember a few faces looking daggers at me," he said, "wondering, 'Why am I paying money to hear this post-adolescent sing about the fact that his latest girlfriend's buggered off?' I suppose that's forever to be the case, and it seems even more so in America. I know a lot of people resent the singer-songwriter, see them as using the resources that were built up and maintained by people in the traditional scene. So when I come to the States, I sense a bit of resentment that the folk scene is so swamped with singer-songwriters."

As the folk revival dissolved in the wake of the disco and punk waves of the '70s, the music went underground, maintained in small coffeehouses by the most ardent activists and lovers of the form. But it was not only traditional people who fought that hard, good fight. Passim, the descendant of Club 47, for example, was run by Bob and Rae Ann Donlin, who were devoted to literate singer-songwriters. On tiny stages like theirs, the folk movement rebuilt itself, but when it reemerged in the 1980s, it was seen almost entirely as a songwriter revival.

Among folk's first new stars was Christine Lavin, who remains among its wittiest and most enduringly popular performers. She said she recently ruminated with Greenwich Village folk patriarch Dave Van Ronk about why so little traditional music has been part of the current folk revival.

"He said, 'Look, if you go to a bluegrass festival, you'll see 10-year-old kids with little cowboy hats and banjos who can name all the bluegrass players from the beginning of time and play all the standards. Folk music today does not have that.'

"And he's right; singer-songwriters don't have that deep, long connection to the traditional music. My theory is that to begin to play folk music, you only need to know two or three chords. You don't have to learn to play other people's stuff first, just to get the technique. You don't have to go to teachers, who would tell you about the masters who came before and have you study their music, the way they do in other forms, whether it's bluegrass or opera. In folk, you can just take off on your own. And it really is to the detriment of the form if new people come up who don't know what came before them."

Lavin also said she thinks it is unfortunate that traditional folkies and songwriters aim their animosity at one another.

"I'm sure that television and radio have helped to escalate the split. Folk gets so little airplay and almost no television, and it tends to be the most popular performers, the ones closest to the pop mainstream, who get what little attention there is."

This strikes at the central tragedy of the schism for David Tamulevich, whose Fleming-Tamulevich is the nation's largest folk management and booking agency. He also performs in the smart traditional and contemporary folk duo Mustard's Retreat.

"I think the real gulf opened when the media decided folk was going to become a four-letter word," he said. "In the '70s, pop culture moved away from the folk revival toward other things, and basically declared it dead. Folk people get all emotional about that, but, you know, it's an impersonal industry, as all capitalist industries are. They want quick money, no investment, and they're always moving on to the next thing."

He is convinced there is as large a potential audience for folk music now as there was in the '60s. As an agent, he is forever helping grass-roots organizations start their own folk venues, watching happily as word spreads from friend to friend, neighbor to neighbor, that folk music still exists.

"Audiences want those roots and welcome them when they find them," he said. "They want all the things that folk music offers; that feeling of connectedness and inclusiveness and tradition. But they don't know they want it until they see it, and they simply don't see it in the media today. It's like the industry and the media just pulled the curtain on it. And that's not the fault of anyone in folk music; it's not the songwriters' fault and it's not the traditional artists' fault. It's the media's fault and the music industry's fault."

Eddie From Ohio is actually a quartet from Virginia, among the hottest new folk bands. Its quirky, hilariously smart-alecky songs are bringing young fans to folk and a welcome spirit of fun to the often-dour world of the songwriter.

Robbie Schaefer, who writes many of the group's songs, wonders if the schism is as wide as many folkies think. He is constantly being warned about "folk police" or even "folk Nazis," traditional purists bent on assailing young neo-folkies like himself. But he has never met one and, in fact, has felt warmly welcomed in even the most traditional folk venues.

"The experiences we've all had tell me the gulf might not be as large as a lot of us think," he said. "I think people who grew up with folk music probably guard it jealously, as they should. It is a precious thing, and it takes nurturing, especially nowadays. As a fan, you really have to seek it out, seek out the CDs, the shows, to be really proactive. This is not a passive form of entertainment. What I think the newer stuff is doing is drawing younger people into folk music who would never have listened to it otherwise—and may not realize they're listening to it now. And I think that's a great thing. Somehow, people have to get their first exposure to the music."

Both Lavin and Tilston said they feel more connected to folk tradition than some purists might give them credit for being.

Tilston said, "I'll hear people say, 'Well, what's the difference between these singer-songwriters and pop singers?' And you could say that, but to me, the overview is that they are carrying on one of the oldest traditions ever, because there have always been singer-songwriters. There have been troubadours going back thousands of years, and they had songs for everything that happened in people's lives. I mean, songs are written by singer-songwriters; that's how they've always been written."

For Andersen, though, the gulf is a permanent feature of the folk terrain. People who discover its vast fields are naturally going to be drawn to different corners, though he made it clear it's not only the traditionalists who think the scales may have tipped a tad too heavily toward the songwriters these days.

"I was in that first wave, when there were maybe six songwriters in Greenwich Village," he said. "Now it's like there's more songwriters than there are ATMs, 7-Elevens, churches, and Wal-Marts put together. But I don't know if this is a gulf that needs to be narrowed. I mean, it's like saying swing music should get closer to free-form jazz or bebop. Maybe the differences are good. That's what makes the form so vital."

—June 27, 1999

The roots of the klezmer revival
Hankus Netsky of the Klezmer Conservatory Band

It was not so very long ago that the surest way to insult a Jewish musician was to call him a "klezmer." It was like calling a country singer a hillbilly, or describing an Irish fiddle tune as bog music. It said a musician was old-fashioned, mired in the provincial and archaic music of the old world.

No more. Thanks to an exciting modern revival of the traditional Jewish dance and ceremonial music called klezmer, it is now widely seen as a still-vital form, as well as a precious part of Jewish heritage, and is heard everywhere from Tanglewood to Hollywood films, television to hit CDs.

In the vanguard of that revival is Hankus Netsky of Newtonville—musician, composer, teacher and scholar, as well as founder and director of the Klezmer Conservatory Band.

The urbane orchestral elegance he brought to the old folk music significantly helped it gain critical and popular acceptance. From his work in films such as "Enemies: A Love Story" to his acclaimed collaboration with superstar violinist Itzhak Perlman on the "Fiddler In the House" PBS documentary and two

I hear the clock ticking away, with all these old klezmer musicians in their 80s and 90s. To share this culture has always been my greatest desire, and my burning desire right now has to do with research...

...we need books on this stuff, we need music and archival documents to be compiled and made available, to understand the roots of the music in ways we don't right now. —Hankus Netsky

subsequent EMI CDs, Netsky and his lush yet captivatingly folksy band have been among the most important and influential forces in the klezmer revival.

Usually, musicians go to school to learn how to be successful performers, but Netsky marked the tremendous success of his work with Perlman by deciding to return to school to get a doctorate in ethnomusicology from Wesleyan University in Connecticut. He hopes to help launch a permanent center for the archival collecting, research and teaching of klezmer music.

"I love performing, but it's always been sort of a means to an end," Netsky said in the happily cluttered study of his Newtonville home, where he lives with his wife, Beth, who works for the Anti-Defamation League, and daughters Leah, 9, and Mira, 5.

"To share this culture has always been my greatest desire, and my burning desire right now has to do with research," he said. "I hear the clock ticking away, with all these old klezmer musicians in their 80s and 90s. We need books on this stuff, we need music and archival documents to be compiled and made available, to understand the roots of the music in ways we don't right now."

As was true for most Jewish baby boomers in America, Netsky, 44, did not hear much klezmer music as he grew up in Philadelphia. His grandfather had played in a klezmer orchestra, and both of his mother's brothers had been in Jewish dance bands. One of those uncles, whose professional name was Harold Karr, wrote the hit song, "Mutual Admiration Society."

"For someone in my grandfather's and uncles' generations," Netsky said, "it was an insult to be called a klezmer. Once you came over to this country, you wanted to be associated with the American music of the day. So, whenever I asked my uncles about the old music, they would say, `Oh, you don't want to waste your time with that.' They felt, if I was going to be a musician, they were doing me a favor by keeping me away from it."

But after finding a cache of his late grandfather's old 78s in the attic, Netsky was deeply drawn to klezmer's dark ebullience and bewitching blend of Eastern European and Jewish folk strains. He attended the New England Conservatory in Boston in 1978 with vague ambitions of composing jazz, but he dreamed of finding some way to pursue his love of Jewish folk music.

On a trip home to Philadelphia, he was invited to an Irish sessiun, or informal music gathering, at the home of folklorist Mick Moloney. In every room, young and old musicians were playing Irish jigs and reels. Netsky was enchanted not only by the music but by how much informal learning was going on as tunes were shared, fiddle styles compared and stories told.

Back at the Conservatory, he began putting up fliers inviting students to his house for what he impishly called a "Klezmer Conservatory," a party to play and explore the old music.

The parties became so popular, a concert was held at Jordan Hall for students and faculty to perform Jewish music. Netsky arranged a few tunes for 15 party regulars, billed as the Klezmer Conservatory Band.

They brought the house down and were immediately inundated with requests to perform. Within a year, they put out a self-made record, and used a share of the profits to fund the Klezmer Conservatory Foundation, which still sponsors concerts for seniors and educational organizations. That record led to a three-album deal with the prestigious Vanguard Records. The band now records for the Cambridge-based Rounder Records.

The Klezmer Conservatory Band was a crucial cog in the klezmer revival then picking up steam, as more and more Jewish musicians began exploring their musical roots. With its orchestral savvy and grand sense of fun, the KCB attracted legions of fans in the folk, classical, jazz and pop worlds.

"There was something for everyone," Netsky said. "The music itself was folky and informal and fun to dance to. But we also had one of the most creative jazz musicians in the country in Don Byron; and singer Judy Bressler brought a wonderful dimension of Jewish theater that attracted the Broadway show-tune people. And because of the level of the musicians and the size of the ensemble, there was interest from the classical people."

In 1995, PBS asked Itzhak Perlman to participate in a klezmer program for its "Great Performances" TV series. He agreed to host it, so long as he did not have to play. Netsky was hired as a consultant. His first directive was to get Perlman to play.

Netsky reached back to his Klezmer Conservatory days. Perlman was invited to a party at a New York hotel room, where some filming would take place. After a few tunes, everyone was having so much fun, Perlman took out his violin and began to play. The acclaimed special, "In the Fiddler's House," followed, along with world tours and two CDs, which sold in the hundreds of thousands.

For an artist with more venal ambitions, this success would have meant that he was beginning to hit the big time. For Netsky, it closed a chapter, one he had begun when he first set out to help klezmer music become seen as a serious form. He found himself eager to open a new chapter, and began to study at Wesleylan under the noted Jewish ethnomusicologist and author Mark Sloban.

Netsky's eyes shine with excitement as he discusses the possibilities for collecting music and lore from old klezmer musicians, now that they no longer feel the need to hide their roles in a music they once believed nobody wanted to remember.

He spoke of Morris Hoffman, for example, a Philadelphia musician he approached 20 years ago for information about klezmer music. He had refused even to see Netsky. "Listen," he barked over the phone, "tonight I'm at the Latin

Casino, playing for the Temptations. And you're what, 25 years old? Well, I'm 75 and I'm telling you that old stuff is gone."

When Netsky was touring with Perlman in 1996, he decided to try Hoffman again. This time, he was not some young student pestering him by phone. He invited the old man to the concert.

"So, Morris Hoffman's reintroduction to klezmer music," Netsky said, "was coming into the Mann Center to listen to Itzhak Perlman play before a standing-room-only crowd of 10,000. And there we were up on stage, playing tunes he had played at weddings 50 years before. Afterward, he said to me, `Come over to my house; we'll talk. Do I have stories for you!' "

—October 10, 1999

Donal Lunny *and the "invention" of Celtic music*

Donal Lunny may be the most influential single figure in modern Irish music. Though little known outside Celtic and Irish music circles, the shy guitar-bouzouki wizard, composer, and arranger is a towering figure within them. From his defining work in the seminal Celtic revival groups Planxty, the Bothy Band, and Moving Hearts, as soundtrack composer for such films as "Eat the Peach" and "This Was My Father," and as a prolific record producer, he has played a crucial role in designing the way Irish and other Celtic-based musics are played today. He is so respected for this legacy that U2's Bono refers to him simply as "the sound man."

For Lunny, the real reward for his legacy lies not in his list of accomplishments and accolades, but in the music he is making now with his seven-piece ensemble, Coolfin.

"Coolfin is closer to playing the kind of music I want to play than anything I've done before," Lunny said. "There are a lot of things I'm trying to get out of my system at the moment, tunes with very unusual time signatures, a lot of syncopation and odd punctuation. That's the kind of thing that excites me, as opposed to the constant 4/4 time that the whole pop-music world seems to be in. A lot of people seem oblivious that other time signatures exist. One of the big ones is 6/8, jig rhythm; you can do five times as much with that as you can with 4/4."

This, in a nutshell, was the problem Lunny confronted over 30 years ago. He loved Irish music but saw the whole world bopping to the happy beats of American rock 'n' roll. First in Planxty, then in Bothy Band and the full-tilt rock of Moving Hearts, he sought common ground between rock-driven popular-music forms and the ancient melodic heart of Irish music. But the roots of this problem were even older than the onslaught of rock.

"Irish music was forced underground by the repression of Irish culture from 1600 on," he said. "The music was nurtured, preserved, kept going, but underground, just on melody-playing instruments. There had been a thriving tradition of harp playing around the courts of the kings, which was wiped out almost overnight. Once the last Irish king was deposed, the harpers had no place to go, and all that knowledge just vanished. It was a gigantic loss; you can only wonder what it was like, because that would have been harmonic playing. After that, the melodic voices were left on their own, so that became the tradition."

The problem in arranging these long-lined, intricately cadenced melodies for modern ensembles was how to add rhythm sections and harmonic playing without disrupting the music.

Lunny's first major contribution, in the early '70s, was introducing the Greek bouzouki into Irish music. It is now so accepted that the Gaelic band in the film "Titanic," set in 1912, is playing one.

"The bouzouki plays more neutral chords, with less color and density than the guitar. I realized a matter of hours after picking one up that it was a better thing with Irish music, because it didn't fill it so much. Irish music has a more limited palette, if you like, than general Western music.

"What makes it different are the things that are absent from it as much as what it's actually doing. The modes leave out notes, and the guitar very often puts them back in. The bouzouki was more transparent, and also a more effective rhythm instrument."

In 1982, Lunny formed Moving Hearts and took on the full power of rock bass and drums. To his mind, the rhythm section won handily, and the group was more a rock band than an Irish one.

"We had a very strong rhythm section that very confidently put rock structures together, and all I could say was, `No, don't play there, don't play the snare on the backbeat.' But I couldn't say what they should play. I learned a lot about musical structures and about how bass and drum more or less dictate to each other what rhythmic structure is played. That's the way of rock music, and it's a glorious thing, beautiful to play. But it's another language. It's as if Irish music has four legs, and rock has two. They just don't run in the same way."

In Coolfin's exuberant airs and clever dances, the melody is allowed to run as it pleases, the rhythm and harmonics forced to ride along. The result is a sound that is always adventurous yet sweepingly melodic and harmonically eloquent. Lunny is not quite where he wants to be, still grumbling about how rhythm chops interrupt the sweet spaces. But he is finally free to let Irish music lead the dance.

"The aim for me has always been to work from the inside out of Irish music,"

When I was 25, I said I never wanted to turn 50, which is coming up, look back and say I could have tried harder. I think I stayed true to that. It's a good feeling. —Bill Morrissey

he said. "I've become more familiar with the function of drums and bass in music that purports to be Irish, and more familiar with how to apply it within the music, as opposed to what happens if you stick rock music on top of Irish music, which robs the music of its intelligence, I feel. There's another way to go round that and let the music just get on with itself. I think this band has the ability to find that way."

—August 14, 1999

Bill Morrissey's *"Three R's": Writing, rural, and roots*

It has taken Bill Morrissey nearly 50 years, but he is finally living inside one of his own songs. Among the earliest and most significant of the urban songwriters to ignite the revival of the 1980s, he has always seemed like a big-city boy with a small-town heart. His evocative, crisply sculpted ballads of life in northern New England prompted novelist Robert Olmstead to dub him "New England's own bluesman," describing his music as "the cabin fever blues of the dead-end jobs and busted relationships, the place where life and consequences meet."

But Morrissey is also the quintessential urban songwriter—in fact, for many he redefined the genre in the '80s and '90s. He writes tight, literate ballads, rippling with tension, conflicted emotions, untold truths and telling imagery.

After years in the folk industry hive of greater Boston, Morrissey now lives in just the kind of squat, well-worn rural home you would expect to find the barflies, unemployed mill-workers and over-the-hill musicians who populate his songs.

You can't find the place without help from him. Even if you get to the tiny village of Tamrack, New Hampshire, at the clenched feet of the Presidential Mountain Range in Mt. Washington Valley—a town so small its two stores are named Remick's and The Other Store—anyone you ask about Morrissey will call him before giving out directions.

"I live in 1963," he says at his kitchen table, with guitars and CD racks to his left, neatly stacked hunting rifles and fishing poles to his right. "Nobody locks their doors; it's a rarity if people take their keys out of the ignition in the cars downtown. You go down to the village and see kids with butch haircuts riding their bikes, parking them wherever they like. You can't make a quick trip downtown, because you always run into two, three people you know."

He beamed like an urbanite bragging about a winning sports team as he described how Remick's keeps a Boston Globe with his name on it for him, letting them stack up while he's on tour. He walks into the CVS, says "one," and the clerk hands him a pack of his brand of cigarettes.

He lived for years in the greater Boston area, where his career blossomed and his record company of nearly 20 years, Rounder/Philo, is based. But when he and his former wife, Ellen Karras, who remains his manager, divorced two years ago, he realized he could live anywhere he wanted.

"I work in cities, but I lived in small towns when I was younger," he says. "It was a concession to move down to Cambridge; I did that for the business. But now with e-mails and faxes and everything, it occurred to me I could live anywhere. When I came up this way to do a gig, I noticed that my blood pressure kept getting lower and lower. It was like a Brigham Young moment: 'This is the place.'"

Morrissey's new record, "Something I Saw or Thought I Saw," is also a homecoming, a return to the stark, bittersweet sound that sparked his career. Sparely melodic and haunting, with a vivid cast of wincingly real people dealing with the careless brutality of changing times, dreams that mock how their lives turned out, it evokes his classic breakthrough '80s recordings "Standing Eight" and "Inside."

Those were the records that gained Morrissey the attention of folk fans outside New England, and among the literati, including fiction editor Gary Fisketjon, who works with Cormac McCarthy and Richard Ford, and edited Morrissey's first novel, "Edson."

"I cannot comprehend a life without writing," Morrissey says while popping open a beer. "I can certainly comprehend a life without touring, but not without writing. It takes me three days after I leave the valley now to get my road rhythm back. I hate leaving here; I bought this place to settle down. I got all the streams I need, some bear and deer and moose. I got my privacy. I've never been happier in a town; it reminds me of being six years old in western Massachusetts."

Morrissey grew up a small-town, middle-class boy in Easthampton, where he lived until the second grade. Then the family lived in Wethersfield, Connecticut "from grade school until the Beatles hit," as he dates it. They next moved to Acton, Massachusetts, then a nearly rural community outside Boston, but close enough for him to discover the folk revival then bubbling to a boil around the fabled Harvard Square coffeehouse Club 47.

"The folk boom was already on; Hootenanny had been on TV and canceled," he recalls. "But Club 47 was hot, and that's where I discovered real folk music. I can't say Woody Guthrie was the first folk singer I heard. I had to go through Peter, Paul and Mary to get to Bob Dylan to get to Ramblin' Jack Elliot to get back to Woody; just like I had to go through the Rolling Stones to get to Jimmy Reed and Muddy Waters."

What drew him first and made him want to pick up a guitar himself was the storytelling in the songs, their bracing directness and honesty. He began paying attention to songwriter credits, figuring out that the songwriter McKinley

Morganfield and the blues legend Muddy Waters were one and the same, that Chester Burnett was Howlin' Wolf. Piece by piece, the trail of tradition became visible to him; still exotically overgrown with myth and mystery, but clear enough to follow.

Then he discovered the gentle folk genius Mississippi John Hurt, cut less from the blues tradition than from African-American songsters, community singers who sang everything from play-party songs to ballads, field hollers to earthy seductions like Hurt's classic "Candy Man." More than any other musician, Hurt's influence defined Morrissey's style, a fact he played homage to in his Grammy-nominated 1999 tribute CD, "The Songs of Mississippi John Hurt."

"It was the simplicity, not just the guitar playing but the way he told stories," Morrissey says of Hurt. "The way the voice and guitar work together is very unique. He's anchoring the bass and rhythm with his thumb, then working around the melody on the treble strings; sometimes playing it, sometimes doing a harmony line, sometimes just being playful. And he's inclusive; he assumes the audience gets it, that he doesn't have to spell everything out."

Like many '60s-weaned songwriters, Morrissey is dismayed at what he sees as a reluctance by many young songwriters today to follow that same trail back to the roots of the form in which they hope to build careers.

"That was not the reason for the record," he says, " but it's always been very important to me that musicians go back and listen to what's gone on before, and I was seeing that not happening. It's like trying to build a house without a foundation. Every great musician knows where the music come from. Bob Dylan can sing you Carter Family songs, Jimmie Rogers songs, Stanley Brothers songs. And it's not just folk music. Charlie Parker could quote Coleman Hawkins and Lester Young note for note. It's like, how can you write a book without having read great books?"

It is suggested that where a lot of young songwriters got the idea that they had to do all their own songs was from artists like Morrissey. Only in the last few years has he been likely to perform any but his own songs on stage. Successful songwriters like him were the role models for the next wave, just as '60s stars like Tom Rush and Dave Van Ronk had been his models. But where he got intriguing smidgens of the traditional masters who had inspired his heroes, Morrissey's acolytes got only Morrissey songs—and wrote at the top of their Career To-Do Lists, "Sing All Your Own Songs."

At first Morrissey glowers at the suggestion, darts off to pour a few fingers of Jack Daniels into a glass and returns to the table. Then his face softens, he nods his head a little sadly, and shrugs.

"To me, the influences are very obvious. I thought anybody who heard me play guitar would think, 'God, he's listened to a lot of John Hurt.' But what I realized was that a lot of younger people didn't know his work, had never been exposed to it. And then I realized I had a responsibility to do something about that, to show people where my music came from."

"I think the mistake a lot of younger people make when they see songwriters like me and Greg Brown and Cheryl Wheeler is that we may seem like we're just writing about our lives, but we're not. We're incorporating what we learned in our lives to write songs about life in general. Whereas they think they can just write about their lives, and it means something to someone else. And it just doesn't. I don't want to read their diaries. I was 21; I know what they're going through, and so much of it is so solipsistic. Except for the good ones."

Morrissey has been a gracious mentor to those he sees as "the good ones." He produced Ellis Paul's first CD, and when Paul asked how much he wanted to be paid, he said, "When you're in my position—and you will be—do the same for somebody who's just starting out. That's how you pay me."

He also gave Paul long lists of songwriters whose work he should study, from Woody Guthrie to John Hurt to Randy Newman. "Paul jumped into it bigtime," Morrissey says with just a smack of parental pride, "and I think he's a much better writer and performer for it. I respect him very much."

When young Bill Morrissey was soaking up influences, shortly after a collegiate career at Plymouth State College that was notable only for moving him to New Hampshire, he sank into what he now knows was a deep and dangerous depression. He would crawl out of bed in mid-afternoon, turn on the record player and grab his guitar, listening and playing for 12, 14 hours until he tumbled back into bed.

"What drove me so nuts," he says, "was that there were so many different styles and voices—and they all worked. There wasn't one way to do it. Here's Randy Newman, who had just put his first album out, and he's got whole songs with 16 lines in them. Which was perfect. Then you've got Dylan singing those long ballads like 'Sad Eyed Lady of the Lowlands.' And there's no Songwriter 101; you have to figure it out yourself."

This was also the early '70s, and folk was beginning a decade-long decline. There were only a handful of acoustic listening rooms in all of New England back then, so Morrissey cut his teeth playing bars, singing to hard-drinking mill workers, fisherman and adrenaline-pumped skiers. That's where he discovered humor, as much as a survival mechanism as career tool.

"I didn't do a lot of covers even when I played bars; it was pretty much my own stuff," he says. "I got away with it by talking, with improv comedy. I would play off what was going on in front of me. By the second set, everybody was drunk and more than happy to offer a comeback. That was how I kept their attention. I wasn't that good a musician then, but I knew if I could make them laugh, they'd hire me back."

He picked up paychecks at notorious dives like the Chit-Chat Lounge in Haverhill, Massachusetts, where he once had a gun pulled on him: "Guy said 'let me play your guitar.' I said, 'No, it's my tool; it's how I make my living.' Guy pulls out a snub-nose .38 Smith & Wesson. I said, 'Would you like a flatpick or a fingerpick?'"

For those first few years, people would shut up when he *stopped* singing, eager for the comic repartee. As soon as he started another Morrissey original, the chatter resumed.

That wasn't as hard to take as knowing, deep down, that they were right. He wasn't writing songs that moved him the way those old folk and blues masters did. How could he expect them to move his audiences? He turned back to his influences, to Hurt and Guthrie, and found the answer not in how they wrote, but what they wrote. They wrote what they knew, what they saw outside their windows every day. Their songs were written about the people they sang them to.

Set to the ambling gait he learned from Hurt, he began writing tight, vivid ballads about life in New Hampshire's dying mill towns and hardscrabble seacoast. Soon, the hush continued after the banter, especially when he said, "Here's a new one."

"That was the life I knew and it interested me," he says. "During dry spells with the music, I worked some mills and chemical plants. People I'd worked with or shot pool with would come up to me and say they liked a particular song, that it rang true for them. The folk audiences dug it and the guys who were living it dug it. I thought I must be starting to get something right."

Morrissey's artistic growth paralleled a growth in the New England folk scene. The Idler in Harvard Square, which had been one of the better bar gigs for songwriters like Morrissey, suddenly blossomed into a premier showcase venue. Its manager, Len Rothenberg, became the Boston revival's principal architect, presenting '60s stalwarts like Tom Paxton along with urgent new stars like Canadians Stan Rogers and Ferron, building them from his club to major concert halls.

At the same time, Tom Rush was producing gala Club 47 reunions at vaunted Symphony Hall, proving that a tremendous audience still existed for folk music. Folk music on Boston public radio stations suddenly flowered into a fulltime presence, making it possible to new artists like Morrissey to be heard. The Boston Globe's Jeff McLaughlin devoted unprecedented space to the new folk revival, trumpeting Morrissey's music at every opportunity.

Morrissey was soon being managed by Rush, along with fellow up'n'comers Christine Lavin, Patty Larkin and Buskin and Batteau. When Cambridge-based

Rounder Records, the largest folk indie in the country, took over the bankrupt contemporary folk label Philo, it aggressively entered the singer-songwriter market. Morrissey was their flagship local artist.

"It was just fortunate timing for everybody," says Morrissey, lighting a cigarette and inhaling deeply, clearly savoring the excitement of those days. "The audience was building, and Rounder had their ears open to that. I've been with them ever since, for nine records. I'm lucky I haven't been traded. The great thing about Rounder is that they trust the artist; I can do the albums the way I want. And I love that they put out so many reissues of traditional artists that otherwise aren't going to get out there, and that don't have any chance of making money."

Morrissey hit full stride with his third album, "Standing Eight," produced by the brilliant Darleen Wilson, who did similarly defining projects for Larkin and Shawn Colvin, and recently co-produced "Cry Cry Cry" for Dar Williams, Lucy Kaplansky and Richard Shindell. Morrissey believed it would be his final record. While his fan base was growing, and his critical praise was unmatched by any emerging songwriter, his records had not sold well, had not captured the visceral charm of his stage shows. He doubted Rounder would pick up his option after their three-record deal was completed.

"With 'Standing Eight,' I wanted to put the emphasis on the songs," he says. "It's like editing; I only wanted what was called for. By only using one instrument or harmony, what I was doing wouldn't get lost in the mix."

"Standing Eight" remains one of the best albums to emerge from the songwriter movement of the 1980s. With a record that was finally as good as Morrissey himself, his career took off nationally, beginning a steady, 10-year climb.

In 1993, he had released three albums in two years, including his Grammy-nominated collaboration with Greg Brown, "Friend of Mine." It seemed like a good time to heed the pestering of friends and fans, including editor Fisketjon, and take a stab at a novel.

It took three years, absorbing him in ways he never expected. He would rise early, make coffee and scurry into his office; not so much to write, but because he had worried about his characters all night and wanted to know how they were doing.

"When I finished the book, I had a postpartum depression," he says, chuckling now at what was then a painful period. "I was losing my friends. They're going away; I'm sending them off to my editor. They were very real to me."

"Edson" was published by Knopf in 1996, to critical acclaim but nothing near breakthrough sales. It is a quiet little ballad of a novel, about a fading minor folk star and the young woman whose interest, and then love, help him reconcile the bitterness of his failed career and, ultimately, to realize why he needed to make music in the first place. It is a book like his songs, chocked with people you may not admire but that you like; and it is easily the most realistic portrayal of the modern folk world ever captured in a novel.

Morrissey's second novel, "Imaginary Runner" is finished but still making the rounds of publishing houses. He is increasingly looking for ways to make what many older touring musicians admiringly call "mailbox money;" ways to make a living that don't require leaving home.

His latest recording resonates with that longing for roots, for a sure sense of place. The drifters are even less attractive than in his earlier work, wearing teen-aged grins on middle-aged faces. When a grumbling, half-drunk old musician watches a young bar band in "Traveling by Cab," he sneers, "That ain't rock'n'roll, that's just vaudeville plugging in." The young bartender who's been humoring him says patronizingly, "Ain't that the way it's always been?" In "Harry's Last Call," an aging drifter and perennial adolescent is viewed as little more than a pathetic hamster, caught in the increasingly meaningless treadmill of his own predictably irresponsible behavior.

There are also the earthy romances that have always been a counterpoint to Morrissey's cynical hyper-realism. But in love songs like "Fix Your Hair the Way You Used To" and "Will You Be My Rose," the longing is less for love than for constancy, a deep-cut yearning for permanence. He may love his new little home in the hills, but everything in this new album says he does not love his aloneness in it.

Morrissey is relishing his growing role as an elder in the songwriting tribe, currently championing a young Boston songwriter named Cara Brown, for whom he will soon produce a premier album as he did for Ellis Paul.

"I feel pretentious calling myself a mentor," he says, popping into the kitchen for another Jack Daniels. "When I was just starting out, I wasn't shy about going to the pros after their shows and asking them to show me a chord progression or to explain something about their lyrics. And they never said no, whether it was Ian Tyson or Arlo Guthrie or Bert Jansch. They all took the time with me, so of course, when people ask me, I'm happy to return the favor."

This perhaps strikes closer to the heart of what annoys him about many of the young songwriters he sees on the scene today.

"I don't understand the lack of curiosity," he says. "I mean, when I was a kid, I just had to know where these songs came from. It wasn't easy finding a Bascom Lamar Lunsford record, but I loved the song 'Mole in the Ground,' and I had to find out what the guy who wrote it sounded like. Because I wanted to be a songwriter. The way you find your voice is to have influences, absorb them, learn what shaped their music, and then work through them to find something that's your own. I'm not saying these guys have to go out and sing 'Death Letter Blues.' But they ought to have heard it."

He said he still returns to traditional music whenever he feels blocked: "It always jump-starts the process."

And it is the process now, more than the product, that enchants him. He is in love with the work, with the ritual, the sense and order of it. He said he puts the time in, a few hours nearly every day, whether the ideas are coming or not. He learned long ago that, even in songwriting, fortune favors the prepared, and that inspiration is more likely to strike when he has a guitar in his lap and his mouth full of music.

"I both need and like the discipline," he says. "When I was 25, I said I never wanted to turn 50, which is coming up, look back and say I could have tried harder. I think I stayed true to that."

He puffs his cigarette, picks up his drink, swirls it in the glass, then puts it back down and nods his head. "It's a good feeling," he says, almost to himself.

—Autumn, 2001
Originally appeared in Sing Out! the Folk Song Magazine
Used by permission, Sing Out Corporation

The little steps of an endless dance Folk Arts Center of New England

A little after 7 p.m. on the last Friday of March, as someone has done every Friday for 41 years, Marcie Van Cleave began writing the evening's dances on a blackboard.

Along with waltzes and polkas, she listed the devetorka, long live London, rrobin ddiogg, tzena, andro and hambo, traditional folk dances from Bulgaria, England, Wales, Israel, Brittany and Sweden, respectively.

While fiddlers, accordionists, guitarists, and assorted flute players from the International Music Club filed into the basement of the First Unitarian Church in Belmont, she folded her arms and looked expectantly at the door.

"Well, all we need now are some dancers," she said, her voice bright but a bit worried.

The beginner level International Folk Dance is a local institution, the welcoming front door to the folk dance community. Founded by legendary dance activists Conny and Marianne Taylor, it has been held every Friday since 1958, first at the Cambridge YWCA, then in Chestnut Hill and in Harvard Square before moving to the Belmont United Methodist Church in 1993. Last month, it moved to the Unitarian Church, where it runs Fridays, except the second one of each month.

Van Cleave had no idea how many dancers would show up. She is director of the Folk Arts Center of New England, a nonprofit organization founded by the Taylors in 1975, which sponsors the dances and coordinates many of the hundreds of regular dances, workshops, seminars and dance camps that make New England one of the folk dance capitals of the country.

Shortly after 8, nine dancers were on hand, enough to form a circle and begin the first dance. By the end of the merry evening, more than 70 dancers and musicians had been on hand. A certain bittersweetness echoed within the buoyant music, laughter and chatty sociability, however. Everyone was having a grand time, but folk dancing is unquestionably in decline, and nobody is quite sure why.

Conspicuous by their absence were members of what Van Cleave called "the missing generation." The crowd ranged from children to adolescents, then skipped to boomers and seniors, but no one in their late teens or 20s.

Van Cleave taught each dance vividly and briefly. Beginners were clearly surprised at how quickly she had them dancing.

"I learned how to dance at these Friday nights myself," she said afterward, "just about 15 years ago, when Conny and Marianne were running them. The vivacity and humor with which they taught made it so enjoyable and formed the way I teach. There are some folk dance teachers who are drill sergeants, and some who go on and on about where each dance came from and what its purpose is. My goal is to make it fun, accurate but fun."

She has an instinct for the one tip that helps people begin figuring things out for themselves. She cautioned them to pay more attention to the right foot than the left, for example, since most movements lead with the right. Offering the useful maxim, "Small steps make small mistakes," she demonstrated how the uncertain dancer can twirl in ways not likely to cause fender-benders in the traffic rotary of the dance circle.

Van Cleave soon had the dancers moving fluidly and, more important, having fun. Each dance ended with laughter and brisk chatter as dancers replayed successful moves and near-disasters with one another. Van Cleave gave her most-satisfied smiles when she saw dancers begin to teach one another.

"There's many different ways of learning," she said. "Some people learn by hearing, some by watching, some by counting. The trick is finding more than one way to convey the information."

She can also count on the fact that not all the dancers are beginners. There is a special sociability to these beginners' events, and experienced dancers often drop by just for fun.

Andy Taylor-Blenis, for example, dances professionally with the Prometheus contemporary dance ensemble, and teaches modern, jazz and folk dance at

Folk dancers at the Falcon Ridge Folk Festival in upstate New York.

There are some folk dance teachers who are drill sergeants, and some who go on and on about where each dance came from and what its purpose is. My goal is to make it fun, accurate but fun.—Marcie Van Cleave

I'm madly in love with dancing. It sustains me, the rhythm, the music, the sociability. Music makes you so excited, the blood starts flowing in your veins and makes everyone so friendly. —Stella Penzer

the Boston Conservatory. The daughter of Conny and Marianne Taylor, she remembers when their Folk Dance 'Round Boston organization, the precursor to the Folk Arts Center, was run out of their Lexington home.

"My parents always said that the beginner is the life of dance," she said, "and to treat them all with care."

She attributed the absence of the "missing generation" to arts education cutbacks in the 1980s. When children don't get at least a taste of folk dancing, she said, they are far less likely to be drawn to it later.

Elgie Ginsburg, still a dance habitue at 70, grew up in Belmont and learned folk dancing while earning a Girl Scout badge. As a troop leader, she helped hundreds of children, including her own, earn similar badges.

"The Scouts don't have a folk dance badge anymore, and it's too bad," she said.

Taylor-Blenis is making sure her own two children are folk-dance-friendly, as they proved when they took the floor with several other youths to do a French-Canadian dance, an acrobatic routine done with brooms. Like so many traditional dances, it makes work into play, tools into toys.

"The dances are fun, but they also show how other people live," Taylor-Blenis' daughter Alexandra, 10, said after her dance. "We learn about the cultures by learning the dance. Like the broom dance, how they made a dance out of sweeping."

"There are Japanese dances that imitate fishing," said 13-year-old fellow broom-dancer Catherine Pixton, daughter of International Music Club founders Tom and Barbara Pixton, who often provide live music for the Friday dances.

"Sometimes there's specific dances for men and women," said Emily Dahl, 13.

"The women's dances have more fluid hand movements, and the men have more stamping foot movements. So it shows how their roles were different."

Asked why folk dancing wasn't more popular, all three simultaneously shouted, "Television!"

During a break, newcomer Sue Grolnic of Arlington caught her breath.

"This is the first time I've folk danced in 30 years," she said. She had gone to dances when attending Northeastern University. Newly single, she was looking for something comfortable to attend alone.

"We're a culture of couples," she said, "and all the years I was married, that seemed OK. But now that I'm single again, it's nice to find someplace you can come alone and still be social. And there really is a sense of community here."

That's what keeps drawing 77-year-old Stella Penzer, who grew up in Poland and has been folk dancing all her life. Still, she savors the easygoing pace of the beginner dances.

"I'm madly in love with dancing," she said. "It sustains me, the rhythm, the music, the sociability. Music makes you so excited, the blood starts flowing in your veins and makes everyone so friendly. I go to more advanced dances, but I enjoy these because of Marcie and, honestly—shall I tell you?—I'm getting a little bit older. So it's nice to do these at a slower pace. The steps are simple. It's not work, just fun. And now you must excuse me. I can't miss the waltz."

—April 4, 1999

Why Ireland's biggest recording star hasn't "gone huge" in America
Mary Black, Karan Casey and Seamus Egan of Solas

It has been a long time since the world viewed Mary Black as only an Irish singer. She has always proudly displayed her roots in Irish traditional music, first as part of the popular folk-singing Black Family, and then with the groundbreaking Celtic revival band DeDannan; but since her first solo record in 1983, she has become Ireland's premier—and best-selling—pop diva. Her seven albums there have outsold even rockers Sinead O'Connor and U2. Throughout Europe and Asia, her wonderfully pure and warm soprano has made her one of those rare artists, like Linda Ronstadt, Barbra Streisand, and Bette Midler, whose stature transcends the boundaries of genre.

Except in America. Here she remains doggedly defined as an Irish singer, which, to most people, means primarily a singer of Irish traditional music. No matter how hot she is elsewhere, the American pop industry pigeonholes her as a specialty artist and is reluctant to play her on commercial radio.

"America is a hard territory to crack for a lot of people, even for pop bands who have done really well everywhere else," she said. "For me, I think it's because I don't fall constantly into any one category. In one song, I can sound like a folk singer, in the next like something more country or bluesy.

"And in America, they really need to box things in, particularly from a radio-play point of view. You've got radio stations that just play this kind of music or that. In Europe, they're generally much more open-minded about music. Different styles of music can sit side by side in a radio program. The measure is how good the music is, not what category it is."

In an odd way, the enormous strength and self-reliance of the Irish music scene in America adds to the predicament. With a sturdy network of Irish and Celtic music programs on public and community radio stations, and a long tradition of fans supporting Irish artists and the independent labels for which they record, Black has found it unnecessary to court the mainstream music industry here.

My parents played and sang purely for the love of it. There was never any other agenda. I'm still like that. If I stopped enjoying the music, I'd have to stop. —Mary Black

"Shine," her 1997 American major-label debut on Curb, was supposed to break her out of the Irish music box. It didn't, and she followed it with a sweetly simple traditional anthology, "Song for Ireland," on Blix Street, North American distributors of her own Dara label.

"I don't know if `Shine' had any huge impact," she said. "I think I have a very strong following in America, most of whom were there before that. The bulk of my audience are people who've been with me for years, moving right along with me."

When you're selling out venues like Symphony Hall, as Black has, it's hard to get too worked up over career woes. Touring with her is the hot American-based Irish band Solas.

It is undoubtedly a sign of how healthy and secure Irish music is these days that so little fuss has been made about the innovations the brilliant quintet is bringing to the old music. Solas's new Shanachie CD, the passionate and adventurous "The Words That Remain," opens with Woody Guthrie's "Pastures of Plenty," and features American folk-based artists Bela Fleck and Iris DeMent.

"I've been a bit suprised there's as little attention paid to some of the different things we're doing," said Solas multi-instrumentalist Seamus Egan. "But when we added some new elements for this record, one of the things we wanted to be careful about was that, at the end of the day, it had to sound like the group not just trying to sound different. We wanted to strike a balance between trying new things, but also making it sound like it was not forced, like it was a natural evolution."

Solas singer Karan Casey grew up in County Waterford and was surprised by how much more awareness there is in America of what is and is not Irish music. Sessiuns, or informal music gatherings, for example, are much more likely to be dominated by Irish traditional music here than they are in Ireland, she said. Both she and Black were quick to say how perfectly understandable this ethnic consciousness is in a country like America, which has so many ethnic and national cultures in it.

"America is constantly in debate over identity, over ethnic backgrounds, color," Casey said. "That seems to be how America sorts people out, where in Europe, they tend to divide people up on the grounds of class. I'm not saying that's any better, but it's what tends to happen."

Black thinks her traditional upbringing gave her the tools to move gracefully from genre to genre, saying the breath control and discipline required for ancient Irish ballads help her adapt to modern pop, country, and jazz. But she said her traditional background gave her something even more important.

"My parents played and sang purely for the love of it," she said. "There was never any other agenda. I'm still like that. If I stopped enjoying the music, I'd have to stop. That's another reason why—and I say this knowing you might not believe me—it doesn't really bother me that I haven't sort of gone huge in America. It's wonderful to come here and sing for people who I know want to hear me do what I want to do. To still have that after 15 years is fantastic; I'm delighted."

—November 13, 1998

Altan keeps its promise **Mairead Ni Mhaonaigh**

With the sole exception of the Chieftains, Altan has emerged over the past 10 years as the world's preeminent Irish traditional band. Almost from the moment fiddler-singer Mairead Ni Mhaonaigh and flutist Frankie Kennedy, her late husband who died of cancer in 1994, left their Donegal homes, they have been seen as more than just budding stars. Veteran Irish players viewed their traditional savvy, along with their youthful charm and exuberance, as proof that the old music would be carried on.

From their debut in 1987, the quintet—which also includes fiddler Ciaran Tourish, accordionist Dermot Byrne, bouzouki master Ciaran Curran, and guitarist-singer Daithi Sproule (Mark Kelly replaces him on guitar when the band is in Ireland)—has honored that trust. In her earliest interviews, Ni Mhaonaigh (pronounced Nee-Wee-Ney) made two brash promises: that Altan would never compromise the music's ancient integrity, and that they would nonetheless someday achieve major-label success.

With their second album on Virgin Records, the wild and lovely "Runaway Sunday," Altan has kept both promises. It is a gorgeous, pulsing delight, its richness driven by the band's traditional instruments. Ni Mhaonaigh's fiddle and soprano anchor the sound, as they always have.

"If you disguise something," Ni Mhaonaigh said from her Dublin home, "people don't hear the essence of it. We have a very strong sense of this music. We were lucky enough to hear some of the best solo musicians ever, the likes of John Doherty and all the Donegal fiddlers, and then people like the great Seamus Ennis. And when you listen to these people, there was no need for backing, for embellishment."

For all their traditional devotion, it was the newness of Altan's sound that made them stars. The Donegal style is unique in Irish music. For centuries, it was isolated by its mountainous terrain, and more recently by Northern Ireland, which lies between much of Donegal and the rest of the Republic.

"Donegal is almost like an island within an island," she said. "It always has been. During the Industrial Revolution, a lot of people started to go to Scotland to work. And Donegal fisherman have always worked off the Scottish coast. They would exchange songs and tunes."

Altan

Altan

This Scottish influence sets Donegal music apart in many ways. While most Irish music is driven by jigs and reels, Donegal's includes Highlands and other Scottish-based tunes.

The fiddle style, displayed in Ni Mhaonaigh's electrifyingly close duets with fellow Donegal fiddler Tourish, is also unique; driving and fiery, it is informed by a mesmerizing drone. The sound is so distinctive, she said, because it is not a fiddle style at all.

"The fiddle style is based on Scottish piping, which has always existed in Donegal. I don't know how, but the connection was always there. A lot of the fiddle tunes are derived from piping tunes, from marches and other melodies that use drones a lot. All the older folk were always imitating the pipes, with the drones blowing at the same time the melody was played. The more you sounded like the pipes, the better fiddler you were. So they'd be trying all sorts of retunings, making the bass string bassier, doing a lot of technical things to imitate the piping sound. A lot of the Donegal technique is based on that."

Ni Mhaonaigh's singing also benefited from her Donegal roots. She grew up in one of the few regions of Ireland where Gaelic is still a first language. Her phrasing on brisk Irish-language songs and slow ballads is graceful; sung in a pure, airy soprano that is as natural as it is beautiful. She sounds as if she has sung these songs all her life, because she has.

"My uncle was a great singer, knew all kinds of songs," she said. "Jimmy was a great man for singing a song that meant something real to him. For instance, he'd come in from the fields and start singing about harvest time. It made the song so alive to me, because he'd just come in from doing that. It was something right there, about something he'd done that day, although the song might have been a hundred years old."

That sort of upbringing does not encourage a young artist to begin thinking of ways to gussy up the old melodies to suit modern tastes. When Virgin Records approached Altan, they were so convinced of their virtuosity, they made a point to say they wanted the band to have complete artistic control. Ni Mhaonaigh is proud of that, of course, but even prouder of the effect Altan is having on many young players throughout Ireland.

"By focusing on our own tradition in Donegal," she said, "it started people thinking about their own parishes or little distinctive styles. In the '60s, there was this great revival of Irish music. There was a dilution of the local styles; they were starting to blend into each other. People were predicting Ireland ould end up with one style; everybody playing the same way. What happened with us has maybe helped refocus things, and now you have people concentrating on the Kerry style or the Sligo style, all the distinct styles within Irish tradition.

"It's refreshing to hear something that's not compromised, that's completely different from anything else that's out there, because it's coming from the true people and the true psyche. The music has obviously developed over thousands of years to this stage, and will continue to develop long after we're gone. You know, we're just part of the present of the music."

—July 17, 1998

Folk music sprouts in the suburbs
Garnet Rogers, manager David Tamulevich, coffeehouse directors Michael Moran, Jim and Beth Sargent

When people call Boston the folk music capital of the country, they don't exactly mean Boston. For more than 50 years, this region has been America's most active and nurturing sanctuary for folk music, but the action these days is mostly in the suburbs. There are a few important urban clubs, notably Cambridge's indestructible Club Passim, and a steady stream of major concerts, but no area in the country can match the vast array of folk clubs that dot Boston's suburbs.

David Tamulevich, who covers New England for Fleming-Tamulevich and Associates, the largest folk music management agency in the country, estimates that more than 200 Greater Boston venues offer folk music, all but a handful of them in the suburbs.

The heart of this grass-roots folk boom is a thoroughly New England phenomenon called the church coffeehouse. The modern folk revival can be traced to the growth in the early '80s of small, grass-roots clubs like the Homegrown Coffeehouse in Needham and the Uncommon Coffeehouse in Framingham; run by volunteers, driven by community-based audiences indifferent to the latest pop trends, and fueled by remarkable performers who eschew the bright lights of pop-stardom for the living-room closeness of the coffeehouse.

Beth and Jim Sargent started their Homegrown Coffehouse in 1983 in the parish hall of their First Parish Church. It is the quintessential New England church coffeehouse, renowned for its friendly audiences and intimate performances.

"In the early '80s, there was just such a drought in the 'burbs for live music," Beth Sargent said. "Acoustic music was something we both loved in college, and we thought other people would love it, too, if they got the chance. Although people of all ages come, our audience draws heavily from the boomer generation. They like that it's something nearby, something they can bring their kids to if they want, something comfortable and social and friendly to do on a Saturday night."

A major misconception about these coffeehouses is that they are second-rate venues featuring beginners or over-the-hill acts. While nearly all of today's biggest folk-pop stars, from Suzanne Vega to Shawn Colvin to Dar Williams, cut their musical teeth at local church coffeehouses, most of the artists who headline these coffeehouses have fashioned careers designed for the small stages. Here is where they feel that this most personal of music forms, which has its roots in family kitchens and hearthsides, is best displayed.

Singer-songwriter Garnet Rogers is a perfect example. A major folk star in his native Canada, he has repeatedly rebuffed serious offers from major record labels, preferring to release CDs on his own Snow Goose Records and to steer his career down the smaller, slower roads that lead to homey venues like the Homegrown and the Uncommon, which he played just last weekend.

Rogers says he revels in the up-close immediacy of the church coffeehouse, most of which have average audiences of 125 to 175.

"Generally, for me, I walk in around 5 o'clock," he said, "and the first volunteers are opening the place up. One of the things I really like about these church coffeehouses is the volunteer aspect; this is part of their social life, they've given up an evening out of their week to make this hall someplace I can play."

"It's like watching a National Geographic special, all these army ants come in with baked goods and coffee and chairs and tables, tablecloths, sometimes candles. A stage gets set up, a sound system, usually a tapestry with the coffeehouse's name hanging behind the mikes. I watch this big, empty church hall turn into a nice little folk club right before my eyes."

It takes a special kind of performer to work these rooms, one who thrives on spontaneity, happy to discard the greatest-hits list and wrap the evening around moments of surprise and discovery. They are what audiences turn out for, those off-script moments that make coffeehouse shows so memorable.

"We try to have a little livelier profile here than at the average coffeehouse," said Michael Moran, whose energetic management approach added new life to the nearly extinct Uncommon Coffeehouse at Framingham's First Parish Church when he took its helm four years ago. "You're never more than 30 feet from the performer, so people can tell if an artist is faking it. There is a connection being made that you're not going to get in a big music hall. You sometimes hear the expression, 'the performer carried the night.' Well, that's got to happen here every time for it to work. In a setting like this, artists have to be able to really move people. If you have that ability, you're going to do great. If you don't, it really doesn't matter what you sound like; you might as well pack it in."

Most church coffeehouses draw heavily from the local community, with ages ranging from teenagers to seniors. For many, the fame of the artist is secondary to the town-social aspect of the evening. Most church coffeehouses have intermissions lasting up to an hour, while people mill around, chatting and sipping coffee, tea and cider. Though the Uncommon occasionally gets a one-night beer license for a dance, the rule-of-thumb at these places is that they are alcohol- and smoke-free. They are valued as friendly, nonthreatening places to go alone, as couples or in groups. It is a guiding etiquette that people can be as social or as private as they please.

Rogers said, "Everybody expects a smooth performance, but coffeehouse audiences also want surprises. That's what keeps drawing me back. A lot of the audience is there for the coffeehouse as much as for me; they come for the season. That lends a certain level of familiarity, because they feel so comfortable there.

"I'll be in the middle of some dither, some carefully honed song introduction, and somebody will respond to something that's maybe a little too worked out, and suddenly the whole thing just explodes in my face," Rogers said. "That joke goes way farther than what you had planned, because somebody just scored off you, and it was real. It adds a real element of danger and chaos to the proceedings that I just love. It's much more like you're working without a net than at the big concert halls."

One reason these church coffeehouses thrive in New England and not elsewhere is a long tradition of viewing church halls as secular spaces. Most halls are simply rented at bare-bones cost to volunteer committees that usually, but not always, include church members.

Sargent, who is a member of the Homegrown's host church, said the word "parish," which is part of so many church names here, was meant in Colonial times to denote that the church also functioned as the town hall. In areas more recently settled, such as the Midwest, the church was the one place people could go to celebrate not just their religion, but their ethnic or racial identity. They are regarded as more private places, and attempts to open coffehouses, even at Unitarian churches known for secular outreach, often fail.

"The parish hall was where a lot of civic and secular work got done," said Sargent, "so there's a long history in New England of viewing churches as secular community spaces. A lot of these coffeehouses are at Unitarian churches, because I think Unitarians are very open to the idea that a spiritual experience does not have to be a religious one in the narrow sense of that word."

Moran welcomes the continuing growth of church coffeehouses. **"What we are really fighting here is that people are used to spending their lives in front of their television sets, letting other people live their lives for them.** I remember when I was growing up, I knew all my neighbors. I only know three of them now, and the reason is that we don't go out. So every time a new coffeehouse comes along that gets people out of their own playrooms and meeting their neighbors, I think we're taking a big step toward fixing what's wrong with our society."

Rogers said, "If you look at the demographic of who goes to the church coffeehouse, they tend to be people who are leading an examined lifestyle. They're people who tend to read a lot, are serious about music. . . . You're free as a performer to express deeper ideas with these people.

"There's more of an organic gardening approach to modern folk music, as opposed to the clear-cutting or strip-mining mentality of the pop industry. . . . Folk music is just a more humane and involved atmosphere; as opposed to getting frisked by a big bouncer as you fall into the Enormo-dome to watch your favorite star on the Jumbo-tron. Do you want that, or do you want to actually be included in the fun? That's what it's all about."

—September 28, 1997

Her *"mom music"* made her a star **Lori McKenna**

Lori McKenna might become a star, if she could only find the time. The 32-year-old Stoughton housewife and mother of four may be the hottest songwriter in town, able to fill the 800-seat Somerville Theater two consecutive nights—an almost unprecedented feat for a local folk act. According to Songstreet Productions, which produced the shows, no local songwriter in the past two years—not Jess Klein, Ellis Paul, Catie Curtis, or Kris Delmhorst— has shown the box-office muscle at the Somerville that McKenna did when more than 200 people were turned away from her first headline show there last winter.

No one is more surpised by this than McKenna, who has stubbornly designed her career to accommodate her chosen lifestyle as stay-at-home mother and wife of Gene McKenna, who works for a Brockton utility company. Her children are Brian, 12, Christopher, 7, Mark, 9, and Meghan, 4 months.

"People will say to me, 'Gee, if only you didn't have kids, you could play music all the time,'" she says while watching Meghan bounce in her jumper. "Now that I've gotten a little success, I realize I don't want to do that. I like being able to watch 'Scooby Doo' with the kids in the afternoon. What I do is a lot easier than if I had to work 50 hours a week in an office. I feel like I have the best of both worlds; I get to have this artistic career and still, most days, stay home with the kids."

It is precisely this level of unselfconsciousness that gives her intimate songs their appeal. She began writing just for herself, during stolen moments between tending the kids and the household chores; personal expressions of the grating travails and emotional roller-coasters all young mothers face. As a result, many young parents feel she is singing their songs.

Her second CD, "Pieces of Me" (Catalyst), opens with the almost defiantly unglamorous line, "There's a hole wearing through this couch of mine." In that song, called "Mars," she realizes she has reached that inevitible parent's moment when her own big dreams fade away and are supplanted by her children's dreams. But she does not admit this without regret, even a little anger. She never sugar-coats the parent's experience. In her darkest songs, she captures the sense of worthlessness and despair that overtakes many young mothers. In that honesty, her fans find healing.

"I got an e-mail from a stay-at-home mom who said I was like her mom music," she says. "You know, the kids had their kids' music, and I was her mom music. I thought that was awesome. Because I know what it is when you first have kids and you're not sure you're doing it right. And the other thing about staying home is that you're not with adults all day, and you're up all night with feedings; it gets really lonely. So it's great that if she's up at two o'clock for a feeding, she could put on my CD and feel like there was somebody else who knew how her life was. And I do; I know exactly how her life is."

In this determination to express her real life in all its blemished glory, she evokes the best instincts of folk music and of the ordinary people who first created it as the self-made soundtrack to their daily lives. In the CD's title cut, she sings, "I have been a poet all my life, with really not too much to say." She goes on to contrast her emotional needs with those of her husband: "I can hold you like water in my hands/ Yet you say that you can't leave/ Still I am dripping wet with things to understand/ And you are trying to believe."

Through this dark recognition of the distances that still exist between them, she comes to quiet terms with what love really is over the long haul. Her ability to build songs around the frayed, imperfect realities of life gives them a visceral power that her fans find both wrenching and redemptive.

She believes that power comes precisely from the fact that she writes these songs just for herself, and she tries to leave them in their raw, unfiltered state.

"You wouldn't edit your journal, because nobody's going to see it but you," she says. "It's the same with these songs; I always just write them for myself. It's a selfish thing; I'm just doing it to make myself happy. I'm really not that clever to think about things like writing songs for airplay or career. The only difference now is that I try to craft them a little better, because I know other people are going to hear them."

The reason these intimate songs never seem self-absorbed is simply that McKenna is not self-absorbed. Even as she explains how she writes just for herself, she pulls Meghan from her jumper with that uncanny prescience mothers of infants have. Meghan is not crying, but she's about to; sure enough, she soon begins to whimper, then bawl. McKenna leaves to change her diaper.

"I never actually think I'm writing songs for other people who are in my position," she says when she returns. "But if I'm going to talk about myself, I'm not going to talk about how everything's always perfect. Because it isn't. When I started singing the songs for other people, I was surprised to find that they could take their own little things out of them, and then thank me for for that.

"It's always amazing to me that people do that, but that's what I do with other people's songs, too. I think that's why it's important that regular people like me just go out and sing about their lives the way they are; not trying to please the radio guy or the record-label guy."

At that, she wrinkles her nose and says with an impish grin, "It's all about me, y'know? It's just all about me." But as she says it, she absently wipes spittle from her baby's chin, bouncing Meghan on her knee to the rhythm of the words.

—December 7, 2001

Singing the praises of family life
Kate Campbell, Maria Sangiolo, Deborah Silverstein, sociologist Alex Liazos

The idea for a special concert of songs about how families really work began percolating in the mind of Regis College professor Alex Liazos after a female student cracked that his "Sociology of the Family" course was good birth control. "Excuse me?" he said.

"Well, you know," she said, "who would want to have kids after reading all this stuff?" "A lot of things I'd been thinking for a while began to crystallize then," Liazos said. "I saw how most of what we teach about family is fairly critical. The textbooks talk about conflicts in families, issues parents face raising children, and problems children have. We focus too much on those problems, not nearly enough about what's good about families."

So Liazos and Regis College decided to present "Families in Words and Music," a concert featuring three songwriters—Kate Campbell, Deborah Silverstein, and Maria Sangiolo—who write about modern family life with uncommon candor and emotional credibility.

As a psychotherapist in Cambridge and the mother of two daughters, Silverstein deals with family issues in her work and songs. She left a full-time music career to begin a family, but still sings professionally with the popular local trio, Taproot. She believes much of the trouble families face today is a painful tug of "fantastic expectations imposed on us by media mythology versus the realities of daily family relationships."

She addresses that in her music by writing about ordinary family moments, parent-child rituals such as nightly walks that can do so much to keep families close.

"Ordinary life shouldn't feel wrong, like a failure, but it does to a lot of people today," she said. "The commercial media is an oppressive force, creating expectations that couples will be wildly happy and stimulated by each other on a constant basis; that all our children will be extraordinary; and that you need great wealth to be satisfied or feel successful. It's hard for us to understand what's ordinary and good versus what's unachievably perfect."

> *In the early spring when the crocus blooms*
> *We'll go in search of the fiddlehead fern*
> *And hear the songs of all the birds*
> *And wonder why they have no words*

"Walking in the Woods," words and music by Maria Sangiolo

photo: J. Frederick Smith

Sangiolo, a regular performer on the local coffeehouse circuit, said she was unprepared for the number of ways parenthood would change her life for the better. She worried she would not have time to write songs but discovered that jotting down fragments while caring for her daughter Sienna, 2, and putting them together during quiet evenings, allowed them to ripen and mature.

She also became closer to her parents, savoring their new relationship as fellow parents and asking them to help her better understand the old family stories she will soon pass on to Sienna. She had no idea how much more deeply felt her life would become.

"You think you wear your heart on your sleeve as a songwriter," she said, "but when you become a parent,

it just gets ripped out of your chest a million times a day. It's wrenching the way you see yourself as you used to be in your child, that pure innocence and truth. You want to get back there so you can be a child with her, be close to her. That's when you realize how much society does to keep us from being close in those innocent ways. Becoming a parent for me has been a process of uncovering that innocence again."

> *Photographs and old 45s stowed beneath a homecoming gown*
> *Pictures of me at sweet 16; but everything's not as it seems*
> *In my mother's house*
> "In My Mother's House," words and music by Kate Campbell

Like many Southern writers, Tennessee songwriter Kate Campbell wrestles with the strong place family holds in that culture. For example, she said she is far more likely to be asked "who my people are" by fans in the South; and she's not at all sure if that's a good thing—denoting a family-friendly culture—or a bad thing—residue from the class system of the antebellum South.

Such dual-edged swords, she said, are why so many writers like her feel they must understand the Southern family in order to understand the South.

" `In My Mother's House' was the hardest song I ever had to write," said Campbell, a full-time performer who is married but has no children. "It's about how parents and children keep these fixed perceptions of each other. You know, my mother thinks I'm eccentric, and I think I'm a very common person. Artsy is the word she uses.

"I never used to know how to deal with that, because underneath it was this hope that I'd come to my senses, settle down, and have five children. I'm fascinated by the process of how we deal with those perceptions, because how we react to them, how we grow through them, really determines who we are going to be."

Asked what they thought threatened the modern family the most, everyone said, in one way or another, that it was time. Many parents are just too busy to create those innocent rituals, those lazy, walking-in-the-woods moments that can keep families close.

Professor Liazos, who has two daughters, now includes contemporary folk songs about family in his class, and sees how clearly they convey what family life looks like when it's working.

"That's what folk music does so well," he said. "It shows us how those good moments feel—better than any sociology textbook I've ever found."

—April 27, 2001

Appearing in a living room near you:
Folk music & house concerts
Barbara Kessler, Susie Burke & David Surrette,
house concert producers Laurie Laba, Neal Ecksteine,
Gary Martin & Barry Kasindorf

It takes Laurie Laba and Neale Ecksteine most of the day to transform their Sudbury home into a concert hall. Gary Martin, on the other hand, can do it in just a couple of hours—but then, he bought his Assonet home with concerts in mind.

House concerts are a growing phenomenon in the grass-rootsy folk-music world. They are a far cry from a simple private party; many of them are well-organized and professionally mounted shows for which people make reservations and attend as they would a nightclub. They are a rewarding and social hobby for those with a yen to entertain in their homes, and an informal alternative for people yearning for a night out that's sociable, affordable (tickets generally range from $10 to $20), and, well, homey.

Ecksteine and Laba have an e-mail list of more than 1,100 people to whom they send announcements of their monthly Fox Run House Concerts, named after the street they live on. Martin's list for his Music by the Bay hovers at around 200, but he draws extensively from the New Bedford area and is frequently seen handing out fliers of upcoming shows at folk concerts there.

Show day begins at 10 a.m. for Ecksteine, a dentist, and his psychologist wife, Laba. He is a one-man stage crew, setting up his first-rate sound system, moving two sofas to the wall in the family room of their contemporary, open-floor-plan home, and arranging 40 chairs. The family room adjoins the kitchen to form an L-shaped space, allowing for 20 more seats.

"I would hate for people to think you need a lot of technical knowledge and gadgetry to do house concerts," Ecksteine said. "I just enjoy this stuff, because I'm an amateur musician myself. Very few house concerts do any of this. What people really have to focus on is the practical side, like how to deal with parking, tickets, taking reservations."

That is Laba's domain. The phone rings almost constantly on the day of shows, which nearly always sell out. Some people inevitably cancel the advance reservations that Laba and most house-concert producers insist upon as friendly ways of screening people before giving out their home address. Then there are calls to people on the waiting list with the good news that seats are available. She also sets up a greeting table, a space for performers to sell their recordings, and the potluck table, a staple of nearly all house-concert series.

Martin, a professor of mathematics at the University of Massachusetts at Dartmouth, keeps the second-floor living room of his contemporary home concert-ready all the time. He just shoves two couches and four rocking chairs to the walls, sets up about 40 folding and director's chairs, and he's there. He has no sound system. Of course, he bought the house for its concert potential.

"I kept telling my real estate agent I was looking for a house for concerts," he said. "She showed me places where the design wasn't quite right; there were bends in the room or the sight-lines weren't good. She was getting a little frustrated and said, 'Well, I've only got one more to show you; but you didn't say you wanted waterfront.'"

He allowed that he had nothing *against* waterfront, and off they went. The moment he strolled into the pine-paneled, slant-ceilinged living room, with its spectacular view of Assonet Bay, he was sold.

Martin puts most of his setup time into preparing coffee and snacks for the potluck table. Most house concerts encourage people to bring food, which enhances the variety of offerings, keeps costs down, and adds greatly to the sociable vibe of the shows.

"I enjoy the fact that everyone brings snacks," said Fox Run regular Adam Rosenoff of Framingham. "It makes it feel more like you're just getting together with friends, more like a party than a concert. As you gather around the snack table, you get to know people. You get e-mailed about shows, and you e-mail them back. It's more social than coffeehouses or nightclubs; here, you're very much invited."

Before a recent Fox Run show, Framingham songwriter Barbara Kessler warmed up in an upstairs guest room. She was grateful for the private space; house concerts don't always provide it.

"You have to go in prepared, because you may be in a social situation from the moment you walk in," she said.

Still, she loves doing them. Like the best contemporary folk songwriters, she writes probingly personal songs from her own life as young wife and mother.

"My songs have a kind of a conversational tone," she said, "so they just seem to work in the give-and-take of a house concert. This music was kind of born there anyway."

Indeed, there is a long history of folk music presented this way, tracing back to rent parties during the Great Depression, when itinerant musicians would host house parties to earn rent money. Irish music first took hold in Boston through "kitchen rackets" in the homes of immigrants, so named for the noise that dancers made on linoleum floors. Hootenannies grew from a tradition of such informal gatherings to become the college fad from which the '60s folk revival grew.

Of course, the history goes back even further. Originally, the term folk music referred to the music ordinary people made for themselves, the self-made soundtrack to their daily lives.

Maine folk performers Susie Burke and David Surette recently did a Sunday afternoon show for Martin's Music by the Bay Concert Series. Their mix of new songs and traditional tunes was wonderfully displayed in the wood-warm acoustics of Martin's living room. During their first song, as if on cue, the sun peeked through the clouds; by show's end, the bay had melted, a gray sheen of ice replaced by blue, rippling currents.

"People come to these with a different air than they do dressing up for a night concert," Burke said afterward. "It feels much more relaxed. Performing in a 500-seat theater, you have to think about size, that some small gesture might get lost on the audience. But nothing is lost on people in a house concert. Everything is seen and everything is shared."

Ellen and Allen Fingeret of North Providence, R.I., think nothing of making the trek for Martin's shows. They heard about them through a Providence coffeehouse they attend.

"The informality tends to lead to people talking to one another a little more," said Ellen Fingeret. "At a coffeehouse, the focus is more on the performers. There's a little more looking around here; it's a lot more casual."

Her husband said that sociability affects the show: "There's more of a relationship with the performer here, because there's no stage. There's no break between them and us."

Martin, Laba, and Ecksteine recommend not doing too much planning in mounting a house concert, because it's impossible to know what you'll need—except chairs. Because the Fox Run series donates proceeds to charity (the $17 ticket price includes $12 for the performer and $5 for charity), they got a good deal from Staples on folding chairs and picked up a coat rack at Bradlee's. Martin, who gives all his proceeds to the performers (ticket prices vary), found director's chairs on sale. No one interviewed was aware of any house concert that is run for profit.

They focused on building their first audience base from friends, neighbors, and co-workers. They all recommend talking to neighbors prior to the first concert, not only to hear their concerns about things that might affect them, such as parking, but also to invite them. The core audience for both series includes neighbors, and both cited new friendships with neighbors as a reward of the shows.

The Internet is the house concert's best friend. Nearly all publicity and reservations can be done by e-mail, and Laba lets people buy tickets through paypal.com, an online money courier. None of the hosts has ever experienced a problem from an unruly patron.

Both the Fox Run and Music By the Bay series represent the high-end of the house concert world. Many people, like Barry and Deborah Kasindorf of Franklin, do much more occasional and informal concerts. The living room of their four-bedroom Colonial home is converted to concert space in less than an hour, using the adjoining dining room for a crowd of around 30. While they have a Web site and small e-mail list, they think of their shows much more as house parties than as the public concert series that Fox Run and Music By the Bay have become.

"If you're doing house concerts, you have to judge how much above the radar you want to be," said Barry Kasindorf, a computer programmer. "Fox Run is way up there; they're everywhere promoting their series. I'm not sure I want to give up that much of my privacy. There's a lot of people who do house concerts and just invite their friends. But however you do it, it's a kick to see one of your favorite performers playing in your own living room, to look around and see how much fun everyone's having, and know you created that environment."

For general information on house concerts, including how-to tips, go online to www.ifolk.org, or www.houseconcerts.com.

—*March 15, 2001*

The Blues Lights His Fires Guy Davis

At first glance, Guy Davis seems like a one-man country blues revival. The 42-year-old actor-singer-playwright has taken the blues to Broadway, appearing in "Mulebone," and drew raves in the title role of the off-Broadway play "Robert Johnson: Beat the Devil." His own one-actor musical, "In Bed With the Blues: The Adventures of Fishy Waters," was also well received in its off-Broadway run and remains an ongoing project. In 1993, Davis was given the prestigious W.C. Handy "Keeping the Blues Alive" Award. Thanks to his wonderful debut disc, "Stomp Down Rider" (Red House), Davis' musical career is keeping him busier than ever as well.

All this activity may seem unusual outside the Davis family, but not to the son of actors Ossie Davis and Ruby Dee. Speaking from his New York home, he said, "My folks have always told me: Son, if you become an actor—and they never pushed me—don't just sit by the phone waiting for Hollywood to call. Go out and make work for yourself."

Too much talk about his many-faceted career, however, doesn't particularly stoke Davis' fires. He is pleasant enough, but almost uninterested. Asked if he has trouble balancing his music career with his acting, he replies, "Well, let's just say it's not as hard as not having the work."

When he is praised for his honest, masterful treatment of rural blues classics

Someday the dust of my bones will be something my great-great-grandchildren will be walking on, and I.look at that in a very positive light. I want to be in the atmosphere, part of what is old. —Guy Davis

by icons such as Johnson, Blind Willie McTell and Leadbelly, he says, "I wouldn't go to a concert hall to hear me sing, I don't think. But I love doing what I do, I just love this music."

When the blues itself becomes the topic, however, Davis heats up. His voice quickens, his passions arouse. It is easy to still see the wonder-struck 13-year-old who first heard Buddy Guy's note-bending blues on a precocious outing to a nightclub. The blues took immediate hold and has not let go.

"It was the guitar at first," he said. "But then I heard Blind Willie McTell, how he'd tell stories when he was playing. I thought that was just the greatest thing in the world, because it took me right back to the tradition in my family, which is telling stories around the supper table, going over to Grandma's and hearing stories. Our family was good for that."

It was when he began to feel the tradition, the history, in the blues, that he knew he was hooked for life: "I love old things. I love old music, old stories, old people, old cups and saucers and tools. I love things that have some dust on them, the dust of time. This goes deep with me. Someday the dust of my bones will be something my great-great-grandchildren will be walking on, and I look at that in a very positive light. I want to be in the atmosphere, part of what is old."

Unlike many contemporary bluesmen, Davis does not fight the oldness of the music. He revels in the folksy, rural cleverness of the wordplay, adding just enough Southern dust to his deep New York voice to phrase the old lyrics easily but unaffectedly. His guitar is just as at home with the many distinct styles of folk blues: the rollicking intelligence of McTell; the raw, sinewy stomp of Robert Johnson; the hard drive of Leadbelly; and the lonely ache of Mance Lipscomb. His playing is so natural it belies the daunting complexity of these masters' arrangements, and his own songs nestle in comfortably. Davis' aim seems always to transport you into the blues experience, never to strut his own considerable virtuosity.

That austerity reflects the deep respect he holds for the blues, both as a vibrant music form and as an emotional expression of the black experience in America.

"If you think about the blues in its most raw roots, it is something that has been with us ever since slave times. Maybe not in the 12-bar or eight-bar form, but if you look at its roots in those field hollers or work songs, you really see the history. The blues moved along with the people, and as a people we've always been concerned with improvement, with getting that next leg up. And improvement sometimes means shucking off the old things and taking on new things. For a lot of people, what the blues was had to go by the wayside the same way minstrelsy did, with the black face and the big white lips. You didn't want to have to be singing about just surviving the hard times, you wanted to look at the good times ahead. So swing music, rhythm and blues came along. And I understand that.

"But this music is treasure, it's gold; part of the process of our people. It teaches us about ourselves, not just the hard times we had, but the things we did to survive and become who we are now."

—*January 12, 1996*

Finding peace beneath the blues Chris Smither

Chris Smither is 52. This will likely not come as comfortable news to the boomers who have followed the boyish bluesman-songwriter since his salad days as a '60s folk star. And it may come as a surprise to his legions of young fans who helped make his last two High Tone CDs the most successful of his career. His latest, the alluringly spare, rootsy "Small Revelations," has hit No. 3 on the college charts.

Smither himself is surprised only that his legendary hard-living ways failed to do him in before he quit drinking in the early '80s. There were no Chris Smither records between 1972 and 1985. In the here-today-gone-this-afternoon climate of the music business, it is astonishing that any artist could have survived such a drought. But Smither, who is doing the best work of his career, believes those hard, killing years may have been his saving grace.

"You have a certain lifespan, mine just got delayed," he said. "So here I am having a pretty good time of it at age 52, when, just in the natural course of things, it might have been over 10 years ago had it gone on uninterrupted. The stuff that's going on for me right now is very exciting. I never thought I'd live to see my picture in The New York Times, let alone People magazine."

Skating on the surface of "Small Revelations," Smither sounds as he always has: a smart, contemporary songwriter and awesome guitarist whose rhythmic groove and melodic sense are banked deeply in the hot fires of the blues. In the lyrics, though, which shine in the tender austerity of Stephen Bruton's production, Smither is every bit the graybeard. Contrary to what many pop pundits preach today, Smither says this maturity is central to his appeal with young fans. They approach him everywhere with the same praise: "You're great, you really say stuff."

"Rock 'n' roll and most blues-influenced music is basically simple," he said. "It's trying to get across ideas that are actually pretty simple with a jackhammer. You cannot avoid it; the whole beat, the whole rhythmic vehicle of blues, which later became rock 'n' roll, is insistent. You just cannot get away from it, and it's an ideal vehicle for making a point. What I've been trying to do is get across some very

You just realize there are no talismans, there's nothing you can hang onto that's going to help you, no sure-fire life preservers. All you've got is your own sense of adventure. —Chris Smither

complicated ideas with elements of that same style. And it's not easy."

Smither's songs often trade in the disquieting uncertainties that are, in the end, life's only certainty. In the title cut, he wrestles with the accommodation and compromise that must accompany lasting love:

Passion is feeling in motion
Compassion is standing still
This isn't justification
Hearing is letting it happen
To listen's a work of will.

In "Slow Surprise," he portrays a love undetectably disintegrating, perhaps for lack of those very accommodations:

It seems so sudden, but it's not, it's only grown
From a seed that long ago was left forgotten in the snow.

This is tough stuff in an industry that wants quick hooks, catchy refrains and a beat you can dance to—all in three minutes. But wonderfully, Smither delivers all that along with the deeper things that led the San Francisco Chronicle to dub him a "philosopher-songwriter." His songs are infectiously melodic, driven by a fluid blues groove, delivered with plenty of hot guitar and sure, passionate vocals.

"Pure rock 'n' roll is a young person's music," Smither said. "It's young because it has absolute convictions. And that is a privilege of youth; those are the only people who can be absolutely sure that they're right about anything. Things that you take as articles of faith when you're 25 you learn much later in life are not necessarily so."

Smither envies few of his more successful rock contemporaries as he sees them trying to squeeze into the ol' spandex, still singing about sexuality with what is hoped will pass for the urgency of youth, but which more often sounds like tired batteries in need of a jump. Smither is grateful now for the hard times that allowed his music to grow up with him; and that there is still a market for those who want to tap their feet and hear the truth at the same time.

"I'm so grateful this success didn't happen to me when I was 25, because I would have been just insufferable. I couldn't have handled it. I would have immediately started to repeat the things I knew worked instead of trying to do new things. One of the nice things about being 50 is you reach a point where you realize nobody can sink you if you've lived this long. You just realize there are no talismans, there's nothing you can hang onto that's going to help you, no sure-fire life preservers. All you've got is your own sense of adventure."

—*March 20, 1997*

Joan Baez looks back at her brand-new career
Joan Baez, Dar Williams

It cannot be easy being Joan Baez. Not entirely unpleasant, to be sure, because for nearly 40 years she has been a major star, among the few folk singers of the 1960s to maintain a consistently viable career. But ever since she climbed on the stage of the Newport Folk Festival in 1959, a shy, nervous 18-year-old in leather sandals and a borrowed coat, it seems that her every song or career move is intensely judged by fans and enemies alike.

She was not even on the bill that year but a guest of folk singer Bob Gibson. She sang only two songs but that was enough. The crowd was enraptured by her almost angelic demeanor (which she now attributes to a stage fright bordering on terror) and what New York Times critic Robert Shelton, in his famous star-making review, described as her "achingly pure soprano."

"I knew I was the little darling of Newport that year," she says now, "I knew that much. That I would be on the front of Time magazine within a matter of months, I didn't get that. I didn't have any idea of the magnitude of it."

From the first, she was much more than a singer. Battle lines in the '60s formed on whether one loved or hated Joan Baez. She was a fiery antiwar activist, and no white musical figure, not even Pete Seeger, was more identified with the Southern civil rights movement. Barely old enough to vote, she was the sweet-voiced icon of the '60s movement, seen by the whole world marching arm in arm with Martin Luther King, and demonized by presidents, conservative religious leaders, even Al Capp's "Li'l Abner."

Since then, her career has been shrouded in the swirl of those turbulent times. Whether she invites it or not (and in recent years she has not), she is still a figurehead for the world's freedom movements. She recently toured Romania, for example. It was simply a concert tour for her, but to those who had fought for democracy there, the coming of the folk diva once banned in their country was a symbol of their hard-won freedom.

Before her appearance, she waited in the wings for hours while every noted folk, jazz, and pop singer in the country sang a song. During her encore, young activists huddled near the front, loudly singing the songs they wanted her to sing until she joined in: "Kumbaya," "Donna, Donna," and "We Shall Overcome."

"I never sing 'We Shall Overcome' in America anymore," the 56-year-old Baez says from her California home. "It's just a nostalgia thing here. But it was very moving singing it there, where they are just coming out of a time of struggle."

Similarly, it is not enough simply to have her appear at the Newport Folk Festival. Though she has returned frequently since the festival was revived in 1985, director Robert Jones urged her to allow a Joan Baez tribute this year.

"I said, well, I'm flattered and let's do something, but maybe you can save the tribute for when I'm dead. I don't feel the need to be any older than I am. But to take the day and make it a celebration of something is perfect."

What she will celebrate as part of Saturday's bill is her recent discovery of the many splendid young songwriters in the thriving subculture of modern folk music.

On her new CD, "Gone from Danger," which Guardian releases Sept. 23, she sings songs by such new folk stars as Dar Williams, Richard Shindell, Sinead Lohan, and Gillian Welch. All will join her at Newport for a "Celebration of Song," along with Janis Ian, Mary Black, Betty Elders, Eric Taylor, and the Borrowers. The CD will likely be heralded as her loveliest and most vital work in years. Her singing is gorgeous, sure, and smart, and she seems more at ease with these songs than she has on recent pop-driven recordings.

"You know, when I went to Newport in 1959, it really was basically a purist form of folk music," she says. "Most of those tents were filled with musicians singing songs that had been passed down by their great-grandparents. Now it's contemporary, period. These new performers write everything they sing. Well, I'm not writing songs. And what works for me is to sing what sounds like it has some kind of traditional roots. So there's lots of music I'm not comfortable singing. It presents an identity crisis when I try to sing music that isn't really home to me. But somehow, these new songwriters are writing songs that are in my comfort zone."

That is in no small measure because Baez's voice has been in their musical imaginations all their lives. It is not just a folk influence she finds comfortable in their songs—it is her actual voice, deeply ingrained in theirs.

Baez hems and haws uncomfortably at this notion, but Dar Williams, 30, who recently toured as her opening act, does not.

"There is an unprecedented mushrooming of female talent out there," Williams says, "and we all started sitting on our beds wishing we were Joan Baez. She was a cultural phenomenon for me growing up. I loved her for who and what she was. I could point to her and say, `this is America, too'—loving the country, hating the war, being a voice against the government while at the same time being a real patriot in the way she embraced the landscape, the musical tradition, the labor movement. Joan was American and a girl—and we all wanted to be her."

Baez recorded two of her songs for the new CD. Williams was also responsible for bringing much of the contemporary songwriter movement to Baez's attention. She sent Baez scores of songs by new writers along with the work of long-respected New York songwriter Richard Shindell. Baez recorded three of his songs, which could help propel his new Shanachie CD, "Reunion Hill" (in stores Aug. 19), into the breakthrough hit the folk world has long wanted him to have.

Like Williams, Shindell, 36, is an intelligent, literate, and often topical songwriter but not political in the same way his '60s forebears were. Still, he is no less committed to the idea that a good song is one that has something important to say.

"I think the songwriters of today are less concerned with politics," he says. "I find it very difficult to write an explicitly issue-oriented political song without sounding trite, sloganeering. I personally have to have some verisimilitude and some meat to it. And if that happens to touch on some political or economic or labor issue, great."

Baez says: "I think these songwriters avoid issues but I think, in a sense, their hearts are bigger. It's like my son. He's not an issue-oriented boy, but I know his heart is breaking for this dying earth. It was really much easier in the '60s, in that the path was cut out for me every morning when I got up. The war was still going on, the South wasn't integrated—the path was very clear. I think anyone who was honest in 1975 admitted there was great confusion about what to do next."

By openly grappling with this confusion, Baez lost some leftist support and artistic direction over the years. That she is rediscovering her voice through these new writers, whose own voices were so shaped by hers, is a wonderful full circle. It is proof that the timeless river of folk tradition still flows through American culture, however subterranean it may have become.

"It really does make me feel like a true folk musician to have my songs sung by Joan," says Williams. "I feel recognized for what I always wanted folk music to be, which is something that turns the wheel. It makes me feel like maybe I'm doing the same thing she was then."

—August 3, 1997

Red House Records: the little label that could
Joan Baez, John Gorka, Suzzy Roche, Utah Phillips, Red House president Bob Feldman

After Joan Baez's star-making appearance at the 1959 Newport Folk Festival, she was flooded with offers from major recording labels and from one odd, little company called Vanguard, known mainly for making obscure classical records.

Her manager, Albert Grossman, desperately wanted her to sign with Columbia, where he would soon bring Bob Dylan. He took her to their impressive offices, the walls dripping with gold records, and begged her to sign an eight-year contract

It was really much easier in the '60s, in that the path was cut out for me every morning when I got up. The war was still going on, the South wasn't integrated—the path was very clear. —Joan Baez

on the spot. Despite being so awed by the place that she actually became ill, she insisted Grossman take her to Vanguard first.

"That's when he realized he had this timid but extremely stubborn 18-year-old on his hands," Baez recalls. "We went over and I knew I was more comfortable there. I was afraid of commerciality, and Vanguard seemed intelligent, oriented toward good music, safe. It took me only 48 hours to decide they were the right place for me: less money, less glamor, less bull."

In that then-controversial move, Baez helped fuel the growth of independent folk labels. Vanguard became for many the very model of the small, principled label. In the lean years after the '60s revival, folk music was kept alive on stalwart independent labels like Cambridge's Rounder and Philo.

Among the most important of those little folk labels today is Red House Records of St. Paul, Minn. It has grown from a vanity label founded in 1983 for Iowa songwriter Greg Brown into one of the most respected folk labels in the country.

John Gorka surprised many this year when he ended his long association with the larger, more affluent Windham Hill to return to Red House, which launched his career in 1987. Gorka said he grew tired of talking formats, market niches, and packaging concepts.

"The way they were treating me toward the end made no sense to me business-wise, personally or musically," he says. "It became kind of a power struggle. They wanted me to do what they wanted me to do, but they had no real vision of what that was. They said I could go more country or more rock 'n' roll, but that if I continued to do what I was doing, they didn't know if they could support me. Then they wanted me to go more toward a light jazz thing, because they'd had some success with that.

"Red House seemed more like a place that was about the music and the people being the bottom line. But yet it seemed like a fully functional record company. It's about making quality records that will make money, but I think the commitment there is to letting people make the kind of music they want to make," Gorka says.

Suzzy Roche of the Roche Sisters decided to take her first solo effort to Red House, after years of seeing her career flounder in the corporate music environment. She sounds thoughtful and sweetly melodic in her CD, "Holy Smokes" (in stores Sept. 16), but fans of the Roches' quirky wit will feel right at home as she ponders life in an eggshell in one song, then longs to be a shoe in the next.

"There is such disorganization at the major labels," she says, "which only works when you're using huge volumes of money. But it doesn't when you're doing something delicate, like I do. I like the idea of working with people who have built their own business, who know and care about all the people they work with. It's just more a way of life than a business."

Red House president Bob Feldman says, "We've always felt like we were on the outskirts of the music business. We don't have the huge money to hype and create demand for our records, so we have to build the foundation with the performers through publicity, touring, seeking out the small radio shows, and folk record stores. I've always felt—no matter how many records we've sold—that we're selling them one by one. We have people who have bought every single record we've ever made. I'm proud of that."

The 61-year-old folk singer, raconteur, and labor radical Utah Phillips says Red House is just where he belongs. He is helping the label compile a long-awaited live CD of his hilarious tall tales.

"Given the nature of what I do, if I had a commercial hit, I would, at some level, have failed," he says. "If I believe the mainstream is polluted—and I do—would I want to end up floating down the middle of it? These little companies like Red House are like the clear tributaries, way up in the mountains. But what cleans the mainstream? It's the pure water coming down from those little streams, so we better take care of them."

—*August 3, 1997*

Having a "John Gorka career"
John Gorka, music manager David Tamulevich

In the humble backstage world of modern folk music, the term "A John Gorka career" is often heard. Like Goldilocks's favorite porridge bowl, the 39-year-old songwriter's career is seen by many as the template of the just-right folk career: not too hot to burn out quickly, not too cold to be measured a real success.

Several times a month, David Tamulevich, whose agency manages Gorka, gets a call from some agent or performer asking how to build a "John Gorka career."

"The best word to describe John's approach to his career is reasonableness," he said. "It's not a greedy, quick career but a long-term investment. He prefers a small room that's full to a large room that's half-empty. He's just very centered about who he is and what he wants, and has managed a very sane balance between work and home, art and business."

An undercurrent of contented joy permeates his seventh "After Yesterday" (Red House). Layers of thick, rhythmic shadow are laid under the songs by Andy Stochansky (Ani DiFranco's percussionist), bassist Michael Manring, and guitarist and coproducer John Jennings, who leads Mary Chapin Carpenter's band. Gorka's milky baritone has never sounded warmer or more convincing, making this his most musically alluring and lyrically memorable record in years.

They said if you want to reach more people, you're going to have to either go more rock or more country. Then they changed that to thinking about the adult contemporary market. It started feeling like they were more concerned about how my hair looked than what my music was like. —John Gorka

The CD seems to tell one long story, ruminating over some recent career upheavals in several tough-minded but ultimately resilient ballads. These are spelled by songs of unabashed wonder at becoming a father. In what Gorka calls his "dad songs," he dotes over the deep, simple pleasures of starting a family, glowing over his pregnant wife, and then, in his deliciously eccentric way, noting proudly that his baby son "looks like Charles Bronson when he cries." He said he counts among the "dad songs," his clever ode to the restoring powers of "St. Caffeine," a sentiment all new parents will understand.

Gorka would be the first to admit that his career path has had its share of bumps and blind alleys. One reason he is making his best music in years is that he finally wrested himself from a long, unhappy relationship with High Street Records, a now-defunct branch of Windham Hill that was supposed to do for the songwriter genre what Windham Hill did for new age music.

"By the end, it just wasn't a healthy place to make music," Gorka said. "I was thinking in terms of making works of art, and they were thinking in terms of a product, and I wasn't going to let them turn what I do into a product."

When Gorka signed with High Street in 1990, he had carefully built a national following from the ground up, by playing small coffeehouses and folk venues. At first, he was the darling of the label, and his early albums were made in an atmosphere of trust and artistic freedom. Changes in the label, most significantly the departure of founder Will Ackerman, left Gorka in the hands of people who seemed neither to understand nor respect the modest but permanent career Gorka wanted.

"They started to want to mess with how I looked," he said. "They wanted to pick the songs and the producer, and it was based more on who the hot artist or producer of the moment was than on my music. They said if you want to reach more people, you're going to have to either go more rock or more country. Then they changed that to thinking about the adult contemporary market. It started feeling like they were more concerned about how my hair looked than what my music was like."

After five High Street CDs, Gorka found a way out of his contract and decided to return to the small, savvy Minnesota label Red House, which had launched his career in the late '80s. There was interest from bigger labels, but their talk sounded queasily familiar. They saw his career as a problem to fix.

"All the other places I talked to, I was hearing the same thing about wanting to take me to the next level. I sat down with Red House, and right away they started talking to me about music. They said, `If you make an honest record, people will come to you.' It seemed like the only place to go.

"I don't feel the need to reinvent myself with every record, and I think that's how a lot of major-label marketing goes. You invent a new image, get a different haircut, different clothes, the Madonna approach. In the folk world, there's more of an emphasis on what we have in common, rather than what makes the artist different from the rest of us. In pop, it seems they're looking for a glimpse into an exotic life, `Enquiring minds' wanting to peek into the lifestyles of the rich and famous. When I write about my life, I don't think of it as anything rarefied or more special than anybody else's life. I'm not saying, `Come look at my life, how interesting and unlike yours it is.' I feel like it's an opportunity to talk to somebody."

—February 5, 1999

The McGarrigle family business
Kate and Anna McGarrigle

The notion of music as a business is really quite new. Until the coming of mass technologies like the radio and phonograph, it was, for the most part, only the well-to-do who could afford to hire musicians. Most poor and working people made music for themselves, singing as they worked and worshipped and courted, gathering around the family fireside to entertain one another in the evening.

For Kate and Anna McGarrigle, Canada's premier folk divas, music has always been more a family affair than a business. They have the discography to prove it: only eight albums to mark their 25-year careers. The sisters became the darlings of the folk-pop world after Linda Ronstadt recorded Anna's "Heart Like a Wheel" in 1974. But despite three critically acclaimed Warner Bros. albums and much touting as the Next Big Things, the McGarrigles always let their lives get in the way of their careers. Anna refused to move to the States, and Kate's children always came first. Their smartly idiosyncratic albums earned them a cult following but never the stardom many thought was theirs for the asking.

"One of the main things you have to do is be in everybody's face all the time," Anna McGarrigle said. "You've got to be touring, touring, touring, and I just don't think I would've been able to do it. Kate says she might have been more willing, but I don't know. The thing is, we're both very stubborn."

Their parlor-piano hearts have never shone as warmly as on the new CD "The McGarrigle Hour" (Hannibal/Ryko), a gorgeously humble hootenanny with family members and friends like Ronstadt and Emmylou Harris; current and former husbands, including Kate McGarrigle's ex, Loudon Wainwright III; and their children, Martha and Rufus, who is a rising star in his own right with a critically heralded new CD on Dreamworks.

"The McGarrigle Hour" grew into the warm family song-swap it is quite by accident, according to Kate McGarrigle.

"We made it very quickly, and that family-round-the-piano thing also came from Anna and I only having chosen three of the songs before everybody got together. So a lot of that feeling is from these being songs everybody knew or had heard; they're not as labored as they sometimes are. I think with technology so advanced now, when people record, they're often going less for performance than perfection. What's interesting with doing it this way is that you don't have time to get too precious."

As a good tale grows in the telling, this CD grew in the singing. Anna McGarrigle had always wanted to sing Stephen Foster's "Gentle Annie" with Ronstadt, and the results are achingly sweet, as are the sisters' singing with Harris of Jesse Winchester's wistful "Skip Rope Song." Harris, for her part, had always wanted to sing in French, and brought along a song by Cajun legend D. L. Menard. Old pop chestnuts alternate with evocative traditional gems like "Green, Green Rocky Road" and "Johnny's Gone to Hilo," wry originals from Rufus and Martha Wainwright, and lovely covers of Kate McGarrigle's "Talk to Me of Mendocino" and Loudon Wainwright's "Schooldays."

The sisters particularly relished watching the youthful fire their children brought to the project.

"You know, Rufus had just come off making the record for Dreamworks," Anna McGarrigle said, "and suddenly he had these studio chops. I mean, the last time we taped anything with him, he was still a little boy, and here he was organizing people in the studio. That was nice to watch. Young people just have a different take; they're not going for the same thing you are, have kind of a lean, eager way of looking at things."

The sisters also inevitably reflected back on their checkered careers, less with regret than with apprehension as they watch their children enter the maelstrom of the music business.

"I think it's so unsettling, this business, because what they do is flatter you to death," Kate McGarrigle said. "It's almost as if they try to destabilize you, and maybe that's what you have to be to in order to be a great artist. When you hear about the Maria Callases and Elvises of the world, maybe that is the extra ingredient, to be unstable or to allow yourself not to have any humility. Maybe that's what people are listening for, taking it that one step, that one godlike step over the edge."

Anna McGarrigle said, "I see Rufus come home from the road and not be able to stay put. He has to leave every couple of days because he doesn't know how to stay home. And I think what's important is to learn where your home is, to have a home. I don't necessarily mean that geographically, but like they say in French, 'Bien dans sa peau,' that you're well in your skin; that you can sit down with yourself and feel comfortable."

—January 29, 1999

One of the main things you have to do is be in everybody's face all the time. You've got to be touring, touring, touring, and I just don't think I would've been able to do it. Kate says she might have been more willing, but I don't know. The thing is, we're both very stubborn. —Anna McGarrigle

I think with technology so advanced now, when people record, they're often going less for performance than perfection. What's interesting with doing it this way is that you don't have time to get too precious. —Kate McGarrigle

Why didn't the music industry jump on the "O Brother" bandwagon?
Emmylou Harris, film directors Joel & Ethan Cohen and Maggie Greenwald, record producer Christopher Covert, record exec Kira Florita, Billboard editor Timothy White

With the stunning success of the soundtrack to last year's Coen brothers film *O Brother, Where Art Thou?*, a lot of industry people, both in Nashville and Hollywood, have their eyes on a quiet little ballad of a film called *Songcatcher*.

But they are not interested in the success of the film about a musicologist who discovers folk music and romance in 1910 Appalachia. Rather, they are watching to see how the Vanguard soundtrack does, believing its success may reveal whether *O Brother*, which has sold more than 1.2 million CDs and spent nine weeks at No. 1 on the country chart (longer than any other CD this year), is a fluke or the bellwether of a trend toward American roots music. With the recent video and DVD release of the film, the soundtrack jumped back to No. 1 on the country chart.

Even among true believers such as *O Brother* directors Joel and Ethan Coen, who describe their Depression-era comedy as a valentine to American roots music, there is skepticism about how much the soundtrack's success says about the music's commercial viability.

Although they are convinced they tapped a genuine consumer interest, they're not sure that an increasingly conservative and youth-obsessed music industry can exploit it.

"A million records is a lot for this kind of music," said Joel Coen, "especially since country stations weren't interested in playing it, and we couldn't get venues like VH1 interested, either. Nobody claimed it as their own; everyone said, 'It's not what we do.'"

Ethan Coen added, "It's not just country radio. Most commercial formats are locked into very mainstream pop formulas, and so much of it is, well, just bad. So if they say this music is not exactly their thing, they're right. I don't know if the people who made *O Brother*, the No. 1 country record are people who traditionally buy country music records."

Emmylou Harris is a tireless champion of roots music, and she lent her heart-melting soprano both to the *O Brother* soundtrack and to the smartly conceived *Songcatcher* CD, which mixes music from the film with contemporary treatments of folk ballads by Harris, Roseanne Cash, and Patty Loveless. Dolly Parton wrote the song "When Love Is New" especially for the soundtrack, as a duet to sing with marvelous teenage *Songcatcher* actor Emmy Rossum. Of these cuts, only Harris's achingly lovely version of "Barbara Allen" is heard in the film.

Calling herself "the poster child for life after radio," Harris said her brilliant and critically acclaimed new Nonesuch CD, *Red Dirt Girl*, was not even sent to country music stations for consideration. Asked why country radio was so resistant to playing *O Brother*, even after its success had proved there was listener interest, she said she honestly didn't know.

"See, you're asking the wrong person. I've never understood that. They're still selling millions and millions of records with their own very narrow format, so I think change is a bit frightening. But ultimately there is going to be some kind of reckoning; you can't ignore the success of a record like *O Brother*, and eventually I think they're going to have to deal with it. But the most important thing is that this music is finding an audience without country radio."

Songcatcher is an historical film designed to present folk music as it existed in the lives of the ordinary people who created it. Beautifully directed by Maggie Greenwald, it is the lyrical love story of a musicologist, played by Janet McTeer, who travels to Appalachia in 1910 and records the centuries-old British ballads the people there still sing.

Like the Coen brothers, Greenwald said the film was always meant to create a context for presenting the music.

"The main character, Lilly Penleric, is really just an excuse for a movie about ballads," Greenwald said. "Throughout the whole project, we'd look at each other and say, 'A cappella ballad singing—what are we doing?' But we all just had faith that if we loved it so much, other people would, too.

"I think there's really a hunger for this kind of music by a significant number of people in our culture; something about the simple purity of the human voice, and music that is so real and raw. It taps a desire to strip away all the mechanics and discover something simpler, more human."

Songcatcher soundtrack coproducer Christopher Covert shopped the CD to labels. Even with talent such as Harris and Parton on board, however, and even with the *O Brother* CD topping the charts, no major labels were interested.

"The big question was, 'How are you going to market this? How are you going to get it on the radio?'" he said. "I mean, if I were a label executive, I would have said the same thing. It's a hard sell, and it all comes down to radio. There's just nowhere to go today with music that's in any way traditional. And unless it's easy to hear, most people aren't going to find it. The hope is that film may be the medium that can break music and artists who are getting lost in the shuffle."

Timothy White, editor in chief of the music-industry bible Billboard, has written glowingly about both soundtracks. He also believes movies may play an increasing role in introducing the public to roots music.

"There's a sense of wonder in both these films, in the way they present us this music as it really existed, but through the eyes of characters who are seeing it for the first time," he said. "Both these soundtracks and films point people back in the right direction, not only presenting this music again, but the stories behind the music, rekindling what went on back then that brought American music to this place. Both of these films sell music in the finest sense."

Everyone interviewed believes that a genuine consumer interest is being tapped by these films. But commercial radio is too tightly formatted to allow the experimentation it would take to bring roots music to mainstream audiences. White believes that those who are bold and creative enough to find ways around the radio roadblock, and bring roots music to the general public, will be extravagantly rewarded—as were the Coens, and before them the creators of the Cuban roots film *Buena Vista Social Club* and the Irish musical *Riverdance*.

At Lost Highway, the new roots division of Mercury that was launched with *O Brother*, people have been watching industry reaction even more keenly. On July 24, they release a CD soundtrack of *Down From the Mountain*, a charmingly intimate and musically breathtaking D. A. Pennebaker documentary film about a recent Nashville concert of *O Brother* musicians.

"There's a lot of people in the industry wanting to hop on the bandwagon," said Lost Highway vice president Kira Florita, "but there's also a lot of people just sitting back and waiting. They clearly see it as a phenomenon, but many think it was a one-time happening. If the *Songcatcher* soundtrack does really well, and if the *American Roots* PBS series next fall does anything like what Ken Burns's jazz series did—then I think industry people will pay attention."

Like so many corporate businesses today, White said, both major labels and commercial radio are under constant pressure to deliver maximum profits on a quarterly basis. Even as both industries lose customers—and are aware that their increasingly narrow formats are to blame—they seem incapable of taking the long-term chances needed to expand those formats.

"I think Nasvhille is having some difficulty with *O Brother*," said White. "It's not what they're about right now, so its success is a little bit like swallowing a doorknob for a lot of people in country music. It really is a strong signal that people like roots-based music and will respond to it. So what I know is that the artists are there, and they're not going to stop, and they are finding audiences. But will this become an industry trend? That's up to the industry."

—June 24, 2001

Boston, a bluegrass hotbed?
Lynn Morris, Matt Glaser, Everett Lilly, Bill Keith, I. B. M. A. president Dan Hayes

Boston may not look like bluegrass country, but a little more than 50 years ago, the high, lonesome sound found a second home here. While it may not be the bull market for record sales it once was, the area remains an important outpost for the Southern folk-based music; home of the largest bluegrass label in the world, Rounder Records; and a valued Northern tour stop for artists.

It is also a hotbed for the informal pickin' parties held at local clubs and community centers that, for many fans, define this most social of music forms.

It was in Boston more than anywhere else that bluegrass first proved it was not just a regional music by attracting sophisticated urban audiences. Rounder has done more than any label to establish bluegrass as a permanent genre with appeal for both Southern and Northern consumers. And when Waltham tenor and mandolinist Joe Val became a bona fide bluegrass star, he proved once and for all that you don't need to be from the South to pick 'n' grin with the best.

The lineup for the Annual Joe Val Bluegrass Festival has many local fans mulling over Boston's crucial role in the music's history. For the first time in 20 years, Everett Lilly, 76, will perform here; and it was the Lilly Brothers who put Boston on the map of bluegrass nation. Also playing is banjo innovator Bill Keith, who rose from the '60s folk revival in Cambridge to join Bill Monroe's legendary Bluegrass Boys.

International Bluegrass Music Association president Dan Hayes, speaking from his Owensboro, Ky., office, said Boston occupies a unique place in bluegrass, though he would hesitate to call it a center these days.

"There's a sizable number of concerts and festivals in that region that people throughout the bluegrass world look forward to every year," he said. "You have Rounder Records and organizations like the Boston Bluegrass Union that keep them in the mix. . . . and it's been important to the music to know it's not just a regional style, that there are people in and from New England who have contributed greatly to the music's history."

The red-letter day in that history came in 1950, when a fiddler and MIT student named Benjamin "Tex" Logan asked West Virginia mandolinist Everett Lilly and his guitarist brother Mitchell about joining him in Boston.

"He booked us a year's worth of work on WCOP radio and the Tremont Plaza," Everett Lilly said. "We went from there to the Hillbilly Ranch, where we stayed 16, 17 years. We never did think that the Boston people would fall for our music, but we were dead wrong about that."

Their first night at the Tremont Plaza, they met Val, whose band swapped sets with them there and at the Hillbilly Ranch. As the '60s folk revival began to boil, a new generation of area college types began seeking out authentic roots music. Some, like Tom Rush, dove into the blues; others, like Joan Baez, into Anglo-American balladry. Bill Keith wanted bluegrass and became a regular at the Hillbilly Ranch. Soon he was performing with Val and the Lillys, and inviting them to play for his fans at the Cambridge coffeehouse Club 47.

"There were two parallel tracks back then," Keith said from the Woodstock, N.Y., office of his Beacon Banjo Co. "There were the Lillys, who were the real thing; and there were a lot of young folk music people like myself who loved bluegrass but saw it through Northern-tinted glasses."

This young, urban audience opened a new path for the music. Bluegrass pioneers such as Monroe and Ralph Stanley soon divided their time between Southern honky-tonks and Northern coffeehouses, as well as prestigious venues such as the Newport Folk Festival. "I remember the Lilly Brothers playing at Jordan Hall," Keith said, "then finishing the night at the Hillbilly Ranch. It was two separate worlds, but Joe straddled them both."

Keith was referring to Joe Val, whose New England Bluegrass Boys became stars, even in the South. Val, who died in 1985, would make anyone's short list of greatest high tenor singers in the music's history. That he was from here became a source of pride for bluegrass fans everywhere.

It was three Cambridge folk fans—Ken Irwin, Bill Nowlin, and Marian Leighton-Levy—who founded Rounder Records in 1970. Taking their cue from the indie label Folkways, they were determined to keep roots music forms such as bluegrass alive by developing an independent, fan-based infrastructure for the music separate from the whims of the industry. They have released nearly 500 bluegrass albums, from superstars such as Alison Krauss and Ricky Skaggs to precious archival reissues of the Carter Family, Monroe, and the Stanley Brothers.

"Rounder is the largest bluegrass record label out there, not only in terms of their longevity but the catalog they've amassed over the years," said Hayes. "They have always had a philosophy that they're not only here to make money but to document the music . . .They're admired worldwide for the kind of music they've put out and helped to preserve."

Among the artists Rounder nursed to bluegrass stardom is Virginia singer Lynn Morris, who performs at the festival. "The Boston scene has a real knowledgeable audience and it's one of my favorite places to play," she said. "In some areas in the South, they get so doggone much bluegrass that they're not as appreciative as your New Englanders."

One of the reasons the music stays alive here is grassroots, fan-driven groups like the Boston Bluegrass Union, which Val helped found 25 years ago.

BBU president Gerry Katz said bluegrass remains popular here because it is such

Joe Val, whose New England Bluegrass Boys became stars even in the South. Val, who died in 1985, would make anyone's short list of greatest high tenor singers in the music's history.

a social music. He estimates that a third to a half of the BBU active membership of more than 400 are amateur or semipro pickers themselves. "It's easy to play at the entry level," Katz said. "Like Irish music, there's a wealth of standard material everybody knows, a common language of tunes people can share. A lot of people who go to festivals never even see the concert stage; they just roam from jam session to jam session."

Matt Glaser, chairman of the string department at Berklee College of Music, is a renowned fiddler in bluegrass and jazz circles. He brings his highly touted bluegrass-jazz ensemble Wayfaring Strangers to the Joe Val Festival, warming up for a June release of the band's Rounder CD. When asked to measure the local bluegrass scene, he did not think first of CD sales or stars coming to town, but of how many people gather informally to play the music. He cited the Tuesday jams at the Cantab in Cambridge.

"There's nothing comparable in New York, where a lot of good musicians get together on a weekly basis, keeping the tradition alive," he said. "Bluegrass is a demanding tradition to master. It's a whole language . . .an emotional language, a language of how to improvise stylistically, of specific approaches to instrumental craft and how to function in a band setting.

"Bluegrass is a real chamber music form, where everyone's role is distinct and different from one another, with a very high level of musical interaction as well as groove and group dynamics. There seems to be a fairly traditional bent to what I would characterize as the bluegrass scene in Boston, which is always a good basis upon which to build. So I feel like there's really a good thing happening here."

—*February 23, 2001*

Club Passim: 40 years of folk in Harvard Square
Patty Larkin, Ellis Paul, Jim Kweskin, Catie Curtis, Betsy Siggins Schmidt

In the simple phrase "Club Passim 40th Anniversary," much is said about why Boston is the folk music capital of the country. As performers gather tomorrow for a concert tribute to the stalwart Harvard Square coffeehouse, their names trace a generational history of modern folk music: Joan Baez, the Charles River Valley Boys, the Silverleaf Gospel Singers, Patty Larkin, Ellis Paul, the Nields, Pamela Means, and Joel Cage. All launched their careers, or had their music exposed to crucial new audiences, in either the '60s folk mecca Club 47, or at Passim, which continued the 47 legacy in the tiny basement of 47 Palmer St., the old coffeehouse's final home.

Club Passim is not, of course, the only reason Boston remains such a folk hotbed. There are hundreds of folk venues here, from suburban church coffeehouses to barroom open mikes to front-rank national showcase clubs, and more folk radio on local public stations like WUMB-FM (91.9) and WGBH-FM (89.7), and Emerson College's WERS-FM (88.9), than anywhere else in the country. But the chain of music linking Club 47 to Passim to today's thriving Club Passim, more than anything else, testifies to the enduring appeal that exists here for folk music. In discussing the club's importance with performers for this weekend's celebration, the curious word "permanence" kept coming up to distinguish the local folk scene from others.

"Passim was the survivor," said Patty Larkin, who rose from its ranks to national stardom in the early '80s, "the club that withstood the disco and punk rock thing when a lot of clubs came and went. When you finally got to play there, and it was not easy to get in, you felt a certain sense of history to the place. That room connected the '60s to the '80s, which was not lost on any of us when we played there. We were all kind of mesmerized by the mystique of who had played there before; it made it an even holier grail for us."

Ellis Paul climbed from Passim opening act to national folk headliner in the '90s, just as Larkin had a decade earlier. He is now trying to repay some of what he owes the club and its indomitable former owners, Bob and Rae Anne Donlin, by sitting on the board of the nonprofit Club Passim, which was formed in 1995, when the Donlins retired. Bob Donlin passed away in 1996; Rae Anne lives in Cambridge.

"Passim was like the Carnegie Hall of folk," he said, "the big one, the place everybody wanted on their resume. But it was also a great place to go and be a student of the music. Not only did you get to see the best national performers in that incredibly close environment, but when you opened for them, you got to watch how they handled different audiences over a six-show weekend. You'd be picking up all the nuances of their presentation and songwriting and guitar playing."

The story actually began a few blocks away, when a nonprofit community club called Club 47 opened on Mt. Auburn Street in 1958, hoping to expose young people to the joys of jazz. The young people came, all right, but they brought their guitars and folk songs with them, and it almost immediately became a folk haven.

Among its first and most influential managers was Betsy Siggins Schmidt, who returned to become director of Club Passim in 1996. She watched her best buddy and Boston University classmate Joan Baez bud into a national phenomenon on the little Club 47 stage. It is largely as a favor to her that Baez, who declined to be interviewed, is returning for this benefit show.

"I think it's terribly poignant to have Joan back as part of the Club 47, Club Passim circle," Siggins Schmidt said. "It means an enormous amount to me personally, to the symbolic importance of this place as a grown-up, permanent institution. What you hear and find moving in young songwriters like Lori McKenna and Catie Curtis strongly connects to the messages of heart and hearth and justice that moved us so much in the folk music we heard way back then.

"Joanie started out as one of a very small handful of women singing English ballads, and that set her apart from the guys, the Tom Rushes and Jackie Washingtons, who were much more into American folk and blues traditions. She was nothing if not charismatic; she just naturally took center stage with the combination of that ethereal, otherworldly voice and her earthy humor, those bare feet onstage and the long hair, riding around town on a Vespa, which women just weren't doing then. But I think she played more and was more comfortable at Club 47 than anywhere during her early development."

Club 47 did not have a house band, though both the Jim Kweskin Jug Band and the Charles River Valley Boys, which then featured bluegrass legend-in-the-making Joe Val, John Cooke, Bob Siggins, and Fritz Richmond, were regulars. They did, however, have a resident washtub-bass and jug player in Richmond, who was paid five bucks by the club whenever he accompanied the nightly act. He was also in the Kweskin band and the Charles River Valley Boys, who reunite tomorrow, minus Val, who died in 1985.

"The folk scene back then was a small town, and Club 47 was the center of town," he said. "We could all just walk down there, we all knew each other, it was wonderful. When I played the new club last year with John Sebastian, it felt a lot like the old place. A guy brought in a washtub bass he'd made, just because he wanted me to see it. That's the kind of thing that would happen at the old club all the time, that kind of sharing of information and music. One of the things we were all trying to do then was just spread the joy."

The club moved to Palmer Street in 1963, due largely to a cranky landlord who disliked the long lines outside the place every night. The City of Cambridge good-naturedly agreed to then-director Jim Rooney's request that, despite there being no other addresses on the street at all, it be numbered 47 Palmer, so the name Club 47 would continue to make sense.

In 1968, it closed, a victim of the waning interest in folk, and the space became McCarthy for President headquarters, then Passim, a bookstore-gallery owned by Walter and Renee Juda. A year later, it was bought by the Donlins. Once again, the young people with their guitars and folk songs came, begging them to resume Club 47's legacy, and, in 1970, the Donlins began booking folk acts. Except for a few months in 1995, when it closed for remodeling and reorganization as a nonprofit community club, it has remained an acoustic showcase club since.

The Donlins became legends in their own right, revered for their stubborn devotion to the music during folk's worst years, through the eras of disco, punk, and MTV, until the songwriter revival took hold in the mid-'80s. Nearly all of that revival's first stars—Nanci Griffith, Suzanne Vega, Shawn Colvin, John Gorka, Greg Brown, Bill Morrissey, and Patty Larkin—credit Passim with launching their careers.

Alluringly soft-spoken and topically fiery folk-rocker Catie Curtis, who performs two sold-out shows at the club tonight, is part of the '90s generation of local songwriters, and credits Passim's permanence for fostering the belief that folk was a viable form here. Many cities went without any regular folk venues for years, or had one after another pop up and then disappear. Those few clubs that did survive, such as the Ark in Ann Arbor, Mich., and Caffe Lena in Saratoga, N.Y., seemed isolated and anomalous, like folk scenes unto themselves.

"I think as I tour around the country, that Boston still has the largest number of people who believe that playing an acoustic guitar and writing your own songs is a viable art form," she said. "In other places, even where there are thriving music scenes like Seattle or Austin, Texas, there's more of an expectation that you have to be in a band to pursue a career in music. But up here, there's a huge number of people who see nothing wrong with just going out on their own and playing solo. I think the fact that Passim seems like it's always been here creates that reality and viability."

But she also stressed, as Paul and Larkin did, that the old Passim was a forbidding mountain to climb. It was hard to get booked, which added greatly to the prestige of playing there, but made it harder for the folk community at large to feel a real sense of ownership about the club. While fans supported it fiercely, Passim was the Donlins' club, its musical personality a reflection of their tastes and penchant for literate, urbane singer-songwriters with pleasing and witty stage ways.

Club Passim now is much more the expansive and inclusive community coffeehouse Club 47 tried to be, a place that welcomes any and all to its stage. It has a Tuesday open mike, which Passim never offered, and a much broader array of music and spoken-word events, offering many more opportunities for local talents, along with its weekend roster of national folk stars.

Curtis said, "Back in the '80s, you really felt privileged to get up on the stage at Passim. It was no small feat to get there. You felt the weight of the folk heroes who came before you; whereas now, there's a whole lot of passion down there to make the place available and accessible to the whole community. But you don't feel that history in the place as much. It's more of a community coffeehouse and maybe a little less of a shrine. To me, that's a real good trade-off."

—*January 15, 1999*

Making a career out of community **Tom Rush**

Tom Rush's name is rarely trumpeted among the folk music giants of the past half-century. Yet it can be argued that the New Hampshire native has been the most consistently influential singer-songwriter to emerge from the '60s folk revival.

Again and again, the folk singer, bluesman, and songwriter reinvented his career, always ahead of the commercial curve. He played a seminal role in the urban blues revival of the early '60s and the folk-rock boom of the mid-'60s. Rolling Stone credited his 1968 Elektra album, "The Circle Game," which introduced the songs of Joni Mitchell, James Taylor, and Jackson Browne, with ushering in the era of the singer-songwriter.

Columbia-Legacy has released a brilliant retrospective of Rush's 37-year career called "No Regrets: The Very Best of Tom Rush." More impressive even than the number of influential songs it includes is the splendid consistency of his style.

As he roamed from form to form, Rush never let the trappings of the day submerge his own sound. His seductively honest baritone remained the same, whether he was wailing old blues tunes, barking out folk-rock, laying the groundwork for the '70s country-rock craze ("Ladies Love Outlaws" was written for him, not Waylon Jennings), delivering starkly commanding covers of Mitchell's "Urge for Goin' " and Browne's "Jamaica, Say You Will," or his own lonely classic, "No Regrets."

"My approach is always to feel like I'm the servant of the song," Rush said. "Some singers, I feel, put the song on like a suit of clothes, and for me, it's more the other way around. You just want to be the window people see the song through."

He cut his teeth in the very traditional Cambridge folk scene that revolved around the fabled Club 47 in the early '60s. His early records were mostly lean folk blues sprinkled with a droll, winking wit that suggested he took the songs very seriously, himself not at all.

"I was always exquisitely aware of the irony of Harvard undergraduates singing about how hard it is picking cotton and working in the mines," he said. "But I think we were all very sincerely enraptured by these songs, because they were so real and gritty and honest. It was not our experiences, though, so something closer to our own lives had a lot of resonance."

That resonance was coming from new folk writers like Bob Dylan and Phil Ochs. While Rush was becoming a star with his blues and original songs written in traditional styles, his attempts at more contemporary ballads were not encouraged: His first Club 47 performance of "No Regrets" was so badly received that for several years he shelved the song that would become his greatest hit. In 1967, Rush moved to New York, where his songwriting was nurtured in ways it

My approach is always to feel like I'm the servant of the song. Some singers, I feel, put the song on like a suit of clothes, and for me, it's more the other way around. You just want to be the window people see the song through. —Tom Rush was not in Cambridge. As he heard new songwriters Mitchell, Browne, and Taylor, he felt he had struck a mother lode.

"I think the songwriter stuff was a lot more accessible to John Q. Public than the coal-miner ballads," he said. "So all of a sudden, there was the potential of selling albums beyond a small coterie of devoted students of traditional music."

"The Circle Game" established him in the vanguard of the songwriter movement, both as writer and interpreter. For years, his career flourished. But in 1975, Columbia, his label since 1970, declined to renew his contract.

He said, "My records were making money for the label, but it's a trendy industry, and they moved on to other things. They somehow decided the record-buying public was between 18 and 25, so they let the baby boom outgrow them. They didn't try to keep up as their tastes evolved; they just let them walk away."

Rush retired to his New Hampshire farm, then decided to fight back. He began promoting his own shows.

"The concert industry, recording industry, radio industry all agreed that folk had no commercial viability," he said. "I guess I just got curious about where the audience had gone. It seemed that just 10 minutes ago, there was a huge audience. They couldn't all have died; it would have been in the papers."

Rush became convinced his audience was still around, just not among the rock-club set. The crowd for his annual Christmas show at the Paradise was declining, so he moved it to Symphony Hall. In 1980, he sold fewer than 500 seats at the Paradise. In 1981, he filled 2,500-seat Symphony Hall—at twice the ticket price.

News of his commercial triumph spread through the moribund folk world, inspiring promoters to try larger concerts at more comfortable venues. The folk revival of the '80s was underway.

Typically, Rush used his annual Symphony Hall shows to introduce new folk stars like Nanci Griffith, Shawn Colvin, and Bill Morrissey, playing as crucial a role in launching the '80s songwriter revival as he had 20 years earlier. He has been in constant demand as a performer ever since.

Asked about his legendary artistic generosity, he shrugged off the praise, making it all sound as sensible as a farmer planting in spring if he thinks he might be hungry in winter.

"You know, an artist needs a context to exist in," he said. "It worked for microbreweries; the more there was a microbrewery scene, the better they all did. It's the same with music. I've always tried to create an environment that I could be a part of, rather than just existing in my own isolation."

—October 9, 1999

Where do old songwriters go?
Jesse Winchester and Loudon Wainwright III

Ever wonder where old songwriters go? In an increasingly youth-obsessed music business, middle-aged songwriters, like old rockers, seem to just vanish from the pop landscape. Is there a Songwriters' Graveyard somewhere, some jungle chasm littered with decaying guitars and skeletons wearing fingerpicks?

Of course, most aging songwriters simply tire of the vainglorious rat race that is the music business, put their guitars in the closet, and find new careers. Faced with declining careers as they hit middle age, though, Jesse Winchester, 56, and Loudon Wainwright, III, 53, two of the '70s' best songwriters, found jobs doing what they do best: writing songs.

"I just got very, very tired of it," Winchester said of the performing and recording career he abandoned 10 years ago. "I seemed to be spinning my wheels. I'm not one of these artistic people who always say they don't care if a lot of people hear their music, that they write for themselves. I don't do that, I write for other people. I want people to like it, and if that's not happening, I get all depressed and disappointed."

But Winchester's smart, wistful songs were being recorded by such major stars as Bonnie Raitt, Joan Baez, Jimmy Buffett, and Emmylou Harris. He decided to chuck the star game and go home to Montreal, where the Memphis native has lived since 1967, when he went there to avoid the draft. He began a prolific association with the hip Nashville company Bug Publishing, and soon Wynonna Judd, Reba McEntire, Elvis Costello, and Sweethearts of the Rodeo joined the long list of stars singing his songs.

"It's a beautiful way to make a living," Winchester said. "You just drop the song in the mail and wait for the checks to come. You don't have to deal with rental-car companies, hotel rooms, half-full houses, any of it."

Wainwright has remained more productive than most of his '70s folk contemporaries, but his 18-album career has been bounced like a badminton birdie between major labels and small independents like Rounder and his current home, Hannibal, where he landed after Virgin Records dropped him last year.

"I made four records for Virgin," he said, "but I guess they decided they needed that money for Janet Jackson's deli platter—which is about how much money they were giving me to make those records. But I've been dropped by the very best labels—Atlantic, Columbia, Arista—so why not Virgin?"

Wainwright can afford to be cavalier about his recording career because he has a steady gig as official troubadour for National Public Radio. Over the past 10 years, he has been regularly commissioned to write songs on current events for "All Things Considered," "Morning Edition," and "Weekend Edition."

"Just the craft of doing it, the challenge, is nice," he said of his NPR work. "When they call and ask you to write a song about something specific, like Tanya Harding or Jesse Helms, you take a breath, go through a moment of panic, and then you say, 'Yeah, I can do that.' Then it becomes not about writing a hit single or a song that's going to make a great video, but just fulfilling that commission."

Wainwright is best known for the sharp absurdist humor he displayed on his biggest hit "Dead Skunk." His new CD, "Social Studies," shines with the same wise-guy wit, but also with a kind-eyed empathy that gives even his goofiest songs a sage maturity and warm emotional resonance.

Winchester has also released a masterful CD, his first in 11 years, called "Gentleman of Leisure," (Sugar Hill). Like the great pop tunesmiths, from Cole Porter to Smokey Robinson to the team of John Lennon and Paul McCartney, he has a genius for writing elegantly catchy songs that shimmer with intelligence, even while traversing such familiar themes as love and loss, spiritual peace, and the sheer joy of a Saturday night spent grooving to your favorite band.

Now that all his chips are not riding on how well this show or that record does, Winchester says he finally enjoys performing. And he candidly admitted he only made a record so he could hear his own take on his latest batch of songs.

"A song never seems to come out the way you heard it when other people sing it," he said. "I just wanted to hear my versions of them. And, you know, there's a lot of greed and guilt and ambition mixed in there somewhere." He laughed at that, the easy laugh of someone grateful that such killing instincts are no longer necessary parts of his career path.

Wainwright is warily watching his children Rufus and Martha battle their own ways through the songwriter maze. As proud and anxious as he is as they fight their way through the tough tangles of the music industry, he also sounded relieved when he sighed that such battles are best left to the young.

"There should be room for older artists like Jesse and myself," he said, "because I think what we're doing is important and valuable; but, you know, there should be world peace, too. Pop music is about new and happening and haircuts, and it's been like that ever since Elvis grew his sideburns."

—October 15, 1999

I'm not one of these artistic people who always say they don't care if a lot of people hear their music, that they write for themselves. I don't do that, I write for other people. I want people to like it, and if that's not happening, I get all depressed and disappointed. —Jesse Winchester

Same job, different uniforms
Utah Phillips and Ani DiFranco

For more than 30 years, ever since that ugly little phrase ``generation gap'' appeared on the scene, our culture has taken it on faith that the interests of youth and age do not meet. From ``Never Trust Anyone Over 30'' to ``Not Your Father's Oldsmobile,'' we have been bombarded with messages that tell us our society is divided not just by income, sex, race, faith and tastes, but by age.

This is just one of the walls 26-year-old Ani DiFranco, the quintessential cutting-edge, Generation-X, neo-folk, radical-feminist songwriter, is determined to kick down. To help her, she could hardly have found better company for her latest recording project than 61-year-old Bruce (Utah) Phillips, raconteur, labor historian, folk singer, songwriter, sometime hobo and proud, professional malcontent.

DiFranco's smart, sassy, furiously radical and often funny songs have turned her into an underground star and bona fide modern-day folk hero. Her recordings, released without major-label muscle on her own Righteous Babe Records, have sold more than 580,000, and she packs major concert halls throughout the world. Her Nov. 23 performance at the Orpheum is sold out, and tickets for the Sunday 5 p.m. show are going fast.

When she decided to expand Righteous Babe's roster, many cultural pundits were bewildered that her first pick was Phillips, an unlikely Righteous Babe at first glance. But then, bewildering cultural pundits is sort of a sport for DiFranco.

``I think Utah and I are really similar in what we do,'' the Buffalo, N.Y., songwriter said. ``Of course, people would never make those comparisons, because people only compare people on the basis of hairdo, sex and age. So I'm compared to any chick out there who sings. But Utah and I share a lot of the same politics and basically talk about the same stuff; just with different uniforms on and different stories to make the same points.''

DiFranco did much more than simply release a Utah Phillips record, though. True to form for both radical artists, ``The Past Didn't Go Anywhere'' is an entirely original, provocative artistic hybrid. While Phillips weaves his marvelous tales, seemingly just chatting as his keenly visual images and free-flowing, often hilarious ruminations unfold, DiFranco adds a very contemporary foundation of rhythm tracks and instrumental music. Say what you will, there has never been a record quite like this.

DiFranco explained her approach, saying, ``People have very little patience for stories in our society today, I think. There's a bit of a lack of respect for oral history and the value of it. So I thought, how could I make it so that people would put this in their car stereo? How could I make it so they'd do that more than once?''

At first listen, many of Phillips' loyal folk fans are likely to be dismayed by the poom-poom of electronic bass and drum, the occasional rap-esque sampling of his voice. But there's much more going on here. With awesome empathy and intelligence, DiFranco has turned this random selection of Phillips' stories, culled from more than 100 hours of concert recordings, into a cohesive set of songs. Yes, songs.

She samples such lines as "The past didn't go anywhere," "You got to mess with people" and "I act out a lot," turning them into refrains that tie the tales together the way a chorus supports a lyric. There is much more to it than the hipping up of an old raconteur for a rock-savvy young audience. "The Past Didn't Go Anywhere" is spoken music.

No one is more delighted by the result than Phillips. He sees DiFranco's approach as a bold, liberating way to bring the spoken word into the contemporary pop arena, much the way the beat poets reinvigorated verse by reciting it to the soft strains of cool jazz in the 1950s. Beyond that, he was enthralled and deeply moved by the stories DiFranco chose.

"I felt that if I was going to go through all that stuff and pick out stories that I wanted to persist if I wasn't around, those are the ones I would have picked out," he said from his home in Nevada City, Calif. "She not only did that instinctively, with no advice from me, but she put them in the right order. I don't know how, but she did."

DiFranco said she just picked her favorite stories, the ones that "most represented him and his journey." But there's much more at work. On one level, "The Past Didn't Go Anywhere" is a fairly straight-ahead autobiographical story cycle. But within each tale, Phillips celebrates the process of seeking wisdom and stories from his elders and passing them along.

He discusses the awakening of his radical populism when he was a young man on military duty in Korea, and his subsequent decision to "never again abdicate to somebody else my right and my ability to decide who the enemy is." He tells this story in response to his son's impertinent but not unreasonable question, "How did you get to be like that?" Phillips forgivingly and accurately translates this as "Why is it that you are fundamentally alienated from the entire institutional structure of society?"

He evokes the wisdom and stories of his own elders, from pacifist-anarchist mentor Ammon Hennacy, who defines an anarchist as "anyone who doesn't need a cop to tell him what to do," to a dying cowboy poet to a one-armed Spanish Civil War veteran to the sagacious old hobo "Fryin' Pan Jack." His tales have a music of their own, which DiFranco deftly plays to, and are marvelously told. But the process is the point; seeking out elders, hearing their stories, then passing them along. It binds tale to tale, hero to hero, generation to generation.

DiFranco said, "I think we live in this culture where there's such a reverence for youth. Our whole culture basically worships youth. Our images of beauty have become 13,14-year-old girls, where they used to be women. Our musical acts get younger and younger, and rock 'n' roll is all about youthful rebellion and once you're past 30, you're just posing or something. I think there's very little attention paid to a lot of the things Utah talks about, which is what we can learn from those more experienced and older than us. As he says, a long memory is one of the most radical ideas, and I think we have a very short memory in this country right now."

Phillips said, "This is the history that didn't make it into the books, and that's why you have to go seek it out. When I was in high school, I got the history of the ruling class; the generals and industrialists and the presidents who didn't get caught. I got the history of the people who owned the wealth, merely owned it, none of the history of the people who created it in the mines, the forests, railroads, wheat harvests, the factories. In order to find that history, I had to go to the people who had lived it. That's a much more exciting and beautiful and ultimately more useful vision of who we are and where we came from than I ever read in any book.

"I remember I said to my wife Joanna once, 'You know, all my elders have died off, all my teachers.' And she said, 'Well, when your teachers have all died off, guess what?' I said, 'Oh no, I'm not ready for that.' Well, but here I am."

Utah and Ani: *the sequel*

Ani DiFranco and Utah Phillips are up to their tricks again. In 1996, acoustic pop's premier radical rabble-rouser and folk's preeminent radical raconteur sent shock waves through the music world with their boldly original CD collaboration, "The Past Didn't Go Anywhere." DiFranco brought all her techno-pop savvy to providing modern musical backings to Phillips' fiery, often hilarious tales of labor history and his own days as a folk performer, sometime hobo, and fulltime anarchist.

On Tuesday, DiFranco's label Righteous Babe releases "Fellow Workers," a marvelous continuation of that saga. As music and as theater, it's even better, recorded before a live audience at the Kingsway recording studio in New Orleans. Where the first CD focused on Phillips's life, "Fellow Workers" offers tantalizing glimpses at the people who fought to establish labor unions in America, epic heroes like Mother Jones and Joe Hill, along with the lesser-known loggers and miners Phillips has culled his stories from over the years. As before, DiFranco frames his songs and tales in exquisite musical settings, adding jazzy smoke and mystery to the mythic moods he sets.

Many were dumbfounded that the 28-year-old DiFranco, whose radicalism is so often associated with her youth, gender, and overall hipness, would reach out to the gray-bearded, 64-year-old Phillips. But she always saw the connection and proudly noted that her fans now cheer wildly whenever she mentions his name.

"You know, my music sometimes gets reduced to, `Oh, it's all just about girrr-ul power,'" she said. "That's sort of the caricature of me, but I'm singing about a lot of the same things that Utah is. I'm more informed by my times and gender—just as he is. So I sing about abortion rights, sexual identity, or gender power. But we both sing about the struggles between power and the powerless. It's just that the similarities aren't that obvious on the surface. We're so different to look at. He's like Santa Claus, and I'm, well, I'm not."

The CD begins quietly, with wet, dissonant jazz runs that congeal, like raindrops on a window, into a haunting evocation of Earl Robinson's 1938 labor classic, "Joe Hill," which Phillips sings a wonderfully wrinkled cover of later. The sound is captivating: new, old, hip, timeless, and thoroughly American.

Through this transporting setting, Phillips offers brief, provocative glances of labor heroes like Hill, whose protest songs were so feared by Utah mine owners, they had him framed for murder and executed, or so Phillips tells it.

His sketch of legendary labor agitator Mary Harris "Mother" Jones is a masterpiece in miniature. "It's hard for the mind to encompass a life that embraced the presidencies between Andrew Jackson and Herbert Hoover," he says, spinning artful webs of wonder. He speaks reverently of her irascibility, of how she singlehandedly stared down the Colorado militia, after which President Teddy Roosevelt called the then-83-year-old "the most dangerous woman in America." DiFranco takes the phrase up, singing it like some undulating and mystical tribal chant.

Phillips thinks DiFranco has done something very important with these CDs, not just in exposing her audiences to the long history of American radicalism, but in the way she has adapted storytelling to the modern music marketplace. He believes she has invented a whole new form to present the spoken word.

"Professional storytelling is heading up some serious blind alleys," he said, "and this is a way out of that. What Ani's done with me proves that it works, and it could work just as well with other people."

DiFranco is forever inventing new forms in her own music, playing with rock, hip-hop, jazz, and folk sounds to frame her lyric points. That was her intent here, and she succeeeds wonderfully. Phillips is a grandly charismatic curmudgeon, casually eloquent, mischievous and irresistibly passionate when discussing the labor movement. But DiFranco's work here is nothing short of brilliant. Her subtle musical settings are entrancing but not overwhelming, casting soft shadows of mood.

"To the ears of a twentysomething hipster at the turn of the millennium," she said, "these stories may seem archaic. What does Mother Jones have to do with me, or how does the 1912 Lawrence textile strike pertain to my life? But if you really listen, I find so much mystery and beauty and importance in them. I mean, the boss today is not the suspender-popping, pot-bellied robber baron; he's like a huge, faceless, multinational corporate entity. But I think that power relationship is still the same; they're no more invested in communities or their workers than those bosses were before the turn of the century."

As the project took shape, Phillips said he began to feel these old labor songs and stories were the most useful things he could give DiFranco's audience.

"Certainly, young people have enough people telling them how to be and what to do," he said. "I didn't want to be another one of those. At the same time, most of these young folks are just going into the workplace, and they never got anything in their school or family or religious experience to tell them how to control the condition of their labor. All they got was you're supposed to enhance your skills so you can make a better deal to get a boss and a paycheck and become a cog in their machine.

"These stories are about people who were almost slaves to the industrial system, treated like animals—they called the loggers `timber beasts.' But they came together, armed only with their sense of degradation, and organized and changed the condition of their lives. That's what this record is about."

There is a revealing symmetry in how Phillips and DiFranco talk about each other. She says people like him and folk singer Pete Seeger, lifetime veterans of the good fight, remind her that the baiting of the press and the disdain of the trend-followers are both the scars and the trophies of that fight.

"You know, I put out a record," she said, "and the mainstream media is like, `Yawn-yawn-yawn, oh, political songs; here's Righteous Babe back up on her horse and we've heard it all before'—as if politics had no place in music, as if people weren't really talking about these things in their own lives. And it blows my mind and it terrifies me.

"Then I'll think of Pete Seeger, getting into his station wagon at the age of 80 to drive eight hours for a benefit for the Western New York Peace Center. With a smile on his face. And he doesn't [care] if the mainstream media doesn't understand or respect that kind of tradition. In fact, when they don't get it, he figures he must be doing something right. The fact that I can and do feel connected to that kind of tradition gives me the strength to continue."

That connection means even more to Phillips, who now suffers from a debilitating heart condition and often grapples with his own mortality. When he speaks of her, he sounds grateful not only for the new fans she brought him, but for being who she is.

"I've learned to respect her enormously," he said. "It's like this: just when you're ready to throw in the towel on this sockful of puppy-poop we have the audacity

to call a culture, ready to chuck the chamois, toss the terrycloth, an Ani DiFranco comes along and says, `It's not over, it can still be changed. We can make valid, self-sustaining, non-commercial art on our own hook, without being part of the Super-Bowl-disco-corporate madness.' In short, she restores my hope."

—November 17, 1996 , May 16, 1999

Rooted in folk music, powered by carrot cake
Brooks Williams, Homegrown Coffeehouse directors Jim & Beth Sargent

They always line up early for the Homegrown Coffeehouse in Needham. For 15 years, the twice-monthly Saturday night folk club in the First Parish Unitarian Church has presented national and local acoustic performers to a loyal audience from nearby and from as far away as Springfield, Boston and New Hampshire.

Last Saturday, the crowd came to see Brooks Williams, a gifted Northampton songwriter with a strong national following. But the many who came early were thinking of another Homegrown attraction. The moment the doors opened, a good hour before the 8 p.m. show time, the 150-seat room was nearly full. The early-comers threw their coats on the chairs and tables that rimmed the small stage, then scurried to the snack table.

They were after carrot cake, so much a part of the club's tradition that a grand, hand-painted banner hanging behind the stage proclaims, "The Homegrown Coffeehouse: Rooted in folk music, powered by carrot cake."

"The first couple of years, we ran out of carrot cake a few times," said Beth Sargent, who founded the Homegrown in 1983 with her husband, Jim, and a few church volunteers. "That's when the early lines started. We almost never run out anymore, but people still make a point to get here early—just in case."

It is a custom that perfectly suits the friendly ambience that has made the Homegrown a favorite stop for performers, and earned it a national reputation as a first-rate folk venue. While people lined up for carrot cake Saturday, the evening's star stood by the stage, guitar under his arm, chatting easily with the crowd. Even if he were so inclined, Williams knows that star trips are suicide dives in a place like this.

"I have seen performers crash and burn in these venues because they don't know how to talk to an audience," he said during a break in his delightful two-hour show. "I mean, look at the setting; it's like a living room.

"When I started playing places like this, I had to get over that edge of intimacy," he said. "It was uncomfortable for me to be so close to the audience. You have to get over the pretense of this being a theatrical event the way a concert hall lends itself to being, and treat it as if it were a living room. People want to get to know you almost as much as they want to hear your music."

The Sargents picked the name Homegrown to emphasize that kind of front-porch informality.

"We liked the name because it suggests a very comfortable setting," Beth Sargent said. "Not a cocoon, exactly, but comfy. We wanted people to feel this was someplace homey."

Like many baby boomers who moved to the suburbs to raise families in the 1970s, the Sargents grew restless in the '80s. It was hard to go to Boston to hear music, and all the local clubs seemed to be rock-loud and youth-obsessed. They noticed small church coffeehouses opening up nearby, as the folk scene revived after its commercial decline of the '70s, and began a fact-finding tour in hopes of opening one in their own church.

As Jim Sargent said, "It looked eminently doable, and it was."

"There really was nothing for people like us to do on a Saturday night," he said. "We thought of this as a community-directed activity, and we Unitarians are forever doing community things. It's one of the church's underpinnings, that desire to do social things within the community. We wanted to create a way for people to get out on Saturday without the hassle of going to Boston. The shows are 10 or 12 bucks; parking is free."

Though they are helped by a hard-working volunteer staff, the Homegrown is very much a family affair for the Sargents. They are volunteers themselves, and deeply proud that the coffeehouse has become a significant revenue source for the church.

During the Homegrown season, from October to June, Jim coordinates the afternoon setup, turning the parish hall into a cabaret-like club with tables and chairs, then emcees the show and runs the sound system. Beth runs the kitchen and bakes the all-important carrot cake, which is not the least bit overrated.

They make booking decisions together and take turns answering their phone, which is the Homegrown hot line and rings ceaselessly on show days. Every two months, they mail out 1,500 schedules to fans and media contacts.

Their 6-year-old daughter, Margaret, already an enthusiatic and savvy coffeehouser, greets folks at the door as their eldest daughter Jennifer, 29, once did. They also have a son, James, 13, who is starting a rock band but still finds time to drop by and help out.

"In the beginning, we were mostly bringing in performers based in Boston, all of which seemed kind of homegrown to us," Beth Sargent said. "That's the musical tradition we have in America, the community-based performer who's a real part of the fabric of the community. I think that's so important culturally. Whether the performers we have now come from here or somewhere else, there's still that ineffable aura about them."

That certainly describes Williams, a spellbinding guitarist and warmly inviting singer. Between songs, he seemed to just chat with the crowd, sharing backstage secrets, explaining how his songs were inspired.

"The secret to songwriting is good eavesdropping," he whispered confidentially to the crowd. Then he confessed that the edgy love ballad he was about to sing came to him when he overheard two middle-aged women arguing at a party, one saying pointedly, "I did not kiss him. We were 17; let it go!"

After the show, he said, "Obscurity doesn't really work here. Coffeehouses force me as a writer to ask questions like, 'What do you mean? How does this impact your audience? So what?' I've always been looking for universal language, for how I can express something that's personal but maybe touches everybody's experience. The coffeehouse is a great place to know whether you're succeeding. There's no place to hide here."

Frequent Homegrown patron Helen Hayes of Westwood was content to wait until intermission for her carrot cake until her husband, Larry, told her there were only a few left. She shot out of her seat, then returned, carefully placing the cake on the windowsill behind her until the break.

She said they first visited the coffeehouse because of the convenience but have learned to relish the coziness. They recently went to the thousand-seat Somerville Theater to see a performer they had liked at the Homegrown, and were disappointed.

"I enjoy that it's a smaller group," she said. "At the Somerville, the artist was kind of far away. This is more fun, intimate, a nice night out. And the carrot cake is real good."

—February 15, 1998

Judy Collins *on her own terms—as always*

Judy Collins is going her own way. This will come as no surprise to fans of the '60s folk star. She has always been a maverick and innovator, among the first to record urgent new folk writers such as Bob Dylan, Leonard Cohen, and Joni Mitchell, among the first to bring full orchestra arrangements to folk music, and to branch out into classic pop and show tunes.

"Throughout my career, I've been breaking the rules," she said, "and getting an appalling lot of flack at different times, whether it was for taking my clothes off, choosing to sing a 13th-century love song with an orchestra or, God forbid, singing 'Send in the Clowns,' from a Broadway show."

Always, however, she was a maverick within the mainstream music industry, recording 22 albums for Elektra from 1961-97, and another dozen for assorted

I had a very long tenure with Elektra, but I realized the big companies are really not capable of doing any kind of nurturing. They're banks, essentially. —Judy Collins

indie and major labels, including Columbia and Geffen. Like so many graying stars today, however, she sees no future in the increasingly youth-obsessed major-label world, and founded her own label, Wildflower, on which she has released two albums, "Live at Wolf Trap," and "All on a Wintry Night—A Judy Collins Christmas."

This summer, she also produces the first edition of an annual summer tour called the Wildflower Festival. It stars Collins, along with guest artists Richie Havens, Janis Ian, and Roger McGuinn, with whom she recorded Dylan's "Mr. Tambourine Man" and Pete Seeger's "Turn, Turn, Turn" before McGuinn founded the Byrds and all but invented folk-rock with electric versions of those songs. The festival was planned for 10 dates, but demand was so high that they will do 50, taking the tour into mid-November, when Collins begins her winter holiday tour.

"I had a very long tenure with Elektra," Collins said of starting her own label, "but I realized the big companies are really not capable of doing any kind of nurturing. They're banks, essentially. And it's not just older artists, it's also anybody who's young and makes a record that doesn't go platinum. I mean, I would have been completely out of the running if that had been going on when I started making records."

That's a powerful statement from a star whose 40-year career includes 16 top-10 hits, six Grammy nominations, four gold albums, and one platinum, not to mention an Oscar nomination for her 1974 documentary "Antonia: A Portrait of the Woman."

She praised the patience and vision of Elektra founder Jac Holzman, who nurtured her career through a slow build that did not produce a gold record until her sixth album, "In My Life," in 1966. She sang a daring mix of modern folk tunes by Dylan and Cohen, along with "Marat/Sade," from the Peter Weiss/Richard Peaslee musical, and the Beatles' "In My Life."

By then, she had emerged from the shadow of folk diva Joan Baez, with whom she was constantly compared in her early years. Collins said she saw Baez more as fellow traveler than rival.

"I was told that I was the version of Joan Baez that Elektra needed," she said, "but I was never aware of that as much as I understood that the nature of our personalities as women, the fact that we were singing in a different way, was very important. It was probably the beginning of the feminist movement; nobody called it that, but that's what it was."

Like Baez, she insisted on following her own artistic and political vision, choosing her own songs and designing her own career. With every groundbreaking album, it became clearer that she was her own woman and her own boss, singing about women's real lives in honest and increasingly uncompromising ways.

"We were pioneers, for sure," she said of herself, Baez, and other strong-voiced female folk stars, such as Mary Travers and Joni Mitchell. "The trick for me, though, was that I had the kind of support I had from Jac Holzman. I mean, yes, it was my personality, my choices, my direction; but he had the guts to say, 'Oh, OK, that's a good idea—let's do Kurt Weill and Bertolt Brecht on a folk album. An all-orchestrated pop album in 1968? Sure, let's try that. "Send in the Clowns?" OK.' But I'll tell you what they were: they were decisions based on music, on what I knew a song needed; and Jac always encouraged me to go for it, no matter how much it went against the grain."

She seems totally energized by her self-run career, planning new albums and a live concert DVD, as well as helping Rhino with its Aug. 8 release, "The Best of the Best of Judy Collins." On Sept. 11, Wildflowers releases her first two Elektra albums on a single CD, called "Maids and Golden Apples."

"Because I feel strongly that I'm someone who's been in this business 40 years and intends to be in it another 40 on my feet," she said, "I just wanted to have the control to do the things I want to do. I think with me and a handful of artists who have been doing it for all these years, we carry with us a kind of history and integrity that is very important today.

"I believe any artist worth their salt is going to challenge whatever the current authority is and move forward. A friend recently asked if it scared me that I've started my own label, and I said, 'No, what scares me is that I might not have.' "

—*August 3, 2001*

She had a song: Ronnie Gilbert of the Weavers
Ronnie Gilbert, Judy Collins, Dar Williams

When America first heard the songs that would ignite the commercial folk revival of the 1960s, it was not the voices of Judy Collins or Joan Baez or Peter, Paul, and Mary that they heard. It was the voice of the Weavers.

From 1950 until the anti-Communist blacklist destroyed their commercial viability in 1953, the Weavers—Ronnie Gilbert, Pete Seeger, Fred Hellerman, and Lee Hays—were the most popular singing group in America. So many songs now associated with the '60s revival, and permanently included in the American folk canon, were first popularized by them: "If I Had a Hammer" (which Seeger and Hays wrote), "Kumbaya," "Twelve Gates to the City," "On Top of Old Smoky," "Guantanamera," "House of the Rising Sun," Woody Guthrie's "This Land Is Your Land" and "So Long, It's Been Good to Know Yuh," and Huddie "Lead Belly" Ledbetter's "Goodnight, Irene," "Kisses Sweeter than Wine," and "Midnight Special."

"Ronnie is historically such an important part of our lives, because she was

We were four very politically motivated people, interested in doing what we could for the music we loved and for social action. Part of social action at that time was to raise the consciousness of any audience to folk music, just to the idea that these songs existed. —Ronnie Gilbert

with the wonderful Weavers," said Judy Collins, who joins Gilbert, Holly Near, Dar Williams, and Linda Tillery's Cultural Heritage Choir in a benefit for the Women's Center of Rhode Island. "I have known her on record for over 45 years; those were some of the first folk music recordings that were available back in the '50s. She was a great influence on me, just because she was a woman singing so strongly in a man's world."

In 1950 and 1951, the Weavers sold more than 4 million records. Time called them "the most widely imitated group in the business," and Carl Sandburg said, "When I hear America singing, the Weavers are there." (Their career is displayed on a superb 1993 four-CD Vanguard set, "Wasn't That a Time.")

At 73, Gilbert is still a dynamic artistic presence, but rarely strays far from her Berkeley, Calif., home. She just finished a run of her musical based on Studs Terkel's book "Coming of Age" at the San Jose Repertory Theater, and remarked that this may well be her last concert appearance in New England.

Tomorrow's gathering of four generations of folk stars—from Gilbert to '60s chanteuse Collins to '70s women's music pioneer Near to '80s-bred African-American feminist folk singer Tillery and '90s songwriting star Williams—offers a compelling study in how strongly the thread of influence runs from Gilbert and the Weavers through the entire modern history of folk music.

In 1949, the four leftist singers had no idea of the legacy they were creating when they accepted a job at the Village Vanguard in Greenwich Village. They simply wanted to see if they could present traditional folk songs in a way that would appeal to urbane, pop-friendly audiences.

"We were four very politically motivated people, interested in doing what we could for the music we loved and for social action," Gilbert said. "Part of social action at that time was to raise the consciousness of any audience to folk music, just to the idea that these songs existed."

They avoided the overtly political songs they knew from their involvement in the labor and civil rights movements, but insisted on presenting folk as a multiracial, multicultural form. Their rise was astonishingly quick; their first single, the Hebrew "Tzena, Tzena" backed with "Goodnight, Irene," was released on Decca after that first nightclub stint. It remained No. 1 on the Hit Parade for more than four months.

But the forces of McCarthyism were just as quick. Red Channels, the organ of the blacklist, first mentioned their leftist sympathies in 1950. Initially, it did not interfere with their string of hits, but by 1953, Decca had dropped them, radio stations refused to play their records, and a television series was canceled before it premiered.

Of course, to the rebellious generation coming of age in the 1960s, forcing music underground made it more alluring. Teenagers like Collins in Colorado and

Near in California devoured their records. Gilbert became a signal beacon in a music landscape peopled with docile pop stars like Doris Day and Patti Page. It was not just what she sang, it was how she sang.

"For me as a female singer looking for role models," said Near, "it was hearing her voice soar above these men's voices. There was something about her enthusiasm, as if there weren't any boundaries on her voice. She just stuck her chest out, threw her head back, and sang with abandon. There seemed to be a kind of body language that was all full of expansion, this kind of `here I am and here I come' stance."

Williams said she believes that strength of purpose is what drew her to singers influenced by Gilbert, like Collins and Joan Baez. To her, it didn't matter so much what Gilbert was singing; the politics was in the stance she took, the way she sang.

"I think the presence of strong women in music—not just politically, but strong in singing songs about life and its meaning—are the reasons I am a folk singer, too," she said. "And my sense is that the women who inspired me, like Joan Baez and Judy Collins, got that from Ronnie. It's all well and good to say women can be strong; it's quite another to have a precedent."

Collins said that Gilbert gave her the hope that she could make music on her own terms. "I've been able to make music in the way I've wanted, to carve out a life in which I write, I sing, write books, and tour," she said. "It's a wonderful gift to be able to do that, and to have had people who showed me that was possible. I think the Weavers' influence has to do with giving people the right to be who they are musically, and to offer kind of a through-line to the tradition of that."

Gilbert was pleased to see so much of the Weavers' repertoire and vocal style shape the early '60s folk revival. It was, after all, what they had set out to do: to place these American folk songs into the cultural mainstream. But it was not until she heard Near's feminist music in the '70s that she was certain their legacy would continue.

"I sat down and my heart just melted over it," she said. "The way she sang, the songs she sang, the form the songs were in, the lyrics, all seemed to be doing in her day and with her issues what the Weavers did with the issues in our time."

Tillery is letting a vocal nodule heal and declined to be interviewed. But in an e-mail response, she revealed a quieter dimension to the web of inspiration Gilbert has spread. She wrote how much it meant when Gilbert, aware of Tillery's efforts to bring African-American folk songs to modern audiences, gave her a rare 19th-century book of songs from the slavery era.

Gilbert stressed that her legacy did not begin with her. She inherited it from labor radicals like Mother Jones (whom she has portrayed in a musical) and from outspoken African-American singers Marian Anderson and Paul Robeson. She sees that legacy blazing now in the politically fired songs of Williams and Ani DiFranco, and knows the sparks she and the Weavers struck so long ago will continue to glow and to be stoked by new generations.

"The strength that people draw from the Weavers, and that Holly talks about in me, is the same strength I found in Marian Anderson and Paul Robeson," she said. "It's about a kind of crazy, singing insistence on being in this world; that we have a right to be here and be heard—and an obligation to be heard. Something of that is in my voice, was in Marian Anderson's voice, is in Holly's voice and Ani's voice and is a tremendously important thing for people to hear. That's our value, and I don't know if we ever do it knowingly; we just do it because that's what came down to us. That's our heritage."

— October 1, 1999

Bittersweet victories: remembering the women's music movement
Holly Near, Cris Williamson

In American music, pioneers rarely reach the promised land. It was up to Louis Armstrong to take jazz to the world, achieving stardom undreamed of by his mentor and teacher King Oliver. Rock pioneers such as Bill Haley and Little Richard never found the success that later stars Elvis Presley and the Beatles did.

That has also been the story for Holly Near and Cris Williamson, pioneering stars of the women's music movement. In the 1970s and early '80s, each sold hundreds of thousands of independently produced albums at a time when no national distribution existed for independent records and such sales figures were simply not thought possible. Each performed nightly for thousands in major halls and women's music festivals throughout North America. Each handily sold out Carnegie Hall.

Along the way, those successes helped prove that there was a viable market for women songwriters writing honestly from within their own experience. Their success sparked the songwriter revival of the 1980s and '90s, but it was left for the next generation of strong women songwriters—Suzanne Vega, Tracy Chapman, Melissa Etheridge, Sarah MacLachlan—to walk through the doors kicked open by the women's music movement..

"Women's music now is a pretty vital idea," Williamson said. "We used to say those words together just so people would put women and music in the same thought. What we did, a bunch of women standing shoulder to shoulder, was to make a road by walking ahead. First it was one or two people on a little deer path, then a few more followed and the road widened."

Holly Near / Cris Williamson *"Bittersweet Victories"* **127**

"What was a movement has become a market now," Near said. "When we first started doing lesbian work, who would have imagined there would be television shows with gay characters? All the things that were secrets when we first started singing about them are now openly discussed on every talk show."

As the civil rights and antiwar movements of the 1960s began to dissipate, Near was already a celebrated protest singer, known for her radical songs about peace and human rights. Like many activists of her generation, she began questioning the culture at large and how it affected her own life.

"What was going on for women who had been working in the labor and civil rights and antiwar movements" she said, "was that they started to see how they were having to fight for their own spaces in those movements. The rebirth of the feminist movement came about as people in those movements began to say we don't want to just change the laws, we want to change our minds, everything about ourselves. That fit so perfectly for women, because we had been living in drag for so long. It came as this huge invitation to say, `Oh, we can decide who we are.' "

Increasingly, Near began to apply the same fiery, heartful passion she brought to her antiwar songs to examinations of what it was to be a woman in modern America, and to what it was to be a lesbian. To her astonishment, her audiences grew.

At the same time, Williamson was pondering her future as a rising pop star—and a lesbian—in a male-dominated music industry. She had an acclaimed debut on the Ampex label, but it went out of business shortly after her album's release.

In 1972, while in Washington, D.C., to do a concert, she met a lesbian activist and musician named Meg Christian. In the early days of the women's music movement, much, though certainly not all, of the energy came from gay women struggling against discrimination.

"Meg was just then formulating an idea called women's music and is the one I credit for thinking up that term. I did a radio interview with these women who were radical lesbians and were saying it was male money and male companies I had worked for. I said they should start a women's record company, and the next day they started Olivia. Meg's record was first, in 1973, then I made `Changer and the Changed' with them in 1974."

That record changed everything, selling more than 500,000 copies, proving there was a viable market for women's music. In it, Williamson brought her beguiling folk-pop craft to outspoken odes to lesbian love as well as sweepingly universal ballads like "Waterfall," one of the finest songs ever written about the intimate, renewable process of human change.

Near was also doing remarkably well, with albums on her own Redwood Records selling 50,000 to 100,000 copies. Women began to create feminist

The rebirth of the feminist movement came about as people in those movements began to say we don't want to just change the laws, we want to change our minds, everything about ourselves. —Holly Near

and lesbian concert series in their communities, first at the local women's bookstore or cafe—or even in people's homes—and then in larger concert halls. As the movement grew, women became concert producers, lighting and sound technicians, creating a solid infrastructure for the music. Their success influenced other noncommercial music in the disco-drunk '70s, inspiring similar fan-driven movements in Celtic, traditional folk, blues, and alternative rock.

Concerts were like town meetings of the feminist movement, rippling with the vibrant, often tumultuous energies of people discovering themselves by discovering others like them.

"They were concerts but also social events," Williamson said. "The buzz was tremendous. You couldn't get them out of the lobby, first of all; there'd be tables everywhere for this cause or that, sign up here, vote for this. You finally get them in their seats and sing something like `Song of the Soul' and they'd all stand up. It was something to behold."

As the songwriter revival of the '80s grew, a new generation of strong women like Chapman, MacLachlan, and Etheridge—all of whom were once opening acts for Near—achieved mainstream stardom. And the women's music movement ebbed. Near disputes the notion that those women could have kept the movement alive by aligning themselves with declining women's music labels such as Redwood and Olivia; believing rather that it was their responsibility to take that next big step. The movement was fading on its own, largely a victim of its success.

Women who had felt like radical outsiders for their feminist beliefs were now creating careers in women's medicine and law, antiviolence work, women and children's rights, feminist history and literature, electoral politics, and countless other vocations that either did not exist or were largely closed to women before the feminist movement of the 1970s. And women's music was the soundtrack to all that change.

"The numbers have dropped way off for everybody that was part of women's music," said Williamson. "But I'd look at that as a mark of success. We should raise our hands as we go over the finish line, saying, boy, we did our jobs well. We fed those hungry women, provided nourishment for their souls and spirits that told them they could go off and lead their own lives on their own terms. So they did. Now they don't feel that same hunger, because they have lives that fill them, and they don't need us anymore. That made me really sad for a long time; then I went, wait a minute, it's because we did our jobs so well."

Like Williamson, Near remains a vital contemporary artist, as she proves on her hotly topical, disarmingly ebullient new CD "Edge" and on a charismatic retrospective called "Simply Love: The Women's Music Collection," both on Calico Tracks. As she sighed philosophically about changing times and her changing fortunes, it sounded much more like a brief breath between sprints than anything approaching a sigh of surrender.

"I'm not taking life quite so personally anymore, which I think is a sign of aging. But I don't for a moment think life would have been better if I had done things differently when I was younger. When I think back at all we did, all the things we just did for ourselves for the first time, I think, my God, how did we have the courage? And it's because we were young and took everything personally. That is the mode of the young warrior, to take it all personally, and society depends on young people to do that; just as it depends on older people to get over that part, so we can be better teachers."

—October 1, 2000

Broadside Magazine: The political spark of the '60s folk revival
Si Kahn, Larry Long, Agnes "Sis" Cunningham, Smithsonian archivist Jeff Place

The 1960s are remembered as an era of great political turmoil and protest, of massive civil-rights marches and antiwar demonstrations. It is also remembered as the time when folk music enjoyed its greatest commercial popularity, when protest songs topped the hit parade and traditional songs formed the living soundtrack for the social movements of the day.

Many of those musical fires were stoked in the New York City apartment of Agnes "Sis" Cunningham and Gordon Friesen, who in 1962 created a small monthly magazine called Broadside. It was devoted to publishing new political songs at a time when commercial radio was dominated by the Beach Boys and the Kingston Trio, and the folk revival centered around traditional music. By offering a publication outlet to young songwriters who wrote uncompromisingly about modern issues, Broadside became the nerve center for the rising wave of singer-songwriters.

Bob Dylan was first published in Broadside's premiere issue, and his classic "Blowin' in the Wind" debuted on its pages. Phil Ochs, Malvina Reynolds, Tom Paxton, Eric Andersen, Janis Ian, Buffy Sainte-Marie, Arlo Guthrie, and, of course, Pete Seeger were frequent contributors to the magazine and to the 15 albums of Broadside songs released by Folkways Records.

Smithsonian/Folkways has released an epic five-CD anthology called "Best of Broadside 1962-1988." It is a vivid chronicle of the 1960s era, the magazine's heyday, offering candid solo cuts of vintage songs by Dylan, Paxton, Seeger, Ochs, and Reynolds, along with fine lesser-known writers, such as Native American balladeer Peter LaFarge, Mark Spoelstra, and Peggy Seeger.

Cunningham, now 92, recalled that the idea emerged from a 1962 meeting of New York progressives, including herself, her husband Friesen, who died in 1996, and Pete Seeger. It took its name from songsheets published in 17th- and 18th-century England and America, sold by street peddlers as "broadsides."

"I never expected it to become as influential as it did," she said. "I'm still very surprised by that, because we thought we were just too left-wing to interest a wide audience. But when Bob Dylan started getting popular, interest in the magazine picked up a lot."

In the anthology, Dylan is glimpsed at his youthful prime. Because Columbia had signed him to an exclusive contract, he was coyly billed as Blind Boy Grunt in Broadside. The two songs offered here were never released by Dylan himself until the 1990s. "John Brown" is a bitter antiwar ballad, furiously sung by Dylan; and his "Ballad of Donald White" is still troubling and relevant, the brilliantly spun story of an institutionalized ex-convict who commits murder simply to get back into prison.

Most of the cuts are performed solo, or done in loose hootenanny-like collaborations, such as a rollicking Ochs and Andersen duet of the latter's Woody-Guthrie-esque "Plains of Nebrasky-O."

Ochs seems more comfortable here than on many of his own recordings, perhaps because his radicalism was so warmly welcomed by Broadside. His wit sizzles on "The Ballad of William Worthy," about an actual journalist sentenced to jail (his conviction was later overturned) for traveling to communist countries Americans were then prohibited from visiting: "Somehow it's strange to hear the State Department say "You are living in the free world, in the free world you must stay."

Smithsonian/Folkways archivist Jeff Place was nominated for a Grammy for his tantalizing CD book, which offers vivid context both to the artists and the issues they sing about.

"Broadside made it more OK for people to write their own songs, particularly protest and topical songs," Place says, "at a time when most folk people were still doing all that collegiate, hootenanny, 'let's-all-sing-together' stuff. Once Dylan clicked, of course, it became very chic to be the troubadour with your own protest songs. But Broadside was the first place offering an outlet for that. I'm not sure that whole movement would have grown like it did if it hadn't been for Broadside. There had to be some fertile garden for these people to grow in."

Pete Seeger's presence is everywhere on the anthology, as it was at Broadside. Cunningham said he supplied the tape recorder used to record songs she transcribed for publication. He pops up again and again, singing songs by obscure writers to lend them his starpower. His droll cover of a then-unknown Tom

Paxton's sassy antiwar song, "The Willing Conscript," is a sage clinic in the use of sarcasm as political weapon. His voice as bright and innocent as a child's, he chirps, "I want to do my duty, but one thing I do implore/ You must give me lessons, sergeant, for I've never killed before."

Many of the most moving moments come from activists singing songs culled from picket lines and freedom marches. The Freedom Singers were an African-American vocal group that led the singing at countless civil-rights marches. They sing "We'll Never Turn Back," written in jail by a teenage demonstrator named Bertha Gober, and which the late Cordell Reagon said inspired him to form the group. Recorded in 1964, it is grippingly authentic, the actual voice of the Southern civil-rights movement at the peak of its power.

Later songs, such as the Reverend Frederick Douglass Kirkpatrick's bitter and militant "Burn, Baby, Burn," show both the civil-rights and political-music movements beginning to fray at the edges. As Broadside wobbled into the '70s, the songs are increasingly less well crafted or convincing, though there are a few gems from Arlo Guthrie and Lucinda Williams.

Broadside always ran out of the home of Cunningham and Friesen, and through the '60s, the most important topical songwriters seemed to come right to their doors. When they no longer did, Cunningham said, they were just too old and broke to seek out the best new writers. Broadside published off and on until folding in 1988.

There is almost no evidence here, for example, of the women's music movement, whose artists, such as Holly Near, Meg Christian, and Cris Williamson, sold hundreds of thousands of records in the 1970s. The best and most popular political writers of the '70s and '80s, such as Near, Utah Phillips, and Si Kahn, are sadly absent from Broadside's pages and recordings.

Kahn recalls subscribing to Broadside in the '60s, but when the grassroots organizer's songs were making him one of the most respected and widely sung political songwriters of the '70s and '80s, he was unaware the magazine still existed.

He said that modern political songwriters and activists like himself often have to fight the great shadow the '60s cast. There is a widespread public perception that political music, and the activism it accompanied, were almost unique to that era. Of course, Kahn begs to differ.

"Politically, the '60s were obviously a time of great foment," he said, "but I don't think they're as different from other decades as they're portrayed to be, either politically or musically. There have been at least a dozen progressive marches on Washington since the '60s that were much larger than the 1963 civil-rights march. I'm sure that many of the feminist artists of the '70s sold considerably more records than most of the political songwriters of the '60s. There's a tendency to either mythologize or demonize that era, and both are really wrong."

His 12th recording, "Been a Long Time" (Sliced Bread), is an urgently fresh and classic set of warmhearted, incisive songs about modern issues of poverty, race, class, and community.

Those are the issues that concern modern political troubadour Larry Long as well. His new Smithsonian/Folkways CD, "Well May the World Go," is named for a Seeger song he sings. Like Kahn, he is a community organizer, and his recent work has centered on bringing elders and young people together to share stories, from which he carves his own musically lovely, emotionally powerful songs. They are brimming with populist anger and topicality, but also with a hopefulness and humanity missing from many of the arch and disdainful protest songs of the '60s.

He said he believes the dearth of topical music in the commercial music world these days actually helps him in his work. "It frees you up," he said, "because it's obvious you're not doing this for money or to be the next Bob Dylan."

"I think political music is heard in communities today more than in the music industry," he said. "Real political music has always been grounded in the ranks of community and neighborhood. We don't hear those songs more because we live in a very capitalistic system which does not promote the common good as much as the good of the individual.

"But in every community, you find good, hardworking people who have given their lives to the common good of others, and who are often overlooked. When you honor these people with a song, that song becomes a nucleus to give praise to all those who have been unsung in our culture. That's always been important work and it always will be; it's the tradition of the troubadour."

—January 28, 2001

Folk festivals: a balm for what ails American cities
The Lowell Folk Festival, New Bedford Summerfest

The cities of Lowell and New Bedford faced similar troubles in recent years. They are the same troubles plaguing many mid-sized American cities whose old industries fled, whose urban centers are aging and filled with the industries' skeletal remains. Both cities are now enjoying a significant urban renaissance, and both have found a powerful ally for that in a most unlikely place: folk music.

These remarkably similar success stories strongly suggest that well-designed urban folk festivals can do wonders to reverse the cultural decline facing many smaller American cities today.

The Lowell Folk Festival is the nation's largest free festival of its kind, drawing nearly 200,000 people every year. New Bedford Summerfest grew from local scallop festival to major music festival when savvy programmers Helene and

Alan Korolenko took over the booking six years ago. Last year, Summerfest sold more than 20,000 of the $5 buttons that offer access to all events. The festival's popularity argues that Lowell's success is no fluke.

"The Lowell Folk Festival brought thousands of people here who otherwise would not have come," said Mayor Eileen Donoghue. "It breaks down those barriers that cities like ours sometimes face: Is it family-friendly, is it a place you want to spend a weekend? The festival has really changed people's expectations about what they will find when they come here."

New Bedford mayor Fredrick Kalisz Jr. echoed Donoghue's enthusiasm about how Summerfest is changing people's perceptions about the port's downtown. The festival was designed to showcase the renovation of the State Pier and the 1996 opening of the 34-acre New Bedford Whaling National Historical Park, the central sites for the festival.

Kalisz, Donoghue, and others agreed that the impact of these festivals go far beyond the events.

"Summerfest has driven so many other projects," Kalisz said, "really driven the arts and cultural development downtown. The Chamber of Commerce, the park, the city and other sponsors build on that success all year long."

Both festivals foster firm deadlines for public and private improvement projects that used to drag on for years. Now they have to be done in time for the festival. After each event, both cities solicit ideas for improving the event—and the city— over the next year.

That highlights the festivals' greatest benefit beyond showcasing the cities. Because they are organized and sponsored by coalitions of city, cultural, and business groups, ongoing public-private partnerships have been created.

"Summerfest has really brought us together as a city," said New Bedford Chamber of Commerce chairman Joel Burns. "We have always been on the end of the Massachusetts spectrum, considered to be a little less than the rest of the people culturally, like in Boston. Now we have this opportunity to show we do have culture here . . . .It's the one weekend people forget there's management and labor and ethnic differences. We come together as New Bedford, and that helps us do other cultural things all year."

So why folk music? Initially, both cities looked at other ideas to bring people downtown, including major pop stars.

Lisa Sughrue, director of operations for Summerfest, said big-name stars tended to draw crowds that only came to see them.

"Bringing in stars didn't do anything for the city," she said. "Now people e-mail us right after Summerfest, asking when it's happening again—and what other things are happening here."

Modern folk music is a vast genre, and both festivals are known for their diversity. Lowell brings in a feast of America's myriad ethnic and traditional

New Bedford Summerfest—April Verch Band

musics, while New Bedford is developing its niche with the best from traditional and contemporary folk.

Because folk is immersed in tradition, it is a grand showcase for these historic cities. Old buildings and cobbled streets, once seen as eyesores, make the perfect backdrop for the music.

As Lowell city manager John Cox said, "The festival turned the oldness of the city from a negative into a positive."

These festivals also draw the sort of mature family people that both cities hope to attract. The Lowell festival took an extensive survey of attendees last year, and found that 69 percent were between ages 25 and 64. An astonishing 98 percent of those surveyed said they would return.

Scottish fiddler and New Bedford resident Johnny Cunningham said these festivals are also very important to the musicians. "Performers get to play for a great mix of people, not just for their fans or the fans of their particular genre. And the mix of music is great because performers of different styles often perform together on the same stage, there's lots of friendly interaction between performers, which is something audiences don't normally get to see."

Because these festivals are financed in advance and offered free or nearly free, the programmers are able to focus on building an artistically successful event, not selling tickets. They offer large lineups of folk headliners and lesser-known acts, presenting a tantalizing array of music. Over time, that tends to make the event itself the main attraction. That, in turn, helps make the cities the stars.

"Folk music lends itself to outdoor summertime venues," said Donoghue. "It's quiet enough, small enough, that you can have different types of music going on at stages all over the city. That kind of festival creates around-and-about strolling, which encourages people to go in the shops and restaurants and museums, to notice the city more."

It is Arthur Motta's job to sell New Bedford to the world as director of the city's Office of Tourism and Marketing. He said Summerfest makes his job easier, since it promotes the oldness which once made the city a hard sell.

"During the down times," he said, "when industries like textiles went south and there was widespread disinvestment, those older buildings were cleared away for new development in wealthier cities. Now, what has stayed up here, and in Lowell, has become an asset. It's being restored and renovated. In tourism, people are always looking for what's new, and in this case, what's new are the cities and towns of old New England that have an authenticity the Disney Worlds do not have."

"The festival has allowed us to believe in ourselves," said Lowell city manager Cox. "When people see 100,000 people here enjoying a festival, they get a different sense about their city. They think, 'Wow, there's something happening here.' I can remember how bleak things were in the '70s. Nobody would have thought we could bring 100,000 people downtown for any reason, with all the old buildings, canals, and streets. Now they say, 'Look at this place, it's gorgeous; it's got old canals, cobblestone streets, lovely old mill buildings.' People love Lowell now for just what it is, warts and all."

—July 1, 2001

What is the sound of **Roaring Jelly** *?*

What on Earth is Roaring Jelly? If you are not in the know, you might guess a rock band with an image problem, or perhaps an ill-conceived breakfast treat from southwest Texas.

But to those in the grassroots world of New England contra dancing, Roaring Jelly is a unique, delightfully folksy dance band with a cheerful mission to make the bandstand as inviting, social, and democratic a place as the dance floor.

Despite its fiercely held nonprofessionalism (members pay $15 annual dues to play), Roaring Jelly has survived for 30 years, hosting monthly dances for nearly as long. As it celebrates its 30th anniversary, there are more than 60 members, as many as anyone in the band can remember.

The March dance in Roaring Jelly's current home, 1st Parish Church on Lexington Green, welcomed more than 30 "Jellies," as they call themselves, playing for roughly the same number of dancers from their 350-tune repertoire of Irish, Scottish, English, and old New England dance tunes.

For 18 years, Susan Elberger of Lexington has been Roaring Jelly's caller, the person who teaches the dances and calls out the figures, or dance moves, for each dance. The term contra, as she explained during a beginner's session prior to the dance, comes from the Latin word for opposite, and describes how couples begin each dance facing each other, then perform a series of figures, as in contra's offspring, square dancing, or its ancestors, English country dancing and Irish set dancing.

As early comers set up chairs for the band and Jellies ambled in with instruments—mostly fiddles, guitars, and an array of wind instruments—Elberger explained the band's role as front-door to the local contra dance scene.

"To me, the idea of folk music is that you don't need to feel polished to participate," she said, "which is not in any way to say it is a simple music. But it is a genre that invites people to participate rather than just watch. This band does that, that's what's special about it. It takes that old social idea and makes it real for people today."

She explained the sheer size of the group encourages the group's egalitarian mission. Beginners don't need to fear being singled out, and in fact, are encouraged to play only the first note of each measure until they get used to the brisk cadence. Everything is smartly designed to offer the comfortable anonymity of a church choir in an instrumental group setting.

"This is not a sit-in band," said president and fiddler Leslie Fuller of Reading. "We encourage people to attend a few rehearsals or gigs to see if it's what they want and if they're ready. When they do come in, we tell them not to get shaken, because the first thing that strikes a lot of people—it did me—is how fast the music goes. I just tell people to play what they can and add more notes as they go on. You do pick it up."

The band's name, by the way, comes from an old slang term for nitroglycerine that became the name of a lively old Celtic fiddle tune also known as "Smash the Windows."

The band opened with a sprightly Irish tune, its first notes arrestingly thick and sweet. Roaring Jelly is not by any means, to borrow from Irving Berlin, "the bestest band what am." But anyone aware of its come-one-come-all membership policy is likely to be surprised by just how good it is—a strong-pulsed, sweetly melodic dance band with an easy, lilting groove.

Everyone interviewed attributed the quality of the band's sound to music director Debby Knight, a busy fiddler and pianist who teaches science at Cambridge Friends School. Only she and Elberger are paid for band work.

"For me, it's very creative to take a group like this," she said, "with players at all different levels, from beginners to professionals, and think how to mesh them all together into a sound that will support and hopefully excite dancers. This is a very social music by its nature, both because you play it in ensembles and because you're playing for dancing. People aren't just sitting there listening. You're providing something where maybe the details aren't as important as the emotion and energy. I've enjoyed thinking about the music that way."

One way she cooked up to conduct subtly is with an elaborate system of cue cards she waves before the band during tunes: "Winds and plucked only," "No Fiddles," and the always helpful, "Smile!" Since most Jellies are sight-reading the tunes, she found these abbreviated commands have the least chance of disrupting the cadence so crucial to the dancers.

Paul Milde, a retired surgeon from Wellesley, is among the band's oldest ongoing members, having joined in 1980. He joined to give his fiddling hobby a boost, and fell in love with the band's sociablility. And he said there is something dancing feet can teach about this music that no books or recordings can.

"The notes are on the page, but the music isn't," he said. "You have to hear it as it's played by other people, get feedback from the dancers. There's an energy that goes when there's a lot of people dancing. It gets fed back to you by the dancers, gets into us, and then we feed it back to them."

He stressed that longtime bass player Andy Riffin was another big factor in the group's long life and current good health. He was seen throughout the evening, putting down his bass and scurrying off to do errands, putting out intermission snacks, setting up and taking down chairs. Milde said Riffin, a Lexington native and owner of the local AR Vending Co., was also instrumental in finding the dance's current home, the band's rehearsal space, and many of the paid gigs it does at neighborhood block parties, schools, and dances.

"What made this system of dancing work so well and hold on so long is that it is so social," Riffin said during intermission. "The farm families, who didn't get to socialize much, would come into town for a Saturday night dance that brought people together in a setting where it was easy to socialize. The music wasn't so loud they couldn't talk, and they got to change partners and mix. It's still that way here."

Newest member Rosemary Green, also of Lexington, is a prime study in what makes this band such a precious part of the local dance scene. A longtime contra dancer, she wanted to stay with the scene, but dancing got more difficult as she entered her 70s, and she began to wonder if her contra dancing days were done. Then she saw Roaring Jelly in action, thought of the recorder she had played off and on for years, and knew she was back in action. She joined the band last month.

"When I heard them, I could see it was such a big group that I could get in there, piddle away, and they wouldn't even know," she said. "Everybody's very friendly, very helpful when you're having trouble with something. I never played that fast before, and I need a lot of help, but it's fun, and I can just play along as best I can. I've always loved the music, and now I'm getting to where I can even play along to it on the radio."

—*March 25, 2001*

Irish music goes American
Seamus Egan, Eileen Ivers, Mairead Ni Mhaonaigh, Mick Moloney, Cathie Ryan

More and more, the big names in Irish music are coming not from Dublin, Derry, and Cork, but from Detroit, Philadelphia, and the Bronx.

Home to artists from supergroups Solas and Cherish the Ladies to solo stars Eileen Ivers and Cathie Ryan to step dancers Michael Flatley and Jean Butler, the land fondly known as Ireland's other shore is now a more vibrant and visible part of that country's musical culture than ever before.

Is this good news? Can these American-born city kids capture the ancient grace and nuance of Irish tradition?

"I've been asked a lot if there is an Irish-American style of playing," said Philadephia native Seamus Egan, whose quintet Solas may be the hottest band anywhere in the Celtic realm. "I don't know that there is. I've heard that Irish music from America seems to have more energy, is faster, a bit more frenetic, and that that's because of the fast pace of American life. But I honestly don't know if that's true."

It is a tricky question because, while the artists in this new wave are American, they are no Paddy-come-latelys to the music. They are part of a generation of Irish-Americans that was weaned on Irish music from childhood as part of an international network of schooling and competition sponsored by the Irish cultural organization Comhaltas Ceoltoiri Eireann.

To compete for what are known as the All-Ireland Championships, held each summer in Ireland, children undergo rigorous and strictly traditional instruction from older players, dancers, and singers. The music is taught in the old ways, orally passed down from old to young. While the idea of music as competition rankles many, these kids learn their traditional chops chapter and verse.

Egan won All-Irelands in four instruments (flute, tin whistle, banjo, and mandolin) when he was 14, a feat never equaled by an Irish-born musician. Fiddler-singer Mairead Ni Mhaonaigh of the Irish-based Altan first learned that Irish music was played in America when a tour of young Comhaltas players from the States toured her native Donegal.

She was stunned by how much more proficient they were in the distinct regional styles of the music than the Irish players she knew. She soon heard about Chicago fiddler Liz Carroll, another All-Ireland champ, whom she claims as a major influence.

"Liz is looked upon as a goddess on this side of the water," Ni Mhaonaigh said. "But all these American musicians are well thought of in Ireland. They're technically brilliant to start with. But I also think people are flattered these Irish-Americans, who could be playing rock 'n' roll or blues, would choose to stick with their own background."

Hot fiddle star Eileen Ivers, who grew up in the Bronx, was the winningest fiddler in the history of the All-Ireland competitions, earning championships in nearly every age group and category from the time she was 8. With her band, which includes an African percussionist and Puerto Rican bassist, she is expanding the boundaries of Irish music with an almost swashbuckling verve.

"I'm really careful that my music maintains its Irishness, that swing and spirit," she said. "But growing up in a big urban environment, you can't help but take it all in. I'd hear things in other styles that worked not just musically but mathematically. The one beat of a jig is longer than the two and the three, and that's what South African rhythms felt like when I heard them. Perhaps only in this country would you hear enough of all this different music to see those connections."

The adventurousness of these Irish-American stars, however, may be less a result of eclectic upbringings than of how they cut their teeth as professionals.

Musician, historian, and folklorist Mick Moloney is perhaps the preeminent scholar of Irish music in America, and did much to focus attention on this new generation of Irish-Americans. Cherish the Ladies, the world's first female Irish music group, grew out of a 1985 tour he produced of young women, including Ivers and flutist Joanie Madden. He has just written a marvelous, anecdote-rich, and vividly illustrated Crown book, with companion Shanachie CD, called "Far From the Shamrock Shores: The Story of Irish-American Immigration Through Song."

Because the venues available for Irish musicians here are so often supported by public arts money, artists have an incentive to learn to play the music in a purer style, Moloney said.

"If someone is promoting an Irish concert with any degree of public arts money," he said, "they'll want the music to be distinctly Irish and traditional in its instrumentation, whereas the music is almost passe with general audiences in Ireland."

Detroit-born singer-songwriter Cathie Ryan, also an alumna of Cherish the Ladies, has earned a global following with her pure soprano, sweet mastery of ancient Irish balladry, and original songs exploring the Irish-American experience. She said public-arts-sponsored concerts give American artists crucial training in how to put the music across to general audiences.

Because this experience often comes early in their careers, it helps form their musical identities, and she believes this knack for winning new fans is the most important thing American artists are bringing to the music.

"When I listened to the music as a child, if a song had 20 verses, they would all be sung," she said. "I'll edit, which I know some purists find insulting to the material. But I believe I'm performing for a modern audience that's used to getting things quickly; I want to present the musical and emotional essence of the song. It's not a night at the fire; it's a concert."

—*March 17, 2002*

Fiddle revolutionary
Martin Hayes, Hanneke Cassel, Lissa Schneckenburger

Martin Hayes does not seem like a revolutionary. His voice is as quiet as his ballad-sweet fiddle bow, the stories he tells of his County Clare boyhood drenched with reverence for Irish music's ancient traditions and wild grace, and especially for the centuries of players who created and passed along the vast canon of traditional tunes, airs, and songs.

But make no mistake—Hayes is the most innovative and influential fiddler on the Irish scene today. His gentle genius is changing the way a new generation of folk musicians performs and thinks about traditional music. His elegantly melodic, structurally ambitious duets with Chicago-born guitarist Dennis Cahill deconstruct Irish melodies in revolutionary ways, opening them up for modern sensibilities in much the same way Miles Davis did with jazz or Eric Clapton did with the blues.

Like those musical revolutionaries, Hayes is not trying to change the old music as much as explore it in new ways. He considers himself less an innovator than an editor.

"What I do is very focused on delivering the core melodic idea and rhythmic idea," he said from his home in Seattle, "and a bit less concerned with the instrument. I'm more concerned with the end result of a piece than with how the execution appears. I am not thinking about whether it is difficult or easy to play, but with how in my own mind I would like to hear pieces come out. I never think of changing a melody so much as heightening the emotional experience of it."

That expresses itself in a nervy willingness to sound tentative as his bow introduces a melody, wandering around it as if peering in to get its sense and shape, then building with captivating emotional eloquence as that essence is examined.

On his latest CD with Cahill, "Live in Seattle" (Green Linnet), an epic 27-minute piece explores 11 melodies with a cinematic sweep and orchestral swell more reminiscent of Aaron Copland's "Appalachian Spring" than a ceilidh of jigs and reels.

Two of the hottest young fiddlers in Boston, Hanneke Cassel and Lissa Schneckenburger, happily claim Hayes as a major influence, though neither is primarily an Irish fiddler. On her debut CD, "My Joy" on her own label, Cassel bases her robust, pulsing style on Scottish and Cape Breton strains. On her CD, "Different Game" (Footprint), Schneckenburger seems equally at home with Celtic or American styles, and her own catchy songwriting. With fiddler Laura Corteze, they are also in the trio Halali.

Cassel, who grew up in Washington, credits Hayes, along with Irish-American fiddlers Liz Carroll and Eileen Ivers, with first drawing her into Irish music.

"After the first time I heard Martin, I told people he can make you cry on a reel," she said. "There's something about his smoothness, and the way he swings the notes, that really drew me in. I love that he has all these great syncopation things he does, where he adds anticipation of a note before it's there, and it drives the tune forward. He's very exciting to fiddlers, because he will play very simply and slowly but can also do all this fancy bow stuff whenever he wants."

Schneckenburger has also absorbed Hayes's use of syncopation and other rhythmic tricks to breathe space into tunes. But she is more influenced by how he thinks about music. The Maine native graduates in the spring from the New England Conservatory.

"I really respect the way he treats music," she said. "I get the feeling he thinks about music very deeply, and that comes across when he performs. He's very careful about how he builds a tune, what ornaments he uses, always presenting it in a way that makes people really feel he's emotionally involved."

Like all innovators, Hayes has his critics. Some traditional music lovers believe his way of deconstructing Irish melody, stripping it from its dance tune structure and exploring it in compositional and improvisational ways, alters too profoundly its innate identity. Hayes counters that much of what he is doing is rooted in older styles.

"Some players I knew growing up would value one particular note in a melody and know that everything hung upon that," he said. "I learned a lot from talking to the old guys about that, but my guiding force in allowing myself some liberty is that the essential quality of the music is an emotion wishing to be communicated through the form. I think the form is subservient to the emotion wishing to be expressed, and you can make the melody as pliable as you need for that to reach the forefront."

To those fearing that may irreparably alter the music, Hayes offers two considerations. First, that change and tradition are, at heart, the same force, as water and current are to a river. Remove either, and what is left will stagnate and die.

The other is that traditional music's survival will hinge, as it always has, on its ability to speak to the emotions of the present, not merely to evoke those of the past.

"I'm convinced that this is an incredible body of music, and I have no fears or doubts about it," he said. "But if you were to say it's locked and steadfast right now in terms of how it's to be played, you would kill it. I mean, who is to say the high point of Irish music is necessarily in the past? It's like a society telling itself their high point is behind them. Wouldn't the most hopeful possible outlook for Irish music be to say that its high point is yet to come?"

—April 6, 2001

How a coffeehouse is born
Greg Greenway, Mozaic Room director Steve Gretz

When Steve Gretz, pastor of the Avon Baptist Church, got the idea of starting the Mozaic Room Coffeehouse, he knew it would be a slow process. He is a sometime folk performer himself, an empathetic and very witty songwriter, so he knew it would take time to build crowds for artists who have never pranced across the MTV screen or topped the hit parade.

Folk music today exists almost entirely beneath the radar of mainstream media, so no TV or radio hype is going to bring people out to see even its best and biggest stars. Coffeehouses must be built by hand, brick by brick, fan by fan.

On a crisp October Saturday, only 35 people came to see Cape Cod songwriter Greg Greenway, a star on the national folk circuit who has no trouble packing established venues like Cambridge's Club Passim. And yet a sense of excitement crackled in the air, a crowd electricity that suggested something was happening here, something growing in this second-floor room above the only Protestant church in the little town of Avon.

Greenway, veteran that he is, recognized it right away and was not the least concerned about the size of the crowd.

"Coffeehouses like this are almost universally volunteer run, and if it's done right—wherever it's done—it tends to kick off and run," he said. "But it's that core of people that makes it work, not the star-power of any performers. What we consider star-power in acoustic music is way beneath the consciousness of mainstream America. People in the folk world talk reverently about John Gorka and Cheryl Wheeler, but the average person has almost no access to their music. So star-power only develops after you have created the community."

He said he has seen this kind of grass-roots growth everywhere he has traveled in his nearly 20-year career. One town will have a well-run coffeehouse, and there will be a public recognition of artists like Gorka, Wheeler, and himself. The next town over, with no coffeehouse, the same names are completely unknown.

In 1997, Gretz opened the Mozaic Room in Mansfield, where he lives. There already is a thriving coffeehouse there, however—the Rose Garden at the Orthodox Congregational Church—and he didn't want to cut in on their act. He also was beginning to understand how little ready-made audience there is for this music. He would have to build it by word of mouth, a fan at a time. Since he had a congregation that was obligated to listen to him at least once a week, the Avon Baptist Church seemed the logical place for his coffeehouse, so he moved it last January.

"I was a little naive when I started," he said. "I thought at least the bigger-name acts would attract crowds. But I mention folk music to most people, and they say, 'Oh, you mean like Peter, Paul and Mary?' They really don't know about all the people who have come up since then."

Greenway is very familiar with the Peter, Paul and Mary syndrome, people having no reference points for folk music after the great commercial revival of the 1960s petered out.

"Folk music came into the perception of the public via people like Peter, Paul and Mary," he said. **"It's almost like vaudeville now, with this whole sub-set of people who have careers going around entertaining, person to person, in these small rooms, with those personal performing skills you don't see much anymore. It's not something you can experience on radio or television.** You have to go see it to know what it's like."

While lines formed across the street at Blanchard's Tavern to see a Civil-War-era mystery, Greenway transformed the sparsely settled Mozaic into his own personal Carnegie Hall.

He said afterward that he had designed his show not only with a consideration of the smaller crowd, but to suit the architecture of the room, a fairly large function room, in which tables displaying used books and bric-a-brac lined the back for the weekly flea market the church hosts. Seated in small groups around large tables, the crowd seemed even smaller than it was.

"I knew right away the collective energy could be very low," he said. "When I see a room situation like that, what I have to do is, in effect, make the room smaller. So I made a very specific appeal to be personal."

The crowd was clearly startled by the chatty, offhand way Greenway began. He asked how they were doing, then patiently, but pointedly, waited until people mumbled back that they were all right, OK, feeling pretty good. Smiling broadly then, serenely in command, he sighed, "Ah, everyone's so polite in Avon," and, as they laughed, pounced into his first song.

"You just want to make everybody confident that you know what you're doing," Greenway said afterward, "that you know where you want to go and how to get there."

Seated around a rear table, having a grand time, were church members and Avonites Joe and Brenda Brooks and Eddie and Shirley Williams. None had been aware of modern folk stars like Greenway before coming to the Mozaic, which they did simply because their pastor had invited them. They are diehard regulars now.

"There's just a nice feeling to it," said Brenda Brooks, a hairdresser in Stoughton. "It's really something you have to come and experience. A lot of our friends who are into rock say they don't like folk music. But they think it's all like Peter, Paul and Mary. They really don't know what happens here."

Her husband Joe, an Avon printer, said getting friends to come once is enough. "They usually come back. There's so many different kinds of music here, and the songs are about everyday things that happen to us in our lives. It helps you look at your life from another point of view."

Brenda said, "Many of the songs are about issues in your own life. Sometimes they're very serious, sometimes downright funny, but the singers talk about what happens in their lives—relationships, marriage, children, death. Real things."

Joe Williams, a retired civil engineer, offered examples. "Drivers on Route 128, Spam. A whole song about Spam."

"Buying new shoes," his wife Shirley added.

"There was one woman who sang a couple of songs about cats, comical things that only cat-lovers would know about," said Brenda Brooks. "We've had songs about Teddy bears and children and barbecuing in the backyard. Sometimes, it's almost like they've seen my life somehow, and written a song about it."

Gretz said that kind of reaction makes the coffeehouse worth all the effort. While it is very much a secular venue, he sees parallels between his ministry and the real-life aesthetics that guide modern folk troubadours like Greenway.

"Among the biggest barriers I face as a pastor," he said, "are that people don't want to show their real feelings. That's a combination of Yankee stoicism and the suburban experience, where we all kind of live in our own private family fortresses. Performers like Greg sing about a lot of the things people come to talk to me about: family, relationship issues, marital problems, a sense of wondering what you're doing on this planet besides just collecting a paycheck and paying off a mortgage. This music is such a great vehicle for sharing experiences, and a coffeehouse makes a great place for people to gather around, a common ground. It's just very human."

—November 14, 1999

Upstaging yourself Vance Gilbert

With his new Philo CD "Shaking Off Gravity," local songwriter Vance Gilbert has come close to doing something many of his fans thought he might never do: make a record as good as he is. For nearly 10 years, Gilbert has been one of modern folkdom's preeminent crowd-pleasers. In a scene so dominated by dour songwriters, his gregarious, mischief-loving stage style has earned him a large and loyal national following. This summer he makes his debut at the Newport Folk Festival and returns to the Falcon Ridge Folk Festival for a third time.

His stage antics and comic tours de force, however, also have overshadowed his impressive growth as an intelligent, emotionally articulate, and important songwriter. In his first two CDs, moments of musical brilliance surfaced, but so did moments where Gilbert seemed to be struggling to find a studio voice that could compete with the power of his stage presence.

"There were a handful of knee-slapping funny songs that ended up being albatrosses for me," Gilbert said. "I don't blame anybody for this but myself, but for a year or two there, I felt like I was just waving my arms around, trying to tell

What's exciting for me is to be somewhere in the middle of an emotion, not at any point of resolution or beginning; and to just be honest about the emotion in that slice of time. —Vance Gilbert

anyone who would listen that I really was a songwriter."

Gilbert grew up in Philadelphia and moved to Boston in 1979, after graduating from Connecticut College in New London. Already, the unique musical stew that would form his lilting and spaciously melodic style was beginning to simmer: snatches of the jazz and pop he grew up with, mingled with the singer-songwriter and folk-ballad styles he found in college.

He started his career in Boston's then-thriving cabaret scene. From 1983 to '86, he sang every Thursday and Friday night at the Starlight Roof atop the Kenmore Square Howard Johnson's.

"I did everything from Jimmy Buffett to Billy Strayhorn," he said. "A lot of it I didn't want to do, a lot of it I wasn't too good at, but I was cutting my teeth. I got my chops together there; got to sing for a crowd that was often indifferent, which can be a great opportunity to learn what you can do, stretch, sing songs you normally wouldn't dare, like Nancy Wilson's `Guess Who I Saw Today?' or Strayhorn's `Sophisticated Lady.' "

After that, Gilbert was a multicultural arts teacher, working with everyone from infants to teenagers. "Teaching kids, I learned how to flow with the psyche of other folks, to impress myself upon them based on how they're feeling and how far they're willing to go with you."

In 1989, he went to the now-defunct Old Vienna coffeehouse in Westborough to hear a budding star named Shawn Colvin. Others were drawn by her whispery voice, alluring style, or incisive lyrics. To Gilbert, it was "the completeness" of her sound. In that moment, his life was set; he wanted to be a singer-songwriter.

He hit the quiet folk scene of the early '90s like a hurricane hits Florida. He quickly became known for his wit and hilarious satires, such as his song about being a country-western rap star. It filled coffeehouses for him, but drowned out the quiet intensity of his serious songs.

"At first, I had to be totally gregarious to get over," Gilbert said. "I'm not sure the audience didn't start getting a little ambivalent about my shows because of that reputation. I would often come close to filling a room—except for the front row. Nobody wanted to be up where they thought they were going to get picked on. Here I was, doing all this to draw the audience in; and people were out there afraid to get close because they were afraid of being singled out. Something wrong there."

His increasingly good songwriting was also demanding he take it down a notch. "Shaking Off Gravity" is Gilbert's finest album; indeed, it is among the finest to come out of the local folk scene in some time. It is also his quietest, most austere, and intimate, entirely dominated by the exquisite emotional honesty of his soaring tenor and vivid lyrics.

His best songs are impressionistic miniatures, freeze-frames of lives in crisis. He trades less in obscure images than ordinary details—fingers tracing a lost lover's name on a dusty table—making the emotional life of the moment wincingly palpable. He rarely offers resolution to these moments; no suns are coming out tomorrow in his songs. There is only the moment and how we face it.

"What's exciting for me," he said, "is to be somewhere in the middle of an emotion, not at any point of resolution or beginning; and to just be honest about the emotion in that slice of time. Those moments are so fleeting in our real lives, and I think one of the jobs of songwriters like me is to take these little slices of our lives and illuminate them. I don't want to tell people what the moments mean or how they should live them. But there are things to be learned by just examining them."

Now that the songwriter is taking center stage in Gilbert's show, he feels the beginnings of that completeness that first drew him to the folk world. "I think people are starting to see that the guy onstage and the songwriter are one and the same. . . . Now I have to figure out how to bring the funny Vance Gilbert back a little, because he's not on this record much. I'm working on a song now, only got one line, but it goes, `They know it's the salt that kills them / But that's exactly what thrills them / Teenage Slugs at the Beach.' Whaddaya think?"

—June 5, 1998

The art of being yourself Ellis Paul

When most of us hear the word stagecraft, we think of big performers, of belt-it-out bravado, grand gestures, and show-stopping sustains. But stagecraft is every bit as crucial on the small stages of the coffeehouse and folk club, perhaps even more so, since performers must engage audiences for entire evenings armed with nothing but their guitars, voices, and songs.

Few modern songwriters understand the importance of stagecraft better than 33-year-old Ellis Paul, and it has earned him a huge and remarkably loyal following on the folk circuit. While even major folk stars carefully ration their drawing power, this Boston songwriter can play a long string of local coffeehouses, then cap the tour with a sold-out concert at the Somerville Theatre, as he did in March 1999 to record his delightful and bracingly intimate two-CD set, "Ellis Paul Live" (Philo).

Paul said he sees this and an upcoming best-of CD as a coda to his career's opening chapters. This summer, big things will surely be popping for him, as his song "The World Ain't Slowin' Down" is used as the love theme for Jim Carrey's new film "Me, Myself & Irene," playing for over five minutes at the film's climax and through the closing credits. That is the sweet spot for music in movies, the place where big song hits are made. The film is directed by Bobby and Peter

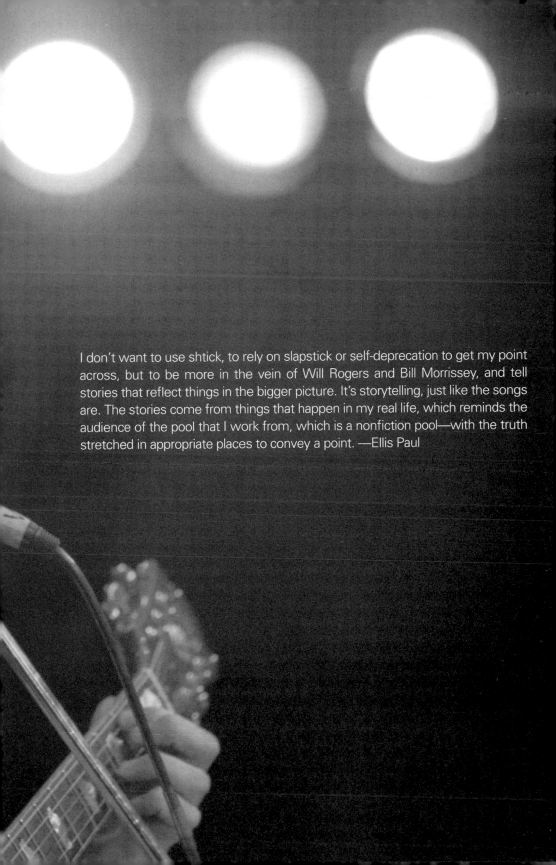

I don't want to use shtick, to rely on slapstick or self-deprecation to get my point across, but to be more in the vein of Will Rogers and Bill Morrissey, and tell stories that reflect things in the bigger picture. It's storytelling, just like the songs are. The stories come from things that happen in my real life, which reminds the audience of the pool that I work from, which is a nonfiction pool—with the truth stretched in appropriate places to convey a point. —Ellis Paul

Farrelly; the latter has called Paul "a national treasure."

The secret to Paul's rivetingly honest performance style is that he culls his stage presence and between-song banter from the same authentic place he draws his songs. He describes the stagecraft of the folk singer as "the art of being yourself."

"Our deal isn't to be larger than life, our deal is to be life," Paul said of the modern folk performer. "It's a lot more naked, less contrived, less focused on what you want people's perceptions to be than on trying to get yourself across honestly. We want to be real, to remind people who they are and what they're going through in their lives, rather than to escape into this kind of Elvis persona they can admire from afar."

Spencer Tracy's famous advice on acting was to "never get caught at it." Paul performs like that throughout his live CD. He tells chatty anecdotes about his daily life that seem unscripted but are as finely crafted as his smartly romantic ballads. In one yarn, he tells of flying in a tiny airplane on a rainy day when he discovers through conversation that his pilot is a huge Grateful Dead fan.

"I don't know if you know the cultural implications of discovering your pilot is a Deadhead," he gulps, "but I broke out in a cold sweat." Settling on a subtle litmus test, he points to the entirely gray horizon out the window and timidly asks the pilot, "You're not seeing color now, are you?"

Paul said he thinks about his stage patter as more than filler between songs.

"It glues people's perceptions of what you're really trying to pull off; it's a foundation for what you want to be as an artist. If I'm telling a poem between songs, for example, I'm reminding them that I am a writer, that that's where my focus is. And if I'm being funny, I want to be something of a humorist, but not a comedian. I don't want to use shtick, to rely on slapstick or self-deprecation to get my point across, but to be more in the vein of Will Rogers and Bill Morrissey, and tell stories that reflect things in the bigger picture. It's storytelling, just like the songs are," he said. "The stories come from things that happen in my real life, which reminds the audience of the pool that I work from, which is a nonfiction pool—with the truth stretched in appropriate places to convey a point."

Paul's stage savvy is not only displayed between songs. There is an alluring theater to his song delivery. His airy voice sounds as if it were whispering in the audience's ears, but that whisper is a wonderfully controlled tenor, tamed to conceal its artistry. His soft song-ending sustains are feats of vocal daring, but done with such apparent effortlessness they seem no more artful than a sigh.

Paul said the road has been a grand teacher. The folk world offers performers a bumpy trail of vastly different venues. Playing the back room of a deli one night, the sanctuary of a church the next, and a 1,000-seat concert hall the night after that, a self-reliant stagecraft is almost forced to emerge.

"You have to come in and kind of make your presence the presence of the room," he said. "You do that by using the songs to make people escape from the room, and your stage presence to help support that escape. I don't prepare set lists too much, because the venues are so dramatically different you have to be able to play each night differently. In a concert setting like the Somerville Theatre, the Orpheum or the Wang Center, the setting provides a frame that is very dramatic, but that doesn't have the nice intimacy and laid-back-ness you have in a folk club. In a coffeehouse, you are the stage."

—*May 19, 2000*

The flowering of **Gordon Bok**

photo: Steve Heddericg

Gordon Bok is not an easy man to know, which makes people want to know him all the more. It is not so much that the singer-songwriter-instrument-builder-woodcarver-sailor from Maine is reclusive, although he is a private man. The mystique is more in what he does offer; vivid and telling glimpses of his edges are sketched into his lyrics. Could he be as bold and eccentric as the old sailors who people his ballads? As tender, ethereal and wise as the sea-creatures about whom he ponders with wonder and affection? There is something deeply rooted, ancient and timeless to his songs, yet he is an utter original. From the instruments he plays to the myths he explores, the music is indelibly his own.

In the manner of his mentors, the shipbuilders and sailors with whom he grew up in the shipyards of Camden, Maine, Bok prefers to do his work as best he can, then keep his own counsel. Friends and neighbors who know him well have noticed happily how much that has been changing in recent years. At 53, Bok is having what can rightly be called a mid-life flowering.

As observed during the 20th Annual Rockport Festival, he is wonderfully present, completely engaged and involved in the world around him. When not performing, which he did solo and as an accompanist for many other performers on the lineup, he could be seen sitting on his sturdy guitar case, leaning back, eyes closed, immersed in the music onstage.

This flowering shows in his recent recorded work, too. Although he has always loved collaborating, notably in seven albums with Ed Trickett and Ann Mayo Muir, the bulk of his work has been alone—during what he now mockingly calls his "do-it-all-yourself period."

Now, more than ever before, he is happily creating group projects, such as the "Ensemble" record, made with many fellow Camden-Rockport musicians and longtime friends, such as Anne Dodson, Glenn Jenks, Bob Stuart and Nick Apollonio.

The latest of his cante-fables shows a new openness, too. These are ambitious musical stories with which, more than nearly any contemporary songwriter, he has explored the horizons of song; of how much a story can be told, of how many characters, textures, sounds can be presented by voice and guitar. But where his best-known cante-fables, such as "Peter Kagan and the Wind," were recorded solo, his latest, "The Play of the Lady Odivere," is a multi-voice musical play. Based on the oldest known version of the Great Atlantic seal legend, around which nearly all his cante-fables revolve in some way, it is a stunning, beautiful work, powerfully successful both as theater and music. With a three-actor cast of Bok as the Seal-Man, Muir as Lady Odivere and Euclid Hanbury, a local doctor, as Sir Odivere, and a five-member ensemble, the work is a masterpiece of folk tradition and contemporary song.

Sitting in his homey, handmade and wood-firm hilltop studio, Bok smiled broadly at the mention of how he seems to be emerging.

"Well, a couple of things have changed," he said in his Maine-crisp bass voice, which is a little bit higher and a lot more casual when he talks than when he sings. "I used to flog myself awfully hard, but I finally came around when my friend, Kendall Morse [sailor, humorist, singer-songwriter] said, 'Life really does go on whether you're enjoying it or not.' That's something to remember when you get up in the morning. It can really change your attitude."

"As my attitude began to change," Bok continued, "I began to enjoy whatever I was doing, even driving in New York City, if you can imagine. I'm looking at a limited life in front of me now. If I thought I was going to live as long as I have, I would have changed my oil. But I'm looking for quality, and that I can change with attitude—how I deal with what comes at me."

The other thing he said had changed was his relationship to his own silence. Like most people who do their best work in solitude, Bok requires a lot of privacy. Much of what people sometimes misconstrued as aloofness was really a combination of shyness and a fear of losing privacy.

"I used to keep people at a distance because I wasn't comfortable with myself as a person," he said. "I was more comfortable with myself as a musician."

"I've learned now to feel good about my silence. I'm never lonely when I'm alone, and my solitude improves the quality of the time that I spend with other people. By giving myself more time to be alone, I can really be *with* other people when I'm with them—not just audiences, but people I stay with when I play, and others I meet on the road. As long as I'm careful to have enough time alone, tend to my needs, get the thinking done I need to get done, then it's a joy to be around people."

"I was also afraid people would turn my head," he said quite sternly. "I didn't want to become a star. What a horrible, false, lonely way of life. It's hard to have real friends when you've got that much between you and other people, and I don't want performing to change me so much that my friends wouldn't like me."

To understand those feelings, it's necessary to backpedal to the early 1960s. Bok was a fledgling folk singer who was also quite happily employed sailing yachts up and down the East Coast, either captaining them for charter, or delivering them for their owners.

Having grown up by the sea, and more importantly, around people whose trades were on the sea, he began to grow weary of the portrait the '60s folk revival was painting of that life. So much of what was sung were sea chanteys and boisterous imitations of sea chanteys, which Bok sneeringly calls "Yo-ho-ho songs." Even contemporary sea ballads, with some notable exceptions such as Ewan MacColl's thoughtful portraits of Britain's herring fishers, sounded more like Lionel Barrymore in "Captains Courageous" than anyone he had known as a boy.

Bok began to write songs drawn from the lives of the people he knew in Maine. His seafaring folk did not speak like characters from a pirate movie; they didn't wax with landlocked eloquence about the gentle beauty of the ocean, and the easy romance of the coast.

The sea in Bok's songs, like all forces of nature, is both provider and killer; thoroughly powerful, benign when treated with proper umbrage, but mysterious, unknowable. The people he sang about alternately loved and hated the sea and their own dependence upon it. Their language was real and honest, their feelings credible and moving.

"It really started with my just celebrating friends and personal heroes,' Bok said, "but so much of my songwriting is just trying to figure out what's going on with me and the world."

These early songs, particularly the starkly beautiful "Bay of Fundy," began to get attention, as did his rich, honest bass voice and fluid guitar. Paul Stookey, at that time riding the crest of the Peter, Paul and Mary wave, produced Bok's first album for Verve.

Bok got a taste of the fast lane—a small one, but enough. One morning, while staying with Stookey, he was told, in some bitter detail, what the life was like.

"Stookey was kind enough to show me both sides of the coin, to tell me what I had, and what I could expect if I was really ambitious. I always felt that being a musician could be a very dangerous job. I didn't think I had what it took morally to keep my honesty in the face of success. So there were times I actually avoided opportunities. I was really terrified of becoming jaded, and chasing this precious thing away before I understood it. I didn't even know how important music was to me at the time. I just sensed it."

Disgusted with the indifference and carelessness of the commercial music business, and genuinely frightened at what success might do to him and his music, Bok went home. He could always sail, he thought, or work in the shipyard, and keep the songs for himself.

The reluctance to continue chasing the brass ring of stardom was the beginning of the Bok mystique. People in folk music began hunting him down like some reclusive old blues legend, wanting him for concerts, festivals.

In 1970, Bok happily succumbed to years of earnest pestering by Sandy and Caroline Paton of Folk-Legacy Records. His honest lyrics, reverence for traditional music, and noncommercial aesthetics were exactly what their small record label was all about. Ten Bok and seven Bok-Muir-Trickett records and 21 years later, they are still in contented partnership.

Encouraged by Folk-Legacy's creative freedom and deep love of the music, Bok got more ambitious in his songwriting. By this time, the sea was not just a subject for chronicling, but a metaphor for his own spiritual and interior wanderings.

"At the risk of sounding regional," he said dryly, "you use what you got. And of course, you are influenced by who you grew up with, where you live, your own vocabulary. When you think of all the different kinds of songs I sing, they're from all over the place. There's really not that high a percentage of sea songs. Not anymore. I've just been broadening my metaphor, really, as I learn from and about other people."

Dreams have always been an important wellspring for Bok, as are the legends and ballads of tradition.

"I believe dreams are my real self talking—sorting out what I've done, what I haven't done, and what I need to do; the things that I've buried as I've gone through life that are still part of me; something that needs to be exercised and honored, just as creativity needs to be exercised and honored. Even at face value, dreams make wonderful stories."

He began wrestling with a mythic tale, drawn from a series of dreams, about the seal-folk. The music was growing into more than mere background or support for the words, though; it wanted to be part of the story itself: the sea one moment, a far-off chorus of seals the next, or depicting the inner-emotions of the characters. The story was drawn from the ancient Atlantic legends of seals who become mortal humans, as in great ballads such as "The Great Silkie of Sule Skerrie."

Bok didn't know much about the lore, though, and was totally unaware it was so rich. What he did know was that he was getting in over his head with the epic shape his ballad was taking.

"It would eventually become 'Seal Djiril's Hymn,'" he said, "but I didn't understand the structure. I just wanted to use this device of song and prose to tell a good story. I was creating a legendary that was already there. Given hundreds of years, I'd have created all the going seal legends—apparently that's what those of us who use that metaphor need. There are legends for wherever you live. For me, that's the sea. I'd have sat there and pounded out what was necessary...thank God, there were a few people around who knew books and libraries."

To sort things out, Bok began to write "Peter Kagan and the Wind," still the best-known of his song-stories. It's the wonderfully simple tale of a sailor caught in a storm at sea, and his wife—really one of the seal-folk—who saves him. Through most of the story, Kagan bravely, but arrogantly and foolishly, battles the wind. It is rich in detail, drama and musical beauty. The music becomes part of the theater in ways that define much of Bok's work: the guitar is the wind turning on Kagan, the waves battering his little boat, the far-off loving call of his wife. It is a ballad in the truest and best sense, but much more than a song.

"I didn't know the word cante-fable until Sandy Paton told me it was what I was doing. But it's not important to know what you're doing; you just have to give yourself room to do it. I would just say that a cante-fable is a story that is sung and told, that has music attached to it that's important. The music does as much work as the words many times. I think it does in Kagan. People who have done 'Kagan' without doing the music are missing a lot. Do the tunes on a pennywhistle, a banjo, a bodhran, whatever. To me, the tunes are integral: the sound of the buoys, the waves, the wind."

Other cante-fables followed. He finally finished "Seal Djiril's Hymn," a gray but lovely meditation on man's estrangement from the world around him, and the dreamlike, album-length "Another Land Made of Water." He wrote the thoroughly merry "Jeremy Brown and Jeannie Teal," a Christmas tale about a goodhearted captain whose boat is, happily for all, a bit brighter than he is.

"The Play of the Lady Odivere" extends the creative marriage of music and story into a true ensemble ballad of nearly an hour's length. It is based on a 90-plus stanza Scottish ballad that is at least 300 years old, tracing back to that mysterious, mystical time when early Christianity and pagan faith collided, struggled, and often commingled.

It is a riveting work, faithful to the rigid rules of honor and magic which prevailed then, yet contemporary in its sympathies both to the tragically victimized Lady Odivere and to the densely honorable Sir Odivere, who earnestly believes himself to be in the right as he uses pagan magic to force her to marry him, then punishes her for loving a seal prince.

The ballad is told in songs, narration, dramatic scenes and musical numbers performed by a properly ancient-sounding acoustic ensemble. Bok clearly relishes the number of creative hands who have made their mark on Odivere.

"A lot of us who are playing it have gone back over the story, being each character, finding each character in ourselves. Smarting for them, cheering for them, grieving for them. It's one of those stories where everybody is right, but it still doesn't work."

"The story was so strong to me, but I didn't know what to do with it. I could have told it in the original—all 94 verses with music. I thought it was out of my realm to put it back into music. I started doing carvings of it. At one point, my idea was, I'll just carve the ballad. But by doing those carvings, I got deeper and deeper into understanding the story. They focused me."

Just as Bok invents a musical structure to suit his needs, in the manner of the necessarily self-reliant Maine people around whom he grew and learned, he has made for himself whatever he could not find elsewhere. And he is proud of that.

He needed a huskier recorded sound to match his music, so he built his Bok-phone. Over 20-odd years, he and instrument maker Nick Apollonio have designed a 12-string guitar suited to the gentle insinuation and cinematic intricacies of his ballad-singing. Bok cheerily praises his good friend's patience with what he calls "Bok's exploding guitars, as over the years, they experimented with how light the bracing could be, how thin the face, how easy the action, before the instrument blew up from the tension of its 12 strings.

He is always a little bit surprised that his creativity is so interesting to others. He is also quite proud of the fact that, unlike so many other contemporary singer-songwriters, he performs other people's work as well as his own. When he finds a good song, he learns it, be it ancient or the work of some new songwriter.

"When I decide I like a song, I sit up and pay attention," he said. "Many times, I won't touch an instrument until the song is pretty well embedded, because, one, I don't know if it needs it; and, two, it's like I could chase the essence away with my habits."

"Songs are a boiling-down of a person's life. They're precious, absolutely unique, no matter what kind of formulas they might be built on; because the human voice is in them. If a person reads a piece of information, they deal with it on one side of the brain; but if it is put in a rhythm and set to notes, you have to use your whole brain for it. This is powerful stuff. The church knows it. Armies know it. Despots know it. When you're listening to a song, you can think about it, or sometimes you can just feel it—let it wash over you."

As Bok enters his second half-century, he finds himself more enchanted with his world than ever before, particularly with the people in it. It took some hard times: the mortality that stares at you when you see the other half of your life getting smaller; the need to pay more attention to health; the dissolution of a long, lovely marriage. All these things, along with his many friends, conspired to urge him out of himself. "You're creating emergencies for yourself," one friend told him, "so that you can emerge."

"I've been working on the present," Bok said peacefully. "I was always thinking of the future, of what I had to do. I've always been very serious about my music, and wanting to have it right. Not that I had anything that I considered right as a model, mind you; no work of art is ever definitive in any setting, or about any subject."

Bok allows himself much more pleasure in the people around him now. One new hobby is forming choruses out of his audiences around the country; taking great delight in, as he put it, "seeing people light up and realize what each other has. Instant community. Wonderful."

If he has a cause, it is urging people to exercise their own creativity; to see it as a vital part of the human spirit that is just as in need of constant use as any of the senses, nerves, muscles or emotions.

"The nice thing about the folk genre is that there isn't a bunch of stardom in it," he said. "Some people prefer to think of a performer as a star, but if they'd realize you're just another person who's paid some attention to creativity, then they'd have to deal with it in themselves."

"By being more accessible, not only do I get to meet interesting people, but I get to hear interesting music. If I were a pop star or something, I wouldn't get the songs I get from other people. Many of them would be too shy, there'd be that barrier. Now it's, 'So, you like Australian songs? Here's a batch.' People will come up and say, 'Now, that song you sang about such-and-such—my experience has been...' And I'll learn a whole new texture about that song. Or just talking to somebody about tractors or boats—I always learn something from a folk audience."

"I meet some wonderful people. The things I hear from them, the ideas that are popping around this country now, are just fantastic. Maybe they always were, but I'm just starting to catch 'em."

"Now I realize that we're all fools in God's garden. I always knew that, but now I really feel it. And I'm a pretty happy fool at that."

Originally appeared in Sing Out! The Folk Song Magazine
Used by permission c. Sing Out Corporation
—Spring, 1992

The Revels' Father Christmas turns 80
John Langstaff

If there is a modern-day Father Christmas, surely it is John Langstaff. Consider the evidence. First, he was born on Christmas Eve, 80 years ago tomorrow. More significant, he is the father of the Christmas Revels— creator and, with his daughter Carol Langstaff, founder of these popular theatrical re-creations of ancient folk celebrating midwinter.

Since the first Cambridge Revels in 1971, it has become a national empire, with annual Revels in 11 cities, including New York, Philadelphia, Seattle, and Berkeley. Thanks to the merry Christmas visions of John Langstaff, Revel-ing is now a holiday tradition for over 80,000 people every year.

Sprawling on a couch in his home here earlier this month, Langstaff talked with a mix of contentment for what he has accomplished and eagerness for the next tasks at hand. The house he shares with his wife, Nancy, a retired music education professor at Lesley College, is just the sort of folksy cottage in which one would hope to find Cambridge's Father Christmas, a converted old carriage house down a winding little road off Linnaean Street.

"I think there's a tremendous need for what Revels does," he said, "creating ways to draw people together through the power of ritual, music, dance, and drama. There's a need for art that connects us to each other. You go far enough back in any culture and you find these rituals, these ways of bringing people together. I think that connectedness is so important to us. It always has been, you

photo: Sam Sweezy

know; the rituals tell us that."

Connection is a crucial word in the way Langstaff thinks about art and culture. Another is participation. Since his early childhood, he has passionately believed that art was not something to be merely experienced from the distant glow of the concert stage, but truly shared. And at the heart of that belief, always, was his love of Christmas.

Langstaff revealed that his Christmas Eve birth was not pure coincidence. His parents were, to put it mildly, fanatics about Christmas, hosting elaborate caroling parties at their home. On Christmas Eve in 1920, his pregnant mother began bolting up and down stairs, moving furniture, doing everything she could think of to induce labor. They simply had to have a Christmas baby.

He grew up in a musical home in Brooklyn Heights, N.Y. His parents mixed classical and traditional music in ways that would mark Langstaff's career as a successful classical baritone and later as music educator and star of Revels.

He recalled tender evenings at the piano, perched on his mother's lap while she sang old English ballads to him, "Wraggle-Taggle Gypsies" and "The Four Maries."

"I'm sure it's because I had these old songs in me from when I was very young that when I came across them again, they drew me so much," he said. "That's why I always say you have to start early with kids and music. When born, the child has the ability to do a lot of things, to match tones, keep rhythms, things that drop away if not nurtured. Music is such a deep part of what it is to be human; it can mean so much to you as you get older. But if you don't get that exposure early on, it's not nearly as likely to become important to you later on."

Langstaff attended Juilliard School of Music, contemplating a career as a classical singer but also deeply interested in music education, particularly in finding ways to offer children the participatory relationship with music his parents had given him.

He was just beginning his concert career when World War II began. Though a pacifist, his innate humanism was so offended by fascism that he enlisted in the Army, rising to first lieutenant in the Pacific forces commanded by General Douglas MacArthur.

Months before the war's end, he and a visiting colonel were discussing the terrain of an Okinawa escarpment he and his men had just secured at great cost. He stood to point something out and was shot through the chest by a Japanese sniper.

Langstaff seems to chart his life more through the people he has known than the events. He told this story by remembering the curious colonel with a bit of understandable disdain, and then a doctor who almost certainly saved his life.

The wounded were sorted on airplanes in prioritized rows, and Langstaff, with both lungs punctured, was placed in a low-priority row of men so severely wounded that intense treatment was not likely to be productive. A doctor strolled by, looked briefly at Langstaff, shook his head and said, "No, I believe we can do something with this case." He was moved to the row for whom immediate and intense treatment was warranted.

"Now that's something," he said. "After the war, I tried to find that doctor for years, but never even learned his name. Why it is these things happen to us is something I often wondered." He stared out the window and was quiet for a moment, then said in a whisper, "I still wonder about that."

His luck improved providentially after that. He ended up being treated by a top lung doctor, and a physical therapist showed him breathing techniques that made him a better singer.

After the war, his career prospered. In England, he became known for his artful mix of classical and traditional pieces, and his first recordings were produced for the HMV label by George Martin, who later assumed the same role for the Beatles.

Back in the States in the mid-1950s, his memories of boyhood Christmases prompted him to mount "A Christmas Masque of Traditional Revels" at New York's Town Hall in December 1957, and in Washington, D.C., in 1958. Both lost money. In 1966, NBC-TV hired him to star in a special of his masque, in which a young Dustin Hoffman played the dragon slain by St. George.

The idea was brilliantly simple and inspired by the difficulties he had trying to present traditional music in the artful environs of the classical concert stage. He wanted to set traditional holiday songs, dances, and rituals in their authentic context but also in a highly professional theatrical setting that would lure modern audiences. There they could see how these old songs and customs were actually used by ancient people, how they brought people together and symbolized their powerful felings about midwinter. It was the darkest, coldest time of the year, so people gathered to lament the dying of the old year, reflect on its joys and sorrows, and then prepare to welcome the returning sun and the dawning of a new year.

In 1971, the first Cambridge Revels was produced at Sanders Theatre by Langstaff and his daughter, Carol, who now produces the annual Revels in Hanover, N.H. Throughout his life, the desire to create participatory art and to place music more prominently in the lives of children have been the twin engines that drive him. Revels was the perfect home for his passions.

"Whenever I am asked to go to schools," he said, "I always tell them, `I'm not coming here to sing for you; I'm coming to make music with you.' That's what I've got to do now, to really develop ways to get children involved in music. So many schools offer no music education anymore. That's just tragic to me."

As Revels grew to include annual Spring Revels and to help promote troupes throughout the country, it became Revels Inc., and produced educational recordings, books, videos, and multimedia kits aimed at helping teachers and community groups mount their own Revels-like shows. The teaching mission of Revels came to consume most of Langstaff's time, and he turned over his duties to artistic director Patrick Swanson, music director George Emlen, executive director Gayle Rich, and director of marketing and public relations Alan Casso.

Looking ahead, he wants to complete a poetry anthology and volume of maritime music to add to his lengthy book credits and is releasing a series of videos called "Making Music With John Langstaff," to show teachers his charming techniques of song-leading and music instruction. Increasingly, he wants to use his legacy to inspire more Revels-rousers like himself.

"Of all the arts, music strikes such a rich, deep chord in us in so many, many ways," he said. "So much of our history can be learned and really experienced through music, how ordinary people actually felt about the times in which they lived. And it gives us that sense of connectedness to each other. We still need that, but we just don't know where to look for it anymore. We need to find ways to put that back into our lives, especially for children. Especially for the children."

—December 23, 2000

Revels goes Victorian—and finds the origins of modern Christmas
David Jones, Revels artistic director Patrick Swanson

We think there has always been a Christmas. But the birthday of Jesus has actually been celebrated only since around the third century. Midwinter holidays, of course, trace much farther back, to the Roman Saturnalia, and even farther (geographically and temporally) to pagan feasts honoring winter solstice and the longest night of the year.

Christmas as most Americans celebrate it today—with Santa Claus bringing presents, trees a-trimming, cards a-mailing, and offices a-partying—is quite new, evolving within a span of about 20 years in the early reign of Britain's Queen Victoria.

This year, the Christmas Revels fete of music, dance, and theater visits Victorian England to watch how our modern Christmas evolved. The Revels have wandered far from that Anglo-American Christmas in recent years, exploring winter solstice in Meso-America, Brittany, and among the Roma, or Gypsy, people.

"It really feels like a visit home for Revels this year," said artistic director Patrick Swanson. "We've been wandering the roads for quite a few years in our productions. This is a theme that brings us back to some of our own Revels roots.

It is not what I would call the quintessential Revels—we really try to dig back to the ancient midwinter rituals that are the roots of the holiday—but it includes a number of things that people would consider very traditional features of our show."

Some have grumbled that, while Revels has been visually and musically splendid the past few years, there hasn't been quite enough of that old familiar Christmas spirit. This year, it will be "Deck the Halls" to the max, with choruses of carolers singing standards like "Hark! the Herald Angels Sing," "The First Nowell," and "Good King Wenceslas."

All the Revels traditions will be included as well, from the "Lord of the Dance" procession to a mummers' play to the Pinewoods Morris Men. Guests include British traditional singer David Jones, the wonderful folk pianist Jacqueline Schwab (whose playing has been prominent in all of Ken Burns's documentaries), and actors Patrick English, Sarah deLima, and Richard Snee.

Swanson said much of our modern Christmas evolved in a frenzy of revived Christmas spirit from about 1840 to 1860. Britain had a young queen the country loved dearly, and she was deeply in love with the dashing Prince Albert. They married in 1840, and he wanted to celebrate Christmas as he had in his native Germany.

"Albert was the instigator in many ways," Swanson said. "He brought the German Yule aspects, started putting up a Christmas tree, as well as exchanging gifts, sending out Christmas cards. It really became a fad among the English people."

The British had been rather sour on Christmas, as were most Americans. Parliament outlawed the holiday in 1647, in fact, seeing it as more a pagan feast than Christian observance. It was beginning to revive a little, both in England and America, when Albert brought his Christmas cheer to the royal court.

The delightful London-born folk singer David Jones has been a feature of every single Victorian Revels production, not only the two here, but in San Francisco and Washington, D.C. His latest CD is the sprightly "From England's Shore" (Minstrel).

"In Britain, Christmas was a big day in the old days, but then died out,' he said. "In strict religious circles, it was frowned on, because so much of the attachments were very hedonistic in their origins, with the mistletoe and the holly and the ivy. Those are all pagan things; the holly represents the male sexual drive, the ivy the female."

He said much of the revival was evoked through the strength of Prince Albert's charisma. He put up a Christmas tree in the palace, so everyone wanted one in their homes. He sent florid and adoring Christmas cards to his wife, so everyone started exchanging them. But the resulting frenzy was not all his doing.

The 1840s were a time, much like our own, of stunningly fast and enormous technological changes. The Industrial Revolution was in high gear, cities were experiencing huge growth as the new industrial workplace changed the way people worked, lived—and shopped. New manufacturing methods made it possible for working-class people to buy such things as Christmas cards, toys, and prepared foods. Workers became consumers. Perhaps not surprisingly, here is where America contributed to Christmas culture in the form of an odd, jolly fat man named Santa Claus.

"If you ask most people today what's a traditional Christmas, they'll mention Santa Claus," Swanson said. "But I think he was an almost totally American invention, a transmutation of the fourth-century St. Nicholas legend. And that also happened very quickly, growing out of the Dutch version of it, Sinter-Klaas, who brought gifts for children. It became a part of some American Christmas celebrations, then Clement Moore wrote the poem `A Visit from St. Nicholas,' better known as `The Night Before Christmas.' Before that, there was a Father Christmas figure; he appears in mummers' plays but doesn't resemble Santa Claus, really, and doesn't bring gifts. Yet almost immediately after that poem was published in 1823, Santa Claus became perceived as this figure from antiquity."

Another important change of the time was a new aesthetic among scholars, artists, writers, and composers that became known as antiquarianism. Life seemed to be changing so fast, so heedlessly, that they sought to hang on to the best instincts of the past by preserving old songs, stories, and customs. Modern lyrics were laid on old folk carols, and ancient visiting rituals, such as wassailing and wrenning, were revived as caroling. Though there had always been carols for

photo: Roger Ide

seasonal celebrations (the name means a song used for dancing), much of the modern Christmas carol repertoire came from this period.

"You have to give the Victorians their due," Swanson said. "They were the original folk revivalists. Antiquarian scholars began to see the need to document and preserve a lot of disappearing folkloric customs and music and dance. Many of these antiquarians took ancient carols and arranged them in very florid contemporary settings, often making the old pagan lyrics Christian, and published them for people to sing in churches and at home. They became very popular very quickly."

What remained constant in the seasonal spirit, from the old winter solstice celebrations to the Victorian Christmas, was a feeling that this was a time to bond together as families and communities. Victoria and Albert were quick to turn the new festive spirit into calls for increased charity, as the prosperity some enjoyed from the Industrial Revolution brought new and even more desperate forms of poverty to others.

Charles Dickens, the great social reformer, immortalized the new Christmas fad in his 1843 classic, "A Christmas Carol." The revived Christmas spirit in Ebenezer Scrooge evoked a newfound love of family, community, and charity. Of course, the first way he expressed his Christmas spirit was to go shopping. But he took care to sing a carol or two along the way.

"I like the audience participation of Revels best of all," Jones said, "and I think that's the reason people keep coming back year after year. It feels like a community sing, with some adornments; something people can really do together. I think that gives Revels more of a feeling of what the season is all about than all these shows where you just go sit and listen. Revels reinforces the idea that you celebrate Christmas together. I know for me, I'm always more likely to remember to call my brother when I'm doing one of these shows."

—*November 29, 1998*

Mother Christmas: how Revels really works
Revels director Gayle Rich

For 15 years Gayle Rich of Brookline has presided over the odd little empire that is Revels Inc., best known for its Christmas Revels at Sanders Theatre, a fete of traditional music, dance, and lore exploring how ancient people celebrated midwinter. For thousands hereabouts, it has become as much a part of Christmas as mistletoe and last-minute shopping.

Under Rich's savvy and creative care, Revels Inc. has grown into a national institution, overseeing Christmas Revels in 10 cities, including New York

City, Philadelphia, Washington, and Oakland, Calif. It produces a lively line of instructional books, songbooks, compact discs, and videos that show people how to do their own Revel-ing at schools, community centers, or simply by the family fireside. There is also a spring Revels produced each year at Boston's Emerson Majestic Theatre.

If you imagine her job falling somwhere between Ebenezer Scrooge with a spreadsheet and chief elf at Santa's workshop, you're not far off. Revels uses a canny blend of arts professionals and volunteers, so Rich's background in music, social work, and arts administration form the perfect Revels pedigree. Whether her daily duties require tough budget decisions, brainstorming pagan solstice rituals, or den-mothering a crew of befuddled volunteers, she is to the Revels manor born.

"I think of myself as a Revels translator," Rich said. "I think about what the organization needs to do to make it work, to make the people work together, the productions work. And yet I don't actually do any of that. It's looking at the very big picture, making sure all the pieces fit together, and, most important of all, keeping the communication lines open."

For example, as the curtain rises this week on a new Christmas Revels, Rich, 58, is planning the next spring Revels, working on a new series of instructional videos, helping launch a Chicago Revels next Christmas, and talking with a woman in Denver who hopes to start a Revels there.

"Gayle is the glue that holds the artistic and administrative groups together," said Revels founder John Langstaff. "She has brought to Revels a wonderfully effective and genial team. We're all very different, but she's responsible to the board, to me, to the artistic people, the administrative people, the audience. We all feel she's responsible to all of us, which is rare and a very healthy thing when it happens."

Rich's background would seem to have prepared her perfectly to walk the fine line between hard business realities and creative cacophony. Single with two grown children, she has worked in music therapy, social work, and arts administration, including a summer with Rudolf Serkin at the Marlboro Music Festival, the Museum of Fine Arts Summer Courtyard Series, and 17 years producing the DeCordova Museum summer concerts. She is a skilled viola player who performed with the Boston Philharmonic, and often brings friends to her home to play chamber music.

Langstaff, who started Revels with his daughter, Carol, in 1970, first hired Rich in 1977, but she left after a year. Despite some hard words exchanged at the time, the Langstaffs soon asked if she would sit on the board of directors. After a few years of doing that, she agreed to become the first executive director in 1984.

"A lot of it was still seat-of-the-pants," Rich said. "The office was in a church basement in Harvard Square, everybody squeezed in there, sharing desks, and an awful lot was being done on a volunteer basis out of people's homes. Communication was not good, and those of us that worked at Revels worked very long hours and long weekends. It was a real burnout job."

For a year she did nothing but listen, listen to Langstaff explain his unique vision of melding folk traditions and contemporary theater, listen to disgruntled volunteers and harried staffers, to actors and musicians, audiences and donors.

Then she began to build a permanent staff and structure, to open lines of communication between the business and creative people, volunteers and professionals, to ensure everyone was clear about their duties, while allowing people the freedom to be creative in their jobs. She moved Revels to a bigger office in Kendall Square, and last year, to Watertown.

Always on her mind was the Revels mission, which is about much more than putting on a first-rate show.

"All these early rituals and traditions we celebrate were done by people in the community," she said. "They didn't hire a professional cast to come into town and plant the seeds, sing the songs, bring in the boar's head or light the yule log. Those were people in the community doing it together. We don't have those kinds of coming-together rituals in the city anymore, so there's really a need to find new ways to do that."

That—not saving money—is the reason Revels uses volunteers along with professionals to stage each production. Community involvement helps create the village personality so central to the homey ambience of Revels. How much the volunteer cast and crew get from their hard-working holidays is as much a measure of Revels' success as ticket sales.

Perhaps nothing underscores the success of Rich's tenure more than the astonishing fact that almost 90 percent of the Revels Inc. budget comes from earned income, nearly half from the 19,000 tickets sold each year for the Cambridge Revels. It gives the company a rare freedom to invest in low-profit projects such as their educational materials and live CDs (including a Dickensian new "Victorian Christmas Revels"), and offer crucial early support to other Revels.

Even more a source of pride for Rich is that nearly all her staff members are the original people she hired as she created new positions. Artistic director Patrick Swanson, music director George Emlen, marketing and public-relations manager Alan Casso, and graphics designer Sue Ladr are the only people who have ever filled those positions.

"My way of administering," she said, "is that when we find that a person who is hired for one area has talents for another, I let them fly. I really expect people to create their own structure within the job. People don't work in the arts because they want to get rich; they want to do something they think is important, that resonates with them and that they love. You have to create an environment that nurtures that."

The nurturing extends to the audience, too. Key to the long success of Revels is that it does not regard its ticket-buyers as consumers, but as part of the community that has huddled together at Sanders, in Cambridge, to celebrate midwinter.

"Revels is not just a show," she said, "it becomes part of people's lives. What it's given to a lot of people is a way of celebrating the holidays. We have lots of people who buy 20 or 30 tickets and come with their cousins, their neighbors, their children, and now even their grandchildren. So at the same time we are recreating these ancient holiday traditions on stage, we are also creating new traditions for all these families. Isn't that a wonderful job to have?"

—*December 5, 1999*

Putting Irish music center-stage
Eileen Ivers

The people cheer, of course, for the dance.

The Irish musical *Riverdance* has already brought millions to a new awareness of the wild grace and exhilarating power of Irish step dancing. But cheers also greet diminutive fiddler Eileen Ivers after her first frisky, free-ranging solo on stage.

Whether the audiences know the 31-year-old Bronx-born Irish fiddler—she has been a star in traditional circles since she was 8—many sense in her clever playing that same point of arrival they see in the dance. However inventive or playful she gets, her fiddle is rooted deeply in pure Irish tradition. As much as the dancers, Ivers personifies the triumph of *Riverdance*.

"I think Eileen's driven first and foremost by her obvious love of fiddle playing and traditional music," *Riverdance* composer Bill Whelan said from Ireland. "But she's also not afraid to push things forward a bit, and that's very important.

"In the dance and in the music, *Riverdance* is really about not being afraid to stray from the tradition; to move forward with the music while, at the same time, being sensitive to the fact that traditional music is sacrosanct. It's part of a new Irish confidence that says yes, we have our music and we love it; but look, we can also do this with it."

Ivers agrees. "Years ago, never would it have been the case that you would get up on a big stage. It was all done in somebody's kitchen where you would have a session and pass on the tunes," she says. "It's just in the last 30 to 40 years with bands like the Chieftains, Bothy Band and Planxty that anybody's really been performing these tunes. It's a fantastic time in Irish life."

Indeed, many of the Irish and Irish-Americans in the audiences cheer in

We've all been brought up, all of us, with the ethic that we're playing melodies that have been passed on for hundreds and hundreds of years. You learn them and play them through your lifetime and then you pass them along. But at the end of the day, it's the music that's the star, not any of us. —Eileen Ivers

celebration of what they see as a significant point of arrival for Irish culture.

Ivers was not always with the *Riverdance* company. In June 1995, the company needed to replace the original fiddler during the London run. Whelan thought immediately of Ivers, with whom he had worked on a stage adaptation of Leon Uris' *Trinity*. He had wanted the musicians more prominently featured in the production, and suspected that Ivers' exciting stage presence would be irresistible to director John McGloglan.

He was right. McGloglan redesigned much of the production to get Ivers on stage, jigging and reeling across the stage with the dancers and soloing in both acts. The audience cheers as loud and long for her as for any of the dances, utterly charmed by the way her entire lithe body seems to play the fiddle; the infectious, dimpled grin that seems to burst across her face in direct response to the quickening music.

At first, Ivers resisted the idea. It is central to the code of Irish music that no one is above the ensemble. It is not the mistake-prone beginner who earns scowls at a seisiun, where musicians gather to play informally, but the showoff.

"We've all been brought up, all of us," Ivers said, "with the ethic that we're playing melodies that have been passed on for hundreds and hundreds of years. You learn them and play them through your lifetime and then you pass them along. But at the end of the day, it's the music that's the star, not any of us."

In that strict traditional schooling, Ivers also personifies *Riverdance*. Like most of the dancers, she began studying Irish tradition as a child, coming up through Comhaltas Ceoltoiri Eireann, the international Irish cultural organization which, like the Gaelic League had done, instituted gala competitions in 1951 to entice young people to the old music.

She went on to win seven All-Ireland Championships, more than any American fiddler, before launching her career, which boasts two successful CDs on the Green Linnet label and stints with Cherish the Ladies, Green Fields of America, Hall & Oates and Sharon Shannon.

Ivers said she often thinks, as the ovations wash over her, of her teacher, the late Martin Mulvihill. He was regarded in Irish folk circles as one of the great fiddlers of his time, but spent his life in obscurity, tirelessly teaching new generations to love the old music and carry it on.

"He had a very hard life," she said, "teaching six, seven days a week, taking the train from the Bronx to Philadelphia, going out and teaching in Brooklyn and all the suburbs. And, you know, teaching a lot of scrapers who would never play again and a few of us who might carry it on. He never got a chance to play the Wang Center and have all these thousands of people applaud him every night. But it's people like him, they're the ones who kept it going. Without them, we wouldn't be here today, none of this could be happening now."

—January 21, 1997

The heart of Irish music: the sessiun
Mike & Larry Reynolds of Comhaltas Ceoltoiri Eireann

It is no accident that Boston's longest-running Irish music sessiun is also its friendliest.

Every Monday night for 23 years, fiddler Larry Reynolds has hosted a sessiun, or informal music gathering, for the Irish cultural organization Comhaltas Ceoltoiri Eireann. Since 1990, the sessiun has been held at the convivial Green Briar pub and restaurant in Brighton Center. Before that, at the old Coach House in Brookline Village, it was one of the best known sessiuns anywhere, a genuine hotbed for the budding Celtic music revival of the 1970s.

"That sessiun was known all over the world," Reynolds said before rosining up his bow for a recent Monday sessiun. "Any traditional or folk musician knew about the Coach House. At the time, there were very few sessiuns around, probably not more than three in the whole of Boston. There was a tremendous interest growing in the music then, and people embraced that sessiun whether they had any Irish in them or not."

There are dozens of sessiuns in the Boston area now, but the Green Briar's is unique for its focus on bringing new players to the music. Reynolds is chairman of the local Hanafin-Cooley branch of Comhaltas and has a passion for promoting the music and inviting new players into the fold. Over the years, the Green Briar sessiun has earned warm and wide renown for its welcoming ways. If there is a front door to the local Irish music scene, particularly for new players, this is it.

A little after nine last Monday, a couple of dozen players began forming a circle around a big table near the bar. For 10 years, Reynolds has shared hosting duties with his son Mike, an accordionist and singer who performs locally with his own band. A few joined right in as Mike began with a bright tune. Others listened, holding tight onto their flutes, guitars, and accordions until they caught the drift of the tunes.

Mike and Larry Reynolds were listening, too. Throughout the evening, they would be seen cocking an ear this way or that, honing in on the musicians. The trick for them is making sure everyone is brought into the circle of players.

"I love to watch people discover this music, play a tune and begin to enjoy it as much as I do," said Mike Reynolds. "That's what makes this sessiun so great: Everybody's welcome, and we play to their levels. Sometimes we get carried away a bit, but we always bring it back to where it needs to be for the group. We want to be sure to get everybody playing together."

The music was nearly all instrumental, though occasionally someone would break forth with a ballad or poem. Tunes are divided into sets of three or four jigs, reels, hornpipes, waltzes, polkas or strathspeys, and the one who leads off the set normally decides what tune to change to and when.

What most players do not notice is how carefully the Reynoldses pay attention to who's playing at which times. Newcomers will usually be asked at some point to lead off a set of tunes. This is in part to welcome them, but also so the hosts can gauge their level and get a sense of what tunes they know. Both men keep track of who knows which tunes, so in the course of the evening, everyone is sure to get a chance to play.

Catching her breath after playing a quick set on her wooden Irish flute, Susan Gedutis of Somerville said this egalitarian camaradarie is what drew her to Irish music and to the sessiuns. She is studying ethnomusicology at Tufts University, plays in the hot local folk-rock band Einstein's Little Homunculus, and has become a Green Briar habitue since discovering its sessiun last fall.

"I studied and played jazz for awhile," she said, "and one of the things I find so attractive about Irish music is that you can just sit down and play, and it's not about being center-stage. It's about playing with other people, becoming a community through playing the music together. People here have been very welcoming to me, telling me the names of tunes, stories about the music, subtly giving me the rules. And there are codes about how to be in a sessiun, about who starts the tunes, when people do solo pieces, things like that. There really is a social culture that surrounds sessiuns."

Irish music is healthier than most traditional forms these days in large part because it remains a living tradition, played socially and passed along from generation to generation. The sessiun is the beating heart of that living tradition, where beginners learn the ear training so vital to any folk form, and where virtuosos return to reconnect with the root aesthetics of the style. For the goal is not to see who's the best player, but for the group to attain common ground, for everyone to play together, trill together, breathe together.

"Sessiuns are so important to Irish music," Larry Reynolds said, "because they keep the music in vogue at all times, keep it being played. And it brings the younger ones right into it."

That certainly happened for 22-year-old James Foley, who lives in Worcester and attends St. Anselm College in Manchester, NH. Whenever he can find a ride, he comes to the Green Briar sessiun, breaking out his guitar to play along.

He was drawn to Irish music through recent mass-marketed productions such as the hit musical *Riverdance*, and through hearing hip young bands, including Solas, whose founder, Seamus Egan, was a Green Briar regular while attending Boston College in the early '90s. Last June, Foley went to the Irish Festival at Stonehill College, eager to hear his favorite Celtic stars on the concert stage. He forgot all about them, though, after wandering into the Comhaltas Sessiun Tent and meeting the Reynolds.

"I didn't go to that festival expecting to find a way to start playing the music," he said, "but that's what's great about sessiuns. This is the best way to learn Irish music. There're so many tunes you can pick up, and you can play right alongside older people who have played the music all their lives. You get to participate at your level, get comfortable with what you're doing and learn. Larry and Mike are great at taking musicians in, making them feel at home. You get the feeling that this is kind of a family event, close-knit, and that you belong, no matter how good a musician you are."

Later that evening, Foley offered a song. Earlier, Larry Reynolds had urged him to sing, but also to wait until the moment felt right, until he was sure he felt comfortable.

"I can actually hear them move from one level to the next," Larry Reynolds said. "Players I've been listening to week after week, I can hear their playing elevate. That's the fun for me, hearing the various people coming up, particularly if they're not Irish, as they really get hold of the music, and it gets hold of them. They become one with it, and you can actually feel the enjoyment they're having. That's everything to me."

—March 21, 1999

Cape Breton's fiddle phenom wrestles with stardom
Natalie MacMaster

"Not true, nope, never happened, I don't even know how that story got started," says Cape Breton fiddle sensation Natalie MacMaster, her normally shy, soft voice turned suddenly testy. As she has grown from fiddle prodigy to international star, a certain folklore has also grown about her beginnings on the far Canadian isle of Cape Breton. The particular myth she was hotly denying, which has been widely reported as fact, is that she was once urged by a record executive to lose her Cape Breton accent.

"I'm asked about that all the time," she said with a sigh. "I think people keep printing it because it sounds good, but it never happened. I haven't come into any pressure along the way, not to talk different, not to play different. That's why my story is kind of boring, I guess; there's no juice, no gossip. It's just really kind of perfect and fairy-tale-ish."

While her saga may not be filled with backstage Svengalis, Machiavellian show-biz manipulations, or tawdry scandals, it is certainly the stuff of a modern-day fairy tale: A little girl grows up in a humble, music-filled, and loving household, going to sleep every night listening to the vibrant Scottish-based traditional music of her

Being a fiddler was never a decision for me, something I wanted to be taught. It was more like learning to walk. Everybody around you is doing it; you're seeing it all the time. You can do it, you just have to practice. That's basically all it was, like a language or any of the essentials. I got this fiddle and knew fiddle music as well as I knew anything. —Natalie MacMaster

Cape Breton home.

One day, a child-sized fiddle arrives in the mail from an uncle in Boston. Anyone who wants to play it can have it, and 9-year-old Natalie scoops it up, as everyone in the family knew she would. Her little head is so filled with the music that she is immediately able to scratch out tunes.

At 16, she makes her first CD, and by the time she is 27, as she is now, she is a bona fide world star who has toured with the Chieftains, been featured on their "Tears of Stone" CD alongside Joni Mitchell, Diane Krall, the Coors, and Bonnie Raitt; and recorded with Mark O'Connor and Alison Krauss, who join MacMaster on her adventurous Rounder CD, "In My Hands."

"Being a fiddler was never a decision for me, something I wanted to be taught," she said. "It was more like learning to walk. Everybody around you is doing it; you're seeing it all the time. You can do it, you just have to practice. That's basically all it was, like a language or any of the essentials. I got this fiddle and knew fiddle music as well as I knew anything."

That organic mastery sparks everything she plays. Her music is passionately joyful, her bow at once raw and tender, muscular and sweet as she drives through ancient tunes that many experts, including preeminent Scottish fiddlers Aly Bain and Alasdair Fraser, believe are closer to what Scottish music sounded like 300 years ago than what can be heard in Scotland today.

That belief comes less from the remoteness of Cape Breton than from how the music remains such a living tradition, played to the thundering pulse of hundreds of clogging feet at square dances. It is pure, single malt, whoop-it-up weekend music.

"It's just real music," MacMaster said. "It comes right from the heart. It's very, very strong in rhythm, because we've been playing for dancers for years. The mark of a good dance player is not based on technical ability as much as it is on rhythm and timing. You've got to be very solid, and once you establish a good groove, you've got to keep it there."

Led by fiery folk-rocker Ashley MacIsaac, who pushed the music into mainstream rock arenas, and followed by dynamic young stars like MacMaster and J.P. Cormier, Cape Breton music is becoming all the rage in North America, Europe, and Asia.

No player better showcases the music's sweeping melodicism than MacMaster. However robust her playing gets, it remains spacious, pristine, heedful of elegant phrase-ending ornaments.

"A lot of the ornamentation comes from the Gaelic language, which is very rich in all sorts of throat noises and different accents on words," she said. "Some of the tunes are actually old Gaelic songs. My grandmother used to sing when I'd play the tunes, and you could hear the same sort of flavor in her voice that was in the tunes. The rhythm, the pacing, and the phrasing of the notes would be the same as the language."

Because it is still such a dance-driven style, Cape Breton music wears the trappings of modern rock, jazz, and world beat better than many other folk forms. Though devoted to the tradition, MacMaster loves to play in modern fields, adding a hip-hop groove to her own ode to the fiddle, "In My Hands," or splashes of icy-blue jazz shadow to a prim old air.

She thanks her lifelong friend MacIsaac for being the lightning rod for any static that might have come her way from these innovations—one more way that, to her mind, her remarkable success story is kind of boring, like a fairy tale.

"Ashley didn't just open the door, he kicked it open. If he hadn't been around, maybe people would be more likely to say, 'What is this? What's she doing here?' Instead, they say, 'Well, she hasn't gone as far as Ashley.' I'm protected by him."

—November 12, 1999

Sol y Canto & the Latin music revival: going deeper than Ricky Martin
Brian & Rosi Amador

For 15 years, Latin American music has had no better ambassadors than Cambridge's Brian and Rosi Amador. With their old band Flor de Cana, and their new group Sol y Canto, they have introduced hundreds of thousands of North Americans to the dizzyingly diverse splendor of Latin music, from traditional Afro-Latin styles to pop hybrids like the tango and bolero.

So now that Latin music is hot, hot, hot, how are things heating up for the Amadors?

Singer Rosi Amador handles the business for Sol y Canto—which performs as a duo, trio, or sextet—and for several other Latin acts. All she's noticed so far, she said with a laugh, was that it used to be the English-language media that asked them why they play the way they do. Now it's the Latin press.

"All of the Latino media now ask me the same question," she said. " 'How come you're not choosing to do a more commercial kind of music so you can make more money now that Latin music is in vogue?' And what I say is, you know, we do the music that we love. We didn't think about switching when it was not popular; why should we switch now because it is?"

But as they discussed their joyful new Red wing CD, "En Todo Momento," shadows of Latin music's new visibility fell over everything they said. They have always been aware of their role as a front door to Latin music. Most of the places they play are not specific Latin venues but folk concert series, clubs, museums, or colleges, where they're often the only Latin act of the season.

Their missionary zeal began when they founded Flor de Cana in 1984. Their shows were panoramic journeys through Pan-American musical tradition, the aim to enlighten American audiences as to the very distinct cultures of the Caribbean, and Central and South America.

One reason they founded Sol y Canto in 1994 was that their own musical vision was getting lost in that eclectic mission.

"While we are still committed to a breadth of styles, we've become more committed to depth," said Brian Amador, the musical director, arranger, and frequent composer. "We want to be able to delve more deeply into certain traditions, and we find ourselves gravitating more towards Afro-Caribbean styles, particularly Cuban. But I don't think we'll ever stop doing a variety; I think that's impossible for us."

They are drawn to the rhythmic complexity of African-influenced styles, and to the intricate vocal harmonies that also inform African-American music. On "En Todo Momento," cadences set by different instruments often captivatingly collide, lapping against each other like southbound waves on a northbound boat. Their sleek, exuberant harmonies can also suddenly change current, Alan del Castillo's silky tenor soaring playfully above Rosi Amador's beautifully pure mezzo.

Latin music's new visibility offers Sol y Canto simultaneous opportunities and challenges. While it is now easier to open conversations with venues, it also presents the problem that most people think they know what Latin music is.

"A lot of the Latin music people are being introduced to is the more commercial stuff, which is pretty much like North American pop sung in Spanish," Brian Amador said. "If you listen to Jennifer Lopez and Ricky Martin, there might be a few watered-down Latin rhythms, but you're not really hearing the authentic Latin groove, which has a strong African element in the drumming and vocal approaches; the call-and-response singing, the way the drums pop, speak, and jump out at you."

Another staple of Latin music that's getting lost in the pop shuffle is the delicate intricacy of the Spanish guitar, of which Brian Amador is a supple master.

"The Spanish guitar was the first guitar used in Latin American music," he said, "and it's largely been discarded for things that make a lot more noise. It has a very distinctive sound, an infinite variety of textures you can create by letting the strings ring or blocking them in different ways. There's such a wide palette of colors and rhythms you can strum, and when you're playing more melodically, it has a warmth no electric guitar will ever have."

The Amadors are convinced the Latin music presence is here to stay, though they suspect some of its high-profile stars may be, as they put it, merely "the trend du jour."

"Because the Latino population is growing," Rosi Amador said, "the culture is more and more in people's consciousness. That made it much easier for Ricky Martin and Jennifer Lopez, and the Buena Vista Social Club, to enter the fabric of the mainstream. People come to us now thinking they know what Latin music is, and I find I have to describe the difference between Latin styles, between what Ricky Martin does and what we do. Which is nice, you know; people have a point of reference now—and they know that this is music audiences want to hear."

—November 17, 1999

Getting it right about roots
Dave Alvin

When Dave Alvin helped ignite the roots-rock revival with his 1980s band the Blasters, he thinks a lot of people missed the point about the roots part. So over his last three recordings, the California guitarist-songwriter has increasingly shone his hot-rocking spotlight on American traditional music.

With his latest Hightone CD, "Public Domain," he pushes listeners headfirst into the deep end of the folk-music pool, devoting the entire CD to songs in the public domain, meaning they are truly traditional, with no known composer or at least no copyright attributed to one. Intriguingly, it is also his liveliest, most rambunctious and fun-loving disc in years.

Though he denies being on a soapbox about folk music, when it's suggested he's become more explicit about traditional music on each recording over the last five years, then devoting a CD to songs in the public domain— as if daring people to miss the point this time, he laughs.

"Well, you may be on to something there. This record is not like I'm Martin Luther nailing the manifesto to the church doors, but there's a couple of little manifestos going on. One is about the interconnectedness of various styles of American music, how these different genres that encompass our folk music all grew up together. They're like sisters and brothers, or at least cousins; they didn't develop exclusive of each other."

To vivify that point, Alvin deliberately cross-pollinated his arrangements, giving a grinding blues feel to the bluegrass standard "Don't Let Your Deal Go Down,"

There is always this drive inside of us for something better, mixed with a loneliness that we don't acknowledge, that we cover up today with television and nonstop media. We're still a frontier society in so many ways, an isolated people who feel strangely disconnected to the world around us. But that same mood runs through all these old songs, so it can show us that a lot of how we feel today, a lot of the concerns we have about community and isolation...It's all right there, in our songs. —Dave Alvin

and a mirthful doo-wop bop to "East Virginia Blues." He brings a tight sense of danger to the string-band chestnut "Railroad Bill," which was written about an African-American outlaw, and underscores the deep anguish in "Short Life of Trouble" by aiming his guitar between the antic groove of white banjo legend Uncle Dave Macon and the dark pulse of black blues guitarist Bukka White. To Alvin, he is merely employing a process of cultural inbreeding that has always shaped American music.

"There's all this debate the last 15 years about multiculturalism, and the reality as I see it is that our folk music has always been multicultural," he said. "These songs are the side of the American story we're not always told, showing how ordinary people really lived, and they tell us that different cultures interacted a lot, enough to share their music."

Alvin's other little manifesto on "Public Domain" is to present these songs not as artifacts of a moth-eaten past, but as vibrant and still burningly relevant meditations on American life. He sings the tragically violent 19th-century ballads "Texas Rangers" and "Murder of the Lawson Family" with a stark intimacy, as if they had happened to him yesterday.

The Lawson ballad in particular speaks to our troubled times, as a man suddenly kills his family and himself. It is eerily similar to stories we read in the news and view as uniquely contemporary signs that something is terribly wrong with our society. In Alvin's whispered urgency, it is as if our ancestors stepped from their graves to reassure us, in their own words, that these senseless tragedies are indeed horrible, but that our entire society is no more infected with some strange malady than 19th-century society was afflicted with whatever madness drove Lawson to destroy everything he loved.

"A lot of these songs were reactions to events larger than the people who created them," he said. "They express the isolation of people caught between preindustrial and postindustrial worlds and have a real connection for us today in the gulf between the pre-technological and post-technological ages. I think that's where a lot of the darkness comes from in the old songs, because what did this new world bring? It brought more money and material comfort, but also loneliness and alienation, the end of community as people had known it up till then."

Alvin hears these mixed feelings coursing through our folk songs; simultaneous feelings of optimism and cynicism, great hope for the coming frontier and longing for the one left behind; a joyful whoop at the open society democracy grants us, mixed with a pervasive sense of fear and alienation. Especially in restoring new life to such over-roasted chestnuts as "Shenandoah" and "Walk Right In," Alvin exquisitely evokes these captivating contradictions in the American personality.

"There is always this drive inside of us for something better," he said, "mixed with a loneliness that we don't acknowledge, that we cover up today with television and nonstop media. We're still a frontier society in so many ways, an isolated people who feel strangely disconnected to the world around us. But that same mood runs through all these old songs, so it can show us that a lot of how we feel today, a lot of the concerns we have about community and isolation, have been part of the American personality from the very beginning. It's all right there, in our songs."

—October 20, 2000

The roots of roots music
Tarbox Ramblers

The crowd seemed to have a plan. The back room of the Burren Pub in Davis Square was packed a good hour before the Tarbox Ramblers started Saturday, people filling in the space around the stage. A tight circle formed, leaving just enough space for a few to cavort, but not enough to turn the club into a mosh pit or disco.

These folks were here to listen, part of a devout and growing cult of fans (Tarheads?) this delightfully rambunctious folk band is building through its regular Saturday night gigs at the Burren and Fridays at the Green Street Grill in Cambridge's Central Square.

The band announced itself with the primal pooming of a tom-tom. Lead singer Michael Tarbox, seated next to his eccentric array of twangy, slidey, and plucky guitars, began to sing a bold but mournful song, the call-and-response lines met by harmonic moans from the rest of the quartet. The sound was rock-solid yet eerily ancient, like some old chain-gang chant or field holler.

Like nearly all of the Tarbox Ramblers' repertoire, it is actually a traditional American folk song with a long history in both black and white cultures, part of what Tarbox calls "the songster tradition." It is "Stewball," a still-popular bluegrass and folk standard, which was also often sung and recorded by African-American blues singers of the '20s and '30s.

"Part of what I really want to do is put folk music back in the barroom where it came from," Tarbox said over a pint at the Burren a few days later. "I think a lot of times, people who are not familiar with it don't know what to make of folk music. It gets a little cute and precious, often done in these pristine presentations. Sometimes I hear it and it's so pretty, I think, oh lord, bring it back home, let it get rowdy again."

By the end of "Stewball," the crowd was bobbing to the beat, some hopping in step, but many also craning forward to catch every moan and nuance. This is hypnotic stuff. The songs they sing come from a vanished America, stomp-down barroom romps about fast women and slow horses, big, bad bosses and high, good times. The band's sound has a blues bounce, but it is not a blues band. It is hard to put a finger on exactly what style the music is, which is just fine with Tarbox.

"People ask us all the time what kind of music we play," he said. "I think it's a good sign when people are perplexed. But it's really pretty specific: We play pre-World War II black and white hillbilly songs, blues, and gospel music."

The key to the band's intoxicatingly original sound is that it scratches beneath the veneer of American popular music, down to its authentic folk core. Tarbox said he gets many of his songs and arrangement ideas from folkloric field recordings made during the '20s and '30s in prisons, churches, front porches, and bars. He wants to recreate the good-time music poor folks made for themselves before they had radios and records, superstars and videos, to do it for them.

"To me, this is such beautiful music, because it's so real, so raw, " he said. "A lot of the songs are about very specific, real-life situations. Like in `Frankie and Albert,' a variant of `Frankie and Johnny,' when it says, `Judge turned to the jury, says it's plain as it can be/This woman shot her lover down, it's murder in the second degree.' That's so understated but outlines this whole, tragic human situation. That verse is just total genius to me."

Scrunched right near the stage, Mark Lyons, 30, of Somerville, said he is a hard-core Tarbox fan. He said this music is his antidote for bad days, just as it was for the hardscrabble folks who first created it. He acknowledged that, at first, it jarred with his preconceptions about folk music.

"Folk has a bad rap, I think, because of all the whiney songwriters out there," he said. "And to be honest, I don't like listening to them myself. But it's not right to stereotype it as just that. This is folk, too, and it's high-energy, fun music. It always gets me in a good mood, gets my feet moving."

His friend, Erica Bernstein, 36, of Cambridge, agreed.

"I'm having fun tonight, which is why I came," she said. "They always get me dancing, feeling good, but it's more mellow than a rock club, and my ears won't be ringing tomorrow."

Tarbox's guitar anchors the band, whether sliding out sinewy blues or power-chording a gospel thumper as if his guitar were some old pump organ. His baritone is convincingly grainy, but also warm and inviting. Like his guitar, it is always on the note, delivering the lyrics with almost no affectation, though he primes the mood with a subtle array of moans and bluesy dips beneath the melody's surface.

Following his lead, the band rocks, embellishing without ever disrupting the plain power of the old songs. Fiddler Dan Kellar, who also works with hot local folk-rocker Laurie Geltman, plays low, chordal fiddle licks that suddenly explode into high, wailing glissandos. Other times, he plucks mandolin-like leads or bows fearfully beneath the lines of violent ballads and dark laments.

Upright bassist John Sciascia is a joyful metronome, often sliding between tick-tocky notes like the wet beats of an old-time jug band. Stan Kozlowski, filling in for regular drummer Jon Cohan, lays heavily on the toms, lightly on the cymbals.

Though Tarbox finds most of the band's songs on recordings of black musicians, he stressed that many belong to a rich and sadly neglected American song repertoire common to both black and white folk music; proof that there is much more of a shared cultural heritage between the races than is commonly believed.

"People have tended to see rural music leading purely into two streams," he said. "There's black blues and gospel on one hand and white spiritual and country music on the other. What slips between those cracks is this shared repertoire of work and play songs, goodtime blues and field hollers. Early professional musicians, black and white, leaned towards them when making records precisely because they knew that everybody knew them."

Lyons said, "They're like a filter for me. I appreciate that these are old blues and folk songs, but it's not like I sit home listening to old records all day. They do that for me, and I come because I always know they'll make me feel good."

A moment later, he was bobbing his head to the backbeat as the band tore into an undulating blues rub of "The Cuckoo," one of the oldest and most traveled songs in the English language (in ancient folklore, the cuckoo bird symbolized adultery, thus the word "cuckold"). After years of being treated as a precious, fragile thing, sung in archly purist ways, the song itself seemed happy to spread its wings and flap amid the rollicking ambience of the Burren's backroom.

"You know, there really is a lot of square folk music out there," Tarbox said. "To me, this music is just the real-est thing I know."

—February 15, 1998

The New Lost City Ramblers: they brought the mountains to the cities.
John Cohen, Mike Seeger, Tracy Schwarz

If you measure success by records sold or hits that topped the charts, the New Lost City Ramblers are not even a blip on the music industry screen. If you gauge their success by how many people they inspired to carry on the musical traditions they championed, however, the trio must be counted among the most successful groups in the history of American folk music.

Almost by themselves, they sparked an urban revival of Southern old-time, folk, and traditional country music in the late '50s and early '60s. That led to a great string band revival in the '70s, driven by new bands like the Red Clay Ramblers and the Highwoods String Band, who nearly all counted the Ramblers as primary influences. Today, thousands of fiddlers, guitarists, banjo players, and mandolin pickers, professional and amateur, trace their musical roots to the exuberant, playful and deeply traditional music of the New Lost City Ramblers.

Founding member John Cohen said, "Jeff Rosen, who is Bob Dylan's manager, once told me that the biggest contribution the Ramblers made is that we showed urban people that you could play traditional music and still be yourself."

That authenticity, both personal and artistic, was a hallmark of the Ramblers's style and approach. The music they played was rural and rustic, wild and raw. The band's members, however, were all urban intellectuals. Cohen and Tom Paley met while at Yale in the mid-'50s. The band formed when Mike Seeger, of the folk-singing Seeger family, joined them on a live radio show in 1958.

"There were very, very few people playing old-time music in the city," said Seeger, "and in the country it was kind of moribund; the old-timers and country music people were giving it up, and didn't really come back to it until sometime in the late '60s. I guess people felt we were kind of a fresh sound. You know, people by then had tried to do about everything they could to this old-time music but play it in the old, original way."

Activists in the folk world felt there was a need for a band of attractive, sophisticated young people who played authentic old-time music, and the trio had a contract on Folkways Records before they'd even thought up a name. For the record, there never was an old Lost City Ramblers; Cohen just liked the contrasting sound of "new" and "lost," "city" and "ramblers."

"That first record might have sold 400 copies the first year," said Cohen, "but it was to people doing folk festivals in Berkeley and Los Angeles and Chicago; it really traveled."

As did they. They were soon crisscrossing America, playing primarily on college campuses, where their authentic sounds and fresh, urbane wit made them cherished figures. It was the era of the pin-striped, crew-cut campus folk group, but where their arrangements were pop-bopping and squeaky-clean, the Ramblers sound was richly informed by the wild dissonance, evocative rural lyricism, and twangy pulse of traditional music.

"We were offended by more commercial acts like the Kingston Trio," said Cohen, "and wanted to make this more authentic approach to the music available. It hadn't been heard in the cities, at least not played by live, young musicians. Nobody was playing fiddle in these folk groups at the time, and Mike bringing in the autoharp—this was all new."

Their missionary zeal was immediately evident. At first, they invited people in

the audience to bring instruments up and jam with them. When they became too popular to manage that, they still accepted invitations to local picking parties and did daytime participatory workshops. Everything about their approach promoted the idea that this music was meant for everybody, not just for stars to sing and fans to admire from afar. This was front-porch, hoedown, hands-on music, and a new generation of players, including Dylan, Jerry Garcia, David Bromberg, and David Grisman, claimed the Ramblers as seminal influences.

Among them was Tracy Schwarz, who replaced Paley in 1963.

"We made it clear we were just catalysts," he said, "that we knew where the music came from, knew the people who made it, but also that we knew who we were playing for. We weren't posing as country boys; we were obviously college-educated, more like our audiences. We showed that you can play this music even if you're not born and raised in West Virginia. The idea of people who grow up the way we did going out and playing this music was pretty foreign and unaccepted then, both by the music business and by academics and folklorists. I think it's less so now, and the Ramblers may have had an effect on that."

The Ramblers never broke up; they just, as Seeger put it, took a few five-year vacations here and there. Their lives continue to be devoted to traditional music. Seeger has gone on to an important solo career, both as performer and presenter of older traditional artists. Cohen has had an equally important career as photographer and filmmaker of the same traditional masters, allowing urban audiences front-porch seats to hear the old music in its natural environs. Schwarz was a driving force behind the Cajun music revival of the '70s.

Seeger said, "When I go to old-time music gatherings and hear good younger musicians playing this music, and see people who just have string bands for their own pleasure, it makes me very happy. And whenever I see a kid in our audience with orange hair and earrings, I think, wow, those are the kids who were listening to us in the '60s; a little rebellious and reaching out for something different. I just think that's great."

—November 20, 1998

There Is No Eye John Cohen

John Cohen has always had a genius for inviting people in. As a founder of the New Lost City Ramblers, he exposed millions of new urban and collegiate fans to Southern roots music. Many of the biggest stars of the '60s, from Bob Dylan to the Byrds to Janis Joplin, cited the Ramblers as chief influences; the Grateful Dead's "Uncle John's Band" was an homage to Cohen.

As a folklorist, Cohen preserved precious traditional songs and tunes, recorded along remote Southern back roads and at rough urban street corners, up hard mountain trails of Appalachia and Peru. He discovered or helped popularize crucial traditional masters, including Roscoe Holcomb and the Rev. Gary Davis.

As an acclaimed photographer, best known for chronicling the bohemian New York art and music scene of the late '50s and early '60s, and as a longtime professor of photography at the State University of New York at Purchase, he has championed an emotionally vivid, naturalistic style poised at the precise crossroads between fine art and photojournalism; one that centers attention not on the photographer, but on the image.

"I've been called a musician, folklorist, visual anthropologist, ethnomusicologist, filmmaker, photographer, ethnographer, visual artist, teacher," Cohen says as he strolls through "There Is No Eye," a retrospective of his photographs on display at Boston University's Photographic Resource Institute.

"I see it all as one work, emanating from one central point in myself. But our society is so specialized that each of these things I do has a name. When you see each thing separately, it may look like I'm a butterfly flitting from flower to flower. I don't see it that way. I say, 'I'm an artist.'"

Complementing the exhibit, Powerhouse Books has released Cohen's equally lovely, provocative large-format book, also called "There Is No Eye." The title was taken from Dylan's mention of Cohen in the cryptic liner notes to the 1965 album "Highway 61 Revisited."

In addition, Smithsonian-Folkways has released a companion CD to the book and exhibit, featuring songs by people in his photographs. The performers include nonprofessional folk singers, alongside intimate solo cuts from folk stars including Dylan, Davis, Holcomb, Bill Monroe, Big Bill Broonzy and, of course, the New Lost City Ramblers.

This multimedia memoir has been four years in the making for the 70-year-old Cohen. After a lifetime showering attention on others, he squirms at the spotlight now falling on him alone.

"I'm a bit puzzled by it all," he says a little sadly. "I'm not used to having the focus on me, having my own interior monologues read by many people. There was a whole page about me in The New York Times. I'm not used to that."

A moment later he is pointing questions away from him again. He bubbles like a teenager recalling the two worlds of his salad days in Greenwich Village.

"This is a shot of the Cedar Tavern, where all the Abstract Expressionist painters hung out. I'd leave my house, walk down there and talk with them and Beat poets and writers like Jack Kerouac and Allen Ginsberg. Then I'd walk down to McDougal Street, where Dylan and all the folkies were hanging out. It was just a scene then; none of these people were great and important yet. But it seemed to me this was an incredible time."

"There Is No Eye" is much more than a celebrity exhibit. Alongside revealingly candid shots of Kerouac, Ginsberg, Dylan, and painters such as Red Grooms and Franz Kline, are unguarded shots of Peruvian Indian women, rural African-American children at play; desolate landscapes and earthy glimpses of poor folks making art for themselves.

As you wander through it, the exhibit becomes less a collection of photographs than a display of captured moments. A visceral connection with Cohen's music emerges: There is not a false note or a contrived shot in the collection. Every picture rings true. If folk songs had shutters, these are the kinds of photographs they would take; of real people engaged in the wonderfully human cacophony of their own lives and times.

"One of the things that attracted me to photography as opposed to painting," he says, "was that you could put your whole life into it; you could walk through the world and record what you saw there, record what you feel. And you really can't do that with painting; it's a life in the studio."

But of course, Cohen is also a musician, among the most influential of his generation. His love of traditional music is everywhere in the exhibit. Gazing at photos of the Greenwich Village folk scene, captured just as it was bubbling to its generation-shaking boil, he recalls how distraught he was at the pin-striped commercialism of groups such as the Kingston Trio and the Limeliters—how they sought to sanitize and urbanize the wild grace of folk music that he found so compelling.

It was precisely to fight that homogenization of folk music that he formed the New Lost City Ramblers in 1958, with Tom Paley and Mike Seeger. They toured college campuses playing Southern traditional music as authentically as they could. In the process they helped to revolutionize the folk revival. Young urban fans such as Dylan, Joan Baez, and Tom Rush took the Ramblers as their ideals, and saw how they could retain their own identities and still perform this music in all its raw, folksy splendor.

"People sometimes describe the Ramblers as the essential folk revivalists," he says. "No, we weren't. We were dissenters from what the folk revival was about, pushing it in another direction. We knew we could never claim to be the music we played; we could not be Roscoe Holcomb or Bill Monroe, so we just let all those streams flow through us. Our job was to introduce the music of those people, to let our audiences see how much they had to offer."

That love of simply laying art out for people, then letting them make what they will of it, is another vital way his musical aesthetics inform his photography. Just as he placed conflicting images against each other in naming the New Lost City Ramblers, he chose "There Is No Eye" as a title in large part because of its ambiguity. He still has no idea what Dylan meant.

"He was referring to a conversation we had while I took photographs of him in 1962. I was flabbergasted he remembered that conversation after many years, because I really don't. What he wrote was, 'There is no eye—there is only a series of mouths—long live the mouths.' I don't know what he was saying, just a hunch, some feelings."

As a title for his retrospective, he likes how it stresses that the photographer—the eye—is less important than the life in the images themselves. "I'm never trying to impose something on the pictures," he says firmly.

He says he enjoys leaving things unexplained, honest moments captured as they happened, then left for us to figure out.

"Thats very close to the way we listen to music, wondering how literally a lyric should be taken. Does he mean he really wants to kill his wife, or is he just working some of those kinds of feelings off? Or is he singing about something that really happened to someone else a long time ago? That's why I had such trouble with the Kingston Trio, because they sort of put it into the context of 'Here's these dumb hillbillies singing a murder song.' And it was never as simple as that."

He is delighted that his exhibit, book, and CD all seem to be gathering extra attention because of the roots revival sweeping the country. He is particularly excited because he sees the interest in roots music emanating from the right place.

"Back then,' he says of the '60s revival, "they put so much glitter all over traditional music to market it. Now they don't want anything to do with glitter;

those people being drawn to roots music want it just as it is. The interest is coming from a hunger for something that's handmade, human scale, not manipulated, a real need for something real. It's a flowering of all these things I've been trying to nourish all my life."

He laughs then, startled to hear himself explain his life in a way that sounds so cogent, so composed. He says he was asked recently what he was searching for in his art and in his life.

"And all I could think of was Pablo Picasso's statement when he was asked if he knew what a painting was going to look like before he started. He said if he knew what it was going to look like, he wouldn't need to paint it."

—Sunday, February 3, 2002

"O Brother, Where Art Thou?" reveals the gulf between folk music and the music biz
Emmylou Harris, Denice Stiff, Norman Blake, Patty Loveless

The *O Brother, Where Art Thou?* juggernaut shows no sign of slowing down. The Mercury/Lost Highway soundtrack to the Coen brothers' film has gone quadruple-platinum (more than four million in sales) and swept the Country Music Association Awards, earning nods for both best album and best single (for "I Am a Man of Constant Sorrow"). It earned six Grammy nominations, including album of the year, best compilation soundtrack, and best producer (for T Bone Burnett). More than a year after its release, it is No. 2 on Billboard's country chart and No. 10 among Sound scan's top current albums, its highest position ever on that chart.

Emmylou Harris is featured prominently on the soundtrack and has been a champion of traditional music throughout her career. She says nobody expected such a hit from an acoustic album of vintage country, folk, gospel, and bluegrass songs. She's now on the *Down From the Mountain* tour, featuring musicians appearing on the *O Brother* soundtrack who were later filmed performing a concert. That second film, *Down From the Mountain,* was released last summer, and its Mercury/Lost Highway sound track earned its own Grammy nomination as best traditional folk album.

"This is really one of those wonderful surprises that comes along and breaks up your cynicism a bit," Harris said. "I mean, this music has always meant a lot to me and the people I hang with, but we all thought it was going to be kind of a regrettably small thing. You always want to believe that if people get a chance to hear the good stuff, they will respond. But I never expected anything like this; none of us did."

The elaborate strategy designed to extend the success of *O Brother* would seem to belie that expectation. With the *Down From the Mountain* film and soundtrack and now the first of at least two national tours, someone must have smelled gold, right?

Quite the opposite, according to Denise Stiff, executive producer for the *O Brother* film and soundtrack and manager of tour members Alison Krauss and Union Station and the Peasall Sisters.

Stiff said it was actually fear of failure that drove Burnett, the Coens, and her to develop such a complex cross-promotional strategy. They were certain that commercial country radio stations would never embrace anything so far from the mainstream sound that dominates their format. If the film fizzled, they wanted other outlets for the music.

"We knew we had a phenomenal soundtrack, but at that time, we didn't know how the movie was going to do," she said. "Sometimes movies like that take off; sometimes they don't. But we all felt the music was so good that we needed to be on the offensive, to take every possible step to get it heard."

Blake, a master of the guitar, dobro, fiddle, and mandolin who is among the most respected instrumentalists in acoustic music, credits much of the soundtrack's success to the spontaneity that Burnett brought out in the players. Blake did his deliciously languid version of "You Are My Sunshine" just to get timing and mike levels, but Burnett liked the take's easy feel and used it.

Blake says he's reminded of the similar breakthrough success of the Nitty Gritty Dirt Band's '70s roots anthology "Will the Circle be Unbroken," which helped make him a star. Both records reached huge new audiences, he says, because they embraced the classic songs savvy traditionalists often eschew for more obscure gems.

"You know, I had never sung 'You Are My Sunshine' because I'd heard it from the cradle up," he said. "I'd never had anything against it; I just felt it was a simple piece that's been done to death. But when you get down to it, if a tune is that standard, there's a reason: It's because people like it."

O Brother is helping the careers of all the participating musicians. Blake has noticed more new fans, especially young people, at his shows. And the attention is boosting sales for his wildly beautiful Red House CD with Minnesota mandolin and fiddle master Peter Ostroushko, "Meeting on Southern Soil."

Though she is not on the soundtrack, Loveless says it's helping her career, too. She brilliantly embraced a bluegrass sound on her recent Epic CD, "Mountain Soul," which received almost no commercial radio play but earned critical raves in places her country-pop career had never taken her, including People, Rolling Stone, Newsweek, and even the Wall Street Journal.

"I think the movie influenced a lot of kids to get more interested in the music," she said. "This form of music is so real, and maybe they're looking for something

This is really one of those wonderful surprises that comes along and breaks up your cynicism a bit. I mean, this music has always meant a lot to me and the people I hang with, but we all thought it was going to be kind of a regrettably small thing. You always want to believe that if people get a chance to hear the good stuff, they will respond. But I never expected anything like this; none of us did. —Emmylou Harris

like that now. It's so different from what's on commercial radio. Even though this music's old to us, you know, it's new to them."

Despite the obvious awkwardness of refusing to play the CMA single or album of the year, though, most commercial country radio programmers still resist the notion that the *O Brother* phenomenon signals any change in national tastes. Stiff worries they may be even more entrenched against it now, because to relent after so long would be to acknowledge they missed the biggest country music story of the year.

So those reaping the benefits of the music's success see its rewards coming in other ways: in more people realizing that commercial radio does not have a corner on all music worth hearing, and in the influence this moment in American music will have on future musicians and fans.

"I believe in people's ability to be moved by music, even if it doesn't happen in a huge way," Harris said. "I started out listening to Peter, Paul, and Mary, thinking that was the most exotic thing I'd ever heard. Then I was wondering who this Bob Dylan was who wrote this great song, and then I was going deeper and deeper to the stuff that's 110 proof. It's a matter of seeds taking root."

—February 1, 2002

News songs from old places
Dave Carter, Tracy Grammer, Joan Baez

If the voice of modern folk music is changing—and many in the folk biz believe it is—it is going to sound a lot like Dave Carter and Tracy Grammer.

The Oregon songwriting duo, who appear at the Boston Folk Festival on Sept. 22-23, are already among the hottest acts on the circuit. They're about to get even hotter, as Joan Baez is singing their songs, showering them with the same star-making attention she gave Bob Dylan in the '60s and, more recently, Dar Williams and Richard Shindell. Baez will record several of Carter and Grammer's songs on her next CD, and tour with them early next year.

Carter and Grammer's folky-sounding but modern songs exemplify an exciting new style emerging from the coffeehouses these days. It bewitched Baez the moment she heard the duo's music.

"There's something kind of Southern-rootsy about the melodies," Baez said, "but there's a very sophisticated feel to the songs, too. Dave is masterful with words, and there's a real spiritual connection in there; nothing direct, it's in the imagery, and that really rings bells with me."

Carter is the songwriter, while Grammer, a sublime fiddler, coarranges the tunes and does much of the business work. Both are lovely, eloquent singers. Their new Signature CD, "Drum Hat Buddha," is stunningly good, brimming with memorable melodies and keenly sculpted lyrics.

"Common cool was a proud young fool in a kick-ass Wal-Mart tie," begins "Ordinary Town," which veers provocatively between dark satire and beatitude. In a wrenching portrait of quietly broken dreams, they sing, "Street poets and vision miners, starry-eyed ambitious / blew like pilgrim leaves through the sad cafe."

"At the festivals we did this summer," Grammer said, "the word we heard most from people was `refreshing.' Which is interesting, because here we are sounding rather traditional, writing songs with sort of a back-to-the-origins approach, and people are saying, `What a relief to hear this kind of music.'

"The idea of folk festivals morphing into rock festivals the last few years may have set the stage for that kind of reaction," she added. "It felt like there was not only a place for the kind of music we're doing, but a real need for it, almost a spiritual need."

That is why many in the folk-music biz see Carter and Grammer not just as rising stars, but also as bellwethers of a return to a more basic folk sound.

But Carter does not write old-fashioned songs; his work is modern, incisive, and intimate. It is in his understanding of song structure, his use of poetic imagery and melodic refrains that his songs wear their folk roots.

That knowledge of the architecture of song came first from studying classical music in college, then from immersing himself in traditional music and the great songwriters of the '60s, particularly Dylan, Leonard Cohen, and Joni Mitchell. He sees similarities between the decline of classical composing and the current desire among many folk-pop songwriters to create music that is new and devoid of influences.

"The greatest composers—Mozart, for example—innovated, but with a strong awareness they were innovating on the shoulders of people who came before," he said. "If you look at the history of classical music, you see that a great deal of wonderful work was done until about 1940, when people decided it was time for a great composer to be completely original and not do anything that anybody else had done before. At that point, the music became just awful."

"I do think innovation is important," he added, "but I think it's a natural process that occurs once you attain a certain mastery of another composer's way of doing things."

Carter and Grammer sing songs from deep within their own lives, but which always leave room for other people to find their own lives in them, too. Of all the folk influences they culled from those who came before, this is the most crucial.

Baez said, "There is a special gift for writing songs that are available to other people, and Dave's songs are very available to me. It's a kind of genius, you know, and Dylan has the biggest case of it. But I hear it in Dave's songs, too."

—September 9, 2001

The greatest composers innovated, but with a strong awareness they were innovating on the shoulders of people who came before....when people decided it was time for a great composer to be completely original and not do anything that anybody else had done before...the music became just awful. —Dave Carter

At the festivals we did this summer, the word we heard most from people was 'refreshing.' Which is interesting, because here we are sounding rather traditional, writing songs with sort of a back-to-the-origins approach, and people are saying, 'What a relief to hear this kind of music.' —Tracy Grammer

Building her own star
Kris Delmhorst

Listen to rising local folk star Kris Delmhorst discuss her career, and the future of the music industry can be heard. It is not a sound likely to warm the cockles of a music mogul's heart.

"People think a record deal is everybody's goal," she says in her Somerville apartment. "I just haven't seen any evidence that would make it an appealing thing for me to do. The number of nightmare record-company stories I've heard vastly outnumbers the happy stories of people actually having a career encouraged and maintained by a record company on any kind of long-term basis. What it comes down to is that I really can't imagine giving that much control of my music and my records, which matter so much to me, to a record company."

There is nothing new about labels that put bottom-line concerns above artistic ones. What is new, and radically new, is that a bright and budding star like Delmhorst has choices that, even 10 years ago, she could not have imagined. Thanks to the Internet, and to affordable new digital recording technologies that make state-of-the-art CDs possible for independent artists, she knows she can build a fruitful, long-term career on her own.

So she declines the offers to showcase for label execs who regularly come the way of such attractive and promising artists: "I always say, `Give it to someone who wants it,' because there's no reason for me even to start down that path if I know for sure that I don't want to go there."

Instead, she put together her sublimely melodic, lyrically smart second CD, "Five Stories," exactly as she pleased, and is releasing it through Catalyst, a new subsidiary of the grassrootsy Western Massachusetts label Signature Sounds, which will distribute and market it. The goal is to create a new kind of collaborative, profit-sharing partnership between independent labels like Signature and self-sustaining artists like Delmhorst.

The new CD charts a stunningly successful period of growth as songwriter, singer, and musician. She was a classically trained cellist and supple traditional fiddler before she began writing songs seriously, six years ago. But the fun-loving folk musician who charmed audiences in the Vinal Avenue String Band, which performed Mondays at Tir Na Nog until breaking up last year, was not heard on her oddly stiff 1998 debut, "Appetite."

But from the bold opening struts of "Five Stories," she displays an appealing

One thing I've learned from traditional music is that it doesn't have to be complicated to be powerful. —Kris Delmhorst

knack for having modern fun with traditional song structures. "Mean Old Hen" turns an old-time fiddle standard into a street-smart meditation on getting others to open their hearts by learning how to open one's own. It is at once incisive and broad, swashbuckling fun.

"When I made my first record," she says, "the different pieces of my music were very separate. All those years playing with Vinal Ave. helped me merge them, so I'm drawing more deeply from my love of traditional music in my songwriting now." Which is not to say she writes old-sounding songs.

"One thing I've learned from traditional music is that it doesn't have to be complicated to be powerful," she says.

Her traditional savvy shows lyrically in a use of everyday images, freshly observed in original and very modern ways. In a soft lament, she sings of having "a love song stuck in my throat." In a moving plea for emotional intimacy, she whispers, "You find me clenched and crumpled like a letter I wrote but forgot to mail." Storm warnings are seen for a couple in a car that is "crowded with all the things that no one's saying."

"Obviously, I'm trying to do new things," she says, "but what I love about the old music is that it's very essential. That's what I hope to soak up from that music—that the more words you need, the further off the mark you're getting. As you get closer, you don't need many words at all—and those are the songs that really kill you. You don't have to make something dramatic if it's getting at some real truth or emotion."

Perhaps the most precious thing she has been given by her decision to mold a career away from the superhighways of the music industry is an uncommonly precocious patience about her art. She sees this CD, like the first, as merely a sign post between then and now; a single cobblestone in a lifelong road she is happy to build one cobble at a time.

"What the industry offers just doesn't sound sustainable," she says. "What I want is to have a happy life as a musician, a balanced life where I can continue to do this for a long time. I mean, I'm a young songwriter; I've only been doing this a few years. I feel like I'm just gaining fluidity with the tools I have, and that I need a lot of space to explore things, grow and go in whatever direction my music takes. I want to have control over my life, and going the industry route feels like stepping onto a big conveyer belt and losing control of where you're going and how fast. I feel very, very lucky to be doing this at this time in the world, when I really can just go my own way."

—October 19, 2001

Is there a gender gap in folk music?
John Gorka, Cliff Eberhardt, Richard Shindell, Bottom Line manager Allan Pepper, concert producer Ellen Friedman, record marketing executive Cindy Byram, music managers Ralph Jaccodine and Carol Young

Is the male singer-songwriter an endangered species? Women songwriters are dominating the pop landscape as never before, from Jewel on the cover of Time to the astonishing success of the Lilith Fair, a tour of women songwriters that played to half a million people and grossed more than $15 million. But the male singer-songwriter that so monopolized the last great folk revival seems almost invisible outside the small, subcultural world of coffeehouses and independent, acoustic record labels.

This is not new. When folk music began to regain its commercial viability in the early '80s, it was women songwriters—Suzanne Vega, Nanci Griffith, Shawn Colvin, Tracy Chapman, and Mary Chapin Carpenter—who led the charge. Their male contemporaries—such as Greg Brown, John Gorka, Chris Smither, Bill Morrissey, and Cliff Eberhardt—went on to fine, folk-sized careers as coffeehouse and small-concert headliners. But it is almost exclusively the women who achieve mainstream stardom. The trend continues as popular male songwriters like Ellis Paul are eclipsed by hot women stars like Ani DiFranco and Dar Williams.

Is there a glass ceiling for the male singer-songwriter?

"I think in general it seems like women have reached a broader audience than the guys," says Gorka.

Eberhardt agrees. "The amount of women who are playing as opposed to the amount of men who can get gigs is astronomical. And I think that's all great. But it's amazing to watch so many talented men struggling to have careers. I think John Gorka and Greg Brown and David Wilcox might be the only ones consistently filling large places, whereas I couldn't begin to count the number of women singer-songwriters who are."

Allan Pepper, who has run New York's influential Bottom Line club for 23 years, says: "Between Alanis Morissette and Shawn Colvin, and Meredith Brooks having big records, and the Lilith tour, and Ani DiFranco out there selling a lot of records without a lot of radio play, there has been a real emphasis in the press and on the radio about women performers. So now the media is keying in on what they sense is a trend."

Ellen Friedman's Cambridge-based Revolutionary Acts/Multistage Productions is the busiest producer of major folk concerts in the Boston area. She urges a certain caution.

"I think the record industry has suddenly become enamored of female singer-songwriters, but I'm not sure there are really more of them making successful careers at the pop level. There are a lot more female singer-songwriters than there were 10 years ago, but 10 years ago, there weren't any. There was Suzanne Vega, and that was about it. So I think for women it's more a question of catching up than taking over."

That said, the question remains, why is it happening? Is it just the natural tendency of pop culture to move in waves, with women songwriters riding the current crest, or is something deeper happening? The contemporary songwriter revival was largely born on local folk stages, notably Club Passim in Cambridge, where Vega, Griffith, Colvin and, to a lesser extent, Chapman, had their careers ignited. Tracing where those first sparks came from offers clues into the energy behind forces that do indeed seem to be changing the face of pop music.

As the folk revival of the 1960s waned, it became dominated by an increasingly bland wave of male folk-pop singer-songwriters like James Taylor, Kenny Loggins, and John Denver. By the late '70s, folk music, and the singer-songwriter, were by and large considered commercially dead.

As often happens when fringe forms lose their commercial appeal, folk splintered into small, self-supporting aesthetic communities, such as Celtic music, political songwriters, traditional music, and bluegrass. By far the largest, best organized, and most successful of these was the radical women's music movement, founded by strong-minded feminist artists like Holly Near, Cris Williamson, and Meg Christian.

As they watched the folk revival become increasingly pop-obsessed, and male-dominated, many women started their own record labels, production companies, booking agencies, lighting and sound services. Women would be a music business unto themselves. During folk's commercial drought years, when even the biggest folk stars had no record deals and could barely fill coffeehouses, women's music headliners like Near and Williamson sold hundreds of thousands of self-released, independent albums and easily were selling out major concert halls.

"I think the women's music movement created a different kind of woman performer," says Friedman, whose Revolutionary Acts grew out of that movement but was never gender-exclusive. "It had an effect in creating the groundwork for presenting women who were independent and who use their own voices, both as singers and as writers. It was that movement that allowed women to sing out, to sing about things that concerned them, to no longer be little girls singing in submissive voices."

When folk began to revive commercially here in the 1980s, female singer-songwriters like Vega, Colvin, and Chapman had an edge over equally popular male coffeehouse acts. It was easier for them to move to the concert level, since that structure already was in place for women's music artists. Though less overtly feminist than stars like Near and Williamson, women's music by and large welcomed these new, pop-fired female songwriters to their stages. As never before, the opportunity existed for women to become major stars on their own terms.

"Today, the women who are doing this are designing their own careers," says Cindy Byram, director of media relations for New York indie label Shanachie. "They are making themselves happen. From being in the music business a long time, I see there's more respect for the women who are succeeding today. There used to be a stereotype, built to some degree from truth, that there were a lot of women in the music industry who were there because their boyfriends were their managers. They weren't taking care of business as individuals, and they weren't taken seriously as individuals. The women succeeding today have tremendous focus; they are not ambivalent about their lives or careers."

Gorka wonders if the different mountains men and women had to climb in the '80s didn't attract different kinds of artists.

"Doors were opening for Shawn and I about the same time," he says. "I think we both ended up in different orbits, partly through the choices of the people we wanted to work with, partly because of the kind of music we wanted to make. I think there was maybe a difference in ambition, too; that the goals were different. For me, I wanted to reach as many people as I could without changing who I was or what kind of songs I wanted to write. As Windham Hill tried to get me to that mythical next level, I think they wanted to make me into a celebrity, a star, and I never wanted that. So I resisted it."

Ralph Jaccodine, who manages local songwriter Ellis Paul, sees some essential differences as well.

"I look at the male songwriters in folk, and I don't know if they're as anxious to push out of that world," he says. "Maybe it's because women were put down so much in this industry that they have had to work harder, be more aggressive."

Eberhardt emphasizes that audience demand, not marketing trends, created the startling, grassroots successes of hot, young songwriters like Ani DiFranco and Dar Williams.

"I think the public wants to hear the political and emotional views of women," he says. "I don't think it's a marketing thing. In the folk world, the opportunities, the audiences, the agencies, are not just there for women. It's just that the women are doing better; they have an original voice and the country is attracted to that voice."

It is not that young males are lacking their troubadours. The recent explosion of alternative rock was in large part driven by the desire of young men and women for smarter, more lyric-driven music. But men seem to be expected to form groups.

Jaccodine also manages the Push Stars, who are about to sign a multirecord deal with Capitol. He is certain the major-label interest would not be there if the band's songwriter Chris Trapper had remained a solo act.

"If they heard Chris alone with a guitar, they would hear the same songs, but they would not want to take a chance with him," he says. "Surrounded by a band, it was easy to hear that these were songs that could get on the radio and be hits."

Carol Young, whose Young-Hunter company manages both Dar Williams and male '60s veteran Chris Smither, says: "I see there being two worlds, the folkie world and the pop world. In the folk world generally, art rules. It's not really gender-based and never has been. In the pop world, up until recently, it was very odd to see an artist, male or female, alone on a stage with a guitar. So maybe women are pioneering something; opening doors they'll let men walk through in a few years."

A bit of that is already happening for Richard Shindell, whose new Shanachie CD "Reunion Hill" may be the breakthrough record the highly respected songwriter has long deserved. Dar Williams brought him to Joan Baez's attention when they toured together. The '60s folk diva recorded three of Shindell's songs on her latest CD and is currently touring Europe with him. He also recently toured the country opening for Williams.

"People need to be spoken for and to with music; they need voices," he says, "and I think that's what's happening with women today. You have a segment of society that definitely has not had a fair shake over the last couple of centuries. All of a sudden these people are empowered and released, and they have a lot to say, and they want to say it in their own voices. The question is: Why are these people who are so excited about this music only now being responded to? Why did it take so long?"

Though he sees no signs of it as yet, Allan Pepper worries that there is often a backlash when a perceived trend fails to sustain its highest high. With Morissette and Jewel selling millions of CDs, will pop moguls turn their back on women artists who fail to do as well?

"That's the danger here," he says, "that some people are viewed not on the basis of what they're producing, but of what gender they are."

Shindell sees nothing but good from all this, and lessons the male songwriters might be learning.

"I was just amazed at the intensity of some of Dar's audiences, " he says. "I watched them while she sang, and it was very moving. They knew every word; I could see them following everything she said and still being moved to tears. She really speaks to them and for them.

"I never considered myself a spokesman for any particular community other than people who appreciate a good song. But seeing what's happening with Dar has led me to want to find the thread that might weave my songs together. Is there a community I could be speaking for, a voice that needs my songs? I don't know the answer yet, but now I'm at least asking the question."

—November 30, 1997

Ferron: a songwriter's songwriter
Ferron, Emily Saliers of Indigo Girls, Shawn Colvin, Bill Morrissey

It seems that the lofty moniker "songwriter's songwriter" is bandied around pretty freely these days. Once it was reserved only for those meticulous, and often obscure, craftsmen such as Townes Van Zandt and Guy Clark, whose work was revered by their peers. Now it seems as if every ardent troubadour capable of remembering the lyrics on stage and spelling them correctly on the CD cover is getting dubbed a songwriter's songwriter by some pundit or press agent.

Ask the songwriters themselves, though, particularly those who ride the modern folk circuit, and a name sure to pop up is Ferron, a 42-year-old Canadian who has never had a hit record, rarely been covered by other singers, and has so far had a pretty bumpy career.

Emily Saliers of Indigo Girls says, "Ferron has an uncanny way of reminding us of what it means to be human." Shawn Colvin praises her ability to find "sympathy for what is hard, honesty for what is inevitable."

Cheryl Wheeler and Ferron

Longtime New England favorite Bill Morrissey, whose keenly sculpted lyrics have justly made him a songwriter's songwriter, said from his home, "Ferron does everything right; she chooses her words very carefully, understands people and situations well, writes passionately without overemoting, writes very visually, clearly means what she says." And in what seems his highest praise, he says firmly, "She shows, she doesn't tell."

Speaking from a Toronto tour stop, Ferron said, "Songwriting is a very condensed language. I've been lucky that I've had a few people over the years watching my work so that I can say the word 'mountain' and it means something. Now, I have no idea what you see when I say 'mountain.' And I don't want you to see what I see, I want you to see what you see. Because over time, when you see those images you begin to see more and more of you. This is what I've learned from people who write to me, that they go back and listen to a song and realize they're not even listening to me; they're retrieving something from inside them. Isn't that a riot? I mean, I think that is a fabulous thing."

Ferron is indeed a very visual songwriter, but she uses those images to connect us with deeply personal emotional and spiritual wanderings. In the soft, wise "Cactus," she describes her youthful obsession with life's dark side: "When I was young, I was in service to my pain. On sunny days you'd find me walking miles to look for rain."

Sung in a captivatingly husky, almost conversational voice, Ferron's songs have an uncanny way of being candid yet universal, introspective to the point of obscurity yet somehow able to resonate within our own experience. She attributes that first and foremost to her primary mission of telling her own truth as purely as she can; also to staying in touch with her listeners, and to her determination to leave enough space in the lyrics for us to fill in our lives and feelings.

"I think the deal is, I get to write songs because I have to, otherwise I just can't live. And the deal is that they are personal enough to mean something, and vague enough that another person can listen and see their own story.

"That's one of the reasons I haven't made a video. I don't want to fill in the blanks with my pictures. After I saw Tracy Chapman's video of 'Fast Car,' with the chain-link fence, I can't hear the song without seeing that fence. There's a real power in the visual. I think the reason we love to read, or at least used to love to read, was because you could see it all your own way. I still care about that."

Particularly since "Driver" was picked up by Earthbeat, which is distributed by Warner/Elektra/Asylum, it has been touted as a potential breakthrough disc for Ferron. She doesn't know about such things, she says, dryly adding that "Driver" is her sixth consecutive "breakthrough" recording.

People in the folk and women's music world have always touted her as a potential breakthrough star, but she has always guided her career to suit her personal goals and to serve the honesty, ideals and human commitment that make her music so ultimately ennobling. At one point, she took nearly six years off to, as she put it, "be sure I was serving the right thing."

"I don't know what the public wants," she said. "I mean, I don't know if they want somebody really young with ripped jeans and not knowing where they're going in life. I don't think that's what's happening with me, but people like that sell in the millions, so I don't know what breakthrough means. Breaking through to what?

"I'm so out of touch with all that. I don't think I'm in service to a pop song. I might not even be in the music business, there's every possibility that I am not. But whatever it is, it's what I do, I like to do it, and people seem to like it. It finally occurred to me that, even if only a thousand people like it, that's fine. So if breakthrough means people might say that's she's a consistent and integrated writer, then that's nice."

—September 30, 1994

Cutting a career to fit her life Patty Larkin

Album titles don't have to make sense. As a result, they are often places where artists have some fun with us, cooking up daffy non sequiturs, clever puns, or funny one-liners. But leave it to Patty Larkin, among the most vivid and succinct of today's folk-pop songwriters, to offer a three-word autobiography for her stunning new Vanguard CD: "Regrooving the Dream."

"I had it as a working title even before I wrote the song that has it," she said. "It was just about reinventing myself, starting with a new record company, the crises that led up to that. During a transitional period like that, you think about what's important to you, why you do what you do, and what impact the next thing you do is going to have on your life."

Larkin has remained a consistently popular and respected songwriter for 20 years but never achieved the mainstream success her thousands of fans—and her consummate skill—have long suggested she deserves.

A troubled six-year stint at Windham Hill/High Street never broke her through to national stardom, despite her songs being recorded by Holly Cole and Cher and featured in hit films such as "Random Hearts," starring Harrison Ford, and "Sliding Doors," with Gwyneth Paltrow. When High Street folded in 1998, she found herself sadly knocking on record label doors again.

But Larkin never writes songs merely to hear herself whine. On "Regrooving the Dream," she turns the recent tumult of her career into parables for anyone in times of crisis and change, making the entire CD feel like an intimate symphony,

When I thought realistically about what I've done and still get to do, I saw myself in this whole tradition of traveling performers, which is where I always wanted to be. —Patty Larkin

a deeply felt and musically gorgeous ode to human resilience.

Stardom may have eluded Larkin because she defies the accepted norm for the female songwriter. She seems closer to the school of guitar-driven writers personified by Richard Thompson or Bruce Cockburn and normally thought of as a male approach to the genre. She was quick to point out, correctly, that Joni Mitchell is very much of that school, as are a growing number of female writers, such as Shawn Colvin and Ani DiFranco.

"I think of myself as a guitar- focused writer, certainly, but I think of myself as a songwriter first," she said. "I find that a lot of people come to my shows because of the guitar playing. Still, the instrumentals I do are sometimes a way for me to say, `You know, I play.' But my focus is having the two blend, so that the guitar is integral to what I'm singing."

She has never done that better than on "Regrooving the Dream." It is an aural masterpiece, songs beginning with alluring licks or tight guitar pulses, which lay an emotionally eloquent carpet for the coming lyric. The bewitchingly complex yet spacious arrangements do not interrupt melodic statements so much as wash up and over them, like water over stones.

Larkin is that rare modern songwriter who sings about mature adult life. "Only One" is a bravely confidential still-in-love song, a celebration of the kind of relationship only couples who have been thoroughly raked over each other's coals—and stuck around to heal the wounds—can know. "You're the only one who is on to me," she sings in an adoring, primally sexual whisper.

But the CD is dominated by songs about people enduring hard changes, sometimes coming through to better times, often just settling for what's left on life's table. It all resolves in "Lost and Found," a wise and tender lullaby for grown-ups. "I'd like to apologize for the world/ Being what it is," it begins, later admitting "No one can save you/ From trials and demons/ Nobody knows what you see." But each tough-eyed verse opens, like flowers after grim winter, into the sweeping chorus, "When all of your dreams come crashing down/ And you stand at the door of the lost and found/ Who loves you now?"

Larkin's regrooving started with Vanguard. They wooed her by being the first label to talk about her career as it was already happening, not something she could have if she played her cards right. Like a character in one of her own songs, she suddenly saw her life for what it was instead of what it might have been.

"This is it, this is the career I'm having and I've embraced it completely," she said. "You know, 35 years ago, 500-seat halls were where Jefferson Airplane played. This whole idea of arena-rock and selling 20 million records the first week is brand new in the history of music. And it doesn't interest me. Playing medium-sized halls, having that immediacy with an audience and the music, is a great way to make a living.

"When I thought realistically about what I've done and still get to do, I saw myself in this whole tradition of traveling performers, which is where I always wanted to be. I feel really excited about the music, because I realize that's all there is, that's all that's important, being able to make music and share it with people who care about it. This is the kind of realization—regrooving the dream instead of getting a new one—that we all have to go through as we get older, realizing what's good about where you are and building up from that."

—November 4, 2000

A master builder of songs
Richard Shindell

When critics praise the work of Richard Shindell, you would think they were discussing an architect or master carpenter, not a songwriter. The New York Times called him a "lapidary craftsman." The Village Voice praised his "endless invention and variation," and Billboard his "eloquent songcraft."

These workmanlike words come easily to mind in the presence of Shindell's exquisitely chiseled, honestly emotional songs. For years, he has been among the most respected of today's new folk songwriters and seems on the verge of gaining the wider audience his peers have long thought he deserves. His brilliant new Shanachie CD, "Reunion Hill," is enjoying brisker sales and heavier radio play than his previous two, and he was warmly received on a fall tour with hot folk star Dar Williams.

Joan Baez sang three of his songs on her new CD, "Gone from Danger," and brought him on her recent world tour, reminding many how she similarly anointed Bob Dylan in the '60s. Even she described his songs in craft terms, Shindell recalled, telling him she liked how "precise" they were.

"It is important to me that people notice I take great care in making sure a song is well put together," he said. "It's what I strive for, but at the same time, I wouldn't want to focus too much on craftiness as distinct from the emotion or actual substance of the songs. It's one thing to be known as craftsmanlike, but that's just part of it. There are crafty songwriters out there whose songs do nothing for me, because they're missing life or empathy or real human emotions."

Shindell is a master builder of songs, yet always leading listeners toward the emotional essence of the moment or character he is evoking. In his CD's title cut, which he wrote for Baez, a widow wanders "Reunion Hill," where a mighty army once gathered and swept her husband away. With hushed lyrics and a plaintively pretty melody, he remembers the tragedy through her eyes, but never reveals exactly what happened there, which army passed by, or even what war it was. It is the interior epic he is concerned with, the emotion of this one moment in the life of this one lonely woman. As with all master craftsmen, knowing what to leave out is as important to him as what he puts in.

"I don't need to give everybody all the details," he said, "because that's not what the song is about. The song is about the people. I'm not trying to make great points about great historical events; I'm focusing on individuals. If things are too specific, the universality is obscured. I try to leave each song as open as possible so people can read themselves into it. I want them to climb into the moment of a song, the way I did when I wrote it. That's why I sing in the first person, even when it's somebody else I'm singing about. I have to be able to be inside the character in order to really believe in a song I'm singing. The people I'm lucky to have as listeners are the kind of people who also want to do that."

Shindell has an uncanny sense of the theater of a song, building his ballads sparely and subtly, set to sweeping, graceful melodies. His timeless sound is superbly displayed on "Reunion Hill," thanks in large part to his lovely guitar work and the gorgeous instrumental accompaniment of producer Larry Campbell, who also has played fiddle and guitar with Dylan, Tracy Chapman, and k.d. lang.

The process of whittling his songs to such sheer essence is excruciating for Shindell. Parents fearing their children may pursue careless lives as songwriters should send them to him.

"I do not like the process of writing songs," he said. "It's not fun. The beginning is hell; I hate it. I feel like an idiot, because I can't think of anything; and when I do, it's not good. I censor myself with constant negative reinforcement and go for long stretches without writing anything, only to pick up the pen when I can't stand myself any longer for not at least trying to do what I'm allegedly doing for a living."

Songs take anywhere from a few weeks to a couple of years for Shindell, partly because, once they truly take form, his pure love of the process overwhelms his dread of it.

"I heard Sammy Cahn on the radio once talking about tidying up a song," he said. "I thought, what a wonderful way to look at it; that you spend time at the end tidying up, moving a line here or there, changing a word. And I do; I obsess at the end of a song, for weeks sometimes, about little, tiny things. I love that moment; it's my favorite part of writing a song. Near the end when you know it's going to be OK, it's going to work, but you just prolong the process, the way you do when you're reading a good book and you don't want it to end. I'll take lots of time to tinker with it. That's perhaps what gets translated into my appearing crafty as a songwriter, but it's really because I just don't want to finish it; I don't want to let it go."

—*January 9, 1998*

Geoff Bartley's *hard-traveled road*

Legendary Scottish folk singer Archie Fisher became such a fixture around his native Edinburgh that a friend once told him, "You'll never be famous, Archie; everybody knows ya.' "

That, in a nutshell, may be Geoff Bartley's problem. The 48-year-old guitarist, bluesman, and songwriter has been a respected fixture on the Boston folk scene for more than 25 years, regarded among his peers as a preeminent guitarist and songwriter. But broader national recognition has eluded him.

After several years that produced only a few homemade cassettes, last year Bartley released "Hear That Wind Howl," a tour de force CD of traditional blues. He's followed it with an equally stunning, deeply intelligent, and beautiful CD of original songs called "One Kind Word" (both on Magic Crow).

Tom Paxton always tries to get Bartley as sideman when he visits New England. In Paxton's 40-year career, he has been accompanied by the world's best pickers, such as Eric Weissberg and Pete Kennedy, and ranks Bartley high among them.

"I love playing with him," he said. "He has the technical chops to play whatever is needed, but he never overplays. Geoff always puts the song number one, himself a distant second. That's true in his writing as well; it's so economical, so un-showy. He's remarkable."

Bartley's guitar work always complements the emotional message of a song. Even his instrumentals tell stories. "Lemonade," on "Hear That Wind Howl," is a sweet, innocent memory of summer days. On the new CD, "Snowfall" wonderfully evokes the quiet, fat-flaked snows of early winter.

"The guitar talks for me," he said. "It's a way of expressing the inexpressible. You sing a line that has a literal meaning, but there are other meanings, too. The guitar helps create context, and then the lyrics have even a deeper, more complex, multilevel meaning. Which is the way the human experience is; things are not linear, nature is chaotic. I might try to remind listeners of that by adding voicings that are ambiguous; notes that are implied but not played."

It is that kind of insight that has earned him respect among songwriters as a master builder of song. John Gorka collaborated with him on "Raven in the Storm" and "Cut by Wire" on Bartley's new CD.

"He has a great sense of structure, of how songs should be put together," Gorka said. "Every note has a purpose, and his songs are always thoughtful, going in interesting directions."

For all his mastery, Bartley writes wonderfully simple songs, molding melodic ideas from traditional ballad and blues forms, his lyrics from the natural world around him. In the spoken and sung meditation "Natural Law," he says, "I need peace and sunlight like a dolphin needs sky/ Breathe in blue, breathe out red/ And

The guitar talks for me. It's a way of expressing the inexpressible. You sing a line that has a literal meaning, but there are other meanings, too. The guitar helps create context, and then the lyrics have even a deeper, more complex, multilevel meaning. —Geoff Bartley

I would sleep deep down beneath every language/ Where old memories come like stones rising in a lake."

"I'm afraid sometimes that people are going to say, this is too simple; this guy is a farmer," Bartley said. "But so much about the natural world is what has informed my sense of beauty, order, values. I feel that the natural world is the source for our definitions of beauty and justice and morality, and that we become very lost if that connection is taken away."

While the recognition Bartley still frankly craves eludes him, he has become a precious resource in the folk world; a reluctant but gifted graybeard who is both an inspiration and a mentor to new writers who seek his approval at his Monday night open stage and Tuesday bluegrass jam in the Cantab Lounge.

Gorka said, "I think Geoff has been very successful on a human and artistic level in what he's done with his music. What he's given goes beyond anything you could put a price tag on. Young performers see in him how much there is to learn about music and performing; that it's not just an image you project."

Bartley constantly wrestles with the dark face of his ambitions and an often deep depression that his halting career has bred in him. Increasingly, however, he is refusing to let that intrude on his talent, and, whether tearing off a hot folk blues or singing a tender meditation of his own, he is making the best music of his career.

"The last few years, I've been kind of lost," he said, "bouncing from this to that, trying to figure out how to live a good life. I don't want to lead a life that's empty and full of ego; I want meaning, fullness. But I have been very much in doubt about my career. Things have not worked out.

"But I know how to play guitar, and I really love words, and there are times when writing a song and singing it to an audience feels like the most meaningful and beautiful and orderly thing. You're emotionally inside the song, so that the ego starts to disappear and the song takes over. What comes out is the song's own tempo, not your own; and it becomes its own organism, with its own colors and rhythms, that you are sending out. It makes me feel full inside."

—*October 2, 1997*

Nanci Griffith *pays it all back*

For folk-pop star Nanci Griffith, sharing the spotlight is not merely a gesture; it's a way of life. Ever since the Texas-born songwriter's salad days touring the nation's coffeehouses in her beat-up Datsun, she has always given much of her stage time to singing the praises—and the songs—of writers who inspired her.

She is a major star now, singing at places like Symphony Hall, rather than the coffeehouses like Club Passim that helped launch her career. She has also written hits for country superstars Willie Nelson and Emmylou Harris, for Suzy Boggus and Kathy Mattea, and for Irish pop chanteuse Mary Black.

But whether appearing with symphony orchestras, on TV, or in large arenas, she still spends lavish amounts of time telling audiences about the songwriters who came before her, the lesser-known writers who labor in the small, subsistence fields of the modern folk world, and of the American folk tradition, from which she is so proud to have sprung. When she took the Crickets on tour with her recently, she was not content to let them be an opening act, but restructured her entire show to feature the now-obscure band that once backed Buddy Holly.

Rolling Stone dubbed her "the queen of folkabilly," referrring to a term she invented to describe her infectious marriage of pure folk strains and rockabilly rhythms. Telegraph magazine recently called her "the torch-bearer of American folk music," a mantle she says she wears happily and proudly.

Griffith's deep generosity and respect for her roots led her to record the Grammy-winning 1993 album "Other Voices, Other Rooms," in which she and an array of guest artists paid tribute to writers such as Bob Dylan, Tom Paxton, John Prine, and the late Kate Wolf by singing their songs. It remains one of the finest and most popular folk records of the decade, and fans have eagerly awaited its sequel, "Other Voices, Too (A Trip Back to Bountiful)," which will be released Tuesday on Elektra.

Fans of the first disc may be taken aback at first by the much more pop-fired, 19-cut sequel. After a few listens, though, its warm spirit and classic song selection will likely make it the same treasure the first one has become. Where the original was austerely acoustic in tone, this is a bright-hearted, rootsy stomp. Griffith calls it "a folk festival on record."

"This one's got so many more voices," she said from her Nashville home. "The cast is doubled. I also think [co-producer] Jim Rooney and I covered some different territory in folk history, that period from the late '50s through the '60s and early '70s, when folk music and rock 'n' roll kind of merged. There was a lot of overlap back then between folk and country and rock; nobody seemed to be afraid of being labeled anything."

Griffith said she knew early in the recording of the first "Other Voices" that a second one was called for, and made song decisions to heighten both the pure folk feel of the first and the rootsy folk-pop sound presented here. It features an all-star cast, including Emmylou Harris, Lyle Lovett, Rodney Crowell, Richard Thompson, Jerry Jeff Walker, Tom Rush, Odetta, and Ian Tyson of Ian and Sylvia fame, along with a host of less-well-known folk and country songwriters, such as Dave Van Ronk, Sonny Curtis of the Crickets, and Texas troubadours Guy Clark, Jimmie Dale Gilmore, Lucinda Williams, and Tom Russell.

Where even the best CDs may offer only a few truly special moments, this

There are a couple of people I've always wanted to be: Sylvia singing with Ian Tyson, Linda Thompson singing with Richard Thompson, and Sandy Denny singing with Richard. I got to do all that. —Nanci Griffith moves from highlight to highlight, as original authors trade verses with Griffith, and contemporary singers duet with their songwriting heroes. Sonny Curtis joins Griffith on a delightfully tender version of his "Walk Right Back," which, Griffith said, includes an obscure second verse not on the 1950s Everly Brothers hit, because they were too eager to record the song to wait for Curtis to finish it.

Seventy-year-old Nashville legend Harlan Howard, who wrote hits for Patsy Cline, speaks the coda to his plaintive "Streets of Baltimore," which John Prine masterfully sings, aided by lonely harmonies from Griffith. She said both she and Prine were afraid they would ruin Howard's take by sobbing when he spoke, but bit their lips and moved from the mike.

No song sums up the CD's playful spirit better than Griffith's wild and mirthful strut of Sylvia Fricker's '60s song "You Were on My Mind," which was a huge hit for We Five. Her voice is somehow girlish and wizened at once, evoking both the brokenhearted theme and defiant ebullience of the song.

She said recording this song was the hardest thing she has ever done in a studio. Despite its simple, direct melodic feel, the bridge modulates, or shifts key, on the word "bind."

"Susan Cowsill was singing with me, who had sung the song when she was 5 with the Cowsills, and it just sent the two of us to the floor with a piece of paper. Here I am, somebody who arranges harmony parts and writes string charts, and for the first time ever, I'm on the floor figuring out how to do this modulation. Emmylou Harris was there and just left the building, shaking her head and saying, 'Uh-uh, I can't watch this.' "

Another sort of storm arose when she invited songwriters Guy Clark, Jerry Jeff Walker, Jimmie Dale Gilmore, Steve Earle, Rodney Crowell, and Eric Taylor to swap verses on Clark's "Desperadoes Waiting for a Train." In this thick fog of testosterone, Walker and Earle commenced to quarrel over who got to sing the line, "And I was just a kid / They all called me sidekick."

"This time, I left the room," Griffith recalled with a chuckle. "Guy sorted it out, and Jerry Jeff won. I don't know how, because, usually, when Steve Earle sets his mind to something, he gets it. It was very funny to see these two grown, big men saying, 'I want to be the sidekick!' 'No, I've always been the sidekick!' I didn't care—I just sang what was left."

Actually, she didn't get a peep in until 2 minutes and 40 seconds into the song, which brings up the only real flaw in this wonderfully vital recording. It's a tough complaint to make, since the clubbiness of these sessions adds so much to the magic here, and many fans will love it all.

But the busy swapping of parts in some personal ballads, like "Desperadoes Waiting for a Train," diminishes the emotional empathy a lead vocal offers, leaving choral anonymity where a unifying personality is needed. Particularly in Woody

Guthrie's wrenching immigrant's lament "Deportees," the constantly changing vocals make it hard to feel the personal anguish the character is relaying. John Stewart, ordinarily a great singer, packs a whole song's worth of emotion into his couplet, which is way too much; and when Odetta moans the song's moral, she sounds more like a preacher sermonizing than like the victimized deportee.

A similar approach is a thumping success on the traditional "Wasn't That a Mighty Storm," where Griffith lets Tom Rush lead the 37-part chorus, and the line-swapping just adds to the fun. Likewise, Dave Van Ronk's bluesy growl leads "He Was a Friend of Mine," which he wrote with Eric Von Schmidt, who is also on hand. The big chorus, including Jean Ritchie, Odetta, and Rosalie Sorrells, crescendoes merrily, like the crowd at some midnight Greenwich Village hootenanny from the early '60s.

All the duets are superb. Griffith sings with Lucinda Williams on an archly pretty cover of Bob Ferguson's "Wings of a Dove." Her duet with Rodney Crowell on the old Johnny Cash hit "I Still Miss Someone" is a gentle tour de force.

In a fine tribute, Griffith had Tom Russell sing with her on his hero Ian Tyson's song "Summer Wages," and then had Tyson return the compliment by singing Russell's Tyson-inspired "Canadian Whiskey." Both cuts are sweeping and beautiful.

Griffith got her own hero-worship shots in, she said.

"There are a couple of people I've always wanted to be: Sylvia singing with Ian Tyson, Linda Thompson singing with Richard Thompson, and Sandy Denny singing with Richard. I got to do all that. Tom Russell, who's known me since I was in my teens, knew what it meant to me singing with Ian. He'd smile at me with this look of, `Well, you're finally getting to do it, kid.' Ian didn't understand what was going on when we only had to do one take of `Canadian Whiskey.' We'd never met before, and he was saying, `How is she matching my phrasing like that?' Well, I've been singing with him on his records all my life."

Despite the symphony of voices, Griffith's vocals shine, all the more so for the many styles she tackled. Like most Texans, she has something of an adaptable drawl, which she notches up or down as required: up to heat her phrasing for brisk tunes, down for more intricate and confidential ballads.

On Sandy Denny's demanding "Who Knows Where the Time Goes," she brilliantly walks the edge between Denny's desolate original and Judy Collins's more ethereal cover. Without surrendering the mystical allure of Collins's more familiar version, she delivers all the tragic, primal hurt in lines like "Sad deserted shore / Your fickle friends are leaving."

She is her most Griffith-esque on gentle, less familiar gems like the sad "Dress of Laces" and the bittersweet coming-of-age ballad "Yarrington Town," for which she had Emmylou Harris and Carolyn Hester sing with their daughters.

"Both of these records have been a dream come true for me, but this will certainly be the last volume," she said, "because nobody can forget the pain and the horror of trying to bring this many people together."

She laughed when she said that, but a little sadly, and her voice grew even more wistful as she discussed her future. It has not been easy being Nanci Griffith the last few years. She feels trapped by the demands of her career and deeply needs to slow down enough to let the music flow into her, as it did during her young days as a budding Texas songwriter. She said that this, her 15th record, would be her last for "a long time," and that it closed not just a chapter, but an entire volume in her life.

"I really want to be off the road," she said very quietly and with a palpable weariness, "to get into a different time for Nanci Griffith. I want to totally change things, and after the tour for this record, that's what I'll be doing. But I think it's important to give back, and this is my way of giving back to this industry that has been extremely kind and good to me, to give back to my audiences, and to pass this music on. I just think it's so important to do that."

—July 19, 1998

Cowboys, outlaws and poets:
the Texas songwriter revival
Guy Clark, Shawn Colvin, Ray Wylie Hubbard, Peter Rowan, Peter Keane

The Newport Folk Festival is in a Lone Star state of mind this year. There is a large posse of Texas pickers and songwriters on the bill, all leading to the first-ever appearance of country legend Willie Nelson. Among the other high-profile stars appearing are Shawn Colvin, Natalie Merchant, Mary Chapin Carpenter, Bela Fleck, and Dar Williams.

But partly to set the right mood for Nelson's appearance, Newport has invited a host of fellow Texans, including Guy Clark, the archetypal Texas songwriter to many, Peter Rowan and his Texas Trio, with Tony Rice, Ray Wylie Hubbard, Peter Keane, Slaid Cleaves, and Stacey Earle.

Country music superstar Willie Nelson at the Newport Folk Festival may seem like an odd combination, but he played a crucial role in reversing folk's decline following the 1960s revival, as ringleader of what was dubbed the outlaw movement of fiercely anticommercial country-folk writers like himself, Waylon Jennings, Jerry Jeff Walker, Clark, and Hubbard.

Shawn Colvin is to many the quintessential East Coast urban songwriter, but she saw the outlaw movement at its peak when she lived briefly in Austin in 1976.

She was so impressed, she moved back to Austin to start a family in 1995.

"There was a whole echelon of songwriter types who didn't seem to be beholden to anything that was trendy," she said of the '70s Austin scene. "Songwriting was a respected form in itself, going back to the balladeers and storytellers. And it still is. The Eastern Seaboard style is probably a little more intellectual, a little more literary, introspective. That's what urbaneness does, maybe, makes you want to go inside and find out who you are. Texas songwriters are bound to be looser, a little wilder, a little more colloquial. And there's much more of a sense of place; the landscape is a big part of the writing."

Texas may seem today like a place that has always had a thriving traditional music and songwriter scene, but folk music was in trouble there in the late '60s, as it was throughout the country with the waning of the commercial folk revival.

Guy Clark came up through the Houston folk scene of the '60s, learning at the feet of such blues legends as Lightnin' Hopkins and Mance Lipscomb, studying cowboy ballads at the Houston Folklore Society. He said that by the late '60s, the folk scene "got to be a little prissy, a little too precious for its own good. Man, it was getting as snooty as jazz; you know, if it's not just absolutely pure, collected from the fields and sung by John Jacob Niles, then it ain't folk music."

At the same time, commercial interest in folk was fading fast. But something exciting was bubbling underground in Austin. Charismatic Texas songwriter Michael Martin Murphy quite noisily left Los Angeles, where he seemed on the brink of national stardom, saying he needed to get back to his roots. With acoustic hits like "Texas Morning" and "Geronimo's Cadillac," he became the center of a rising storm of rebellion against the commercialism of folk-pop music. Soon he was joined by folk-based songwriters Jerry Jeff Walker, B. W. Stevenson, and Ray Wylie Hubbard, whose raucous "Up Against the Wall, Redneck Mother" became an early anthem of the movement.

"There was quite a folk music scene in Austin before Willie came," Hubbard said. "There was a whole bunch of folk singers like Murphy and Jerry Jeff, and all of a sudden people started using bands and playing clubs. Everybody was getting record contracts, filling clubs; there was such a camaraderie to it."

In 1972, Nelson sent shock waves through Nashville by moving to Austin, proclaiming country music hopelessly corrupted by its own commercialism. This was no dismissible folk renegade like Murphy or Walker. No writer in Nashville had the mainstream credentials Nelson did, as the writer of breakthrough hits for crossover country stars Patsy Cline and Ray Price. When Nelson (who declined to be interviewed about his Newport appearance) grew his hair long and moved to Austin, what had been a localized songwriter boom became a bona fide cultural movement.

"It seemed to make it all legitimate," Hubbard said of Nelson's move to Austin.

...by the late '60s, the folk scene got to be a little prissy, a little too precious for its own good. Man, it was getting as snooty as jazz; you know, if it's not just absolutely pure, collected from the fields and sung by John Jacob Niles, then it ain't folk music. —Guy Clark

"The hippie folk people just loved him, and when he started doing his annual picnics, these big outdoor festivals, it started to feel like a real movement. He'd have hip young guys like Kris Kristofferson and Billy Joe Shaver play, but he'd have these old country stars, too, like Floyd Tillman and Ernest Tubb. It was remarkable to see beer-gut cowboys in the same crowd with these tie-dyed hippie girls. It made it OK for all of us to like each other's music."

That unlikely coalition of country music rednecks and unrepentant hippies, then called cosmic cowboys, fueled the outlaw movement. No one is quite sure how that term came to define the revival, but Clark said it always referred more to the anticommercialism of the music than anything else.

"It applied to the music industry mostly, to not doing the mainstream thing, the string arrangements and that slick, overproduced sound Nashville was using back then. This was a raw, wild, rocking sound; Telecaster cowboys was another term they used back then, named from the Fender electric guitar."

The outlaw movement became nationally famous, fizzling out, as most such grassroots revivals do, when it became too popular, too imitated. By the time it fueled the urban cowboy fad of the late '70s, it had become a parody of itself. But by then it had done much to restore the underground luster of folk music and of the singer-songwriter. Like the Texas songwriters, folkies all over the country began to wear their un-commercialism as a badge of honor, and the stage was set for similarly rebellious folk and songwriter revivals in the '80s and '90s.

Peter Keane came up through the Boston folk scene of the '80s, but found his rootsy approach to songwriting did not fit the urbane template of the Boston songwriter. Moving to Austin in the mid-1990s ignited his career. He said there are deep-rooted reasons that city remains such a vibrant music center.

"Music is more a part of the fabric of life here. You can walk into so many restaurants, bars, and barbecue joints and find live music. You go to cities like Boston and New York and find a lot of people who say music's just not something they do. Not here. Music is on everybody's radar screen in Austin. Any Joe on the street has their favorite local acts they go to see."

Colvin said, "There's a big dance-hall scene with bands doing the same dances they were doing 100 years ago. Traditional music doesn't come and go in Texas the way it does in some other places, so even if you're some cutting-edge original songwriter, it's not beneath you at all to go to the Broken Spoke and do the two-step to the Derailers."

To instrumental wizard and songwriter Peter Rowan, who was born in Wayland, that unbroken tradition defines the Texas music personality. He now lives outside Austin, in a little town called Blanco, just a stone's throw from the old Chisolm Trail.

"Right up the road from where I live, every weekend there's bands I've never heard of in my life playing two-steps and polkas and waltzes," he said. "There's still a remnant of neighborliness and individualism that helps combine into the Texas personality. You bump into somebody outside the post office, you're liable to have an hour conversation, because people just like to visit down there. And language is not just functional in Texas; it's also a celebration of poetic terms. People still talk country, still talk Texas."

"You spend time there and you can't help but feel it somewhere along the line. You eat enough of that Mexican food, feel that sense of place, and that big old sun takes such a long time to get across the sky. Suddenly it's like a click inside you that happens, and you realize you're on a different time zone. It's a wide, deep groove; like [Lone Star rock icon] Doug Sahm used to say, Texas is a groover's paradise. And that all reflects in the music, all mixes together like a good Texas chili—some spice, some sweet, some beans, and some good, honest meat."

—July 30, 2000

photo: Jackie Ahlstrom

The tangled roots of the cowboy
Connie Dover, Skip Gorman

There may be no music that Americans think of as more uniquely their own than that of the 19th-century cowboy. But like all American folk repertoires, it is a child of mixed blood. Ancient Irish and Scottish ballads about shipwrecks, saucy sailors, and fair lassies became plaintively simple songs about stampeding cattle, dying cowboys who knew they'd done wrong, and wistful senoritas waiting. Fiery Celtic fiddle tunes were relaxed by the lazy gait of the cattle trail, sweetened and spiced by Hispanic influences, and reinvigorated by the robust frail of the African-American banjo.

Few American artists understand the Celtic roots of cowboy music better than Missouri singer Connie Dover and New Hampshire fiddler-guitarist-singer Skip Gorman.

Dover is among the most respected American-born singers of Irish and Scottish ballads. Her three beautiful Taylor Park CDs were produced by Scottish music legend Phil Cunningham, and feature such Celtic all-stars as Manus Lunny, Christy O'Leary, and Aly Bain.

Gorman is one of the most savvy and authentic cowboy folk artists in the country. His two Philo CDs of traditional cowboy songs and fiddle tunes are at once plain-spun and sweepingly lovely. The two met in 1992, singing around prairie campfires at the 90,000-acre High Island Ranch in Wyoming, which invites people to work an authentic 19th-century cattle drive during the summers. She had just launched a solo career after years singing for the Celtic band Scartaglen.

"I started hearing songs around the campfire that were very much like the Scottish and Irish songs I'd been singing," she said. "It was clear these songs were connected, that the musical cultures weren't that varied. When you actually stand around a campfire in Wyoming and hear old Nate Brown from Grass Creek sing a song you heard an Irish traditional singer do on an old recording—but Nate's singing about a cowboy—you see how this music traveled and adapted to suit the lives of people."

Gorman said: "So many of the actual working cowboys were of Irish descent, fresh from fighting the Civil War and working on the railroad. These were the guys who had the gift of gab, the poetry, the sweet songs—and that all poured into cowboy culture. Add to that the black guys who wandered into the cow camps after the Civil War—with their work songs and field hollers and spirituals and bringing the banjo with them—and it made for some pretty powerful music."

These cowboys were also influenced by the music they heard from the Hispanic-Americans with whom they lived and worked, often adding an alluring forward lilt to the languid pace of the ballads. But Gorman said the Celtic influence is everywhere.

"When I studied the fiddle tunes the cowboys played, I started retuning my fiddle, using cross-tunings the way they used to. A lot of these guys didn't know how to play the fiddle, so they'd tune it up low, with these haunting drone sounds that reminded them of the bagpipes they heard in the old country."

Dover's approach to both Celtic balladry and cowboy songs is rivetingly austere: Her pure soprano floats from melody note to melody note, concluding in clear, open sustains, where Celtic vocal tradition is based on line-ending ornamentation and emotional midline trills. Just as experiencing the rigors of trail life affected Gorman's fiddle, it influenced her singing.

"I was singing outside every night, around a campfire at high altitudes, in a stiff wind, after having hauled water, built fires, ridden horses, and cooked since about 4 in the morning. My voice got stronger, and I think it also made what I sing a little simpler. Sometimes ornaments get lost in the prairie; you don't want to waste your energy on grace notes."

She said her austere style began with a desire to never sound like she was trying to imitate Irish or Scottish singers, to never, as she put it, "brogue up" her voice. As she experienced a taste of cowboy life, and when she read old diaries and letters by frontier folk, she came to embrace that simplicity as a hallmark of the American folk style.

"I just sing what's pleasing to my ear while trying to remain true to the spine of the song," she said. "But there is some part of me that is maybe tearing away the gossamer a little. I think maybe I'm willing to strip away a few layers of gauze and look at these songs in their essences: simple, clear, and authentic, the music of real people, just as the music of the American frontier was. So I'm less inclined to window-dress and to just let the stark simplicity and beauty of what's offered in the song shine through. It was those embellishments and ornamentations that got left aside as people traveled west, just as they threw their good china and teapots out the back of the wagon but kept their wooden bowls. They left their piano by the side of the trail but remembered the songs."

—November 27, 1998

Solas: *The birth of America's best Irish band*
Seamus Egan, Winifred Horan, Karan Casey

The noise came before a note was played. No Irish band in recent memory has had its coming so loudly trumpeted. Before they had ever stepped on stage as Solas, the young quintet of Seamus Egan, Winifred Horan, Karan Casey, John Williams and John Doyle was being almost universally touted as the Next Big Thing in Irish music. Before the release of their first Shanachie CD, the New-York-based band was heralded as "among the most exciting bands anywhere in the world" by the Irish Echo; "The first truly great Irish band to arise from America" by the Boston Herald; and "an Irish traditional band bearing all the marks of greatness" by the influential Irish critic Earle Hitchner—and this in the Wall Street Journal, if you please.

Their performing debut was at Georgetown University, in a fete sponsored by respected folklorist-musician Mick Moloney; their second appearance before a public radio audience of millions at a 4th of July folk festival broadcast from the mall in Washington, D.C. They did not disappoint.

Now sporting their second Shanachie CD, the entirely lovely "Sunny Skies and Scattered Showers," Solas is bringing exciting youthful passion, a globe-spanning compositional elegance and sophisticated urban savvy to Irish traditional music, but in ways that seem to be pleasing nearly everybody. They are the rare modern folk band equally welcome at very traditional folk festivals and urbane nightclubs. At the heart of their success, and of their exhilarating, gorgeous sound, is a deep and abiding respect for the wild grace of ancient Irish melody. Unlike many more experimental folk bands, they never make the tune or the song bend to fit the whims of modern ideas or technology. Quite the opposite.

"We're never intentionally trying to change the music," said fiddler Winifred Horan, whose classically-informed ideas add graceful counterpoint and harmony to the group's arrangements. "We're all thinking counterpoints and what could go underneath or on top, but never to detract from the main melody. We're just trying to make it a little more appealing or beautiful, but we're constantly thinking about what came before us. We often refer back to where it's come from in making our decisions. With us, it's the music first. We're never coming to show off, never coming just to show we can be different. It's always the music first, definitely the music first. That's the motto."

"We're there to serve the song, you know," said vocalist Karan Casey, "the song isn't there to serve our egos. And that's a tricky balance, because obviously our ego is involved. But I think if we just think of the song and what it says to the audience, we'll be kept in our place."

That almost militant humility is just one of the characteristics these young traditional masters have carried with them from their years of training in Irish music and dance. In so many ways, they are the product, the legacy, of generations of dedicated teachers and cultural activists who devoted their lives to preserving Irish culture, both in Ireland and North America.

All of Solas, except guitar and mando-cello player John Doyle, cut their musical teeth in the many competitions Irish cultural organizations like the Gaelic Athletic Association, Gaelic League and Comhaltas Ceoltori Eireann sponsored to lure youngsters away from their radios, record players and televisions in the 1940s and '50s. It may have been a trick—using the shiny lures of trophies and bragging-rights to bribe children to study traditional music and dance—and many have criticized the notion that such precious things as tradition should be ejudicated like horse races or spelling bees.

But it worked. It has given Ireland new generations of savvy, impassioned players and dancers. Despite what your thoughts might be about the commercial sheen of *Riverdance*, it is a remarkable concept; one few other cultures could even attempt. They have been able to draw from tens of thousands of teen-agers who know ancient Irish step dance from the heels up; strictly trained in the rigorous rudiments of traditional dance.

The musicians in Solas are, in some essential ways, traditional musicians at heart. They learned the old music in the old ways; orally, by example, from master musicians and teachers, beginning when they were seven and eight years old.

And they learned to play, sing and dance in rudimentary, disciplined ways. The competitions are judged by very strict criteria, for which they are often and roundly criticized. But these kids learn their chops.

Seamus Egan won All-Ireland Championships on four separate instruments—flute, tin whistle, banjo and mandolin—all by the time he was 15. He bristled at times at the stringent judging criteria, and came to intensely dislike the whole notion of music as competition. As with other members of the band, it contributes to a an attitude of almost fierce self-effacement in the group's personality. None wants to be seen as a show-offy or tricky player. Still, Egan thanks the competitions for both his technical mastery and for his deeply ingrained understanding of the music.

"There's such a tremendous focus on technique," he said. "That got me minding the technical aspects of the music. But to some degree, the competitions could be very rigid, to a point where it made me want to hear more, to be open to more; to hear the music in some different ways. But certainly the benefit of growing up in the competition atmosphere was the motivation to get your technical skills developed. And certainly it helps you play it however you want to when you understand it from the ground up that way. You can do different things with it then, expand it, because you have sort of an understanding of the inner-workings of it. That allows you to do some things naturally, almost instinctually."

It was evident from Egan's first recording, a Shanachie record released when he was just 16, that he was struggling to hear Irish music in more complex, compositionally structured ways. But he has always been strikingly melody-driven; drawn more to slow airs and long-lined graceful tunes than to quick, brisk acrobatic numbers. No matter how quickly he is playing, he seems always to be mindful of how a melody breathes, finding sweet ways to lay gentle musical boughs beneath it, airy trills above. From his first recordings, he remained entirely faithful to the music's timeless melodic grace, even in his own pieces; but increasingly his ideas were becoming sophisticated, informed by jazz and classical compositional techniques. The results were often sweeping, almost cinematic in their texture.

It was precisely that quality that drew director Ed Burns to use Egan's music entirely for the soundtrack of his acclaimed sleeper-hit, "The Brothers McMullen." How this happened is a remarkable story of good luck and good deeds being rewarded. Egan's soundtrack success came entirely by accident, through the providence of a broken-down van.

Egan was appearing on the "Young Turks of the Banjo" tour in 1993 with Tony Furtado and Dirk Powell when their van broke down in Connecticut. A nice couple who had been at the show offered to put them up until the van was fixed. As a thank-you gift, Egan left his 1990 Shanachie record, "A Week in January," behind.

Some time later, the couple's son, who was on the "Brothers McMullen" crew, mentioned the director was having trouble finding the right music for the soundtrack. He wanted something very Irish, traditional-sounding, but with a certain modern orchestral texture. They suggested Egan's record. Ed Burns ended up using Egan's music entirely for the film.

By that time, Egan was working frequently with Winifred Horan, who had joined the delightful Irish women's ensemble Cherish the Ladies as a dancer, but soon became its fiddler, replacing Eileen Ivers when she moved on to her sparkling solo career.

Horan had also grown up in the competition life, winning nine North American dance championships at the annual Oireachtas contests, under the tutelage of Brooklyn teaching legend Danny Golden. As her musical passion for the fiddle grew, however, her father urged her to receive formal classical training; not out of any disdain for Irish music, but so she would have the skills and education to follow her muse wherever it called her.

But classical music did draw her away from her Irish roots. She attended the New England Conservatory, graduated in violin and prepared for an orchestral career. A short-lived but severe bout of tendonitis, as though sent by some ancient Celtic god to rescue her, sent her back to New York, and she began attending Irish sessiuns, where players gather informally at pubs to share tunes. The amount of classical training she had can be fatal to a traditional career, but even deeper in Horan was her training in traditional music; particularly its ancient pulse, which had entered her through the dance. Still, at first her classical training blocked the older instincts.

"My ears had developed in a different way," she recalled. "I had become dependent on sight-reading. I'd be able to sit in a sessiun for 10 hours if I had my book in front of me, you know? But my ears had closed up; not to the beauty of it, but to the ability to follow a tune instinctively. The technical part wasn't difficult to get back, but I was so far removed from the traditional-ness of things—ornaments and the difference between Sligo style and Clare style. And Seamus was the one who made me aware of that."

Egan met Horan in the New York sessiun scene. She remembered awkward moments when, unable to pick up the sense of a tune but wanting to contribute something, she would lay in some low, viola-like chordings. Some would scowl at her, the sessiun ethic being for everybody to play in unison. Egan, however, was fascinated by her rich textures, the classically informed splashes of mood and color she added. He also knew she had to get her traditional chops up to speed again, and sent her a tape of "10 tunes you MUST know." Like a born teacher, he rewarded her quick mastery of those ten with a tape of another ten, then

Solas, 2002 line-up

another.

He also challenged her to begin playing gigs with him. He would also often bring in guitarist John Doyle, with whom he was playing in the inventive Irish folk-rock band Chanting House. With his long-lined chordal pulse anchoring the rhythms, the nucleus of Solas was in place, though none was thinking about a band. Horan was soon off with Cherish the Ladies, but they played together whenever they were all in town.

"I tend to hear the countermelody first, before even the melody," Horan said, explaining her approach to building arrangements. "When somebody plays a tune, I immediately start hearing what can go under or on top of it. And then John will start hearing longer lines that can be supporting. That's the key word: *supporting*, never going beyond that to where it overwhelms."

"I think the classical background helped me with that. You can listen to any good symphony or concerto, and there's lots of things going on in the orchestral background, the undercurrents, that never, never detract. It adds to it, propels it; it should always push the piece forward, never pull it back or ride on top of it. I love playing that role; it's very comforting to me. Sometimes I can actually hear something lift when the right line comes in underneath; I love that feeling."

The three enjoyed playing with Chicago Irish music sensation John Williams, who had many of the same chordal ideas about his button-accordion and concertina playing; and was in great demand for his ability not only to rip off a dizzyingly quick solo, but to offer rich support. The four are all present on Seamus Egan's "Brother's McMullen" work, and appeared together at the Lowell Folk Festival in 1994. Their sets there felt so good to them that they began thinking about forming a group.

Master instrumentalists all, however, none wanted to proceed without a singer to anchor the sound.

"I don't know if we would have ever formed a group if we hadn't found Karan," Egan said. "Having a singer, and the right singer, was one of the most important ingredients. It gives you so much more opportunity for material, and exploring the arrangements of songs is every bit as challenging as trying to play the tunes. The way you're sort of reared in Irish music, learning all the tunes, you really don't come round to playing with songs until you've played for a bunch of years. You have this one particular way of playing ingrained in your mind—at a session, you're sort of just barreling ahead, with everybody trying to play the same thing. But accompanying songs is a different kettle of fish altogether. You're trying to find something that makes sense musically, but doesn't detract from the story or the singer."

That problem is even more pointed in Irish music. Traditionally, most singing was done unaccompanied; both the intricate sean nos ballad style and the freer, chorus-driven folk songs. Melodies are created with instrumental portions already built in as vocal ornamentation. "The trick," Egan said, "is to create interludes without making them a distraction."

Karan Casey was the perfect singer for Solas. Horan said the first time they heard her, singing with Atlantic Bridge at a festival, both she and Egan snapped their heads toward the distant stage and hurried over to hear her. It is impossible to capture in words, but there is a sandy silkiness to her airy soprano that billows with much the same rounded texture Egan's flute does; and a deep resonance to her lower notes that reverberates with much the haunting timbre of Horan's low, droning chords. More than that, though, with her own jazz and classical background, Casey had long wrestled with how to sing these old songs to the groove of more contemporary rhythms—without disturbing the intricacy or delicate wildness of the melodies.

"I think in jazz I learned to lay back a bit, a bit off the beat, and to relax," she said of her years singing in various jazz groups. "I tried to learn things like Ella Fitzgerald and Sarah Vaughan solos. With jazz, so much of it is about rhythm; there's more emphasis on how you say things time-wise. So I suppose that must have creeped in somewhat."

As a child in Country Waterford, Casey competed in vocal contests sponsored by the Gaelic Athletic Association, coming into contact with the locally well-known Foran family of singers and cultural activists. They helped instill not only a love of the old songs, but the traditional singer's unshakable belief that the song comes first. This, above all, made her the perfect singer for Solas. Her shimmeringly pretty soprano seems always to be just telling the song's story; her deceptively elaborate trills and soaring ornamentation always in service to the song.

"I tend to be very dramatic at times," she said, "so sometimes at rehearsals the lads'll be looking at me, like, *Jeezus*, you oughta be on *Broadway*! But any hint of pretentiousness just shines through in this music. The melodies are so strong, the lyrics have lasted so long. I think it's fascinating that they've lasted, that they can come down from generation to generation to still be here, intact. I just think it's brilliant, you know? Really brilliant."

Speaking of what made Casey right for Solas, Egan said, "She has the quality of voice I've always enjoyed listening to, sort of high but strong. And she knows how to sing, she doesn't gesture with her voice. She's certainly placing emotion into the song with her interpretation, but she's not in any way bludgeoning the point. If it's a good song, people are going to know what it's about."

Another thing Casey brings the group is a fiery populist voice.

She said, "I dislike when a singer—and it's become so popular—is just involved in his or her love life;

whether or not they're in love or out of love or how many times they've been heartbroken. I just think there's so much more to love and to life than that, and so many other things that can be spoken about in song." I try always to do a song that will talk about the conflict in Ireland, that takes colonialism in Ireland or imperialism and discusses it in what I consider to be a progressive way. Then I'll try to do songs that have women in a good light or are sensitive to women's stories, that are enlightening about women. And, you know, I suppose I like to do a few weird ones, too; I like ghost songs, ones that are a bit quirky. Just different kinds of things, and that's certainly all there in the traditional repertoire. It's amazing when you start to delve into it, all the little strange goings-on that people have thought to make a song about."

While she finds sharply modern themes in the old songs: portraits of women heroines and bold Irish rebels, wise and foolish lovers —and she certainly sings her fair share of good ol' love-gone-wrong songs—she never is at odds with the oldness of the old songs. She never seems to be trying to give folk songs a modern swing or twist. She loves them for just what they are. That palpable fondness shows in her wonderful way of wrapping herself around the quaintness of old phrases like *"When Jimmy set a-sailing, lovely Nancy stood a-wailing"* or *"Their love it is tempestuous as the wavering wind"* from "Adieu, Lovely Nancy," which closes the new Solas CD. She embraces the sweet archaic charm of the lyrics, able to have some warm fun with them without ever seeming to be condescending, cloying or precious. She attributes much of that quality to one of her mentors, folk singer Frank Harte, who taught her to appreciate the old elegance of the songs.

"I love lines like those in "Adieu, Lovely Nancy," she said. "I just think they had great ways of saying things. I mean, I really do like it—I don't just think it's quaint or old; I appreciate that other people have other ways of saying things, and they're to be valued. I get the feeling that , no matter how old it is, with a good song, they didn't set out to do anything but try to be honest and write it as it was. And that's very much the way I want to sing it."

It is hard to get the members of Solas to discuss their virtuosity, or even their technique. Getting them to expound on their virtues is very reminiscent of what often happens when one tries to compliment an old traditional musician. Praise the old-timer, and he'll say, "Yup, that's a great tune." Say, no, you meant the way he *played* it, and he'll say, "It's a great melody; been around for years." Insist again that you are referring to his *technique*, and he'll say, "Learned that from my grandfather. He was a lovely player; you should've heard *him*!" Say again that you loved how *he* played it, and he'll mutter, "You want to hear another one, or you wanna just talk all day?"

This is more than mere modesty, both in those old-timers and in young Solas. It reflects a studied attitude of reverence for the music, a deep belief that that is where the attention should be placed. It is why Horan's sophisticated harmonies were sometimes met with scolding glances at sessiuns, and why showoffs, however skilled, don't last long at them. There is a desire to serve the music that is deeply imbedded in these young masters and informs everything about their approach to Irish tradition. Sophisticated as their arrangements get—and they are state-of-the-art, both compositionally and technically—they never seem to be doing anything but playing the tune, singing the song. At rehearsals, they all said the the most dreaded critique from another band member is, "That's a bit over the top, isn't it?" They don't seem to mind being virtuosos; they just don't ever want to get caught at it.

Horan said, "Irish music has been considered over the years a very linear music. With the introduction of all these nontraditional instruments, like guitar, banjo, bouzouki, it's great to find new ways to introduce other things in ways that don't offend or detract from where the music is actually coming from. But I don't like to see it get to where the tune itself gets torn apart."

Egan said he reminds himself sometimes that it was not the purely traditional music that initially drew him, but the more contemporary treatments of seminal revival groups like the Bothy Band. Then he followed the bread-crumb trail back to the purest traditional players, with the help of scores of patient, dedicated teachers and players. But most of them told him he had another responsibility, as sacred as the one to respect the old music, to also honor the music he heard in his own head and heart. Music is a living thing, they told him; it either breathes and grows, or withers and dies.

"People are always keeping an eye on whether or not you're destroying some aspect of the culture, and it's a hard thing to know," Egan said. "I personally don't think innovation is a destructive element, but there are certainly folks who do. Ultimately, you can't end up playing the music you want to hear if you pay a huge amount of attention to all the different angles different people have. Ultimately, you're not going to please everyone anyway, so as a consolation prize, at the very least try to keep yourself interested."

Originally appeared in Sing Out! the Folk Song Magazine
Used with permision, Sing Out Corporation
—Autumn, 1997

America's piper of record
Jerry O'Sullivan

Only the harp is more immediately recognized as an Irish musical instrument than the uillean pipes. These small bagpipes, which are played using a bellows inflated by pumping the arm, deliver the same wild, note-bending sound of the large bagpipes, from which they evolved, but also a delicate intricacy that makes them among the most distinctive of folk instruments.

In this country, the piper of record these days seems to be Jerry O'Sullivan of Yonkers, N.Y. Whether you are an Irish music fan or not, you undoubtedly have heard his pipe mastery. He has done commercials for AT&T, Texaco, and Pizza Hut, recorded with James Galway, Sinead O'Connor, Dolly Parton, *Riverdance* fiddler Eileen Ivers, and Cherish the Ladies flutist Joanie Madden. He was the main piper for the film "Far and Away" and was featured extensively in the recent PBS documentary "Out of Ireland."

O'Sullivan superbly displays his command of the uillean pipes on his merrily genre-jogging new Shanachie CD, "The Gift." He struts his traditional chops on furious sets of jigs and reels, including a stunningly wild, close duet with Boston-area fiddler Seamus Connolly, with whom he frequently performs.

But he also performs several pristine slow airs by Appalachian banjo player Tony Ellis, a raw, riveting moan of the American folk classic "Wayfaring Stranger," some cool jazz tunes, and an elegant set from Bach's Suite No. 3 in D Major.

O'Sullivan has become something of a scholar on the uillean pipes, and relishes exploding some of the most cherished myths about its origins. The word "uillean," for example, is Irish for "elbow," and most assume it was named for its arm-pumped bellows. O'Sullivan has a more intriguing theory.

"In an early 19th-century Irish-English dictionary, I found that an older, alternate definition for `uilleann' was `the elder plant.' Well, a light bulb went on for me, because the early uillean pipes were made out of elder wood. Elder is a native plant that's perfect, because it's very, very hard and the center is hollow. So to me, it makes a lot more sense to think of them as the elder pipes, rather than the elbow pipes."

O'Sullivan is passionate when it comes to the oft-told tale that the smaller uillean pipes evolved because the British banned the larger war pipes. Supposedly, a law was passed banning the playing of any instruments standing up.

"The reasoning, according to the tale, was that it was some legal sleight of hand intended to ban the playing of martial instruments like the bagpipes," he said. "The first problem with that story is that you can play the bagpipes sitting down; a lot of pipers do it in Cape Breton [Nova Scotia]. The other problem is that I've looked for it and asked about it, and would pretty much put my neck on the block

He keeps an old woodcut of a piper who was hanged "for playing seditious tunes" to remind him of laws that banned speaking the Irish language, saying Mass, and singing patriotic songs. But mythologizing Irish music with what he calls "ha-ha bar stories," like the legend of banning the pipes, is to miss the real miracle of it.

to say that law never existed."

The trouble with the tale, O'Sullivan said, is that it glosses over so many of the innovations that make the uillean pipes such a lovely, distinctive, and complex instrument. It was not just the development of the arm bellows that forged it.

"The most important thing that happened was that the inner bore of the chanter, which is cone-shaped in a conventional bagpipe, became narrower and more tapered," he said. "When you do that, two things happen. One is the instrument gets quieter; the other is that you get more notes in the high octave.

"It's similar to what happened to the shawm, the medieval wind instrument that evolved into the oboe. When they took this one-octave bagpipe, made the bore smaller and the taper more gradual, they started getting notes in the second octave. As they continued to narrow it, they got a full two octaves, and found they could use the same system of keywork they were using on flutes and oboes, which allowed them to get chromatics."

O'Sullivan stressed this same revolution was happening throughout Europe in the 17th century. In France, it led to the development of the similar, bellows-driven musette pipes.

At the same time, regulators—closed keys opened with the wrist or heel of the hand—were developed, enhancing the pipes' percussive possibilities, as well as adding harmonic tones to the drone that make the instrument so uniquely haunting.

"Basically, what you had was a folk instrument that evolved for playing what was the Top 40 music of the day," he said. "Books of 18th-century pipe melodies had Handel arias along with Irish and Scottish and Northumbrian dance tunes. The instrument kept getting beefed up to make it more flexible."

O'Sullivan is extremely mindful of the horrible oppression and poverty British rule imposed on Ireland. He keeps an old woodcut of a piper who was hanged "for playing seditious tunes" to remind him of laws that banned speaking the Irish language, saying Mass, and singing patriotic songs. But mythologizing Irish music with what he calls "ha-ha bar stories," like the legend of banning the pipes, is to miss the real miracle of it.

"These tales reduce Irish musical history to something very simplistic, when the truth is much more fascinating and complex," he said. "I find it frustrating, because it dismisses the instrument and what it can do, as well as the music and how it evolved. I know there was incredibly violent repression, but in the face of all that, it's all the more remarkable how the music and the culture continued to flourish. To not love the music for its own sake, and take the instrument on its own merit, just seems to me a lack of respect."

—June 12, 1998

We all came as strangers: the African and Irish immigrant experience
Sparky Rucker, Robbie O'Connell and Mick Moloney

We all came as strangers to these shores. In the vast canon of American folk song, perhaps no single truth shines more clearly. The songs immigrants brought with them, and those they made up as they migrated westward, echo with the loneliness of the stranger and the promise of better lives in a new home. It is now widely believed that even those Native Americans who met the European settlers (and the African slaves they brought with them) first came here in some prehistoric odyssey, seekers who left old homes for the uncertain promise of new frontiers.

Regis College is presenting a provocative concert exploring the migrant folk songs of the Irish and African-American experience, featuring three performers—Irish musicians Mick Moloney and Robbie O'Connell, and African-American folk singer James "Sparky" Rucker—renowned in the folk world as entertainers and educators.

Moloney, a superb tenor banjoist, is among the most respected scholars of Irish music in the world, a doctor of folklore and author who was a musical consultant and performer for the PBS epics "Out of Ireland" and "The Irish in America: The Long Journey Home." Born in Limerick, now living in Philadelphia, he is writing a book on Irish music in America for Random House.

"There are literally thousands of Irish songs written on the theme of leaving," he said. "Even love songs; an awful lot of them have themes of separated lovers, and often they are separated by one of the lovers emigrating. And they're not all sad, either; many are just brimming with hope and adventure. In the 19th century alone, close to 5 million Irish people left for America. The present-day population of Ireland is only just over 4 million, so this was an enormous exodus. Because we stored a lot of our cultural memories in songs anyway—as a colonized people there were only a few limited ways you could publicly express your point of view—the number of songs heavily reflecting that experience is only to be expected."

Of course, that bittersweet commingling of loss and hope is everywhere in African-American folk music. Rucker, who lives in Knoxville, Tenn., has made a career of tracing black history through music; not just blues and gospel music, but the woefully neglected treasure-trove of African-American work songs and ballads that profoundly influenced all American popular music.

"In my mind, there were at least two major migrations of black populations in America, three if you count the original trip over here," Rucker said. "After slavery ended, there were the Exodusters, which was the major migration westward after the Civil War. The whole black cowboy tradition—at least a third of 19th-century cowboys were black—came out of all these people who were heading west in wagon trains.

"The third major migration was of black people moving north, going up the river from Mississippi to St. Louis, Kansas City, up to Chicago; and the Delta blues becoming the Chicago blues."

Rucker said no songs are known to exist describing the horrible journey of slaves from Africa to America, since all use of native languages, music, and other African cultural expression was forbidden. But he argues persuasively that the spirituals and work songs of the slavery era, with their Biblical symbolism wrenchingly articulating the horror of slavery and the longing for freedom, occupy the same place in the African-American canon that emigration ballads, with their tales of oppressive landlords, evictions, and famine, do in the Irish tradition.

"That's why spirituals have to be part of any examination of black migration," he said. "This was not a planned migration, of course, but the only thing that united these people from various tribes and languages was the condition they were all in. The only outlet they were given for expression was through the church; they could only gather in groups or sing together through the Bible and the English language, so they used that as their way to communicate and build a culture of their own."

O'Connell is among the most respected guitarists in Celtic music and toured for years with his uncles the Clancy Brothers. He is also an eloquent songwriter and often performs for schools and folk societies on the Irish experience in America.

"My experiences as an immigrant have given me themes for more songs than anything else," said the Waterford native, who now lives in Franklin. "As an immigrant, you're really a displaced person. No matter how long you're here, you're never quite accepted as an American. But if you're away long enough, you become a bit of an outsider back in your own country.

"I wrote a song called `Two Nations,' about an Irish-American who travels to Ireland and confronts this ingrained notion that he is not Irish, because he was born in America. But when I sing that song, other immigrants—Germans, Japanese, Chinese people—come up to me and say it's true for them, too.

"All immigrants seem to have the same problem when they move away from their country. They stay here for a long time and then feel like outsiders when they go back. So when I hear that in the old ballads, that sense of being a stranger wherever you go, it resonates. And it's still true."

On the westward migrations of the 19th century, Irish immigrants and African-Americans often worked together, first in the rugged Southern mountains, where the African-derived banjo met the Scotch-Irish fiddle to form the roots of country music. As they worked the great sailing ships, built the canals and railroads, and traveled as cowboys on the great cattle drives, their musics melded to form new and uniquely American sounds.

The melodicism of Irish music and the call-and-response structures of African work hollers are heard in hundreds of sea chanties, canal, and railroad songs. Many cowboy ballads are variants of old Celtic songs, mingled with the plaintiveness of African-American balladry and the gentle lilt of Hispanic music.

"When you think of it, African-American music is the first truly American folk music, because it was created here," said Rucker. "Slaves were prohibited from playing the drums, singing the songs they brought with them, using their native languages or dance. So they had to totally reinvent what they were doing here, as opposed to other migrant groups who brought their musical traditions with them intact."

As various ethnic styles hybridized into American popular music, Irish and blacks—as well as Jewish, Italian, German, and other immmigrant cultures—became victims of racist caricatures on vaudeville and minstrel-show stages. As much as we rightly decry the crude stereotypes of the minstrel and "stage-Irish" songs, however, both Moloney and Rucker stressed that much good also came from them. Both groups used the stereotypes, and the access to the popular stage they brought, to propagandize on their own behalf and to make crucial inroads into the cultural mainstream.

"In the cities, because of variety theater and vaudeville," Moloney said, "a whole new tradition of songs arises: songs about the Irish in politics, in tenement housing, protesting discrimination and the plight of the Irish. There were songs that caricatured the Irish much like blacks were, but the huge body of songs were about Irish city life, and were powerful tools in building the Irish machinery of urban politics."

O'Connell said, "We take so much for granted now. I mean, the distance is still great, but we can always pick up a telephone, fly back for a visit. In the 19th century, the journey took up to six weeks; many arrived with nothing, had little or no English, nowhere to go, no one they knew. They were leaving behind famine and dire poverty; and yet, as little as they had, it was often the money they sent back that kept the family back home alive. They were heroic people."

Even through the horrible veil of slavery and the unending racism that followed it, Rucker said there is much to hear in these migrant songs that speaks well of the American experiment.

"When you listen to these songs—not just the African-American, but the songs of the Irish or any immigrant groups— you see how this nation was built by such strong, special people; people willing to leave the known for the unknown and strong enough to survive—and, of course, that includes those able to survive the passage from Africa, the time of slavery, and the great black migrations afterwards.

"We are all descended from people who were willing to strive for that frontier, who left what they knew hoping for something better, and who were strong enough to survive all they had to endure. I think that explains why we're such a powerful nation, I really do. It's just in the genes here, in everybody's genes."

Moloney said, "It's not just Irish or African-Americans, of course: All Americans need to know how tough it was for the first generations of immigrants, how we all faced exactly the same issues in adjusting to life here that immigrants today are facing. I firmly believe that if Irish-Americans, or any other Americans for that matter, knew the full extent of what their own people went through in coming here, it would be impossible for them not to be deeply sympathetic to immigrants today."

—Friday, February 25, 2000

From holocaust to homecoming: the odyssey of the Sephardim
Flory Jagoda, Voice of the Turtle's Judith Wachs

Voice of the Turtle does not merely find it surprising that it has reached its 20th year as an ensemble; to the group, it is a bona fide miracle. As artistic director Judith Wachs prepares for Turtle's 20th annual Hanukkah concert, she is a bit shellshocked about it all. What began as a personal quest to unravel the intriguing puzzle of Sephardic folk music evolved into a career leading to what many regard as the best and most influential Sephardic music group in America.

"To tell you the truth," she said, "I never expected to have any anniversary. When we started Turtle, it was just for the pure pleasure of musical discovery. We had no idea that a group, much less a career, would evolve out of our saying, `Let's see what this music is about, where it comes from.' "

The other members are Derek Burrows, Lisle Kulbach, and Jay Rosenberg, all versatile singers and multi-instrumentalists who perform the music of the Sephardic Jews who were expelled from Spain in 1492 and Portugal in 1497.

The Sephardim were welcomed by the Ottoman Empire and resettled throughout its domain, in Turkey, Greece, Rhodes, Morocco, Jerusalem, and the Balkans. They assimilated the cultures of their new homes, but kept their Judeo-Spanish roots alive, including the medieval Spanish language of Ladino, in which the women spoke to one another and sang their tenderly preserved ballads, lullabies, and seasonal, holiday, and work songs.

In 1977, Wachs was at a rehearsal for Quadrivium, a Boston medieval music ensemble, when a member sang a Sephardic folk song as a suggestion for an upcoming show. Wachs was riveted, feeling this song was unlike anything she had heard before, and yet strangely like everything she had heard before, with its medieval European sound and unmistakable Jewish texture.

Unraveling the puzzle of that Sephardic folk song would fill Wachs's life, and she did not really find the key until she met older traditional Sephardic musicians like Bosnian singer-accordionist Flory Jagoda, who joins Turtle Saturday with her family of musicians. When Jagoda offered her the key to the puzzle, it was, actually and literally, a key.

Jewish culture in the States has always has been dominated by the Ashkenazic tradition of Central and Eastern Europe, whose language is Yiddish. Jagoda, for example, who left her native Bosnia to escape the Holocaust, was then singing Jewish and European folk songs for Jewish organizations around her new home in Ohio and later Virginia, but not the Sephardic music that had filled her life as a girl in the mountain village of Vlasenica.

"Ladino did not exist here," she said. "Nobody even knew what that was. I felt that what I knew as Judaism was very new to these people. Speaking Spanish? That's Jewish? It was just not accepted here, so I gave up the idea completely."

Wachs had grown up in a typical Jewish-American home, with its roots in Ashkenazic culture. Scouring local libraries, she found little about Sephardic music until her Hebrew teacher suggested there were folkloric discoveries being made in Israel, as Jews from around the world returned to their ancient homeland. Perhaps the key to her puzzle was there.

Folklorists and musical archivists in Jerusalem were indeed beginning to unravel the miracle of the Sephardim. For the first time since 1492, Spanish Jews gathered in one place, and amazing things became clear when their traditional repertories were compared. For one thing, Ladino had been been perfectly preserved everywhere the Sephardim settled. Along with it, a huge and astoundingly similar repertory of songs existed throughout the Sephardic world, the Ladino lyrics unchanged, though the melodies were subtly shaded by the Balkan, Turkish, Middle Eastern, or Mediterranean sounds of their new homes.

This has been an epiphany not just for Jewish scholars, but for all folklorists and anthropologists; proof that the memory of oral tradition can be more indelible and flawless over hundreds of years than many had believed possible.

"These communities wouldn't have had anything to do with each other for centuries," Wachs said, "and yet they shared so many songs, so much language and culture. A musicologist there, Shoshana Shahak, let us make recordings of this firsthand material, made by actual singers from Sephardic communities. That was the turning point for us as a group, to hear the actual singers, their inflection, ornamentation—and emotions."

The miracle of this preservation was women's work. As Jagoda described it, the women preserved the Judeo-Spanish heritage, while the men assimilated the culture of their new homes. Ladino was considered a Jewish tongue, written in Hebrew and called "la lingua de la madre," or "the mother's language."

"Mothers spoke it to their daughters," she said, "nonas to their granddaughters. But it was not just songs; women had their own prayer books in Ladino. They considered this old Castilian Spanish a Jewish language. To them, this was the music and language of their Jewish faith, the music of their prayers, their holidays and lullabies, their daily life, family life."

For Jagoda, music would literally become a matter of life and death when, in 1941, her father put her on a train to the Dalmatian coast to escape the Nazis. He told her to sit at the back of a train car, play her accordion, and not say a word.

At that time, it was fashionable to have sing-alongs on train rides. Since she was the song leader, no one bothered to check her identity papers. The conducter got so busy singing he failed even to take her ticket; and so she traveled safely to the coast and, finally, to freedom in Italy. There she married an American soldier and came here to build a new home and family.

"If you sang or played an accordion, you had an open door," she said. "My father knew I would be all right if I just sang. So I hugged my little accordion and played; and it's always been my very best friend, helped me in every imaginable situation."

While she abandoned her Sephardic repertory here, she kept writing Ladino songs for herself, as her private way of mourning and remembering her Vlasenica family, all of whom, except her mother, were killed in the Holocaust. One day, she got a call from people organizing a Sephardic folk festival in Washington, D.C. They had heard she was Sephardic, since she sometimes mentioned it at her shows; did she know any Sephardic songs?

One of the original songs she sang there—and at other Sephardic events as the music was revived through groups like Voice of the Turtle—was "La Yave de Espanya," or "The Key of Spain," about old black keys Sephardic families often kept in their homes. When Wachs learned the story, it unlocked for her the puzzle of the Sephardim's long, bittersweet odyssey.

The keys, like the Ladino language and Sephardic repertory, were at once metaphors and carefully preserved realities, keys taken from Judeo-Spanish homes and synagogues in 1492.

Voice of the Turtle learned the song after meeting Jagoda at a Sephardic festival.

Over the years, she has become the nona, or grandmother, to Turtle and other Sephardic revival musicians throughout the world; happy and proud to answer questions, help with pronunciations and melodies, explain the stories behind songs and how they were used. It was through her, and other traditional singers Wachs met in Jerusalem, that she finally understood the puzzle of Sephardic music; why it sounded the way it did, and why it had been so faithfully preserved.

"Flory has given us a personal sense of the importance of music to life," Wachs said. "And a sense of handing off, of passing on tradition. She is more realistic about what is being lost than I am. She says Ladino is a dying language, and that's just a fact. But she also says there are ways of keeping things alive which are still important, even though they cannot be re-created or reinvested with the kind of life that had been. Even though you cannot go back, she's taught us, it is still critical and nourishing to remember where you've been."

Jagoda said, "The songs of my family may be in Ladino, but they're Balkan songs now. The same with the keys. Whenever they would give you a gift, they would say, `Watch it like the key in the drawer.' That had tremendous meaning. They had these big black keys that were part of the household. They were supposed to be from their ancestors in Spain, but, I mean, who knows? It was five centuries ago. But it was a symbol of freedom.

"A cousin of mine, I just brought her here from Belgrade after this messy war, and she said, `I left everything; I have nothing that belongs to me anymore. But I have the key, I still have the key.' "

—December 6, 1998

She taught America to sing its own folk songs: Ruth Crawford Seeger
Mike Seeger, Peggy Seeger, biographer Judith Tick

American composer Ruth Crawford Seeger (1901-53) always seemed to be living in her own shadow. She was a leading figure among the classical avant-garde of the 1920s, among the most inventive and critically respected modernist composers of her time. In 1930, she became the first woman to win a Guggenheim Fellowship for composition, although her work was rarely performed in mainstream classical settings.

Yet her most important and influential work came in the form of two simple anthologies called "American Folk Songs for Children" and "Animal Folk Songs for Children." It is almost impossible to overstate the importance these humble books had in helping restore then-vanishing American folk music to mainstream consciousness in the late 1940s. They became standard texts for parents, music teachers, librarians, and children's performers. And they helped to infect the postwar generation with the zest for traditional music that expressed itself in the great commercial folk revival of the 1960s—a revival very much led by her stepson Pete and her children Mike and Peggy Seeger.

Because of the long shadow each of Crawford Seeger's careers cast on the other, her brief life of 52 years is too often told as tragedy, according to author, music historian, and Northeastern University professor Judith Tick. Tick's major biography, "Ruth Crawford Seeger: A Composer's Search for American Music," was just published by Oxford University Press. She also wrote the notes for and helped put together a new Deutsche Grammophon CD of Crawford Seeger's modernist orchestral works, piano pieces, and classical song settings, called "Ruth Crawford Seeger: Portait," with Oliver Knussen and the Schonberg Ensemble, New London Chamber Choir, pianist Reinbert De Leeuw, and soprano Lucy Shelton.

"I can't tell you how many times I've heard classical music people say, 'It's so tragic she stopped writing music,'" Tick said. "And then the folk people say, 'Isn't it wonderful that she finally saw the light?' The virtue of Crawford Seeger is that it's never either/or. She brought everything she could to every experience. That's who she was—one size fits all. Whatever you're doing, that's what you put your whole self into, whether it's teaching kindergartners folk songs, composing an orchestral suite, or writing songbooks."

In 1930, already a respected composer, Ruth Crawford went to the equally avant-garde composer Charles Seeger to study "dissonant counterpoint." They fell in love and were married in 1931.

This is where much of the myth of her tragic life begins. Charles Seeger was a towering figure, a fiery radical who all but invented the field of ethnomusicology (he did coin the term) and who had a profound impact on the study of American folk culture. So some see her composing career sacrificed to her husband's work; the dutiful wife toiling as music teacher and folk-song scribe to feed his muse and their growing family. They had four children: Mike, Peggy, Penny, and Barbara. His children from a previous marriage included folk singer Pete Seeger.

In fact, it was Crawford and Seeger's simultaneous disenchantment with modernism that drew them together. They began seeing it as elitist. Daughter Peggy Seeger recalled them both scornfully calling it "music for musicians." As the hard times of the Depression deepened around them, and both parents had to work to support the family, their progressive radicalism led them to folk music, which they saw as the true American music and as a potential bridge to connect the classes. Even as they fell in love with one another, both were falling hopelessly in love with American folk music.

"I know the formal composing cadre condemned her for going into folk music," said folk singer-songwriter Peggy Seeger. "But I think some of her greatest work was done in folk music. She was trying to wed the disciplines and, of course, there are purists in both camps who say this shouldn't be done. But her idea was to get the songs back into popular usage."

In the 1940s, radios and record players were slowly drowning out the ancient sounds of traditional music, particularly among the urban middle class. After transcribing some songs for Carl Sandburg's "American Songbag," she worked with influential folklorists John and Alan Lomax, scoring their seminal song collections, "Our Singing Country" and "Folk Song, USA."

Working from roughly recorded field collections culled from America's farms, villages, prisons, and places of worship, she brought all her awesome compositional technique to her folk music work. She deeply wanted these songs restored to the center of American family life, and she struggled to find accessible ways to encode into her accompaniments the spirit and playfulness of American folk music that had always been relayed orally, from singer to singer.

"She would listen to those field records over and over," Peggy Seeger remembered. "It would drive her crazy trying to figure out how to write down the way singers would slide notes. In her own books, she learned to write the melodies simply and to suggest the mood from her piano accompaniment."

Noted local pianist Virginia Eskin has recorded a CD of Craword Seeger's piano pieces, due out soon on Albany. She included 10 folk song settings.

"I feel she's an extraordinary woman composer," Eskin said, "because she is a sandwich of this very intellectual, lunar, drifting kind of classical music that is so complex, and then she did so much work using all her knowledge as a sophisticated composer to capture the charm and nuance of folk music. Her arrangements of folk songs are brilliantly conceived, reminiscent of Bela Bartok's work. They sometimes veer on atonality, but because of her genius, a song like 'Sweet Betsy from Pike' really comes to life. In that one, she puts together a C-natural against a C-sharp, which could cause unease in a child, but it's so playfully and artfully done."

Crawford Seeger's intent was not to be artful but to attempt to transfer the emotional energy of the songs to readers, most of whom she knew were novice players. She constantly sang the songs with her children, at nursery schools, and kindergartens. Mike and Peggy Seeger remember her music constantly filling the house in Chevy Chase, Md.—folk music during the day, classical piano at night.

"She was trying to not just transcribe but to actually describe the music in written notation," said Mike Seeger, among the most important traditional musicians and collectors of the '60s revival. "When she wrote the books, she was trying to be a translator for people who had not heard this music, to give them some feeling for the music from the kinds of arrangements she made. She was trying to get the songs back into currency."

Tick said: "The one story that Pete Seeger told me over and over is how he used to watch her transcribing, listening to the same song over and over, asking everybody, `Is that a B-flat or a B?' Or `How can I capture the vitality in the way this note is played?' Alan Lomax talked about how upset she would get trying to capture these elusive qualities in the arrangements."

"American Folk Songs for Children" was published in 1948, "Animal Folk Songs for Children" in 1951. In 1952, with her youngest child in school, Crawford Seeger returned to composing with the acclaimed "Suite" for wind quintet. All her roads seemed finally open to her when, in 1953, she died of cancer.

Tick said: "When you go into schools today, everybody is singing this material. Children are learning American folk songs. We just accept it as natural, something that always happened, but it isn't. She did an awful lot to bring about that change. Remember, she was working in an era when you could read in music education books that America had no folk music. She helped figure out how to turn this music from being a regional curiosity into an essential element in American identity."

As to any tragedy in her mother's life, beyond its brevity and economic travail, Peggy Seeger is having none of it.

"She loved, loved, being a mother. Is it a betrayal of oneself to become a mother? It seems to me it's putting women down rather badly to say that. She was wonderful singing with us, could get us to do anything by singing a folk song about it. She wanted you to put your galoshes on, she'd sing a verse about it and on would go the galoshes. I do that with my grandchildren now—it still works."

Tick said: "There was a tragedy in that she was not able to see herself as an entitled artist who would make her own creativity a top priority. That is a tragedy, and it's a woman's tragedy, but it's not about the music she produced. She was an artist of profound accomplishment and profound humanity who did not believe in notions of high vs. low culture. As the folklorist Bess Lomax Hawes said, `Ruth took it pure.' "

—*October 19, 1997*

What Is Folk Music?
From the New England Folk Almanac.
Pete Seeger, Ani DiFranco, Dar Williams, Tom Paxton, Dave Van Ronk, Guy Davis, Bob Franke, Jack Hardy, Lui Collins, Rounder Records exec Marian Leighton-Levy, folk radio host Dick Pleasants, concert producer Ellen Friedman, Scott Alarik

(Author's note: From 1991-1997, I had the pleasure of editing and writing for an odd, properly eccentric little bimonthly paper called the New England Folk Almanac. Hands down, the most fun I had was compiling a segment for every issue called "The Question." I wanted to get right at the community nature of folk music today by doing a roundtable interview in which I asked a variety of different artists and folk-biz people the same question. It took me five years to summon the nerve to tackle the Big Question: what is folk music? By then, several performers had told me if I ducked answering that one myself, they would...well, let's just say the threats were dark, fearful and highly creative. Seriously, I took up the challenge, and it was the only Almanac Question I ever answered.)

Pete Seeger. I think I'd preface my statement by saying I'd just as soon the term was no longer used except by professional folklorists who know what they're talking about. But if it is to be used by journalists, I always point out it's music that has more of the traditional element; whether it's gospel music or Chinese or Jewish music or even Appalachian music with a Scotch-Irish background. I might end up saying, just call me a river singer. You have mountain singers and western singers, why not a river singer?

Ani DiFranco. Sounds like the million-dollar question. Drum roll, please...what is folk music? *That* stuff? I think folk music is sub-corporate, community-based music o' the people. That's kind of why I'm interested in it. The make and model of folk music isn't so much interesting to me in terms of how it sounds—that it's acoustic instruments or, oh, it's so damn *folky*. The form it takes doesn't speak to me as much as the whole context in which it's created. It just tends to be unpretentious music that's uncommercial, made by unpretentious people who are not interested in moving units so much as revolution or communication. That's what I really, really like about it.

Bob Franke. Since the oral tradition has changed its spelling basically, to aural, I think that folk music is music about living in community. Mostly, it comes out of communities; sometimes they're intentional communities, sometimes they're ethnic or geographic communities. But that for me seems to be the guideline.

Dave Van Ronk. The first thing I wonder is, who really cares? The term is flung around and pinned to all kinds of music, and I wonder why the question persists, I really do. Because the term has become so meaningless. I suppose that's the very reason why people want a definition, because it's gotten so broad.

I take the narrowest possible view, that is oral transmission, anonymity, the folk process. Which is to say, there is no more folk music with the exception of dirty songs, jokes and, to a certain extent, rap and toasts, things like that. Mostly only insofar as they're obscene [are they created and passed along that way]. Because they're obscene, the commercial interests won't touch them, so the folk process continues unimpeded.

Because what's happened is that the whole process has been short-circuited as consumer capitalism moves into more and more fields. A hundred years ago, the music biz, media and so on, were just getting off the ground. So yes, there was folk music then and yes, there could be folk music again. If for some reason or another, music ceased to be in the context of the market economy, it would probably revert to folk music. But folk music isn't a sound or style. I mean, is flamenco a folk music? Yes it is, but it doesn't sound anything like southern mountain ballads, and that's folk music, too. So no, I'm not a folk singer. Jean Ritchie is a folk singer, and a few others like her. But when that generation goes, that's probably it.

Dar Williams. First of all, folk music is something that gives me more freedom than any other name. People think that's funny, because you'd think it was defined by its limitations. But for me, it just means people let me do whatever i do. I'm sort of guided by what I observe, but that can take any form I want.

I want to say this includes the singer-songwriter phenomenon as well. Folk as a term obviously serves me better if I abstract it from its technical roots, because then I have more freedom as a sort of sound sculptor. But what Lawrence Lazare, who was a booking agent at Fleming-Tamulevich, said, I think is really true.

And that is that folk music is really defined by its listener's; it's the way people come to a concert, the way they want to listen to things, and the way they want to feel at the end of a concert. People come to coffeehouses, and there is the certain framework of a certain kind of show that they are prepared to be part of. They don't talk, they're all facing you, it's generally a nonalcoholic event. And I think there's some hope that there will be words that will be uplifting, as opposed to just entertaining or clever or numbing.

I think folk music is sub-corporate, community-based music o
the people...unpretentious music that's uncommercial, made by
unpretentious people who are not interested in moving units so much as
revolution or communication. —Ani DiFranco

Lui Collins. First of all, I think as humans we label and categorize in order to understand and simplify our world. It's neither a good thing nor a bad thing, but it seems to be an essential part of what we do.

I find people asking me all the time, what kind of music do you play? So I'm seeing this question in terms of that: how do we understand? Historically and globally, folk music, I believe, is the music of the common people. This would include both vocal music, which would tend to tell stories and history and speak of the lives around the people; and instrumental music, which is often connected with folk dances.

It's something that's passed along orally from generation to generation. Folk music in its purest sense can only be sustained where you have a nation, as opposed to a political state, that has its own integral language, belief system and culture, which would include the music and dance.

But in this present-day technological society, folk music, if it can exist at all, has to take on a whole new meaning. Because what one might call the common people now have access to music from cultures all over the world through radio and television and CDs and tapes and computers. The world is just so complex, the influences are so diverse, that folk music, at least in modern western technologically society, can't be understood in the same way.

I think to clearly define folk music for us, in a way that would allow one to say that this or that specific piece of music is or is not folk music, I think is impossible. So what I came up with as my working definition—and this is, I think, inclusive as opposed to exclusive—is music that comes from the heart and that speaks of and to the world as the musician experiences it. That would be number one.

Number two is music that deals with what is real. Of course, that's defined by the individual doing it, but it is [music that does that] as opposed to doing what might be commercially viable.

Three, I think folk music is primarily acoustic, as differentiated perhaps from pop or alternative music. I would include, you know, electric basses, pickups, p.a. systems, but I think of it as primarily acoustic. I see it as music that's primarily simple, that doesn't require years of intensive formal study to perform, and i want to very heavily acknowledge here the technological proficiency of vast numbers of folk musicians. But I see this proficiency generally more the result of more informal training that comes from playing with others, listening, practicing; as opposed to going to school to study. As opposed to classical music, which, of course, going back to the historical and global perspective, was the music of the elite rather than the common folk.

The fourth thing I have is that it is music that's open to interpretation by other performers—what we call the folk process. It's music that changes and grows, depending on who is playing it, and when it is being played. Because the understanding is that the performer interprets it depending on his or her own view of the world and belief system. As opposed, for instance, to classical music, where the composer writes it, and everyone tries to play it as close as they can to what they think the composer wanted it to be.

The final thing that feels really important to me is that folk music is music that encourages the development of community; whether it's through live concerts and people joining together singing or dancing, or through the content of the music. It's music that encourages people to come together. That's the one I really feel defines it in a large way.

Nerissa Nields. I think what makes folk music folk music in this day and age is the audience. That's maybe always been true, and is why what is basically a rock band can play at folk clubs and folk festivals all across the country. Because there's an audience there that knows us and likes us. It's as simple as that. There's no one thing you can point to in our music. I know that's sort of a Nields-centric point of view, but I've been thinking about this a lot, and I don't think it's about us. It's about something else.

What attracted me to folk music from when I was a kid was the inclusiveness, both of the music and of the movement. It's a very unusual genre in that the people who support it are so committed to the music, and to what the music says. It's more than music, it's really a community, a movement; in the '60s, it certainly was very connected to a movement.

I think that's really important. And it's not about money, as I think rock and country music have become. I think those genres are about money, and the beauty of folk music is that it's not; it's about an experience and a passion.

When I was a kid, I was kind of afraid of rock, because there was something very much like "you can't be in our club" about that kind of music. It sort of dared you to be part of it; whereas, folk music was the opposite. It was very inclusive and welcoming—you know, everybody can sing along. When you get to be a teenager, that challenge of rock'n'roll can seem very appealing; it's exciting, and I think that's a natural feeling.

What amazes me now, as an adult who makes this music, is to see the wide appeal of folk music. For example, to see how many kids come to our concerts— and by kids, I mean teens to preteens to five year-olds who are really excited about this music, really into it. So as a rock band, what we try to bring to a show is that inclusiveness that I learned from folk music when I was a kid; how important it is to be welcoming to an audience. I mean, it's important to challenge them, too, and that's certainly part of what we do. But there's also a big part we take from folk music. I mean, we don't often say, "Hey everybody, sing along!" But that's just implied; that you're the audience, so you're part of this."

Marian Leighton-Levy. I am definitely not a purist: I think of folk music in the broadest possible sense. The main thing to me that is important is that it be music that speaks directly to the experiences of people in their everyday lives. In the performance context, I would say it's music that communicates directly to the audience. I don't think that needs to be limited to, for example, singer-songwriters or solo performers. It can be bands. While it may tend to overall have a more sort of acoustic-y feel, it doesn't need to be limited to that.

Ellen Friedman. I had a really hard time thinking about this, because I was thinking of the way songs we regard as folk songs are converted to pop songs. "From a Distance" was part of the folk idiom when Nanci Griffith sang it, and then when Bette Midler sang it, it became a pop song. So there's a question there.

Part of it, I think, has to do with presentation. Part of it is that a folk song has a narrative vein in some way or another, though that vein I certainly not restricted to folk music. Another part is the simplicity of it. But a larger part is the presentation, the ability to perform with just a guitar, or in your basement for people to sit around and sing it. So both the simplicity and the accessibility of it is important. We're looking at what makes something folk music, rather than a folk song, because a song can be treated in such a way that it's not a folk song, or that it leaves the realm of what most of us would think was folk.

Guy Davis. If I put it in the broadest possible definition that I can give it, I would extend it as far as rap music, as far as certain pop songs. Even a song as established and old as "I Wonder Who's Kissing Her Now?"—well, what's the difference between that and "Kisses Sweeter Than Wine?" You had a guitar and four voices [the Weavers] on "Kisses Sweeter Than Wine, and on orchestra on "I Wonder Who's Kissing Her Now?"

So in a way, my very broad definition almost invalidates itself, because it completely unscrews the question. So I'm going to have to narrow it back down into a slightly more practical vein, and I'm going to put politics in it and say folk music for me tends to be a bit more non-commercialized, and tends to use acoustic instruments; instruments that can be used anywhere, such as schools, hospitals—community places where you don't have to make a big to-do out of a sound system. Now, my definition is based on its availability to folks more so than what you use to perform it with.

Getting back to rap music, to me it's actually brilliant to think of some black young man taking the turntables in a disco, and turning what was on them into music by scratching back and forth on the grooves, and creating this weird out-of-rhythm, in-rhythm thing. Now that is folk music, it is—it's an honest-to-God thing created right there.

Dick Pleasants. One of the ways I'd like to describe folk music as I know it these days—and this is only in my terms—is by listing a few people I consider folk musicians: Utah Phillips, Bob Franke, Rosalie Sorrels, Bill Staines, Ramblin' Jack Elliot. These are people that, to me, really represent what I call troubadours of folk music today. These people really understand what bringing music to communities today is all about.

And I guess the center of what folk music is today is community. If you take away what I think now is an archaic description of it—the music traveling down through generations—as we have to describe it today, it represents something quite bigger. It represents a community where music is grown, changed and adapted—and traditional music is sustained as well. But it now covers a much wider spectrum than it has been in the past three or four hundred years.

We don't have front porches to play on anymore; we generally don't have picking sessions and dances in the kitchen. Generally, things are organized outside the home, and you need audiences to pay for it. When I represent folk music on the radio, I try to stretch it as much as possible, because I like to see different influences on it. I think folk music is something that is roots-based, but then taken from there.

And I would also say folk music is Flatt & Scruggs, Tommy Jerrold, Muddy Waters, Professor Longhair, Dr. John. Those are people I think represent music particular to different areas of the country. That's another thing folk music is now.

It's an emotional thing for me more than cerebral. I like to think I can look at it in an intellectual way as well, but I don't think folk music was ever made to be intellectual. It was a people thing, for people to play, feel, dance to; not to analyze. Musical theorists can do whatever they want, but I don't think what they do creates more folk music or enhances it. I generally would much prefer to listen to the music than to analyze it. I work with it, I'm a fan of it, and therefore I like to see it grow.

Jack Hardy. My definition is always where the song is more important than the singer or the style. And the song I define as stripped down to its bare essentials, a wedding of melody and lyric. In an ideal world, the melody must be something you can and would like to whistle going down the street, and the lyrics would be something meaningful to yourself, and somewhat memorable in their own right. Everything else—whether it be style, production in terms of recording—is gravy. If you don't have the stripped-down beginning of it that could actually be done a cappella, then you don't have a song.

That's my definition of folk music, where often in rock'n'roll you know the style, you can identify the singer, you know the personality, you know whatever he or she wears. You know everything, but you can't think of or whistle a single song they do.

These things are not mutually exclusive. Applying this definition, I would consider most of the early Beatles folk music; applying this definition, a lot of what passes for folk music these days I would not consider folk music. Because they rely too heavily on pretension.

But I consider what is folk music to be the true poetry. I mean, poetry was never meant to be on a written page; it was meant to be sung. It's only in the last several hundred years that the conceit of putting poetry on the printed page, and the subsequent control of it by academia, has taken it out of the realm of things that were a), memorized and b), sung. I think the best poets writing today are folk singers. The rest is all categories, and category is something that was sort of perpetrated on us by academia.

Tom Paxton. The first thing I do when I begin to answer a question like this is skip graduate school. I don't feel I have to meet some kind of academic discipline in this. For me, it's a subjective judgment. I have certain criteria that I automatically apply: The song has to be around for awhile and, while I'm not rigid about it, I have to sense that the song was written for other than pecuniary motives. It's probably not a song that was written first of all for the market. Now, there are just a thousand exceptions to that.

But for me, a song like "Green, Green, Rocky Road" that the Kingston Trio did—this was a song that was written to get recorded by a hit folk group. Yes, there are some people you might hear singing it now and then, but it's not a folk song. Whereas, Bess Hawes' "Charlie on the M.T.A." is to me a folk song. It was written to help get someone elected mayor of Boston, and did it by telling a funny story. I mean, who remembers George O'Brien besides his family, but everybody knows that song. It's still the most requested song in the Kingston Trio's repertoire.

So I think the song has to have been around for awhile, or be one that gets in the tradition. A perfect example of that would be Michael Burton's song "Night Herder's Lament." Don Edwards, the great cowboy singer, did an interview where he said that no sooner did that song appear than every cowboy in America knew it and sang it. Burton, apparently, is an Englishman, but that song was instantly adopted by the guys who punch cows.

A song like that, in my unscholarly way, is an instant folk song; it is sung by people who don't know Burton and never will. They have no idea who the guy is. People take the trouble to learn a song that feels like their own thoughts turned to song.

I should add that these songs are free from the obligation to make sense. "I've Been Working on the Railroad" makes no sense. I mean, how working on the railroad has anything to do with Dinah in the kitchen is more than I have ever been able to figure out. But I defy you to start singing it without going to the end. "Shenandoah" is totally illogical. What Shenandoah has to do with the Missouri River is more than I can figure out. In one verse, Shenandoah is the girl he loves, in the next it's the father of the girl. It makes no sense—but it's arguably the greatest American folk song.

So if it's a modern song, it's written to be sung, to contribute to the collective songbag. Then if anything commercial happens to it, great.

Scott Alarik. I've found that by beginning with the historical definition, many of folk music's modern aesthetics make more sense. Why is it more of a real-life music? Why more community-based? Why more intimate and honest? Why more political?

The term was originally coined to distinguish this music not by style or content, but by class. "The folk" was a term that referred specifically to the lower classes, peasants, the poor and working people. And folk music was the music they created for themselves, for their own use in their own lives.

For nearly all our history, folk music was the only music of, by and for the vast majority of ordinary people everywhere in the world. Only the nobility and the wealthiest elite could afford to have what was called "art music;" that is, music composed and performed by formally trained professional musicians. There were exceptions—itinerant folk musicians gifted enough to have careers playing for other folks, or even hired by the gentry. In the main, though, folk music was made nonprofessionally, by the same people who listened to it. It was then passed on in an endless creative cycle called the folk process, passed from singer to singer, player to player, generation to generation, culture to culture.

Technology changed all that, first with published song sheets called broadsides that were sold to the masses; then with sheet music for parlor pianos; and later with records, radios and television. With mass-market technology, it became possible for music to be profitably sold to the folk, and that industry became known as popular, or pop, music.

What were once functional and precise definitions that distinguished folk, pop and art music have now become aesthetic ones. People are still drawn to the real-life qualities of folk music, whether it is made by a cowboy-turned-singer, or a rich'n'famous singer-songwriter. The songs tend to be about more than just dating and mating, like so much pop music is, because life itself is about more than that. The folk sang songs about courtship, of course, but also about work, their community, history, children, parents, pets, politics. Music was made for dances and wedding and funerals, to mark the changing of the seasons, celebrated holidays, and to worship.

Much of folk music retains a topical, populist edge, because it was originally a class-defined music. Since it so honestly and movingly portrays the hard lives of poor people throughout history, it naturally draws listeners to a desire for social justice. It may not be innately a political form; but I believe it is an innately populist one.

It also tends to be more personal when it speaks of matters of the heart, because the old folk love songs were not written to sell to other people, but to express deep and private feelings. Then as now, people used the vocabulary of the love song to examine their interior lives; to express their deepest feelings about both love and life. The songs were not crafted to conform to any market trend or commercial taste, but simply to express the individual heart, and perhaps explain that heart to those closest to it. The songs that lasted did so because they somehow touched something in all hearts. Those that expressed only a mood of the moment were soon forgotten.

Of all the definitions of folk music I have heard over the years, my personal favorite came from my niece Caitlin Park. She was 10 at the time, I believe, and I had sent her Suzanne Vega's first album as a Christmas present. She told me how much she liked it—and that she could tell right away it was folk music. "How could you tell it was folk music? I asked her.

"Because all the songs are *about* things." She said.

—February, 1996

Sing Out! The folk music magazine at 40
Pete Seeger, Mark Moss

Forty years ago this month, an amazing little firebrand of a magazine called *Sing Out!* was born. Dedicated to fanning the flames of folk music, it took its title from "The Hammer Song," written by two of its founders, Pete Seeger and Lee Hays, who were then members of the Weavers, America's most popular singing group. "I'd sing out danger, I'd sing out warning/ I'd sing out love between my brothers and my sisters, all over this land."

Even during the halcyon days of the 1960s folk revival, *Sing Out!* never sold more than 10,000 copies an issue. But the little quarterly was never designed for mass consumption. It has been written for folk music's hard core devotees. It features articles about well-known and lesser known folk artists. It also includes columns about where to find jam sessions and hootenannies, folk festivals, how to find rare songs, children's performers, Celtic music, storytelling and the folk process.

And it publishes songs. From the very first cover, which printed the lead sheet to "The Hammer Song," *Sing Out!* has included songs—from Woody

Guthrie's topical ballads to the first new songs from a young Bob Dylan, from ancient Scottish ballads to politically fiery songs of the Latin American New Song Movement, from the best of today's young songwriters to centuries-old broadsides and work songs.

"*Sing Out!* never sold a whole lot because it's not about pop music," said editor Mark Moss from the magazine office in Bethlehem, Penn. "It's not about what color socks Peter Yarrow is wearing or how to write to the Suzanne Vega fan club. It does not approach folk music as a passive medium."

"*Sing Out!* is printing songs for people to sing for themselves, telling them where to go to participate in folk festivals, folk music camps, learning experiences. It's about putting responsibility for culture and entertainment back in the hands of the people who are reading it."

To estimate its value, then, just as to estimate folk music's value, merely looking at the numbers misses the point. While never read by millions, *Sing Out!* has had an enormous impact on those who have been most involved in folk music during the past 40 years.

It would be difficult to find a hard core folkie, be it a professional performer, coffeehouse manager, agent, record producer, record company owner, or just aficianado—for whom *Sing Out!* was not, at one time, crucial in their change from casual fan to one whose life revolves around folk music. That was always the idea.

Speaking from his home in Beacon, N.Y., Pete Seeger said: "*Sing Out!* really grew out of a little newsletter I started in 1946 with Lee Hays, Woody Guthrie, Alan Lomax and a batch of others. We called the newsletter People's Songs. It was just intended for people like us to stay in touch with each other. We just expected a couple hundred readers, but to our surprise it grew to 2,000."

People's Songs went bankrupt in 1949. Seeger put out an interim newsletter until *Sing Out!* was formed in 1950. The new name was used partly because outstanding debts prevented them using the old name, but also because times were changing.Seeger said, "It got to where if you used the word 'people,' everyone started looking for the Reds under your bed."

Throughout the '50s, *Sing Out!* kept printing its songs, instructional columns and articles. Seeger carried copies on tour, getting them into the hands of a new generation of folk music fans. Seeger proudly recalls a small concert he gave in Palo Alto, CA, during the late '50s which he later found out had greatly inspired both the Kingston Trio and Joan Baez. In Minnesota, a young Bob Dylan searched its pages for Woody Guthrie songs.

With the '60s, interest in the magazine grew but and, as *People's Songs* had, the magazine overextended itself with a combination of over-optimism and business naivete.

We're always searching for ways in which music can help the human race survive. Sometimes that's a song, sometimes it's a way to use a song. —Pete Seeger

Mark Moss first saw the magazine at a *Sing Out!* booth at the 1970 Philadelphia Folk Festival. He was just beginning to discover folk music. "This was my food," he said, "just exactly the stuff I liked: Finding out about the roots of music, how things were inter-connected. So I said those immortal words, 'Can I help?' "

Throughout the '70s and '80s, when commercial interest in folk music waned, *Sing Out!* struggled with mounting debts, constant restructuring and raging debates about how and for whom it should be written. In August, 1982, it ceased publication.

As he had in 1949, Pete Seeger wrote and printed an interim newsletter. He also licensed the magazine's anthem, "The Hammer Song," for a British tea company jingle and contributed the money from that to get the magazine to publish again.

Moss became its editor in April 1983. Under stable management and profiting from the renewed interest in folk music, circulation is now nearly at the '60s high of 10,000.

"I think our fundamental reason for existing is the same as it was in 1950," Moss said. "It's expressed in more defined ways maybe; but we're still basically talking about the re-empowerment of people with the music that is at the core of their culture and their lives, and learning that folk music is a form of expression that is theirs to use, not just to watch on VH-1 or MTV. I think that's always been the *Sing Out!* party line."

Seeger said, "We're always searching for ways in which music can help the human race survive. Sometimes that's a song, sometimes it's a way to use a song. Izzy Young, who used to run the Folklore Center in New York City, said there are music magazines that are more exciting than *Sing Out!*, ones that are more dancey and funnier. But at some time this peaceful, wide umbrella covers them all. That's how I see *Sing Out!* Except I don't want it to be too peaceful. As you probably know, I like to see some arguments."

—*May 24, 1990*

A life of vernacular music
Chris Strachwitz & Arhoolie Records

When Chris Strachwitz founded Arhoolie Records 40 years ago, he had no idea he was going to help revolutionize the way America views its own folk music. In fact, to hear him tell it, he was barely aware he was he was starting a label at all. And he's still uncertain Arhoolie is a folk label at all.

True to his idiosyncratic vision, Strachwitz applies a unique definition to the music he records, one he picked up from California folklorist Archie Green.

"What I call the music Arhoolie puts out is vernacular," he said from his office in El Cerrito, California, "authentic regional music; downhome, down-to-earth, real people's, working-class music. And by vernacular, I mean what the lowest class, the poorest people play."

Since Arhoolie released its first record of African-American songster and bluesman Mance Lipscomb in 1960, the small California label has been in the vanguard of a radical change in the way folklorists, musicians and the recording industry perceive, present and hear America's vast, multicultural music riches.

Before the 1960s, it was difficult for Americans to hear the traditional music of their own country at all. The music industry largely ignored the regional, ethnically-specific music found in poor and working-class communities. Most people outside those communities understood folk music to be either the professional music made by interpreters such as Pete Seeger, the Weavers and John Jacob Niles, or "field recordings" of mostly nonprofessional musicians collected by folklorists such as John and Alan Lomax.

Folklorists at that time often overlooked the music performed in roadhouses, dance halls and streetcorners by itinerant professional musicians. Their interests tended to be more more historical and anthropological; more in the roots of various traditions and what their evolution revealed about the societies which created them. Traditional musicians were often recorded in very artificial circumstances, asked to plumb their memories for long-forgotten songs and playing styles of their youth or, worse yet, provided material previously unknown to them, but deemed authentic by the folklorists themselves. The few small-time commercial producers who recorded vernacular music usually created equally artificial environs, bringing in slick studio musicians to provide the external trappings of whatever fit the current pop sound.

The African-American, Cajun, Hispanic and other ethnic artists who made music for their fans and neighbors in isolated regional communities did not themselves regard what they played as folk music. According to Strachwitz, blacks called their music either "downhome blues" or "lowdown blues," and it was marketed to them by small record companies as "race music." Cajuns in Louisiana thought of what they did as "French music," and Hispanics called their music "border" or regional music.

"These different groups considered what they played as simply *their* music," Strachwtiz said. "The term folk was imposed on it by outside people."

Arhoolie has just released an epic 6-CD collection called "Arhoolie Records 40th Anniversary Collection: 1960-2000. The Journey of Chris Strachwitz." It is a stunning documentary, breathtakingly vivid and intimate, brimming with splendid music and evocative, gripping and often deeply charming real-life moments. Some of the most influential roots musicians of the past half-century are captured in wonderfully relaxed and musically supple moments: black music legends Lipscomb, Lightnin' Hopkins, Big Mama Thornton, Mississippi Fred McDowell, Katie Webster, Booker White; Cajun and zydeco virtuosos Dewey Balfa, Clifton Chenier, Beausoleil and the Hackberry Ramblers, traditional country and bluegrass greats J.E. Mainer, Rose Maddox and Del McCoury; Hispanic masters Trio San Antonio, Narcisco Martinez, Lydia Mendoza, Don Santiago Jimenez, Sr., and his children Santiago, Jr., and breakthrough Tejano star Flaco, who Arhoolie first introduced to national audiences.

Throughout, the set is a convincing testament to the validity of Strachwitz's vision, his mission to record these artists precisely as they chose to perform their music; not slicked-up for commercial purposes nor folked-down to fit some outsider's notion of what was authentic. In a single sentence, Strachwitz captured the radical new ethos he and his generation of folklorist-collectors brought to traditional music: "Who am I to tell these guys what to do?"

Strachwitz was born in Germany and immigrated to the United States as a boy shortly after World War 2. He was immediately entranced by the vastly different regional musics he could pick up late at night on his little radio: hillbilly and Hispanic music, blues and New Orleans jazz.

"Back home, the only difference between people was whether you were Catholic or Protestant," he said. "This was all something brand new, and I was very drawn to how many varied cultures existed here. I was amazed by the variety and soulfulness of this regional music; it had such a bite to it."

At first, he was drawn primarily to the professional music of regional bands and singers he heard on the radio and became an avid collector of the obscure records they made. He would scour neighborhood record stores, garage sales, flea markets, even seeking out juke-box operators and buying discarded records by the boxload.

He began recording off his radio, poking around his neighborhood in Pomona, haunting jazz clubs, sometimes sneaking his tape recorder in under his coat.

But the idea of this being anything but a hobby never occurred to him, and he became a high-school teacher. In 1960, the Los Angeles public school system made a significant contribution to the history of modern folk music: it fired Strachwitz.

"My whole passion was geared toward this music, but I never saw how I could make any living with it," he said. "When they fired me as a teacher, it was sink or swim. I had to figure out a way somehow to make a living from this music."

By then, he had met other collectors of vernacular music, and went with collector Mack McCormick to Texas, seeking out blues legend Lightnin' Hopkins, who folklorist Sam Charters had just discovered living in Houston. On the way, they passed through Washington County, mentioned in "Tom Moore's Farm," a stark song they had heard on a Hopkins record. They asked around if anyone knew Tom Moore and were soon sitting in his very office, asking if he knew any blacks nearby who sang. They were led to Mance Lipscomb, who they found perched on a tractor, finishing up his day's work. That evening, they recorded Arhoolie's first album.

McCormick told Strachwitz they had made a crucial discovery, not only of a brilliant and previously unrecorded talent, but of a vital link to the all-but-extinct songster tradition.

"I didn't like Mance at first," said Strachwitz, "because he was kind of nice and sweet; not the nasty, rough blues I was used to. He did play some blues, but he was from the older songster tradition, which was very common from the end of slavery until the beginning of the commercial blues craze in the '20s."

Songsters were essentially the village minstrels for rural black communities, performing at parties, dances, weddings, funerals, religious and seasonal celebrations. Their repertoires included everything from children's play-party songs to bawdy blues and dance tunes, spirituals and hymns to historical ballads and pop chestnuts. As the blues became a commercial craze in the '20s, it displaced and all but eradicated this older, more varied tradition.

"The folk process is a very cruel bully," Strachwitz said. "When the folk discover a new instrument or form, it often wipes out what was happening before. The accordion wiped out the fiddle in zydeco and made it secondary in Cajun music. In Mexican music, it wiped out all the little regional orchestras, with their clarinets, violins, guitars. The folk process will grab whatever is available; that's why all the early blues guys were developing their styles on electric guitars as soon as they could lay their hands on them."

Hearing Lightnin' Hopkins perform live charted Strachwitz's course permanently. Asking around, they found him in a small Houston beer joint. Hopkins had been tipped that some white guys form California were looking for him, so the moment they walked in, he improvised a verse: "Whoa, this man come all the way from California just to hear poor Lightnin' sing." Strachwitz was stunned.

"That was really the turning point for me," he said. "I had heard him on record, but not like this. That night, he sounded better than he had on his best record. All I remember was one long number, and he was making up one verse after another about what was going on that night; wondering why this woman was dancing right in front of him, things that had happened to him that day. I knew right then that I wanted a record company that captured the music this way; the way it really sounded in its own communities."

Back in California, he settled on a name, which should prove a useful parable for any who presume to know too much about other folk's cultures. The moniker for this most authentic of roots labels is, in fact, a misnomer. Someone told Strachwitz that "arhoolie" was a slang term for a field holler, the chanting songs African-Americans sang while working in the fields. It seemed to capture the vernacular spirit of what Strachwitz wanted to do. It is also wrong. He has never encountered anyone else familiar with the term, though "hoolie" is occasionally used for "holler." He speculates now that what was probably heard was just somebody saying, "This is a hoolie."

For any considering a life like Strachwitz's, it should also be instructive, if not cautionary, to know that while Arhoolie always showed a profit, he has earned more money from side vocations. In the early days, his vintage record collecting became a full-fledged business, catering especially to European hobbyists.

But publishing earned the greatest financial windfalls. K.C. Douglas's "Mercury Blues," recorded and published by Strachwitz in 1959, was later recorded by rocker Steve Miller and country star Alan Jackson, whose version was used in a Ford commercial. With the royalties, Strachwitz started the Arhoolie Foundation, dedicated to the preservation of roots music.

In the '60s, a Berkeley antiwar activist and folk singer asked if Arhoolie would record his new protest song so he could make it available locally. Strachwitz agreed, though he had no interest in the song himself. The activist had no money, so Strachwitz said, "Tell you what; I'll take publishing rights instead of a fee, how's that?" Country Joe McDonald was grateful at the time, though he has had second thoughts since his "Feel Like I'm Fixing to Die Rag" became a generational anthem after its inclusion in the film "Woodstock." Those royalties helped support Arhoolie through the lean years following the the decline of the '60s revival.

It took awhile, but Strachwitz finally recorded Hopkins in 1961. The seasoned blues master, who had enjoyed some minor R&B hits in the '40s, was notoriously—and quite understandably—wary of record producers. He had been badly ripped off by producers waving money and big promises at him. But Strachwitz insists that was all just business, and that the widespread myth Hopkins had a prejudice against white people is nonsense.

"I never felt anything like that from him," he said. "He just didn't trust most people, like most country folks don't. They figure city people are all a bunch of slickers who are going to beat you somehow. But he took me all around the joints in Houston, and we traveled to Europe together; I don't think he had nothing against white folks."

On one of those Houston tavern-trawls in 1964, Hopkins took Strachwitz to hear his cousin, the brilliant zydeco accordionist Clifton Chenier, whom Strachwitz immediately agreed to record. Increasingly, as word spread about Arhoolie's devotion to recording this music the way artists liked to perform it, people flocked to him with leads about whom he should record.

Archie Green began introducing Strachwitz to Hispanic border musicians, and the CD box includes cuts from the lilting Los Pinguines Del Norte, the irresistibly charming Trio San Antonio, stunning Tejano chanteuse Lydia Mendoza, and the remarkable Jimenez family, including Tejano star Flaco Jimenez, whose album "Ay Te Dejo En San Antonio" earned Arhoolie the first of its two Grammy awards.

Strachwitz's best finds, like Lipscomb, were often a combination of pure serendipity and a willingness to follow his hunches. Strachwitz rediscovered the seminal cajun band The Hackberry Ramblers in 1963, when he drove past a sign pointing to the little town of Hackberry, Louisiana. "Worth a shot," he thought, having heard old '78s of the classic band, but not knowing if any of them were even still alive. He stopped at a cafe and was directed right to leader Luderin Darbone's house in nearby Sulphur. Darbone pulled the old band together, dormant for years, and they recorded the next day. Knowing that, their crisp, fun-loving "Crowley Waltz" is even more remarkable.

The recording quality of all five CDs is wonderfully clean and inviting. Because of Strachwitz's determination to capture these artists performing as naturally as possible, there are wonderfully vivid moments. Hopkins sings at his long-lined, sensually eloquent and acidly witty best. Mississippi Fred McDowell performs a dizzyingly close guitar-harmonica duet with neighbor Johnny Woods, and Big Mama Thornton brings a robust, often hilarious sexuality to "Little Red Rooster." Trio San Antonio are gently charismatic and spry, and the New Orleans Ragtime Orchestra provides a sweet, evocative bridge between 19th-century ragtime and traditional jazz.

Strachwitz said it was the idea of co-producer Elijah Wald, who also wrote the cinematic, anecdote-rich CD book, to include only tracks Strachwitz personally recorded. As a result, the box plays like the grand, sprawling adventure his life has been; full of fun and surprise, loping serendipitously from zydeco to salsa, hillbilly swing to German drinking song, gospel thumper to searing blues.

As the great commercial revival of the '60s faded, Strachwitz was a leader among the new wave of folklorists and folk labels devoted to presenting roots music as its interpreters actually performed it in their own communities. The new availability of authentic Cajun and Tejano music, blues, bluegrass and traditional country music spurred grassroots revivals in all those forms, igniting the quieter, less commercial but more permanent market for folk music that still exists today.

Strachwitz is, of course, delighted to see the world and roots music booms of recent years, though he hotly laments how often indigenous musical styles are made "market-friendly" by being stapled to conventional pop and rock rhythm sections.

"I wish our simplistic, goddam boogaloo beat would just stay out of it," he said. "So much of it all sounds like a boom-box to me. I really don't know why that happens; I imagine it's just that the average person can't identify with the really pure, authentic stuff. And you know, I'm a typical example of that myself. When Sam Charters first played me the old blues records—Blind Lemon Jefferson, Willie McTell—I didn't like them, because they didn't have the depth of quality soundwise that the more recent ones like Lightnin' or Sonny Boy Williamson had. It sounded tinny to me, and I couldn't identify with it at first. That's why performing is so important; once you see them in person, you get it."

Strachwitz also departed from commercial and folkloric producers of the past in his commitment to singles. While he never made money releasing singles, he felt it was his duty to distribute these records not only to roots music fans, but within the artists' own communities. He helped revive many important regional careers by placing new singles on jukeboxes where those artists lived and performed. To Strachwitz, it was simply a matter of returning this music to its rightful owners, and he took great pride in seeing a neglected conjunto or Cajun artists regain local respect when their songs blared out of jukeboxes at local taverns.

Along the way, Arhoolie also became deeply involved in making documentary films about regional musicians and culture, and to preserving the archival recordings that represent the roots of American vernacular music. As he gets older, he takes great pleasure and pride in helping young Americans trace their cultural roots through music, and set up the Arhoolie Foundation to promote that work.

So does he recommend young people pick up the Great Vernacular Trail he has been blazing for 40 years? Are there still traditional treasures to be found?

"I think there's always plenty of music out there. In regard to ethnic traditions, most of them are constantly changing, so there's always the chance to find some wonderful performers preserving the music from the past."

He offered his own recent forays into the Rio Grande valley on the Texas-Mexican border as an astonishing proof. For a new CD, "The Devil's Swing," he has been collecting a spate of freshly composed Mexican corridos about drug smuggling, and in particular about drug lord Pablo Escobar, recently killed by the federales.

Long accustomed to inquiring about older traditions wherever he goes, Strachwitz and his guide, University of Texas professor Jim Nicolopulos, asked some Mexican cowboys if they knew any corridos about the 19th-century cattle drives to Kansas. "Oh yeah," one said, "about the 500 steers. We know that one."

And they sang it, a long, plaintive ballad about a foreman explaining the death of a cowboy to the young man's widow after a drive from Chihuaha to Kansas.

"It's about how the steers had pushed him into a corner and crushed him," Strachwitz said. "It still rings true to in that rural region, where most people work with cattle, so it's still sung, still passed along. We did some research, and it is the oldest corrido ever collected. It's not known to have ever been recorded before, just passed along from cowboy to cowboy purely within the border community, for almost 150 years. And we found that last year; so yeah, there's still lots of great stuff to be found."

He encourages people to start close to home, doing oral histories in their own neighborhood, even within their own families. This music, since it has little broad commercial appeal, often remains within specific ethnic communities. He suggested asking older people how they used to socialize, where they went on dates, what kind of music they listened to, what they called it, what kind of dances they did. Do you know anyone who still plays that way? Do you have any old records of that music?

Often, old-timers to these traditions are skeptical about interest expressed from younger people, suspicious they might be just making fun of them. So any advance research that can be done to show your interest is genuine and informed is helpful. Once the bond of interest is established, most keepers of old traditions are eager to pass along their knowledge; delighted and flattered that someone else cares.

In exploring more deeply into communities, Strachwitz suggested some people—folklorists sometimes call them "key informants"—who are good places to start. Religious leaders, for example, are usually knowledgeable about their congregations and would know if any used to be musicians or still are; if there are or were any ethnic dances in the neighborhood. Owners of local restaurants, taverns and ethnic clubs are also often plugged into local ethnic dances and musical happenings. Ask where the elders of local cultural and ethnic groups tend to gather to socialize, and go ask them the same questions. Strachwitz also recommended scanning local radio stations, particularly smaller AM ones, that still offer ethnic programs, usually on weekends. Local DJ's of those programs are often cultural activists within their communities.

"If you don't know where else to start," said Strachwitz, "just get your tape recorder and go talk to your parents, grandparents, aunts and uncles. Where did they go on Saturday nights? What kind of music did they like? What about the older folks way back then; what did they like to go hear? Are any of those musicians still around?

"Because vernacular music ain't written down, and neither is the history of it.

It all comes from ten million personal experiences. You gotta go get it from the people."

Originally appeared in Sing Out! the Folk Song Magazine
Used by permission, Sing Out Corporation
—Spring, 2001

What do folklorists do in the 21st century?
Massachusetts state folklorist Maggie Holtzberg, Joe Cormier

When most of us hear the word folklore, we think of old wives' tales, herbal remedies and fiddle tunes. So, why is Massachusetts state folklorist Maggie Holtzberg poking around the garden outside Carmela Farina's Newton home?

Since being hired by the Massachusetts Cultural Council in April 1999, Holtzberg has launched an ambitious statewide survey to document the Commonwealth's diverse folk cultures. But to her, that means something much more vibrant than old fables.

"A lot of people think that folklorists are mostly concerned with dead or dying art, stuff that's gone," said Holtzberg, whose official title is Folk and Traditional Arts Coordinator. "But this survey is dealing with living traditions. We want to find living artists and workers, tradition-bearers who certainly have a link with the past; but what we're most interested in is how people came to a tradition, how they learned it, whether that's a traditional fiddler or a Big Dig tunnel worker."

Holtzberg also lives in Newton and first heard about Farina from a neighbor. While she confessed some of her questions were practical, since she is having trouble with her own backyard garden, she was most interested in the stories about how Farina learned to garden and do embroidery, how she came to live in her house 52 years ago, in the Nonantum part of Newton, still heavily populated by Italian-Americans whose roots are in San Donato.

Farina told how her parents came from San Donato, settling in Nonantum to be near relatives—valuable information about local immigration patterns. When Farina said both her father and husband worked for the City of Newton, Holtzberg gained insight into the role government played in aiding immigrants.

As she discussed the statuary in the thick of her flowerbeds, she revealed how Italian-Americans use urban gardens to honor their Catholic faith, but also to mark their own lives. She pointed to grand iron "geranium trees," with flower pots dangling, that her husband had welded for her, and explained that the large bottles filled with bright blue water were to remember how he and her father both made their own wine. A statue of a little girl sewing represented Farina herself, a memory of learning to embroider from her mother.

"When you look at any group of people that has a sense of belonging to something," Holtzberg said, "whether it's their language, the music, where they're from, or the work they do, there are unspoken rules that make them feel they belong to that community. When you learn through family or from elders, you pick up much more than just the skill; you pick up values, aesthetics, cultural history, the rules and behavior that make you an insider in that community. That knowledge is ephemeral; it doesn't always get documented by mainstream historians. Wonderful bodies of lore, song, dance, ways of doing work, will all get lost unless it's documented."

Farina explained that urban gardening is very much a social tradition, done not just to please herself and her neighbors, but as a vehicle to visit with them. She loves to tend her flowers and chat with the people who pass by.

"I think flowers represent the beauty of God in this world," she said. "There's a lot of ugliness, but flowers and birds are the beauty of God that He's given us to enjoy."

Holtzberg's next visit was with Stow stonemason Kenny Barnes. She said that the information from this survey will do much more than satisfy scholarly curiosity. She is hoping to launch an apprenticeship program like the one she began when she was Georgia's state folklorist, in which public funds are used to pay master craftsmen like Barnes to pass along their lifetime of knowledge. After all, there are still stones in New England fields, still walls lining the roads that need tending.

"A lot of this gets to economics," Holtzberg said. "Still-useful vocations are vanishing. This information can be used to employ people; not just to document old and vanishing trades, but to preserve them and create new ones. It's not just lore that's being lost here, it's jobs."

Holtzberg was intrigued by the stone walls, but more by the work Barnes did—and how he learned it. She asked a favorite folklorist's question: Whether older workers in his trade played any pranks on apprentices. She explained that these are often used not only as practical jokes, but also as rites of initiation, after which new workers feel more like insiders themselves.

Banks laughed and confessed that as long as he has been around stonemasons, newcomers have been urgently dispatched to piles of stone searching for a "No. 2 stone." By the time they get the joke, they have also learned a key lesson in the trade—that each stone is unique. It's a lesson especially vital to building dry stone walls, so called because they are built entirely from free-fitting stones, with no caulking or cement.

"Something we say is that there is no such thing as an ugly stone," he said.

"Each one has some value, some use."

Asked about the future, he said, "It's a dying trade. Everybody's going into computer work. But we have a backlog of people waiting for us to work on their walls. Some people call a year ahead for us; I actually have too much work."

Then it was off to Waltham to visit Cape Breton fiddler Joe Cormier, one of the real success stories of folklorist-run traditional arts programs. Though always a fixture on the Cape Breton dance scene, in recent years he has become an international folk star and winner of the prestigious National Heritage Fellowship Award, an honor he shares with bluegrass progenitor Bill Monroe and blues legend B. B. King.

Cormier has benefited greatly from publicly funded festivals and touring programs, fondly mentioning folklorist Joe Wilson of National Council for the Traditional Arts, which brought him to the National Folk Festival, the Lowell Folk Festival, which the council still helps program, and a Masters of the Folk Violin Tour.

Without the funding public-arts folklorists like Holtzberg bring to traditional music, music like Cormier's would often remain entirely within small, ethnic communities.

To Cormier, a retired electrician, his illustrious new career as a folk legend is not quite the departure you might expect. Between ripping off sprightly dance tunes at Holtzberg's request, he explained, "When I was young, we lived in a little fishing village, a poor village, and the fiddler was a little celebrity. That was the entertainment; they put you up on a table, on a stage, and you were the focus of the party. That seemed like a good deal to me at the time."

Then, winking softly at Holtzberg, he said, "Still does."

Holtzberg thinks the survey, which is just in its opening phase, will be ongoing, and grow into a permanent mechanism for documenting and honoring traditional culture. In these noisome and strangely isolating times, she sees great relevance to her work, not just for those being surveyed, but for all of us.

"In a very real way, modern folklore is the study of human community, how it forms, what keeps it together and what threatens it, how it is communicated and how it can be preserved.

"The way our lifestyles are changing, people don't stay in the same community they grew up in so much, and both parents are often working. People don't have access to the kinds of extended families and lifelong neighbors that were once fairly common. If we are going to keep community a living part of our culture, we need to understand how it works. That, in a nutshell, is what folklorists do."

—*May 28, 2000*

New England's saloon singer laureate
John Fitzsimmons

Back in the 1970s, it seemed that every fern bar and singles pub had its own folk singer. Wedged in between the cigarette machine and the jukebox, with a potted plant hanging threateningly overhead, he'd belt out standards by James Taylor, Bob Dylan, Joni Mitchell, and John Denver, occasionally attempting to sneak in an original song or two. The music these earnest warblers provided was merely romantic background for desperately seeking singles, and they often sounded as though they wanted to be anywhere but where they were.

Occasionally, however, a true master of the form emerged; someone who was proudly a pub singer, able to mesmerize disparate crowds of drinking, chatty people as he led them from the hits they knew to the more obscure treasures of tradition that are the root and heart of the folk genre. These entertainers were happy just where they were, always relishing the challenge of winning over the crowd. Many ardent folk fans began their musical journeys under their exuberant tutelage.

A wonderful throwback to that tradition is John Fitzsimmons, who holds cheerful court every Thursday night at the Sit'n'Bull Pub in Maynard. It is a Thursday tradition Fitzsimmons began 15 years ago at the Colonial Inn in Concord and moved to the Sit'N Bull last August.

"I love pub singing," he said after the show. "The night's long enough to get to know your audience, and I've learned that is the key to this kind of entertaining. And I don't mean knowing them as in being able to read a crowd, but actually knowing them, knowing their names and a little bit about their lives. Then people give you the benefit of the doubt. They don't mind hearing some of the same songs every time, and they trust you when you give them one they may not have heard before."

Fitzsimmons mistrusts all the trappings of stardom and resists anything that separates him from his audience. Shortly after moving to the Sit'N Bull, which features rock, country and blues bands on weekends, he abandoned the large nightclub stage for a little corner in the front room. There, perched on a stool in front of a modest green backdrop, he can chat more easily with the crowd, as he did Thursday, often on a first-name basis.

He began in familiar folk terrain with a rollicking cover of Dylan's "Don't Think Twice," followed by a merry strut of the old railroad song, "John Henry." His rich baritone is a marvel of honest restraint and casual phrasing, but with an alluring satin resonance shimmering underneath. Though he would never want people to think so, he is a superbly disciplined singer.

Fitzsimmons is a true Yankee original, an iconoclastic, often stubborn man who loves hard work, but hates when that work becomes business. In his 40 years, he has been a farmer, sailor, carpenter, street singer, horse handler, teacher, camp counselor, children's entertainer, and youth minister. He turned his back on 15 years at the Colonial Inn when the new owners, to his mind, unfairly fired the Thursday bartender. (He is on good terms with the inn again, and returns to sing occasionally.)

"Rightly or wrongly, I sort of claimed an ownership of those evenings," he said. "I'd played for so long there, it was almost part of the rhythm of my life. It was the place I saw people who I came to consider friends, business travelers passing through once or twice a year, local people I never saw anywhere but at the inn. It became known as a safe place for people to come and socialize and have some fun, never so much a performance as a shared experience, something we were all making happen together. I'm hoping to build that at the Sit'N Bull."

Fitzsimmons is accompanied every Thursday by Seth Connolly, one of the most respected acoustic guitarists in the area, and supple bassist Rick Maida. On March 26, he happily sang any requests he knew, and twice promised to learn songs he did not. To his mind, there is no such thing as a chestnut; any song that can become meaningful to someone is a good song.

"The value of music to people's lives supersedes my opinion of it," he said. "The fact that I might think a John Denver song is schmaltzy doesn't mean it's not good. If it has value and importance in people's lives, it's a good song. To start thinking your taste and and opinion is the most important thing is a bad drive down a bad road. I've learned over the years that if a song can move someone, anyone, it's a good song."

Fitzsimmons acquired much of his musical egalitarianism on long trips through Asia and Russia busking, or singing on street corners, for tips. They were the only interruptions in his 15-year run at the Colonial Inn, except for a six-month stint taking people on sailing cruises off Martha's Vineyard. He is building his own boat now, in between his job as shop teacher and wrestling coach at the Fenn School in Concord, his Thursdays at the Sit'N Bull, and his increasingly busy schedule as a coffeehouse performer. This month, he is to move into a house he and his wife, Denise, bought in Maynard.

Fitzsimmons is also a counselor at Camp Sewataro in Sudbury, which is how he got to know Sit'N Bull owner Ted Epstein, who gave him a standing offer to come play after hearing him sing for his fellow counselors at the pub a few summers ago.

It is in his writing that Fitzsimmons' serious side emerges. His songs and poems are informed by a quietude that makes them rivetingly reflective, brimming with vivid images of backwoods wanderings and inner wonderings. He has a warm and wise poetry book, "Raccoon," and a splendid compact disc of his own heartfelt ballads called "Fires in the Belly."

At the Sit'N Bull, however, he was reluctant to indulge his muse much. Mostly, he sprinkled familiar 1960s and '70s hits like "Early Morning Rain" and "Gentle on My Mind" with older traditional gems. At one point, he honored a request for "Ain't Misbehavin'," which turned into a grand strut of folk legend Jesse Fuller's "San Francisco Bay Blues."

Again on request, he sang Gordon Lightfoot's familiar "Wreck of the Edmund Fitzgerald," which led to an ebullient cover of "Lead Belly" Ledbetter's blues classic about the Titanic. That inspired a brilliantly conceived medley of Ledbetter's famous "Pick a Bale of Cotton," spiced with hot verses from his lesser-known antiracism song, "Bourgeois Blues."

Beneath the surface of Fitzsimmons' friendly charisma is the heart of a purist, gently leading people from the songs of their lives to the timeless traditional folk songs he loves so well.

"Bad folk songs just don't exist," he said. "Bad interpretations of them do, but the very fact that a song has been deemed a folk song, that it's gone through the mill, been handed down again and again and survived, gives it value. They're like people that way, and I've always been drawn to people who've been through the mill. There's something about experience that I'm drawn to, in the way I live my life and in the people I like. And a folk song to me has experience."

"I think music is meant to be used," he said almost sternly. "I've never been refined about it. I treat my guitars like an old pickup truck, and my songs the same way. Songs are meant to carry people somewhere."

—*April 5, 1998*

Lead Belly *and the children: the tender side of a hard man*
Smithsonian Folkways archivist Jeff Place, folklorist Tony Seeger

Today, Huddie "Lead Belly" Ledbetter (1888-1949) is regarded as one of America's greatest and most influential folk musicians. His brilliant guitar playing, marked by driving bass lines set against quicksilver treble fingerpicking, helped popularize both the Texas blues style and the 12-string guitar. Even those who no longer remember his name know his songs and the songs he made famous, among them "Goodnight, Irene" "Cotton Fields," "Midnight Special," "Take This Hammer," "Pick a Bale of Cotton," and "Rock Island Line."

Yet we almost lost his most precious gift to American musical culture, the hundreds of traditional African-American songs he picked up along the hard roads of his fiery, myth-enshrouded, and sometimes violent life. The groundbreaking little 1941 album called "Play Parties in Song and Dance as Sung by Lead Belly" opened up new career vistas for Ledbetter, however, through which nearly his entire body of songs was eventually recorded.

The humbly produced six-song record had an equally powerful effect on the man who released it, Moe Asch, who went on to found Folkways Records, the single most prolific and arguably the most important of American folk labels.

It has been re-released in its entirety on a new Smithsonian Folkways CD, "Lead Belly Sings for Children." (His moniker has also been rendered as Leadbelly, but scholars in recent years have reverted to writing the nickname in two words, as he preferred it.) Also included in the 62-minute disc are a live children's music concert Ledbetter did in 1945, some of his lively radio appearances with such guests as Kid Ory and the Golden Gate Quartet, and several stirring solo versions of Ledbetter's best-known classics.

It is a remarkable record, musically superb and deeply informative, both in the intimate glimpse it reveals of Ledbetter the performer and in the knowledge he conveys about the roots of the songs he sings. It is striking how utterly comfortable he seems around children, talking to them without condescension, explaining honestly and movingly the hard times from which the songs came.

"This really isn't a children's record in the conventional sense," said Smithsonian Folkways archivist Jeff Place, whose savvy liner notes add immeasurably to the CD. "What Lead Belly did was present American folk songs for children, showing them and teaching them about spirituals and blues and work songs, not just the the usual play-party and ditty songs you associate with children's music."

By 1941, Ledbetter's music had been obscured by his legend. He was a minor star who had recorded for Columbia, Stinson, and RCA's race label, Bluebird. But he was tragically stereotyped by his infamous past. He had gone to prison twice for fights that resulted in the death and near-death of his opponents.

Ledbetter was discovered in Louisiana's Angola Prison in 1933 by folklorists John and Alan Lomax, who went there to collect prison songs. Upon his release in 1934, he came to New York, where, first under the sponsorship of the Lomaxes and later on his own, he found himself billed as "the Savage Singer from the Swamplands," and was often made to perform in prison garb. Record companies regarded him either exclusively as a blues artist or as a primitive novelty act. The genius beneath the legend was in danger of being lost forever.

Enter Asch, who was introduced to Ledbetter by Broadway producer Sy Rady. At the time, Asch was a recording engineer who had released a few records of local Jewish music. He loved Ledbetter's music, but despised the way he was being presented.

Smithsonian Folkways director Tony Seeger said, "Moe thought Lead Belly was being stereotyped, presented with a very limited view of his repertoire and this single facet of his history. And he felt Lead Belly was an intellectual, just like himself."

In a brilliant marketing stroke, Asch confronted the stereotypes head-on, determined to humanize Ledbetter to the public. He had spent a delightful afternoon listening to Ledbetter perform for children, probably at the progressive Little Red School House in New York. By recording these gentle, playful songs, he hoped to force the music world to see this man for the musical genius and genuine folk scholar he was.

What he did not expect was to have a hit. Shortly after its 1941 release, however, gossip columnist Walter Winchell smeared the obscure producer for recording a convicted murderer singing children's songs. The notoriety made the album a bestseller.

Seeger said, "This record really made Asch. It turned him from a small provider of specialized music into a record company. It sold well enough for him to have the money to make other recordings, and he began to issue music from other parts of the world, and other folk communities here. He started recording Woody Guthrie, my uncle Pete Seeger, and other folk musicians, which led to his founding Folkways Records in 1948."

It also helped Ledbetter break the shackles of his pigeonholed career. From then on, he was seen even by major labels as more than a novelty. He continued to record on occasion for big labels, but returned to Asch over and over to preserve his encyclopedic treasury of African-American folk music, among the most extensive and brilliantly performed traditional song collections ever recorded.

The 1941 cuts are digitally remastered with astonishing clarity, showcasing Ledbetter in superb form, performing bright children's tunes as well as fiery blues and work songs.

But it is the live recordings that provide the best glimpses of the man behind the legend. He clearly wants to show children something of the hard truths that shimmer beneath the bouncy melodies and clever lyrics. His explanation of the blues, how it is rooted in hard times, is wonderfully crafted for young listeners. He follows it with an equally ingenious musical essay, in which he asks them first to simply feel the blues through his eloquent guitar playing, then sings a simple lonesome blues any child could empathize with.

In another cut, he sings a lovely medley of hymns from various faiths, making the point that, as he puts it, "We're all in the same boat, brother." In the CD's most charming moment, he sings his classic work song "Take This Hammer," explaining how the exhaled "Whah!" at the end of each line accompanied the driving of the hammer. He then asks them to join in, and the children enthusiastically pant along until giggles overtake them—and very nearly Ledbetter. You can fairly see them swinging their imaginary hammers to his powerful vocals.

Seeger said, "Children's music today is often made up of infantile ditties that don't address terribly serious issues, or do so in a rather contrived way. But here he is singing songs about life and death and hard work and insect plagues driving farmers out of their homes, really tough stuff. This record is kind of a revaluation in how you can relate to kids. They may be small, but you can treat them straight on, talk straight at them and present your music the way it really is, and they go right along. You don't have to create a purple dinosaur or a green bumblebee; you can just be a real person and sing real songs and let them learn about life."

—April 11, 1999

A little muscle: honoring the songs of Malvina Reynolds
Rosalie Sorrels

Looking back on the remarkable career of songwriter Malvina Reynolds, it is hard not to conclude that she would be much better known today if she had been a man. As political songwriters, only Woody Guthrie and Pete Seeger cast larger shadows on the folk revival before the 1960s; it can be argued that her unique blend of personal and political had even more influence on many in the next generation of folk writers.

Her songs were among the most popular to emerge from the early days of the folk revival, including the wistful parents' hymn "Turn Around," a huge 1950s hit for Harry Belafonte; and "Little Boxes," a wry satire of middle-class conformity that Seeger made famous in 1963. Her politically precocious songs about the environment, feminism, and the homeless both predicted and helped ignite those modern social movements.

"Malvina was one of the first who was a female and wrote political songs," said folk singer-songwriter Rosalie Sorrels, whose new Red House CD, "No Closing Chord," is a candid and musically haunting trib ute to Reynolds, produced by Nina Gerber and featuring Bonnie Raitt, Barbara Higbie, Terry Garthwaite, and Laurie Lewis. Sorrels was also curator of two Smithsonian/Folkways CDs of Reynolds singing her own songs. The first volume, "Ear to the Ground," came out last summer.

"There was really a sense at the beginning of the '60s revival that it was the province of the male society to write the songs; that Judy Collins and Joan Baez were very fine, but basically girl singers using male songs. Malvina helped teach us how to take our personal feelings into our songs; that you recognize what's funny or meaningful about you as a woman singing about these issues and put that into your songs."

Sorrels is now among the first ladies of American folk song, but she was a wild child of the '60s when she became a friend and protegee of Reynolds. She credits her with turning her rebelliousness from a destructive force into an artistic one; and with literally saving her life, since Reynolds was the first to warn her of the dangers of cancer and teach her about self-examination. Sorrels is now recovering from breast cancer.

"Malvina was determined to live a useful life," she said, adding that the lifelong progressive left the Communist Party because all they wanted her to do was type and make coffee. Even being a radical was not considered woman's work in those days.

Still, her politics got Reynolds blacklisted in the 1950s. It was her determination to speak her mind as a woman that led her to song writing. She was over 40 when she wrote her first song.

Reynolds became equally adept at simplistic rally songs, often written for specific issues, protests, or causes, and sweepingly universal anthems, such as her environmental classic "What Have They Done to the Rain?," which was recorded by Sorrels, Baez, Collins, and a host of other '60s folk singers. But unlike many of her contemporaries, she also wrote with a keen empathy for differing points of view, illuminating the gray space between the blacks and whites of hotly debated issues.

In "Rosie Jane," written more than 30 years ago, she argues for a woman's right to choose in a musical dialogue between a woman who has an unwanted pregnancy and a patronizing doctor. It succeeds because it refuses to take sides by portraying the woman as victim or heroine. The sheer complexity of the dilemma makes the case for women needing to make this decision for themselves.

Sorrels always suspected that Reynolds wrote the song about her after once mistakenly assuming she was pregnant. Reynolds always denied it, but after Reynolds's death in 1978, her daughter acknowledged that she had but had not wanted to hurt Sorrels's feelings by saying so. The song is on both CDs, and Sorrels's version is a droll comic masterpiece, brimming with affection.

"She was able to identify what it was to be a human in whatever situation she was writing about," said Sorrels. "One of my favorite children's songs of hers goes, 'Everybody says sit down, sit down / I can't sit down, I can't sit down/ My feet are full of runaround.' Now if that isn't a perfect description of a kid, I don't know what is. In everything she wrote and did, she cut through all the bull, made you get specific about what you liked and didn't like and what you wanted to change."

One of Reynolds's favorite terms was "A Little Muscle," which became the title of a posthumous ode by Janet Smith, sung beautifully by Sorrels on "No Closing Chord."

"The word muscle was important to her because she was a woman and old and therefore often shunted aside," said Sorrels. "She meant by it intellectual muscle and insistence, saying, `You have to listen to me, because I have something important to say.' People tried to ignore her; it was not possible. And also, she was talking about the kind of muscle that evolves from people doing things together; how you feel weak and helpless all by yourself, but when you all get together and work and insist, you can get something done—you have muscle."

—November 10, 2000

Columbine's anthem: the troubled trail of a song
Cheryl Wheeler, Rounder Records executive Brad Paul, radio program director Dave Benson, gun control advocate Douglas Weil

Today in Littleton, Colo., Ann Kechter will listen to a song called "If It Were Up to Me," written by New England songwriter Cheryl Wheeler. She has listened to it every day since late April, when her 16-year-old son Matthew was one of 13 people murdered by two Columbine High School classmates. For her, it has become a ritual in a healing process she knows will never really end.

In a letter to Wheeler's manager, Tony Gottlieb, she called it "a true to the heart reflection of all the pain, anger, sorrow, frustration and the realization of absolute senselessness of gun violence I have experienced as a result of the Columbine massacre."

The road that song traveled between Wheeler and Kechter was remarkable, marked by tragedy and controversy, offering glimpses of the media and the music business at their best—and worst.

Wheeler is one of the most popular performers in folk music, but her songs are rarely heard beyond that small world of coffeehouses, public radio stations, and independent labels like Cambridge's Rounder Records Group, on whose Philo division she records. "If It Were Up to Me" was written in March 1998 as a response to the schoolyard killings in Jonesboro, Ark. Once again, she thought to herself, children are killing children. As Wheeler often does when she has nowhere else to pour her feelings, she picked up her guitar and began to write.

"I think what really got me was the media discussion about why this might have happened," she said. "I started compiling this litany of reasons I was hearing for why violence occurs."

"If It Were Up to Me" begins with her chanting those reasons: "Maybe it's the movies/maybe it's the books/maybe it's the bullets/maybe it's the real crooks." After 64 more reasons, including drugs, TV, parents, and the Internet, she ends by singing, "If it were up to me, I'd take away the guns."

"We'll never stop being able to think up reasons why people go nuts," she said. "If we could understand why people become violent, that would be great. But all we know is that the reason these people are dead is that they had bullets go through their bodies. So while we're trying to understand these other things, all we can do is control the access to very deadly weapons."

Two weeks after the Jonesboro shootings, Wheeler was performing the song to very strong response. Gottlieb rushed a tape of it to Rounder, and Brad Paul, vice president of national promotions, felt something special should be done to get it heard beyond the usual folk-friendly radio stations.

"This is an intensively competitive world, and it is extremely difficult to get major-market commercial radio stations to pay attention to any records," Paul said. "But it was not a novel idea to tie a song to a good cause to get that attention. Rykodisc did it with a Bruce Cockburn song a few years ago, offering to donate a sum of money to a group seeking the banning of land mines every time the song was played. This was a song that cried out for that kind of approach."

It seemed like marketing at its best, tying a little social altruism to the usual promotional glitz. The Center to Prevent Handgun Violence was Rounder's first choice as a place to donate the money. The nonprofit gun-control advocacy group, part of Handgun Control Inc., is chaired by Sarah Brady, whose husband, James, then President Reagan's press secretary, was shot by John Hinckley.

Rounder officials contacted the center's research director, Douglas Weil, who they knew was a Wheeler fan. He reported back that the center loved the idea. But he also had a warning for them.

"The center has dealt with lots of people new to this issue, with victims and their families in particular," he said. "So when anybody wants to become more public and speak out on this issue, we let them know they are likely to hear from people on the other side, people with very strong voices."

Rounder launched the campaign in February with the release of the CD the song was on, "Sylvia Hotel." In radio trade publications such as Billboard and the Gavin Report, it advertised its pledge to donate $5 to the center every time the song was played. Rounder also posted the pledge on its Web site, along with a list of 175 Adult Album Alternative stations to which they had sent the single. Rounder urged customers to call local radio stations requesting the song.

The response was swift and strong, but ran over 8 to 1 against the song and the promotion, and included pledges from customers that they would never buy a Rounder record again. What surprised the folk label most, given its fairly progressive fan base, was an almost complete lack of positive responses.

Among those disturbed enough to write to Wheeler was David Popowitch, a software product manager in Akron, Ohio. In a phone interview, he said he is not a gun owner but is troubled whenever government regulation, such as gun control, is offered as a solution to our social troubles.

"What I think is being created is this great Orwellian system, in which we're having tabs kept on us constantly," he said. "We have gotten away from the true moral fabric, the proper procedures and ethics of people in this country. And all I can attribute this violence to is what children are not being taught today by schools, and also what they are being taught by television and video games. It's total irresponsibility on society's part to let that take place."

The Rounder promotion ran throughout February. Not one major-market commercial station responded.

On April 20, Dylan Klebold and Eric Harris walked into their Littleton high school and opened fire, killing 12 students, one teacher, and themselves. At KBCO, a commercial adult-rock station in nearby Boulder, program director Dave Benson pondered what to do. He had read about the Rounder promotion.

"I dug the CD out and listened to the song," he said, "and got what I can only describe as goose bumps. I thought it said exactly what we were trying to say. At almost that same moment, our afternoon announcer came in and said he'd just gotten a call from a listener requesting the song."

Benson programmed the song once an hour for the first two days, then once every few hours for the next eight weeks. The reaction was as strong as anything Rounder had experienced, but in the wake of the Columbine massacre, very different.

"The phones started ringing and never stopped for two days," Benson said. "And the reaction was 98 percent positive."

Rounder reinstated the promotion when it saw the resumed interest in the song. The officials worried they might be viewed as exploiting a tragedy, but decided it was more unacceptable to not honor the pledge they had previously made. This time, the response doubled, from 240 plays in February to 500 in April, including a few commercial stations like the local WXRV-FM (92.5).

A friend gave Kechter a copy of Wheeler's CD, and the mother began her daily ritual of listening to the song. Kechter declined to be interviewed, but she gave permission to quote from her letter, in which she offered to help get a video of the song made.

She wrote: "It is comforting and amazing to me that someone so far removed from the core of the chaos can accurately voice the same despair and anxiety I have experienced. . . . Every day, I listen to the words as part of my healing and growing conviction to make a difference in our innocent children's lives."

The promotion is over, though a video of the song is in preproduction. Paul thinks the campaign overall was a failure. Less than $4,000 was raised for the Center to Prevent Handgun Violence. Apart from that brief flurry of response after the Littleton shootings, he doubts if any stations played the song that would not have done so anyway.

Wheeler has responded to the often vitriolic criticisms she received, including some threats, by becoming even more outspoken as an advocate for gun control.

On Monday, Columbine High School was reopened to students for the first time since the massacre. The night before, someone had scratched swastikas on walls and restrooms in the school.

Benson had not heard about Kechter's response to the song. When told, his normally jocular radio voice grew very quiet.

"Well, to me that makes it all worthwhile," he said. "If we, in any way . . . I mean, those poor people."

Paul stared blankly at the walls of his Cambridge office, pondering his experience with the song and the promotion.

"I think the saddest aspect is that this all will have happened, and our short memory spans keep getting shorter, and nothing will come of it," Paul said. "We just move along to the next tragedy. I read that heart-wrenching letter from Ms. Kechter, and I asked myself, what am I doing now? I've moved on. I'm consumed by the records we have coming out in the fall, what I'm going to do to help get the word out about them. I'm on to the next thing. I think of her letter, and then I wonder, am I any better than those other people who didn't want to get involved?"

—August 20, 1999

A love song for the ages: **Terry Egan** *builds a garden to honor his wife*

It began as a simple promise. Keeping that promise has become a second life for Terry Egan of Waltham.

In 1992, his wife, Mary Egan, was dying of leukemia. "The only thing she asked for," he said, "was that a patio be built for future patients. She'd be in a hospital room for two weeks at a time while she was treated, and she wanted people like her to be able to go outside, see the trees, hear the birds, get some sun. It would have made a big difference to her, she said."

This Friday, almost 10 years after promising her he would build a garden in her honor, the Mary Egan Memorial Garden opens as part of the new Beth Israel Deaconess Cancer Care center at Deaconess-Waltham Hospital.

"Terry's whole story is like some great old folk ballad about true love, a pledge, and all these obstacles that have to be overcome," said Ann Ormond, director of community relations and marketing for the hospital. "He was raising four children alone, had a full-time job, and still found a way to do all this. You just don't see that every day. It's a very sweet story."

Ormond was the first person Egan asked if the hospital would be interested in a garden patio. His wife had been treated at Newton-Wellesley Hospital, which couldn't incorporate a garden into its cancer unit, so Egan turned to Deaconess-Waltham.

"Waltham is my community," he said. "I'm third-generation here, so I approached Deaconess, and they took a shine to it."

That was not until December 1997, however. His first obligation was to care for his four children. The youngest were only 6 and 9 when their mother died, so the idea of flitting about town doing fund-raisers was out of the question.

Egan, who is 47 and director of software development and customer support for the Computer Corp. of America, has a few passions that fire his life: family camping, hockey, and local folk music. Whenever he took his children camping, often to hockey hives like Ottawa and northern Vermont, he would poke around record stores, looking for CDs by local artists. Something about the homemade, personal songs of community-based folksingers pleased his own reflective, familial nature.

After one such trip, his son Kevin, then 14, said, "Dad, you should do something with music to get Mom's patio built."

Egan decided to produce benefits featuring musicians he had discovered through his travels. The first was in 1997, with a few locals, such as country star John Lincoln Wright, along with Ottawa bluesman Rick Fines and other Canadian artists who had never performed in Waltham.

It was a total flop.

"Terry learned the hard way that you can't just hang out a sign and expect the hall to fill itself," said Fines, who has performed at every one of Egan's benefits. "By then, I knew he was going to make that patio happen if he had to build it himself. So after the show, we all started talking about what it was going to take to make the next concert work."

Egan enlisted Deaconess-Waltham Hospital for help promoting the shows.

The new cancer care center had not been conceived when Egan approached the hospital about the garden. Both the center and garden will be dedicated Friday.

The idea for the center dovetailed with Egan's garden. As cancer treatment is increasingly done on an outpatient basis, the goal was to put all treatment facilities in one place, and to make that place as patient-friendly as possible.

"With cancer treatment, patients often come for a lot of visits, as many as 60 over a six-week period," said Stewart Berman, head of radiation oncology at the hospital. "The patients are going to see a lot of our facility, and you know how anxiety can build in a waiting room, so the garden will provide people with a more natural, pleasant environment."

"Diagnosis of cancer has a lot of emotions associated with it," said Jackie Felt, program director for the center. "It's very difficult for patients and their families to work through those emotions, and the garden will give them an area of peace and calm where they can can go while they're here."

At every step of the process, Egan remembered his wife's ordeal and why the idea of a garden was so important to her. Annie Gallup, a songwriter who performed at a benefit, recommended Michigan sculptor-designer Wendell Heers, who had done a garden for the Assarian Oncology Clinic in Michigan.

"Terry's idea was for something to help people with cancer find some sort of peace while they undergo treatment," Heers said, "a place they can go to that's not just chairs and walls. There are rocks to sit on, and two fountains that form a stream with a pond, like a river of life with a beginning and end."

Landscape architect Shinichiro Abe of Sudbury's Zen Associates was brought in to design the vegetation.

"The most important thing for Terry was that it have a very natural feel," he said, "with running water, lots of color, evergreen shrubs, and trees that everyone could appreciate even in the winter. He wanted people to see things growing all the time, new shoots and buds, that kind of natural energy."

Egan was active for years in Little League and youth hockey, and acts more like a coach than concert producer when planning shows. He asks artists to play on each other's songs, even suggesting songs he'd like them to learn. As the shows became known for their off-the-cuff, jamming vibe, attendance climbed. Last year's show attracted more than 350 people.

"There's always a lot of people playing together at these shows, a lot of variety," said renowned Waltham fiddler Joe Cormier, who met Egan years ago through the Waltham Youth Hockey Association, for which Egan coached and served as president.

Egan has clearly enjoyed arranging these concerts, working with his favorite musicians, making new friends and forging new communities from those he enlists to help with the garden.

And his work is not over. He said he has not yet raised enough to cover all the garden's costs, and plans to keep producing concerts. Mary Egan's garden has flowered into a whole new life for him, and one can't help but wonder if perhaps she knew it would. Heers is certain the opening of the garden, the keeping of the promise, will not close the book on that new life.

"This guy is magnetic, so full of enthusiasm, and this project is something that goes very deep within him," he said.

"He's very much in love with Waltham, too, a real hometown boy. I'm sure he'll just keep on doing these kinds of things."

—April 22, 2001

photo courtesy Aine Minogue

Irish harpist is too busy for the big-time
Aine Minogue

For Arlington harpist Aine Minogue, Christmas is becoming a second career. Since its 1995 release, her tenderly lovely seasonal CD, "To Warm the Winter's Night" (Evergreen), has become a cherished part of the holidays for thousands of folk and Irish music fans.

The time between Thanksgiving and New Years' Eve is now the busiest season for the Irish-born harpist, averaging five shows a week, eclipsing even March, often dubbed "St. Patrick's Month" by harried Irish musicians.

"This time of year, people can tune into the kind of music I play in a way they can't the rest of the year," she said. "Despite all the distractions of the shopping and chores, there's an attunement to the ideas I find in the old Celtic music, of giving and acceptance, being reflective, sharing with your fellow man and being part of the natural world around you. There's more a sense of interdependence and community, because, even though it's a busy time for many people, it's the darkest time of year. People are more aware they need each other."

The rise of her Christmas career helped her resolve conflicts she felt about her beckoning stardom and the homey, rooted things that first drew her to Celtic traditional music. Last year, she walked away from a promising four-record contract with the major label RCA.

"It's kind of strange because in my recording career I've been working at a national level," she said over tea in her spacious Arlington Heights dining room, "but I'm still very much a community musician. I usually work close enough to Arlington that I can be home that night. I'll fly away for a big concert or festival now and again, but not too much anymore."

That is largely due to her desire to be home for her family, husband, Brian Myers, and 14-year-old son, William. But it is also because of the ancient values that first drew her to Celtic music and spirituality. She loves the ritual nature of the old music, its ceremonial uses, how particular tunes, songs, and carols were used to mark important events—winter solstice, weddings, the coming of spring and births. To her, performing for a wedding was as vital an artistic expression as filling a concert hall.

"To be in concert all the time, you have to develop an ego, a certain shell to put on a big show," she said. "I didn't want to develop that on a full-time basis. When you're part of a ritual, you're not central to the event the way you are on a concert stage. Everything you do is about contributing to the larger event in the purest way you can. I'm not saying ego is a bad thing. I love doing concerts, just not all the time."

While wrestling with the lure of the concert stage and the proddings of her record company, who saw genuine star potential in her entrancingly melodic harp playing and beautifully airy soprano, she talked to a Zen Buddhist friend of hers.

"I told him I knew I shouldn't be doing weddings and parties when I'm supposed to be touring and doing big concerts and all that," she said. "But I just love doing things like weddings. He said to me, `You have two people committing themselves to each other for life in a ritual. You love the ritual, you love the music and you love providing the music for that ritual. What's out on the road that you can't have here doing that?' "

Apart from money, she couldn't think of a thing. So she amicably negotiated an end to her RCA contract, focused on performing locally at coffeehouses, concerts, weddings and private functions, and founded Druidstone, her own production company. She is busily releasing records, both her own and anthologies, for sale in record stores, but also for the burgeoning market for acoustic CDs in bookstores and gift and specialty shops. The latest is "The Vow: An Irish Wedding Celebration," an unabashedly sentimental, deeply pretty set of Celtic airs and mushy old love songs like "The Rose of Allendale."

She said it was the startling success of her Christmas CD, "To Warm the Winter's Night" (available through her Web site, Minogue.com) that made her believe she could have the kind of cottage career she dreamed of as a girl in Borrisokane, Tipperary. She comes from a large musical family, and her father ran a local music club, so players from far and near would be found fiddling and piping in the family kitchen at all hours.

She lacked the confidence to contemplate a music career when she came to America in 1990 and found secretarial work at a Boston law firm. In fact, she didn't even bring her harp.

"I realized pretty quickly that people loved Irish music here," she said. "So I got a harp and people really responded. I developed a confidence here that I didn't back home, coming from such a large family of very good musicians. Here, there's such a feeling of individuality, a belief that you can pursue your own dream. Back home, the mold for a woman was that you became a nurse or a teacher. One of the things America gave me was the confidence to believe even the craziest things could work if you wanted them and were willing to work hard."

She said she also became deeply drawn to Celtic spirituality, to the beliefs that shaped the aesthetics of the old music. One reason "To Warm the Winter's Night" has become such a part of so many people's holidays is that she artfully placed it at the ancient crossroads where the Christmas holiday mingled with the older celebration of winter solstice. So many holiday rituals—the burning of logs and candles, bringing evergreens like fir and holly into the home, visiting neighbors with food, drink and song—trace back to those older winter holidays.

"People have this problem with Celtic music and myth," she said. "They see it as very new-agey, airy-fairy stuff, but it's not. It's very practical. People considered fire sacred, for example. Well, if the fire went out, you were in big trouble. You had to make it almost a mortal sin to let the fire go out, because your lives depended on it. And the rituals where you'd visit neighbors were important for everyone's welfare, especially during this time of year when it's so cold and dark. They set these rules in place for good reasons, and it's a very contemplative way of living because everything has a sacred meaning, a sanctity to it."

During December, more than any other time, she said, people are receptive to the warm, ancient mood of the Celtic music she loves. As an experiment, she performed an old Irish Christmas air once every month last year, just to gauge the response.

"Most of the year, it didn't have any particular effect at all. But if I play it in December, you can hear a pin drop. The people who created this music really knew what they were doing. I firmly believe there are specific keys that have a mood-altering effect that works more strongly this time of year."

"I look forward to December in a way I don't even to March, though I enjoy a bit of the March madness. I get a lot of job satisfaction out of seeing people come in so frazzled from their chores, and then say to me when they're leaving how they feel so good and relaxed and contemplative. That's the way this music makes me feel all the time, so when people come in just dying for me to make them feel that way, well, it's like . . . ."

And she rubbed her hands together with glee.

—December 10, 2000

From the Clancy clan to Celtic stardom
Robbie O'Connell

Up a narrow hilltop road in Franklin lives one of the busiest Irish musicians in the world. At 47, Robbie O'Connell is among the most respected guitarists, singers and songwriters in Celtic music. Those who know him only from his album credits, however, might think there are several Robbie O'Connells in Irish music.

The intricate finger-style guitarist whose ornate open tunings influenced a generation of Celtic players in traditional ensembles like Green Fields of America could not possibly be the same boistrous chord-banger who backs up the world-famous Clancy Brothers. And how could the sharp satirist who penned such hilarious pub standards as "You're Not Irish" be the same one who writes tenderly pretty ballads that seem ancient and timeless?

But they are one and the same. And it suits O'Connell fine.

"If you don't stretch yourself, put yourself in situations where you're challenged a bit, you get into a rut," he said.

It does present some logistical problems, though. He admits to some difficulty keeping track of all his careers. For example, he has three new CDs out: his own hilarious and long-awaited collection of "Humorous Songs—Live," a bold and ballad-sweet nautical disc with Liam Clancy, O'Connell and Donal Clancy, and the warmly gorgeous RCA record "All on a Christmas Morning," with his quartet Aengus. He didn't count Green Fields of America as an active group until he suddenly recalled he was doing a concert with them soon at New York's Town Hall.

"So I guess you'd have to count that as well," he said sheepishly, as Roxanne, his wife of 24 years, surpressed giggles across the kitchen table of their Franklin home. And how does she feel about being married to this musical whirlwhind?

"It's very binary," she said. "Either he's here or he's not. But when he's home, he's really home. It's good for our four kids to have the male role model so available when he's home; although I'm sure they sometimes see it as a mixed blessing. And I get a wife when when he's home. I get to come home at seven and say, `Honey, what are we having for dinner?' "

She works as corporate marketing director for the Blue Dolphin publishing group. Together, they run and are guides for Celtica Tours, music-drenched Irish vacation tours.

There's nothing about O'Connell that suggest his madcap career pace. He was soft-spoken and relaxed as he recalled his boyhood in an interview the day after Thanksgiving. His mother was the Clancy Brothers' sister, and the family ran a small hotel and pub just outside Carrick-on-Suir in Country Tipperary.

"I was never very aware of them the first 10 years of my life," he said, referring to his famous uncles, who popularized the Irish folk song repertoire during the '60s folk revival.

"After they'd really made it big in the States, they used to take the summers off and come back," he said. "My parents had a guest house, so they'd often stay there, and lots of their performing friends passing through would stay there. We had a Saturday folk club in the hotel starting around 1962, all set up like a Greenwich Village coffeehouse, with fishing nets on the ceilings and candles on the tables. It was great."

That's where he started his musical career, playing with his sister as the club's regular opening act. There were lively sessiuns, or informal Irish music gatherings, every night. He rarely remembers actually going to bed, only being at sessiuns, thoroughly enjoying himself, then waking up the next morning in his bed, having been carried there after dozing off.

For years, he was adamant about not wanting a career in music, though looking back, he's not sure why. At the time, he said lofty things about not wanting to corrupt his music, but thinks now he was just frightened by the long shadow of success cast by his uncles. Soon after coming to the states in the early '70s, though, he was singing in Irish pubs, both solo and then in a popular folk duo with his wife. It was in these rowdy climes he developed his gift for humorous songwriting.

"That was my uncles' influence," he said. "They're always very conscious of entertaining their audiences; that if you engage the audience, you get so much back from them."

In 1977, his mother died, and he returned to run the hotel for a couple of years. That convinced him he was not cut out for the business world, so he sold the place, returned to America and began hooking up with Irish musicians like noted folklorist and tenor banjo master Mick Moloney, with whom he founded Green Fields of America, an ensemble celebrating traditional Irish music as it has been preserved and performed in this country.

In 1979, the O'Connells bought their home in Franklin. The town's quiet charms then reminded them a little of Carrick-on-Suir, though it's changed over the years.

"Franklin was the fastest-growing town in the state for two or three years in a row in the mid-'90s," he said. "It's changed a little with all that; but it still has a nice small-town feel I like. There's lots of lovely areas around to go cycling and hiking, which I like to do when I'm home."

Around that time, he was invited to join his uncles in the Clancy Brothers group. Sadly, that is one ensemble he must now drop from his list. Paddy Clancy died last month at the age of 67. Tom Clancy passed away in 1991, so O'Connell is certain this will close the curtains on the most successful Irish folk group in history. But he still performs some of that rollicking repertoire in Clancy, O'Connell and Clancy,

The upside of this kind of career is that there's no chance to get bored. The downside is that it seems you're no sooner getting somewhere than you're off somewhere else. —Robbie O'Connell

which features Liam, the best singer among the brothers, and his son, Donal.

With charismatic young fiddler Eileen Ivers and accordionist Jimmy Keane, he founded Aengus in 1993. Ivers left to play in the hit musical *Riverdance*, and was replaced by Chicago fiddler Sean Cleland. Filling out the roster is piper Pat Broaders.

O'Connell loves to find obscure traditional songs and reinvigorate them, as his uncles did so well. Almost immediately after founding Aengus, they began performing lesser-known Irish Christmas and midwinter carols. They are now on their 5th annual Christmas tour, and perform at Boston College Saturday night.

Having a whole month of Christmas suits his Irish tastes.

"One thing I miss about Christmas in Ireland is that from Christmas Eve to New Year's Day is one long holiday," he said. "We'd always have big sessiuns and family gatherings every night. Of course, in Ireland the big day is Boxing Day, the 26th. Our hotel would be the starting and ending point for the ritual of hunting the wren. We'd all dress up in costumes and go from pub to pub, singing and visiting and collecting money for local charities. Then it was back to our place, where there'd be a huge sessiun till four or five in the morning."

After a long Christmas tour, O'Connell is ready for slow walks in the Franklin woods, cooking up a few holiday meals, catching up with the O'Connell clan—and hosting a few all-night kitchen sessiuns.

"The upside of this kind of career is that there's no chance to get bored," he said. "The downside is that it seems you're no sooner getting somewhere than you're off somewhere else. It does tend to be a bit confusing, but I've gotten used to that over the years. It all keeps me fresh."

—December 6, 1998

Cherish the Ladies
Joanie Madden, Aoife Clancy

It seems incredible that it was only 10 years ago that Cherish the Ladies, the first all-women's Irish music ensemble, came into being. Women on an Irish music stage seem so matter-of-fact now, not just as singers but as instrumental stars, like Sharon Shannon and Eileen Ivers. Yet just 10 years ago, Cherish came as a revelation in Irish music, helping spark a lively, largely amiable revolution in that historically male-dominated world. In traditional music, which is content to wait two or three centuries before making up its mind about a tune, this must be seen as cultural change at something akin to warp speed.

Cherish the Ladies is now among the busiest, best, and most popular Irish music groups in the world, as likely to be singled out for being American as for being all-female. From the group's ranks fiddlers Eileen Ivers and Winifred Horan, now with Solas, and singer-songwriter Cathie Ryan have emerged. Founder Joanie Madden, 32, has become a preeminent Irish flute and whistle virtuoso, constantly in demand for session and commercial work.

It is very much due to Madden's steely determination, devotion to Irish tradition, and business savvy that Cherish grew from a one-time revue into a bona fide Celtic supergroup.

"I have always had the same philosophy when I get on a stage," she said. "I don't want to look at my left and right and see a pack of girls. I want to see powerful musicians, a good vocalist, good accordion player, good dancers. For me, the all-girl aspect is really the least important fact about us."

Still, it was only in 1984 that Madden became the first woman ever to win the All-Ireland Championship on the flute, and was still being told by some hard-line old duffers that women lacked the lung power to master the instrument. She has gone on to become both a dazzling technician and spellbindingly articulate interpreter of slow airs. Her hauntingly gorgeous solo album of airs, "Song of the Irish Whistle" (Hearts O' Space), has sold more than 150,000 copies, and she displays a range of texture and emotion that many singers could envy.

"You hit a certain plateau as a flute player where you've pretty much gotten as good technically as you're going to get," Madden said. "After that, I think you become more in tune with what's happening around you. Before Cherish, I never used to care much about a song; it was just something to break up the tunes. But when I started backing them with the group, I realized you can't just try to belt out the line. You have to be with the singer, to follow her mood as well as her melody. I think that's helped all my flute playing."

The current singer for Cherish, fittingly enough, is Aoife Clancy, daughter of the Clancy Brothers' Bobby. She shares their famous honesty of style, but where they are boisterous belters, she is a clean and subtle interpreter, as she shows on her warmly pretty Ark solo CD, "Soldiers and Dreams."

She said it would be a mistake to think Irish music was a man's game, even in the Clancy household.

"My grandmother Hannah, we all called her Mammy Clancy, was very shy, and my father said she always had to be encouraged to sing. But definitely, it was she who encouraged the music in the household, she who encouraged them all to sing and who knew all the songs. And there was a woman named Annie Roche, who looked after them when they were children. She had a huge influence, taught them a lot of the songs they still sing today."

Cherish the Ladies is now seen for what Madden always wanted the group to be, genuine ambassadors of Irish music, dance, and song. Onstage, the group

My grandmother Hannah, we all called her Mammy Clancy, was very shy, and my father said she always had to be encouraged to sing. But definitely, it was she who encouraged the music in the household, she who encouraged them all to sing and who knew all the songs. —Aoife Clancy, offers samples from the whole vista of Irish music, from sweet piano solos to hot fiddle and flute reels, soft old ballads to dazzling step dances.

All that is vividly displayed on the new "Cherish the Ladies Live!" CD, the first on their own label, Big Mammy. It is that rarest of live records that captures the raw energy of concert performance without sacrificing anything in audio quality.

It was recorded over two nights last March, the first at the Palace Theater in Manchester, NH, the second at the Flynn Theater in Burlington, VT. Madden brought in first-rate New York engineer Paul Whicliffe, who has done live recordings with everyone from DeDannan to Tito Puente. What she did next offers a glimpse into the unique savvy with which she propels Cherish.

"After the first night, it was good, but you could tell we knew we were being recorded," she said. "So I went to the group and said, `Listen guys, everything we got last night was great. So tonight, let's just play.' Well, we wound up taking 98 percent of the record from that second night."

Madden is clearly proud of her role in gaining acceptance for women in Irish music, as well as in establishing, once and for all, how important a role they have always played. But as with the Clancys, this music has always been, first and foremost, a family affair for Cherish the Ladies.

"Every one of us comes from musical families," she said. "Accordionist Mary Rafferty's father Mike is one of the greatest flute players I ever heard and was a huge idol for me growing up. My father Joe was Mary's idol on the accordion. What you need to understand is that we have to answer to them before we answer to anyone else. And believe me, they let us know if we're not hitting it right."

—September 5, 1997

An Irish music legend is reborn Joe Derrane

A legend lives on Grove Lane. You wouldn't guess it to see the small brown-shingled house in Franklin where he has lived with his wife Anne since 1959, but Joe Derrane is among the most influential musicians in the modern history of Irish music.

Tunes he wrote more than 50 years ago are required study for accordion students as far away as Ireland, Australia, and Canada. He has played his button accordion at the White House, Wolf Trap, and major Irish festivals at Stonehill College, Milwaukee, and University College Cork. He has headlined the Lowell Folk Festival and Celtic Colours in Cape Breton. He performed at Symphony Hall as a guest of Irish superstars The Chieftains and will play at the Kennedy Center in Washington, D.C., in May.

His story is all the more remarkable given that, for more than 30 years of his adult life, he did not play a note of Irish music.

Derrane will turn 70 this Thursday, the day before his St. Patrick's Day concert at the Fuller Museum of Art in Brockton. He still seems a bit shell-shocked at his return to Irish music stardom over the past six years, which Earle Hitchner, music critic for the Wall Street Journal and Irish Echo, called "the greatest comeback in the history of Irish music." Sometimes staring wistfully out his kitchen window at Norroway Pond, where his children learned how to skate, and sometimes clenching his knuckles white with excited memories, he told his story.

He was born in Boston in 1930 to Irish immigrants. He first heard Irish music on the local radio show "Terry O'Toole, the Boy from Ireland." But O'Toole's tenor was not what drew him.

"The radio could be playing all day," he said, "but as soon as the accordion started, I'd come running from wherever I was to sit close by or jump up and down to the music, totally fascinated. I don't really have any recollection of that, I was only four or five, but it's what my parents told me."

He does remember pestering his parents into getting him a melodeon when he was 10. He now plays a two-row button accordion, which is chromatic, or playable in any key. Single-row melodeons, like harmonicas, can play only one key.

His parents called the radio station and found out O'Toole's accordionist, Jerry O'Brien, was also a teacher. Derrane's talent was clear from the start, and the two were soon inseparable. O'Brien began taking him to house parties, called kitchen rackets because people danced on loud linoleum floors.

"Having to play in a real dance tempo," Derrane said, "the discipline of the music really started to enter my playing. Jerry broke me in slowly; he'd be right there listening and saying, 'Now remember, they have to dance to this.' "

Derrane recalled kitchen rackets that were so crowded he had to play on counters, with his feet in the sink.

By the time he was 16, Derrane was a local star, already a brilliant accordionist and a fixture among the fabled dance halls of Dudley Street. He was appearing regularly on "The Irish Hour" on radio station WVOM. People began going into the Irish record store and travel agency owned by O'Byrne DeWitt, asking for records by the people they heard on the show.

DeWitt formed the Copley Records label and made 78 RPM records of local Irish stars. Derrane was paid a single fee for each of the 16 tunes he recorded through the early '50s. He joined the Johnny Powell Dance band, who played Thursdays and Saturdays at the Inter-Colonial Ballroom, and worked during the day as an administrator for the MBTA.

The Dudley Street scene declined sharply in the late '50s, a victim of changing times and the growing popularity of rock 'n' roll. Derrane traded his button accordion in for a piano accordion and began playing top-40 music. At first, he sneaked bits of Irish music in, but nobody wanted to hear it.

"It was a complete divorce, if you will, but not my choice," he said. "People have often asked me why I gave up Irish music. Well, it's not that I gave it up; it gave me up, gave all of us up at that time. No one was at fault; it was just the changing times, social structure, all these things."

For the next 30 years, Derrane played in a variety of Top-40 show bands. He played weekends at the Am-Vets Hall in Randolph with a trio called the Mello-Tones, and at Ritter's in Whitman with Avon guitarist Lou Pelaggi in a duo called Lou Joseph. In the '80s, he had a quintet called Nitelife with his son, Joe Jr., that became the house band for the old Hugo's in Cohasset.

In 1989, he retired from the MBTA and from music, too. "I just assumed the musical part of my life was over," he said.

But a new generation was reviving Irish music, forming into hip, vibrant bands that combined the energy of rock with the ancient pulse and melody of traditional music. The popularity of these Celtic bands renewed interest in the roots of the music.

In 1993, Rego Records reissued the old Copley tracks on a CD called "Joe Derrane, Irish Accordion." Unbeknownst to him, the old 78s had traveled far and wide in the '50s, and many of his own tunes, as well as his version of traditional ones, had become standards in the Celtic accordion repertoire. He had become a mythic figure, since no one knew what became of him.

People began to track Derrane down. The prestigious Irish Festival at Wolf Trap in Vienna, Va., called to ask if he wouldn't mind just coming to do a lecture on the Dudley Street era. "Or you could play if you'd rather," they said. Of course he'd rather play music than talk about it, he told them. "Great," they said, "we'll send the contracts."

"Well, I hung up the phone and said, what did I just do?" Derrane said. "I hadn't played Irish music in over 30 years."

On an accordion given him by friend Jackie Martin of Norwell, Derrane began practicing six hours a day, seven days a week.

On May 29, 1994, he performed a triumphant comeback concert at Wolf Trap. His children had never heard him play Irish music and were there weeping and cheering, along with his wife and everyone else in the crowd. He was immediately asked to make a new CD for the respected Celtic label Green Linnet.

Three acclaimed recordings followed. The latest, "The Tie That Binds," (Shanachie) features such Celtic superstars as DeDannan founder Frankie Gavin, Solas founder Seamus Egan, and piper Jerry O'Sullivan. With Boston guitarist John McGann, Derrane now frequently plays concerts, weddings, and private functions, when he's not being whisked away to some grand festival or performing arts center. He has begun teaching, and in the eager eyes of the young players, he sees reflected not only the boy wonder he once was, but a safe future for Irish music.

"The music itself has not basically changed," he said, "but the approach the musicians take has. For instance, there were no guitars with the bands in my day. The music, I think, is much more energetic today, thanks to young groups like Solas, Lunasa, Dervish, Reeltime. They let it all hang out, which is very much the way I've always felt about Irish music. It's full of life, full of energy. Other people say, `No, it's sweet and old.' But to me, it's the fire; it's always been the fire."

—Sunday, March 12, 2000

Where the song is the star
The Boston Folk and Traditional Singer's Club

Before the fiddle, guitar and piano, before even the drum and the horn, there was the voice. In these days of electric guitars, synthesizers and musical pyrotechnics, it can be hard to hear that original musical instrument, the human voice in its unadorned splendor.

That is precisely what draws people to the Boston Folk and Traditional Singers' Club, where they spend their Wednesday nights huddled in the cozy, third-floor room of Paddy Burke's Pub at Boston's North Station.

The goal is to create a local gathering place for professional and hobbyist singers to swap songs in a convivial, noncompetitive environment.

At one such gathering April 11, the club felt more like a very musical book club than a "sessiun," the informal gatherings of traditional and primarily instrumental musicians that flourish at many local Irish pubs these days.

The club was founded two years ago by Dublin-born guitarist and singer Shay Walker, who has hosted local sessiuns for years, and also hosts a Thursday sessiun at Matt Murphy's in Brookline. He and then-partner Mick Murphy, who recently returned to Ireland, modeled the Boston Singers' Club, as its members call it, after a popular singers' club at the Trinity Bar in Dublin.

"There's lots of good singers here who just don't get an opportunity to sing," Walker said. "There's at least two singers' clubs in Dublin that I know of, and more in Scotland and England. People want a place where they can just go sing."

Cornelius "Connie" McEleney, at 67, is the club's unofficial graybeard, spinning vivid tales about his Irish boyhood between songs. He is also the one most likely to decide when between-song chit-chat has gone on too long, returning the club to music with a hotly whispered, "Song, song, song."

A Donegal native who has lived in Medford since 1957, he recalled the Boston house parties of the 1950s, sometimes called kitchen rackets, where Irish immigrants gathered in each other's homes to dance and sing, and from which emerged the best musicians of the legendary Dudley Street ballroom scene.

"Every weekend, there'd be house parties somewhere," he said. "That's where the old songs were mostly heard, some of them going back 250 years. I'd say a lot of those house parties would be 75 percent singing, the rest playing and dancing. You go to most sessiuns today, and you get four or five hours of music and maybe only four or five songs."

Throughout the evening, Mc Eleney, a retired MBTA machinist, plumbed his vast, lifelong repertoire of Irish folk songs, singing in an alluringly honest, leathery baritone. His first offering was a plaintive immigrant's ballad pondering both the bright and dark sides of "growing old in a new world." Later, he sang a sentimental portrait of an "Irish Harvest Day"; and a wrenchingly credible parent's lament about a son killed in the American Civil War, which he said he learned as a boy in Donegal, where singing was a way of life.

"It was all songs that were handed down from your father and grandfather," he said. "You just picked up the tradition from them. It started early; when you were 7 or 8 you started learning songs. There was no pastime at night, so you just sat around the fire singing. And when you'd go out to work in the fields, the day went on faster if you were singing. It was all singing all the time."

While most traditional music styles are enjoying healthy revivals these days, older singers like Mc Eleney worry that folk song repertoires are being neglected. In most folk traditions, the instrumental, or tune, repertoire is separate from the song repertoire. Tunes, like jigs and reels, were played mostly for dances or informal gatherings like sessiuns. Songs were sung a cappella, at home or as a break in the dance or sessiun. That old, intimate style of singing is increasingly rare these days.

It was that intimate, song-driven ambience that drew Medford writer and Emerson College teacher Peg Aloi to the club.

"I like that it's all songs here," she said after delivering a pretty love song by Scottish poet Robert Burns. "Unless people know you or ask you to sing, it's not considered polite at a sessiun to say, 'Hey, let's sing some songs.' It's hard to get a chance to sing, but this is a very supportive environment for learning and trying out new songs."

The emphasis is on the songs, not the singers. Everyone's vocals were straightforward and unaffected, as if no one wanted to get caught being a crooner or a diva. The happy result was that even the most untried singers were pleasant to hear.

"Often when somebody sings a song," said Walker, "it'll remind someone else of one, so you end up digging up songs. Sometimes we'll go a whole evening just singing on one theme, like somebody running off on their lover, or sea chanties, or drinking songs. And we'll often get to talking about the history behind the songs, where they came from."

Intriguing historical tidbits peppered the between-song chat. Gary Martin, a math professor at the University of Massachusetts/Dartmouth, sang only songs that mentioned April, and at one point several songs were sung with a heroine called "lovely Nancy," prompting club president Judy Predmore to quip, "Boy, she gets around."

Predmore, a computer programmer at State Street Bank, said the active membership of the club numbers 31, but rarely do more than a dozen show up for any Wednesday gathering; she would like to see more regular members. That Wednesday, there were never more than a dozen people in the song circle.

"Here at this club," she said, "it's more like it is in Ireland and the British Isles, where more people are brought up singing. They're exposed to relatives and neighbors who know songs, and nobody expects you to be Streisand or Pavarotti. People just learn a song they like, and they're not judged on whether they're great singers, but if it's a good song."

Brian Reynolds, who works at MIT, said the Singers' Club helped him overcome a lifelong shyness.

"My wife swears I would never have got the nerve to ask her to marry me if it wasn't for the club," he said. "I used to be just scared to death doing anything in front of people."

"He's a lot more relaxed around people now than when he first came," Walker said, nodding at the blushing Reynolds.

Aloi said clubs like this are popping up in Europe more and more. She regularly visits a British folk music newsgroup and notices announcements of new singers' clubs almost every week.

Musing on this, the singers wondered whether their desire for this oldest and most social of musical exchanges had placed them all on the cutting edge of some hot new cultural trend. Then McEleney whispered, "Song, song, song!" Heads spun about, trying to recall whose turn it was, until Aloi cleared her throat, tossed back her head and began to sing, *"If I were the king of Ireland/ With all things at my will . . ."*

—*April 22, 2001*

Beyond Steeleye Span
Maddy Prior

This time, says Maddy Prior, it is official. The 50-year-old singer has often wandered away from Steeleye Span, the seminal British folk-rock band she helped found in 1969; for solo projects, for two epic "Silly Sisters" records with fellow folk diva June Tabor, to front the brilliantly mischievous Carnival Band, and, most recently, to sing with keyboardist Nick Holland and piper-guitarist Troy Donockley. But now she says she has, formally and finally, quit Steeleye Span.

"We've had quite a lot of changes in lineups," she said. "It's just that I've been the one who stayed. I figured it was my turn to go. It was a choice about work in the end. I wanted to do all the things I was doing, but I can't. And I felt I'd sort of covered the ground with Steeleye."

To judge by her most recent work, she made the right call. Her new Park CD "Flesh and Blood" displays her most vital work in years. There is no tug between the ancient ballads at which she excels and her own provocative songs, written with husband and former Steeleye bassist Rick Kemp. She built strands of song into a cycle called "Dramatis Personae," which she called a meditation on human personality.

But on this record, as throughout her career, it is with the ancient English ballads that she stakes her turf as one of the finest traditional singers in the English language. Her earthy mezzo is a superb ballad voice; marvelously austere, shaded by subtle ornamentation and a mesmerizing drone texture she says was influenced by ancient wind instruments like the pipes.

When a traditional singer like Prior talks about ballads, she does not mean a soft love song. She is referring to the narrative folk ballads that date to the dawn of literate civilization and before, and that form the roots of both song and poetry in nearly every culture on earth. The ballads Prior sings come primarily from a collection of ancient Anglo-Scots balladry compiled by Harvard professor Francis James Child (1825-96); a work so respected that its 305 selections are still referred to as "Child ballads."

Prior sings three Child ballads on "Flesh and Blood," two of them in the very old quatrain form, with repeating second and fourth lines. Central to her allure as a singer, and to Steeleye Span's success in melding traditional music to rock, is how rivetingly she embraces this repetition, wrapping her cadence and vocal shadings around the refrains, warming them gradually as the passion of the story crescendos.

"These ballads have different layers," she said, "and when you sing them all your life, which is how they were supposed to be sung, you see different depths

These ballads have different layers, and when you sing them all your life, which is how they were supposed to be sung, you see different depths and angles in them, see them from different psychological and sociological perspectives.
—Maddy Prior

and angles in them, see them from different psychological and sociological perspectives.

"I don't see the costumes anymore. I'm not distracted by the fact that they're wearing long skirts and riding horses. I think a lot of people are drawn to that romantic aspect, but because I've sung these songs for so long, that's not there for me. I'm more interested in the fact that they are about what people do. Because they emanate from a time when our society was being set up, from the 12th and 13th centuries, they say a lot about our society; not just historically, but psychologically. They have a lot to say about the way we relate to each other."

She bristles at the notion that the ballads are sexist because they portray a society in which women were oppressed. She said all the ballads she has come across deplore the mistreatment of women. In fact, because so many ballads have women as central characters, she believes Sir Walter Scott's theory that many were authored by women.

"A lot of the ballads show women as the active person in the situation, the men as these rather bland images," she said. "Which is quite the reverse of how most history would have you believe things were then. Women were supposed to be totally cowed and subdued, but that's not the image you get from the ballads at all. This is like an alternative society of the day being revealed, one in which women did have some power. I'm not saying they weren't kowtowed as well, but nothing is quite as simple as all that. In loads of them, it's the women who drive the action; and, of course, the power of mothers and hags absolutely terrified the life out of men."

When asked what she was proudest of about Steeleye Span, it was not the group's hits or longevity. Instead, she recalled how she had sneered at the Victorian parlor settings of English folk songs she heard as a child. It was a reaction against them that led her generation to rock the old songs up.

Now, she said, a new generation of folk lovers sneers a bit at Steeleye's rock approach and is returning to more traditional styles. But they are finding the songs through her body of work, just as she found them through the prim parlor treatments of prior generations. To her, it means Steeleye did its job.

She said, "I think the great thing about what we did was to take some of the music back to the people. I like to think we took one or two songs, like `All Around My Hat,' and put them back into use; so they're not known as folk songs, just as songs that everybody knows. And that we carried on the tradition of reviving the tradition."

—June 19, 1998

Making old songs new **Kate Rusby**

Husky-voiced Yorkshire singer-songwriter Kate Rusby may be the Next Big Thing in British pop. At 26, she is already spearheading a significant folk revival in the British Isles, bringing moody modernity to the old ballads, and writing in an alluringly sensual, neotraditional style.

This year she won the BBC's Folk Artist and Album of the Year awards, and her first two CDs, "Hourglass" and "Sleepless" (available here on Compass), each sold over 50,000 copies in the United Kingdom alone.

So is folk music getting hip again? No newcomer to the old music, Rusby resists any notion that her success represents some hot new trend.

"The mainstream media kind of peeks into folk music every five years or so in Britain," she says in her syrup-thick Yorkshire accent, "The last time they did, there was this surge of young people playing the music, like myself, Kathryn Roberts, and Eliza Carthy. But that was not because we had suddenly discovered it; we were all the children of '60s folk revival people. The media got all excited about seeing these young people performing traditional music, and all these magazines that would never talk about folk music at all were saying this must be the new thing. We all felt lucky with the timing of it all, and now we've got people from all different walks of life coming to our shows, which is brilliant, lovely."

Rusby grew up around the music, daughter of folk-singing parents who also run sound for the summer festivals that keep the music alive in Britain between those peeks from the mainstream media. Her upbringing gives her an innate understanding of folk music similar to that found in purely traditional singers.

She says she has known most of the folk songs on her first two CDs as long as she can remember. Like traditional singers of old, she has an almost primordial memory pool of folk melody, which gives her singing a riveting naturalness and her writing a timeless grace astonishing in so young an artist.

"I learned most of the songs the old-fashioned way," she says, "from word-of-mouth, hearing somebody sing them. They just keep popping back in my brain kind of half-known, and I can't remember where they come from. So when I start to sing them, I already know them."

On "Sleepless," she sings the droll "Cobbler's Daughter" with a languid sassiness and lends a lonesome dignity to the old sailor's chant "The Wild Goose." Her voice is all husk and honey, the emotions emerging organically, as if she is feeling them for the first time. She said it is that emotionalism—immediate, personal, and universal—that draws her to the old songs she sings.

"I don't find any other form of music that has the effect, that kind of breaks your heart, like the old ballads do," she said. "I guess I just like to hear music that gets me upset and sad. The whole way they were written is so beautiful, because it's people's music; it wasn't scholars writing it, so it's quite simple but really captures what people went through. It's about people's emotions, about people falling in love and dying and leaving, and of course, those are all things we still do."

That passion for emotional honesty marks her writing, to which she brings a rare understanding of folk aesthetics. She says that when she writes, she is often just noodling on the guitar, pulling things up from those deep pools of melodic memory, when she suddenly realizes she is not recalling an old song but writing a new one. That is precisely how scholars describe the song-creating process among ancient traditional musicians.

John McCusker, who accompanies Rusby at a sold-out Lexington show Sunday, is a brilliant 27-year-old fiddler and cittern player who has been with Scotland's venerable Battlefield Band for 10 years. He watched Rusby's star rise first as a fan, then friend, and now as record producer, sideman, and fiance.

"Kate gets more young people at her concerts than any other folk musician or band I've ever seen," he says. "I think part of the reason is that they see this girl who looks fairly trendy, wears normal clothes, but is singing songs that are hundreds of years old and really singing them from the heart."

And that may indeed signal a new trend in the long history of folk music. Like the best songwriters of her generation, Rusby brings a new definition of "authentic" to folk music. Her parents' generation sought to preserve dying musical traditions by performing them authentically, by which they meant adhering to how they were played in the past. Rusby's generation seeks to reinvigorate the old music by singing it authentically, by which they mean honestly, intimately, in their own voice and emotions.

"What draws me is the authenticity of the feelings in the song, not how it might have been sung years ago," she says. "In order to get the song across, you have to find a way to feel it yourself, perhaps change it a bit so you really, really believe it yourself, or else how will it have an effect on other people when they hear it? You have to make it your own song."

—November 17, 2000

photo:Adam Nash

Growing up in England's first family of folk
Eliza Carthy, Martin Carthy

Eliza Carthy is almost certainly going to be a star. She is already one of the finest traditional musicians in England. What is not at all certain is whether she will ever be able to be both things at the same time.

Warner Bros. signed the 25-year-old singer, fiddler, and accordionist, daughter of British folk singers Martin Carthy and Norma Waterson, to a deal designed to break her as a major star. But she can leave her fiddle bow at home; she will be playing no traditional music for them. Warner wants only her silky voice, darkly quirky folk-pop songs, and alluring stage charms.

"They're a major label," Carthy said, "and every time a major has tried to get hold of traditional music, as far as I'm concerned, they don't quite know how to deal with it. Because innately, it's kind of anticelebrity, which leaves them scratching their heads going, `What?' It's just not very exploitable in a mass sense, I don't think."

Carthy was literally born to the tradition, and plays the old songs and tunes with a rare organic grace and youthful zest. Her father may be the most influential guitarist in British folk music, a superb ballad singer who has played a seminal role in reviving and sustaining traditional music as a solo artist, and with Steeleye Span, Albion Country Band, and Brass Monkey.

The Watersons have been England's first family of folk ever since the progressive Topic Records heard the family quartet do a guest set during a Carthy show in 1962 and immediately signed them to a contract. Norma Waterson married Carthy, and gave birth to Eliza in 1974.

Eliza Carthy cannot recall a time when she was not surrounded by traditional music. By 16, she was touring in a folk duo with Northumberland fiddler Nancy Kerr and with her parents in Waterson:Carthy. By 19, she was a rising presence in British folk and rock with her own band and the grandly rowdy Kings of Callicut.

But she said she was drawn to a music career less by the music than by the thoughts that ran through her head as a little girl waiting for her father to come home from tours.

"I knew he was away doing music, which was intangible and exciting to me," she said. "And then he would come home with his arms full of gifts. It was something I always associated with music that wasn't actually musical. It's that glamour thing: Dad's home from Sri Lanka and Malaysia, and he's brought all these wonderful shadow puppets and beautifully painted things. It was totally exotic. I don't know what it was like for him, all that touring, but it was a real boom time for me."

The whole pop-star thing is kind of irrelevant to the traditional music. It will always be my passion. For me, it's like your ancestors whispering in your ear, telling you what went on and why and how they felt about it. History books can't tell you that, academics can't tell you. If you want to know how somebody a hundred years ago felt, you can find it in a traditional song. —Eliza Carthy

Her parents don't see her new pop career as being quite the disparate thing it might appear to her traditional music fans. For one thing, she had it written into her contract that she can still tour and record with Waterson:Carthy.

More important, they don't see her songwriting rooted in traditional music. Even before she played music, she wrote precociously brooding and odd little poems. She also said she thinks this is the wellspring for her pop songwriting.

Eliza Carthy is already a minor star in British music, but the subcorporate folk industry simply does not have the marketing muscle or media visibility to push her further.

Waterson painted a bleak picture of how the pop industry dominates British musical life. In the '80s, she said, funding cutbacks forced most schools to give up music education. But fledgling pop bands are brought in for free concerts. By the time a band's first CD is out, kids already have their photos and are signed up to their fan club.

"We used to learn folk music in schools, so people accepted it as a part of life," she said. "Now you don't get exposed to it at all, not in schools or television or radio, and youngsters grow up thinking that all music sounds like pop music."

Martin Carthy said, "Nobody's ever been able to package and sell traditional music in a mass way, and I must say, part of me gives a huge sigh of relief. As long as it doesn't shut itself away, it can continue to develop and be interesting. But that's the crucial thing; the music does actually have to breathe real air, to make itself heard in front of ordinary people, rather than just in little clubs for people who know what it is."

Listening to Eliza Carthy rave about the old music, it is hard to believe she will ever leave it behind.

"The whole pop-star thing is kind of irrelevant to the traditional music," she said. "It will always be my passion. For me, it's like your ancestors whispering in your ear, telling you what went on and why and how they felt about it. History books can't tell you that, academics can't tell you. If you want to know how somebody a hundred years ago felt, you can find it in a traditional song; it's like you can ask them yourself. If you want to know about your culture and where you come from, the place to go is traditional music. And if there's nobody left to do it, if there are no structures or platforms left for playing and hearing it, how's anybody ever going to know, except just by reading dusty old books?"

—November 26, 1999

Mouthpiece for the common man
Ewan MacColl

Ewan MacColl will turn 73 in January. He is home in Britain these days, laboring over an autobiography which he calls "the most unrewarding thing I've ever done, a very lonely occupation, but quite interesting. You remember things you never remembered before."

There is a lot of MacColl to remember. While he is best known in this country as a prime founder of the British folk revival, as a songwriter and powerful interpreter of traditional ballads with his wife Peggy Seeger, he is known in British theater as an experimental playwright, founder with Joan Littlewood of the influential Theater Workshop in 1945, resident dramatist and art director of that company for seven years. His radio ballads for the BBC, musical documentaries about working people's lives and art, did much not only to spur the British folk revival, but also to change the way people perceived radio as a medium. His political songs, often times anthems delivered to specific events and causes, have long been sung on picket lines and at rallies. His love songs, like "The First Time (Ever I Saw Your Face)" and "Sweet Thames Flow Softly," have long been standards in the folk music canon.

Particularly these days when, in preparing the autobiography, his whole life is spinning through his mind, MacColl sees folk music as the common thread binding all his work together. He learned to love the old songs through his family; his mother in particular was known as a traditional singer. When MacColl talks about theater, about radio, about politics, he talks about folk music. And, natural as the flow of a river, when he talks about folk music, he talks theater, talks politics, talks art.

"I see what I do as one work," he says quietly. Those familiar only with the bold, ringing Scots baritone of his ballad recordings would be surprised to hear him speak: softly, invitingly, in an expressive, rather high voice.

"It's difficult to make people understand how that could be. The world of singing and collecting in the field of folkloric studies appears to be a long way from the world of theater. In some folk circles, I'm regarded as a ballad singer, by which I mean the straight narrative songs of our tradition. Another group looks at me as a signer of political songs. And there are those who know me only as a songwriter. I'm constantly being amazed when I go places. There's always someone who comes up to me and says, 'I've never heard of you except that you wrote "Shoals of Herring," or some other song. Then there's always a few who say, 'I didn't know you wrote songs.' But to me it is quite simple: My career has been a constant attempt to try to find a way of being

a mouthpiece for the common people."

"I worked in the theater for a long, long time, starting with the street theater in the late 1920s, then into experimental theater of all types. I more or less made my mark as a playwright. I was regarded as a writer's writer, taken up by people like Sean O'Casey and George Bernard Shaw. But it seemed to me that, although we'd had a certain amount of success, we were appealing to that very tiny segment of the population which goes to the theater. I really was keen on creating theater for the kind of popular audience the Elizabethans worked with, a broad spectrum of the community."

"I thought that perhaps the secret lay in the kind of language we were using. Then I came across a paper by Bela Bartok. It said that artists of the 20th century are in a tremendous dilemma. Poets write for poets, composers compose for composers, and so on. He said if we were to find a way out of this, we must learn to create the way the folk create. That came as a blinding revelation to me. I began thinking deeply about what folk music was, what the texts were like. So when I began seriously to work in what has now come to be known as the folk revival, it was to some extent with the intention of trying to find a language to write for the theater."

Around about 1948 or '49, Alan Lomax came to Britain. He was working on a big project for Columbia Records, a series called 'Primitive Music of the World's People.' He'd gotten my mother's name as a traditional singer to look up, and I met him, later recorded for him myself. I knew a number of singers in Scotland, so I took him there. Later, I went to Italy collecting with him. That was the beginning of collecting for me. I found it fascinating work, a bit like being a literary detective, poring through ancient manuscripts. But it's much more exciting, because you're meeting people."

"I immediately went on a collecting tour for BBC in Yorkshire. When I met Peggy, we got interested in working with Gypsies and the nomadic peoples of Britain. The two of us went into Scotland, and we recorded lots of travelers, particularly a family we found that possessed pure gold in the way of folk material: traditional stories, songs, ballads, riddles, the whole shoot, you know. From them we met others, and we've gone on collecting ever since."

Both MacColl and Seeger share a deep commitment to the great ballads of the English language, whose roots lie deep in the folk tradition and were collected most completely and comprehensively by Francis James Child, the 19th-century ballad collector. His collection, titled "The English and Scottish Popular Ballads," became such a definitive text that its 305 ballads are still known as Child Ballads.

"I think a folk revival in any English-speaking culture needs the ballads as a touchstone against which you measure all other songs," MacColl says firmly. "Our song tradition is largely a narrative one. Unlike, say, the French or the

Italians, we don't have many songs which are about emotions; we have a lot of songs about situations which create emotions. We have songs about lovers, but not many about love."

"Most of our songs are stories with cause and effect, with a good, unassailable logic behind them. Nearly all the best songs to come out of the revival are narrative songs, in structure, anyway. That ballad structure is more apparent than any other form in the revival, so you need it as a model if nothing else. If you divest your culture of what is most typical of it, you're at a loss to know how to create."

MacColl the playwright sees the ballads in terms of theater, just as MacColl the singer sees them in terms of music.

"The ballads are brilliant examples of song construction," he says. "They are as important to people today as the plays of Shakespeare or Moliere, just as much complete works of art as anything we have in written literature. I think all the ballads in the quatrain form, such as 'Lamkin' or 'Tam Lin,' were very calculatedly composed, as carefully constructed as 'King Lear.' I think they they are that closely textured and intricately conceived. And I do think they were individually written. Not only that, but as I've gotten to know them very well, several of them appear to be by the same hand."

"They are altered then in two ways, up and down. They are altered by reducing the story—cutting subplots, eliminating minor characters. And they're altered by changing place and time. And, of course, they are altered by accidental changes due to lapses in memory. But my feeling is that most of the changes that occur in the texts take place purposely."

I think that the theory of the lapse of memory arises out of the belief that the singers right through history have been idiots who have made no contributions themselves to the songs. It's the old kind of upper-class idea that the traditional singers are apes who can sing, rather than people who can create. Memory may account for some, but by no means all—and by no means the majority—of changes in texts. I've known quite a number of singers who, in the course of time, will admit to having made changes in songs because a certain line lies easier in the mouth. For example, you can switch the 2nd and 3rd lines without altering the sense of many of the old ballads.

"The more I work on ballads—and I do work on them, it's not just a simple matter of learning the text and putting a tune to it—the more it seems to me that one must have the ballad in one's mouth many, many times to really know it. The way it works with me, apart from the handful of ballads I learned from my parents, is that I will have sung a ballad for one or two years, perhaps two or three times a fortnight. Then I drop it completely. A couple of years later, I start all over again learning it. That time, the process is much easier. Now, the *third* time I do this, something very strange will happen. I will begin to dream about the structure of the ballad, to see it as architecture; the way one would see a stage divided up into areas of action, the way Stanislavsky would divide a play for actors."

MacColl is referring to Konstantin Stanislavsky, the great teacher of acting, whose incisive, psychological training system laid the groundwork for the school of acting known as the Method. Again, MacColl returns to theater for his explorations of the ballad, just as the theater calls him back again and again to the ballads. He often uses Method acting techniques in teaching the art of singing the great old ballads.

"I remember a signer was having trouble with 'Gypsy Davey,'" he says. "She'd been singing it for four years, and it had lost all its qualities for her. She could no longer whip up any enthusiasm for it, yet she was constantly being asked to do it as a request. It was at a meeting of the Critics Group, part of the old Singer's Club in London.

"We said, 'Let's suppose you are the mother of the girl who goes away with Gypsy Davey, and you're singing about something that happened 20 or 30 years ago. All the people present know something of the story, but not the entire story. So you're telling them.'"

"After we'd done that for awhile, we said, 'Now suppose you're the girl herself.' Or, 'Suppose you're a member of the Gypsy tribe that was supposed to have gone away with this lady, and you're singing the song triumphantly to a company of non-Gypsies. How would you approach it then?' It was quite extraordinary how different the interpretations were. And suddenly, the singer would slip into the role of a singer again."

"The best thing is to suppose you are the person who wrote the song, and you are singing it for the first time. You're nervous, you're wondering if it's going to work. And yet you've been in the grip of the story for such a long time, you feel it's bound to work. And sure enough, by using this technique, we were able to make songs live again for singers."

"For folk singers today, I think it's important to immerse yourself in the old songs, and learn to think in the way that the people who made them thought. That is not as difficult as it sounds. There are techniques: find out what the songs are about; not just the simple stories, but each layer of the sandwich on which the song is composed. Dream it, live it. Tell yourself that you're dealing with a great mass of inherited stories that can be told in thousands of ways, so long as you stay within the disciplines of the music itself."

What MacColl is stressing, more than anything else, is that these ballads, and for that matter, all of the traditional folk songs that have been good enough to survive this long, are great works of literature, worthy of being treated as an actor treats Shakespeare. But he also reveals the secret all great ballad singers know: that in this respect, this understanding, this discipline, comes the freedom to interpret—

and change—the ballads to suit a singer's individual style and strength.

"There are so many subtleties a singer has to master in the singing of ballads," he says. "It's very hard to understand just how important the pauses are until you've been singing them a long time. The fact is, you're working in a very narrow compass, and the disciplines necessary are enormous. You have a tune which is repeated over and over for 16, 20, 30 stanzas. You're not in the position of being able to make radical changes inside the tune. You can create modern ornaments, providing they don't interfere with the tempo of the ballad."

"You're having to create inside this very rigid discipline, but a discipline which calls upon the singer to exert the maximum imagination. How much do I thin out the line here? how do I bring this very critical line out—especially in the Scots ballads where you get what we call anchor lines: lines of tremendous poetic strength that serve as signposts inside the ballad? These are things you move from and move toward, always keeping them in your sights. And they tell you which emotions are to be used. Looking for ways to keep a song alive—even if you've sung it a thousand times, that's what makes it a really interesting and fulfilling job to do."

Within these disciplines, MacColl thinks it is not only permissible, but virtually obligatory, for modern singers to alter words and even lines in the old ballads, seeking words and sounds that lie easily on the tongue, and that phrase naturally for the singer. Of course, he believes it is important to preserve both the story and spirit of a ballad, but also that it sound like it is coming from the person singing it now, and not as an echo from the past.

MacColl also turns to the ballads when he writes songs. He is not of the school that believes the old songs should be kept on shelves, that today's creativity cannot be applied to them or that they cannot be used to make new music.

"It is important to remember that the old songs are what they are because people did tamper with them," he says. "Anything that I've ever written that has had any impact has been grounded in these old songs. They provide a wonderful base on which to create new lines, new songs, new melodies. I used them particularly for my radio ballads, when I'd have to write 15 or 30 songs for one project."

"'Shoals of Herring,' for example, was built on a tune from a Scots setting of 'Famous Flower of Serving Men.' I can hardly recognize it anymore, but that's where it started. I would take a melody line, then sing into it the line I wanted to use, and stretch it or shape it until it fit. When I took 'Shoals of Herring' back to the old fisherman about whom it was written, he said something I found shattering. 'Boy,' he said to me, 'I've known that song all my life.' Within two years of my ballad about traveling people, 'Freeborn Man,' going out on a radio, folklorists in Ireland were recording it, and there were people in the field who *swore* they'd known it all their lives."

"The point is, once you begin with the old songs that way, there is something that makes people respond. There is a kind of collective memory which operates, making the song immediately accessible to a lot of people."

"Both Peggy and I have always functioned on the basis that folk music is a continuum of the old and the new, and that it has to be a continuum to work properly. I'm very careful, for example, to separate my political songs from my traditional songs. But yet, they are the same in the sense that they're both part of the continuum."

It may be difficult to see MacColl's and Seeger's urgently modern political songs belonging to an ancient continuum. But MacColl knows what a long, outspoken history of political music exists in the British folk canon.

"The oldest tradition we have in Britain is that of popular political songwriting," he says. "The first big collection of songs we have is a collection of songs about ecclesiastical politics in the time of Edward II. We have gone on producing songs like that right through the ages. Some of them are good, some of them are bad. The best of them have gone on into the tradition. Often they've been transformed, lost their political significance, the way 'Barbara Allen' did. It began as a political satire about the Duchess of Reading, last mistress of Charles II. In its time, it was probably a very valid satire. Today, it's a very valid romantic song."

"A lot of the political pieces I have written are obviously ephemeral. They will disappear when the political situation that gave rise to them disappears. Some of them have already disappeared. Others, which are political in the broadest sense of the word, and much broader in their feelings, might survive."

"The songs I like best are the traditional ballads. Now many of those were political songs in their times, and some of them, like the Jacobite songs, were very anti-populist songs. They were on the wrong side, as far as I'm concerned, but they wrote the best songs. So I'll make that point when I sing them. I'll say, 'These are brilliant examples of political songwriting. They're very witty or they're very moving. But they're not my politics.' After all, if a guy writes a song about his political beliefs two or three hundred years ago, his ideas deserve to be respected. I hope someone will respect my ideas in times to come."

When he is asked if he thinks songs can change people, he pauses for a long moment; longer, one senses, than he might have as MacColl, the young firebrand playwright, the cocksure folk singing radical. Not because his beliefs have changed or grown milder, but because his respect for the power of the old songs has deepened so; ripened in its maturity into something wiser, more complex, and even more filled with awe and wonder.

"Songs are very potent things," he says slowly, softly. "I'm not sure they can actually change people, but they *can* reinforce people's vision of themselves. I hope people will look on these old songs as life belts that they must hold on to in a world that is increasingly artificial. Human beings can't manage without creating, without being active participants in art. Once you get to the point that you're just pushing a button or turning a lever, then the art form is doomed, and the people are as well. People without creative roots are very vulnerable people."

"This music is all that is left of the dreams of generations of working men and women, and it is absolutely vital that it not be allowed to die; that it be kept alive so that it may reinvigorate future traditions. The only way I can think of doing that is to become good at it, to work bloody hard at being able to do it justice."

Originally appeard in Sing Out! The Folk Song Magazine
Used by permission, Sing Out Corporation
—Winter, 1988

The sound and spirit of Ellen Kushner

Ellen Kushner has made a career out of wondering. Her weekly WGBH-FM program "Sound and Spirit" is heard by more than 150,000 people on 110 public radio stations nationwide. Each week, the Somerville resident hosts a thoughtful, amiable, and provocative music- and story-filled journey through such topics as "Cycles," "The Spirituality of Work," "Ghosts," "Harvest," and "Sacred Spaces."

Kushner roams from ancient folk ballads to classical pieces, world music to urban songwriters, poems to folk tales, hero myths to chatty personal anecdotes.

The aim is never to define or answer the questions she raises, but simply to wonder about them as she explores the different ways people throughout history and across cultures perceive, celebrate, fear, and love the same vital forces.

"The whole point behind 'Sound and Spirit,' " she said from her offices at WGBH, "is that I'm trying to show that humanity has some very basic needs: food, clothing, shelter, heat. But that after that, there are certain things everybody goes through, whether they're in a high-rise in Manhattan or a hut on the tundra. You've got to deal with the great issues and questions of life: birth, death, grief, joy, dreams, laughter. What is all this about and what can we do about it?

"And what people do about it is they make art, poetry, music, myth, and they make complex systems of religious and spiritual belief. Now, they're all different: The clothing may be different, but it's all clothing that covers your body and is used to signify who you are.

"Everybody wants to put something on, and what I'm doing in the show is saying, OK, spiritually, musically, culturally, what is it that we're putting on? Why are we putting it on? And let's look at all these extraordinary things we have found to wear. And let's realize that all of those different ways answer the same need in a different way."

Where others might feel adrift in such vast and general seas, Kushner has never felt so cozily at home. In her 43 years, she has worked as a folk singer, book editor, Plimoth Plantation pilgrim, and late-night disc jockey.

She is an acclaimed novelist whose first book, "Swordspoint," launched a whole new school of fantasy fiction. She has hosted radio shows before, notably her irreverent stint with the Nakamichi International Music Series, but always felt constrained, no matter how much format room she was allowed. With "Sound and Spirit," it is finally her job to roam and wonder, ponder and explore, hop from century to century and culture to culture.

Early on, she realized she was simply too curious about too many things to focus the way the world expects most people to. She found any attempt to confine her college education to a major limiting, first at Bryn Mawr and later Barnard and Columbia, and confessed that the only reason she settled on anthropology was it seemed to allow practically anything in the way of tangential study.

"I am the eternal generalist," she said, "and I never wanted to major in anything. So I settled on anthropology, and that's where the `Sound and Spirit' story begins. I was saturated with world cultures and a relativistic view of looking at the ways different people deal with the same thing.

"I remember having this idea that my life's work was going to be to figure out what every culture had in common, and that somehow this was going to unlock the key to human society and the human heart, and I was going to understand everything, and everything would, in some way through this understanding, be fixed. It's hard for me to remember now just how I thought all this was going to happen, but I was enchanted with the idea of there being this common thread throughout humanity, despite the very great differences in the way it is perceived and practiced. And that is exactly what `Sound and Spirit' is."

She always sprinkled into her cultural explorations a deep love of history, which, in turn, led her to folk music.

"I wanted to touch something old and something mythic and something that wasn't my everyday life," she said, referring to her fairly typical Jewish-American childhood in Cleveland, Ohio. Her father was a doctor, her mother a social worker.

"I was always looking for oldness and authenticity, something real and yet plugged into something somehow eternal. It had nothing to do with kings and queens and formal political history; it had to do with life in the past. I'm always trying to re-create in my own mind what life in a pre-industrial society was like, whether that's in the years 700 or 1820. I feel like the past is another country, one we can travel through and learn things from, particularly about what is eternal."

After college, she worked as a book editor in Manhattan, mainly because she couldn't settle on what she, herself, wanted to write about. She worked on her first novel for five years, editing other science fiction and fantasy novelists, and writing five "Choose Your Own Adventure" books along the way. Finally, fed up with the corporate publishing world in particular, and New York City in general, she moved to Boston in 1987, with no plan.

It is when Kushner has the fewest plans, however, that she seems to do the best. Within a few months, WGBH hired her for the midnight-5 a.m. on-air shift. Right after that, her first novel, "Swordspoint," was published and became an overnight sensation in the fantasy world. Its blend of modern sensibility and classic fantasy spawned a whole new genre of fiction called "Mannerpunk."

"I like to think of 'Swordspoint' as 'The Three Musketeers' written as a New Yorker short story," she said with a grin. "My favorite review was that it was as if Noel Coward had written a vehicle for Errol Flynn."

Suddenly, she was having success precisely because she was all over the map, mixing genres in her writing and attracting radio fans by following Mozart concertos with Peruvian harvest songs, Beethoven with Celtic jigs and reels.

She produced a series of Jewish holiday specials for Public Radio International that are still played nationwide. PRI loved how she pushed the focus beyond Jewish culture, tying Passover, for example, to liberation songs from other cultures. Again, her refusal to stick to the topic was winning her fans. PRI producer Melinda Ward approached her about a weekly show.

"She wanted me to move through myth, storytelling, world cultures, not just spiritually, but on a variety of themes," Kushner said. "She's one of those people who really has her pulse on what people are ready to hear.

"A lot of Americans right now are saying, 'My needs aren't really being met,'" she said. "My need for connection, religion, music, whatever. What else is out there that might suit me?' I think we really are in a sort of shopping-cart mode for spirituality and culture right now, and I think there's something out there for everybody."

With producers Jon Solins and Helen Barrington, and a staff of researchers, Kushner assembles and hosts 52 one-hour shows a year.

"This is really an organic process to me," she said. "It's like composing. Sometimes people describe what we're doing as a cultural documentary, but that makes it sound like a news show. To me, every hour of 'Sound and Spirit' is a work of performance art that combines words and music, but is bigger than either of those things alone.

"It's like I'm leaping from stone to stone across this river, and sometimes the stones are music and sometimes they're ideas and sometimes they're stories. But they have to work in tandem to move the show forward."

She said she tries not to inject too many of her own opinions or conclusions into the show, hoping instead that her sense of wonder becomes contagious. Her fondest hope is that, by seeing the myriad ways people express their lives, loves, fears, and faith, listeners might be enticed to more actively create and participate in their own culture.

"I think making art is our birthright," she said. "If you wanted something on your wall, say, a rose, you used to have to paint it. It didn't matter if it was a perfect rose that you painted, or even that it was a good rose. It was your rose, and then it was your sister Ann's rose, and then it was your ancestor's rose. That's where the value came."

"It's pompous to assume you can answer one of the big life questions in a one-hour radio show, just stupid. It's the journey, what you learn and experience along the way."

—December 27, 1998

All folk, all the time
WUMB-FM radio manager Patricia Monteith

On top of Forbes Hill in Quincy sits an old castle tower. Over a hundred years old, it once held city water but has been abandoned for years. Jutting skyward from its eerie old brownstone turrets, however, are strangely modern signs of life. A radio tower and satellite dish broadcasts the signal of one of the country's more unusual radio stations, WUMB-FM of the University of Massachusetts in Boston.

It is among the smaller urban stations in the National Public Radio system, drawing about 55,000 listeners weekly in a population area of 1.3 million reached by its signal. But it is the nation's only regular daytime folk music station, and as such it is a crucial bellwether for the viability of acoustic music as a format.

The tower atop the tower marks just one in a long string of improbable solutions to seemingly insurmountable problems that WUMB's general manager, Patricia Monteith of Randolph, has overcome in building the station from a record player in a cafeteria into the nation's busiest folk music radio station.

"It still surprises me when performers tell me how much people talk about us in other parts of the country, how important we are in the folk world," Monteith said. "I've always seen WUMB as a community station. We didn't set out to do folk, we set out to serve a community."

In fact, she never set out to run a radio station at all. She grew up in Watertown, the only daughter of a single, working mother. She displayed a talent for mathematics and dreamed of working for NASA. But radio was drawing her in even then.

"I was home alone a lot, because my mother worked," she said. "I still don't understand why I turned to radio so much more than television. But I did; radio was my main companion."

Perhaps that is why, in 1968, when she was attending UMass-Boston, she responded to a flier seeking volunteers to start an on-campus radio station. Her life was never the same.

"I really don't think I've ever made the decision to have a career in radio," she said. "It was just one problem to be solved after another. I am a problem solver, that's the mathematician in me. I've got a lot of patience and a lot of tenacity. And that's really what running a radio station is all about, just solving one problem after another as they come up."

At first, they were just playing records in the cafeteria and hard-wired into a few student offices. Monteith became intrigued by the possibilities. It was fun going to all the music-biz agents for free records and invitations to backstage parties.

She began to dream about WUMB becoming a real radio station, broadcasting to the public at large, but she was told emphatically that there was no room on Boston's jammed radio band for even one more station. She saw it as just another problem to solve.

But it was not until 1981, 13 years after signing on with the station, that WUMB was granted 91.9 on the FM dial by the Federal Communications Commission— the last FM signal granted anywhere in eastern Massachusetts.

"It was during those years that I learned about the politics of radio," she said. "It got nasty at times, absurd at others. It took a year-and-a-half to convince the university that it wanted a radio station, and over the next 10 years, we applied for five different frequencies, only to be shot down by larger stations who didn't want more stations in the area."

Over those years, Monteith also did hard thinking about what kind of radio station she wanted, about how radio could still be a companion to people and serve a community. At first, she wanted to be as diverse as the public she was broadcasting to. But as she earned a master's degree in mass communications from Emerson College, she began to realize how modern radio worked.

"I learned that it was foolish to try to do all-things-for-all-people radio," she said, "because that's not how people listen. No matter how good your format is, they just won't switch around the radio dial to tune in their favorite programs. That's how they watch TV, but not how they listen to radio. People listen to a radio station, not a radio program."

In 1981, just after the Boston folk station WCAS had become a Christian station, WUMB did surveys to help decide on a format.

"I had been a WCAS listener myself and knew how many people there were who missed having an all-day acoustic music station," she said. "I remember feeling really moved by the thousands of people who felt like they no longer had a home. We had always wanted to be an alternative to what was on the radio, but we wanted to be an alternative with some listeners. We said, 'Look, here's an unserved community. Let's do folk music.' "

Initially a 100-watt station, WUMB reached mainly Dorchester, Quincy, and adjoining communities. Monteith moved to Randolph to be able to listen to her station at home.

In 1985, an ownership change of the land where WUMB's antenna was forced Monteith to seek a different site. She went to the office of Francis X. McCauley, then mayor of Quincy, which offered them the Forbes Hill tower. That coincided with a boost to 200 watts, and suddenly WUMB could be heard throughout the Boston area. In the last few years, repeater antennas in Worcester and Falmouth have made it accessible to folk fans in most of Massachusetts, and parts of Rhode Island, New Hampshire, and Connecticut.

"The mayor's office really came to the rescue," Monteith said. "The folk fans of Cambridge and Somerville can thank the City of Quincy for being able to get our signal."

Almost overnight, WUMB became a crucial resource for the area's burgeoning folk music scene. Their community events calendar, which is announced several times a day, mushroomed as more coffeehouses and concert venues opened, confident they could get the word out and that their artists could get airplay.

WUMB is enjoying its largest audience, more than 55,000 regular weekly listeners, its largest paid membership levels (4,600), and its best financial numbers. Its last three fund-raising drives earned more than $100,000 each, an almost unheard of amount for such a small station in such a large market.

In addition to contributions, the station gets a quarter of its cash support from the University of Massachusetts and a quarter from the Corporation for Public Broadcasting.

But Monteith still has plenty of problems to solve. Threats to federal funding of public broadcasting resulted in severe limits on which stations receive support from the Corporation for Public Broadcasting. WUMB's listenership falls below that threshold, according to Arbitron ratings. Monteith expects to avert disaster by working with consultants, under a two-year agreement with the corporation, to further build her audience.

The station's numbers are steadily rising, and listener loyalty is intense. But as folk programming throughout the nation is cut or moved to late-night slots in favor of classical and news formats, WUMB's future remains uncertain.

"Our surveys show that folk people are exactly the same people who also listen to news and classical music," Monteith said. "In short, it's the target public radio audience. In most parts of the country, though, they can't find that out, because they only give folk a chance late at night, when just 1 percent of any station's audience is listening."

In many parts of the country, cutbacks in federal funding have already meant the end of folk radio. For Monteith, it is just another problem to be solved. "Folk is diversity within diversity," she said. "There are so many genres within the folk genre that it never stops being fun for me. And it's real-life music; the songs are about real people and real issues. A lot of radio today, like TV, talks at me. I like to feel I'm having a conversation. That goes back to when I was a child and and turned on the radio when I was lonely. I want to believe that radio can still be a companion."

—*February 8, 1998*

From rock drummer to folk-biz revolutionary
Phil Antoniades

Who could have guessed that folk music's best friend would turn out to be a rock drummer? Ever since Bob Dylan went rock 'n' roll at the 1965 Newport Folk Festival, drumsticks have drawn the battle lines for many folk lovers. But for literally hundreds of up-and-coming singer-songwriters in this area, a 33-year-old drummer, music manager and computer-age Renaissance man, Philip Antoniades has provided the jumper cables they needed to self-start their careers.

His Framingham company, Artist Development Associates, is in the business of helping artists help themselves. Not a talent agency, not a record company, it offers professional services for musicians that, just a few years ago, only major management agencies and record companies could provide. Self-managed musicians turn to his company for everything from low-cost compact disc and cassette manufacturing to graphics work, 800 numbers, World Wide Web pages and on-line record sales.

Artist Development is fueled by Antoniades's remarkably prolific energies, far-ranging talents and deep belief that artists should own their own art. Thanks to the computer revolution, he believes that it is more possible now than ever.

"You used to need a record company to track everything you did," Antoniades said from his Framingham home and office. "Record sales, air play, promotion— artists really couldn't do those things for themselves. Now, if you have a database, you can build your own career. I've helped performers develop computer programs that work the way they think, that even remind them of the things they need to do to build their music as a business. What we're doing is designed to suit the touring, independent artist who is not with a major record company, maybe not even with a booking agency."

Antoniades discovered the local folk scene in 1990, when he founded the influential Acoustic Underground with music manager Bob Lafee and agent Rhonda Flashen. Its annual songwriter contests and CD anthologies helped put the folk scene on the pop-music map, offering crucial early exposure to budding stars, such as Ellis Paul, Laurie Geltman, Jim Infantino, Catie Curtis and Barbara Kessler, who met Antoniades through the Underground and married him in 1996. They have a 10-month-old daughter, Emilia.

"I had no clue what folk music was until Acoustic Underground," he said. "We expected it to be sort of an MTV `Unplugged' kind of thing and found this exciting underworld of folk music that's just thriving in the Boston area. I really liked the new songwriters like Barbara; the idea that instead of a song coming from this whole band sound, it came from a good melody and good lyrics. I liked that the subject matter of songs got a little deeper.

"To be a great folkie is to write great songs, not to be a star. I love that about the folk world."

Antoniades has a grand "Let's-fix-up-the-old-barn-and-put-on-a-show" attitude that is tailor-made for the grass-roots, sub-corporate world of folk music. After years drum-rolling around in the comparatively mean-spirited and money-minded world of rock, folk was a place he felt good about applying the business skills and technological savvy that were second-nature to him.

"I was always a pretty scattered kid, always getting into things," he said. "They didn't label it back then, but I was certainly hyper and certainly active. I was always building things, taking things apart. I have to be doing a lot of things at the same time. That's why I love the drums."

Antoniades grew up in Berkeley, Calif., the son of a research chemist and a high school teacher. By the time he was in the third grade, he was performing recitals as a guitar prodigy, but his frenetic energies drew him to the primal and creative chaos of the drums.

He was equally prodigious tinkering in his garage, and by 14 was running his own auto body shop, approved by three local insurance agencies and making some $2,000 a week.

But music kept pulling him. After touring Japan with a big band, he sent a tape to the Berklee College of Music to see if there was any point to his applying there. They responded by offering him a full scholarship, and he moved to Boston in 1985.

Not even the vast musician's playroom that is Berklee could contain his tinkering energies, however. A job as apartment manager led to his own contracting business, using musicians as workers. But Berklee did expose him to the new world of synthesizers, computers and other high-tech music tools.

"The synthesis department was just growing then," he said, "so there was a lot of creativity and discovery going on, exploring new sounds and technologies."

Antoniades graduated from Berklee in 1989 with degrees in drumming and music synthesis. Where some saw the new technologies as a threat to acoustic and traditional forms, such as jazz and folk, Antoniades believed that these tools could allow artists to control their careers in unprecedented ways. To many musicians, the new world was a terrifying frontier of cold machinery and forbiddingly expensive new technologies. To Antoniades, it was a just a garage full of new toys that needed to be put together in ways that helped the creative artist.

"A new Macintosh has the power that only a handful of people in the world had 10 years ago," he said. "There's a very nice living to be made for a lot of people in music that wasn't thought possible just a few years ago. If you can manage your own business fairly well and handle a personal computer, you can do it. You may never be a star, but you'll stay creative and in control of your music. You will be able to tour nationally, sell CDs and make a good living. What we've created with Barbara is an artist on an independent label who's selling records in the 20,000 range and touring nationally up to 250 dates a year."

Only a few years ago, many feared that the expense and complexity of the new music technologies might doom noncommercial forms like folk. Antoniades is in the business of making sure just the opposite happens—and happy to report that business is very good. His company is averaging 20 to 30 projects a week.

"What I love about the folk world is that there are people in their 50s still making a living on the club level," he said. "In the pop world, I've seen so many artists who started out wanting to be stars, made a successful first record, then stumbled with a second and their label dropped them. Their whole career was through.

"But if you can start your career on your own, building your own tours, making your own records, you build this core world from the bottom up, from fans who have seen you live. They are loyal to you, not responding to industry hype. If there are companies like Artist Development to help them along, to help them develop their own art, then they can do this forever."

—November 16, 1997

Folk music as a business **Ralph Jaccodine**

Ralph Jaccodine is not your father's folkie. At 38, he is among the most important movers 'n' shakers in Boston's burgeoning singer-songwriter scene. He owns Black Wolf Records, which launched the career of Ellis Paul, among the very best of today's brash and literate new singer-songwriters. He also manages Paul, hot folk-rockers the Pushstars, and, until recently, handled the shooting-star career of Martin Sexton.

With Black Wolf's ambitious and cutting-edge songwriter anthology, "This Is Boston—Not Austin," Jaccodine did much to put the local songwriter scene on the map nationally. As in the 1960s, the Boston area is in the vanguard of the folk revival.

But those couched in the comfy, slow-paced world of the last great folk revival would hardly recognize their old hippie selves in the casually power-dressed Jaccodine, in his congenial cockiness or serenely sure business smarts.

"I think that in the past, being a savvy businessman was frowned upon in folk music," Jaccodine, who lives in Cambridge, said. "Lawyers and contracts and even managers were almost seen as impurities. This new generation of songwriters can look in hindsight at the mistakes made by previous generations of performers and say, look, you've got to be armed to deal with this world if you want to play in it.

"In the past, I think a lot of artists lost control of their songs and their careers. There was a feeling that people with business experience could manipulate their way around musicians like a hot knife through butter. That's changing."

Like most of his contemporaries, however, Jaccodine takes exception to the notion that today's folk music is very different from that of past generations. If boomer-bred folkies think the most important folk aesthetics do not drive artists like Paul, Jaccodine will suggest, as younger generations always have to their elders, that they are just not listening.

Asked what the new songwriters carry from folk tradition, Jaccodine said without a moment's hesitation, "truth, passion, simplicity. There's not a lot of bells and whistles to folk music. At its best, it can be a very simple medium, which is what makes it so damn complicated as a business. You're not selling a lot of gimmicks."

When Jaccodine was growing up in Allentown, Pa., folk music was even further underground than it is now. It existed almost entirely beneath media view, the frail flames fanned at isolated venues such as Godfrey Daniel's coffeehouse in nearby Bethlehem. It is a club long renowned for its welcoming ways.

High-schooler Jaccodine wandered in one night because he'd heard there was an open stage where anybody could sing, and he was burning to try out his brand-new, $75 Epiphone guitar.

New to the folk scene, he was a big wheel in local rock as president of the Allentown Council of Youth, which had a municipally sanctioned monopoly on rock concert production. At 16, he was promoting concerts for such '70s superstars as Kiss, Hall & Oates, Linda Ronstadt and Bachman-Turner Overdrive.

Even with all that noisy charisma ringing in his ears, however, he immediately fell in love with the quiet folk scene he found at Godfrey's.

"The folk world invites people in," he said. "I felt like I could function in the folk world, as a fan and a performer. In the rock world, I was a fan and a promoter, but I didn't feel like I was a member. This was the '70s; these were big rock stars, with big drug problems and big alcohol problems and huge egos. At Godfrey's, I could talk to the performers after they left the stage, get their autographs and old guitar picks. They were very inviting to me as a little guy just checking out the scene. It's a very different vibe than I found in rock. There was a lot of humility, a lot of community involved."

After high school, he attended Notre Dame, majoring in economics, still producing big stars as student concert director. Another way Jaccodine contrasts with many older folkies is in how free of rebellion his path was. His father, a physicist, was deacon of their Catholic church in Allentown, and Jaccodine is also an active Catholic; he has taught catechism for 14 years at the Boston College church where he worships.

"It might be contrary to a lot of people who get into folk music," he said, "but I'm not that political. I'm not an activist type person, though I do believe in right and wrong."

A brief sales job for Wrangler jeans brought him to Boston in 1982. He dabbled around the edges of the folk scene, taking in occasional shows at Passim, but began a career in real estate after leaving Wrangler. It increasingly ate up his time without filling his soul. Rebel or not, contended capitalist or not, Jaccodine was having a crisis of conscience.

"I like to sell things I believe in," he said. "I believe in music; I didn't believe in real estate. But I like to negotiate, I like business, I don't think any of those are evil. I like to make money, I don't think that's evil. Artists need someone with those skills to be on their team, and that's what I do as manager."

One night around 1990, he wandered into the Nameless Coffeehouse and was spellbound by the invitingly melodic, intelligent and very contemporary songs of Ellis Paul. Just as he had felt the artists at Godfrey's were singing the songs of their times, he felt Paul was singing the songs of Jaccodine's.

A series of remarkable circumstances, including a prophetic dream and winning a $1,000 church lottery, led to his founding Black Wolf Records in 1992. Paul's debut disc, "Say Something," was its first release. Jaccodine soon left real estate to pursue his new career.

The second volume of "This Is Boston—Not Austin" is hot off the presses, and already gaining national attention. Like its predecessor, it is urban-edged, lyrically smart and rock-friendly, though heavily acoustic. It is truly revolutionary in its inclusion of local performance poets, such as Boston Globe columnist Patricia Smith, Tim Mason, who is also Passim's music manager, and local poet-activist Richard Cambridge. He sees the same fires that continue to light folk music in this street-smart, underground art movement. Describing why it excites him, Jaccodine went a long way toward defining folk's value in today's corporate-dominated, market-driven, music world.

"Like folk music, it is about being stripped-down, honest, portable, and judged by what it says," he said. "And it's very alternative, underground; you don't see it on TV or hear it on the radio.

"I don't see the past generations of the folk world as anything we're clashing with," he said. "I see us evolving through it.

"You know," he says, referring to Paul, "I manage a guy who has a tattoo of Woody Guthrie on his arm. They believe they're keeping those traditions alive in their own way by keeping the music accessible and portable and human. Above all, by keeping it human."

—April 13, 1997

The tools they are a-changin'
Roger McGuinn, Christine Lavin, Bob Franke

The pop music world seems all in a tizzy about our new computer age. Rock stars and record labels are furiously hunting down and suing download-enabling outfits such as Napster and MP3.com, complaining that these newfangled machines are going to mean the end of the music world.

Wait—isn't that folk music's job? Aren't folkies the Chicken Littles of music, forever whining about the latest musical invention, be it the electric guitar, the synthesizer, or—heaven forfend—the digital phase sampler?

But as the folk battalions gather for the last great camp of the summer campaign, the Boston Folk Festival, much of the talk is about how digital and computer technology is revolutionizing the music industry—and all the news for folk is good.

Roger McGuinn has been in the front lines of bringing new technologies to traditional music ever since he picked up an electric 12-string guitar in 1964 to twang out Bob Dylan's "Mr. Tambourine Man" with his band the Byrds and invented folk-rock. He is now an ardent pioneer and champion of the digital technologies used by Napster and MP3.com, on whose behalf he recently testified before Congress. He has an ongoing deal to provide new tracks for MP3.com customers to download as part of his ambitious Folk Den project to preserve traditional folk songs on the Internet. Like all the other Boston Folk Festival performers interviewed, he thinks the information age is the best thing to happen to folk music in decades.

"These new technologies are cutting the major music corporations out," McGuinn said. "It bypasses the middle man, and they are the middle man. They've had a stranglehold on artists all these years, and finally there's an alternative, somewhere else artists can go when they believe there's an audience for their music. It's like a new folk tradition, using an electronic medium for an oral transmission of the music from singer to listener, the way folk songs have always been passed along."

It must be said that the pop industry has a point in its objection to Napster and MP3.com, which enable people to download rec ords in ways that skirt paying legally required royalties to labels, publishers, and artists. The courts so far have vehemently agreed with the industry, levying hundreds of millions of dollars in penalties against both companies.

Songwriter-comedienne Christine Lavin is among the most popular performers in folk today. She recently attended a music industry conference on new computer technology, which included a symposium of industry lawyers pondering Napster and MP3.com.

"There was never any mention of the artist, the songwriter, the content of the music or what effect the technology might have on the quality of the music," she said.

Instead, the talk was entirely about how the major music corporations can gain control of the technology and begin profiting from it, she said. It reinforced her theory that it is not the piracy of the downloads that offends them, just that the pirates are not sailing under their Jolly Roger.

"These new technologies make them superfluous," she said, "and I think that's a very good thing for all the music. They have had such a stranglehold on what people can hear on commercial radio today, and it's all so homogenized, boring, so lowest-common-denominator. It's just a product to them, like all we're doing is making parts for a CD player."

Because folk music is, at heart, a performance-driven medium, Lavin loves the idea of people downloading her songs—Napster lists 100 Lavin downloads— whether she is paid or not.

"I think of Napster as a whole bunch of tiny radio stations that are now playing our music all over the world," she said. "Because I have confidence in the music, I believe that if people hear it, they're going to want to hear it more—and to go hear it live. And it's onstage where I make my living, and where all successful folk artists make their living."

The Internet is also making folk music much easier to hear on the radio. Local public folk station WUMB-FM (91.9), producer of the Boston Folk Festival, began Internet broadcasts last March. At their next fund-raiser a month later, nearly 10 percent of what they raised came from Internet listeners who tune in from as far away as Israel, Japan, France, and Switzerland.

The Internet has also transformed the way folk music does business, making it much easier for performers to stay in touch, not only with their agents and venues, but with fans and fellow performers. Longtime circuit rider Bob Franke, among the most respected folk songwriters in New England, has enjoyed a big career boost through the Internet.

"The way my career always felt to me is that I'm not a national performer, I'm local in a lot of places. There have always been pockets all over North America where I did well, because someone heard about me and took a chance. So I become a regular performer in that area's folk scene. Now these isolated pockets are much less isolated, all these folk scenes talk to each other over the Internet, which is good for them and good for performers who know how to put on a good show."

It is already commonplace for folk performers to have their own Web sites, chock-full of information about their tours and records, but also of chatty news about their recent doings and ways for fans to e-mail them directly. These are not only great career assets for the artists but, because the best folk artists see their fans more as friends than consumers, the sites are used as a way to continue the conversation begun onstage.

"Folk music is and always has been based on audience reaction," said Franke, "while popular music, industrial music, has been based on gatekeeper reaction, the gatekeepers being industry and radio executives who decide for audiences what they're going to hear. Gatekeeper reaction is always more conservative, because they're worried about investing large sums of money. I think the era of the gatekeeper is over, at least as we've known it. Now any musician with a computer has access to, if you will, the moral equivalent of airplay through technologies like MP3. The net result is going to be a tremendous democratizing, favoring those artists and musics that rely on word-of-mouth more than marketing."

And what of the brakes those gatekeepers are putting on companies like Napster and MP3.com? McGuinn has been watching the music industry from the inside out for 40 years, always pushing the envelope forward yet always putting his new ideas to the service of the best instincts of the folk music he loves. For him, the future has never looked brighter.

"What I think all these lawsuits are about is that the big companies want to stop all these little guys and then take over their territory. Well, they may be able to stop the big ones from doing it, but what about all the college students who are doing it on their own? It's just too widespread, too democratic to stop. Ain't that great?"

—*September 17, 2000*

Rebuilding the folk music movement Utah Phillips

For Bruce "Utah" Phillips, congestive heart failure has turned into a great career move. Thanks largely to radical folk-rocker Ani DiFranco, the 64-year-old folk singer, songwriter, and raconteur has earned thousands of new fans since his performing career was severely curtailed by the condition in 1994.

DiFranco produced two collaborative CDs with Phillips on her own Righteous Babe Records—"The Past Didn't Go Anywhere" and "Fellow Workers"—showcasing his fiery populism and vivid tales about labor history. A new generation of fans fell under the spell of his rakish wit, rabble-rousing charms, fiercely stated humanism, and devotion to America's radical past.

But there is another side to Phillips, one only glimpsed on these CDs: the hard-traveling folk singer, songwriter, and showman who played a crucial role in redefining the folk form after the collapse of the '60s folk revival. That performer comes splendidly to life on a new Red House CD of yarns and repartee called "The Moscow Hold & Other Stories," culled from old concert recordings. It will be released Tuesday.

Phillips's radicalism informs everything he does, but this CD highlights the hilariously folksy humorist and stage-smart entertainer who helped teach a dour postrevival folk world how to laugh at itself again—and how to put on a show.

"Watching performers playing the small coffeehouses back then," he said, "I encountered a great casualness and carelessness about the stage. It was almost as if it was part of the folk canon to pretend it wasn't theater. I would say over and over, 'If there's a stage, a microphone, and an audience, it's theater. Why ignore it? Why not learn how to use it?' "

The skill of a theatrical and comedic master is everywhere on "The Moscow Hold." Phillips's artfully offhand banter is punctuated with keen one-liners ("He was madder than a boiled owl"), daffy place names, double-entendres, and bald-faced lies. In the title yarn, he claims he began a wrestling career (under the name Kid Pro Quo) by defeating a professional bully's dreaded Moscow hold. It's just an old barroom joke, turned epic by his swaggering treatment.

In the robust tradition of American tall tales, the fun is in the winding road to his

I worked with lots of old drunks only fit to shovel gravel, but they all knew songs, and they showed me how to play them. The reason I wound up doing what I do now, I guess, was that the songs these guys sang were so close to their lives, to what they were experiencing in their work and loves and afflictions. —Utah Phillips

punch lines. Phillips rambles about places like Two-Out-of-Three Falls, Idaho, and his current home, Nevada City, Calif., which he says is such a trendy new-age hive ("Got so many healers there it makes me sick"), the local Catholic church serves high-fiber, low-calorie Communion wafers marketed with the brand name I Can't Believe It's Not Jesus.

One reason Phillips sounded such a rousing wake-up call to the sullen folk world of the '70s was that he arrived on its stages a mature, savvy raconteur, skilled radical organizer, and accomplished songwriter whose songs had been recorded by Joan Baez, Flatt and Scruggs, and Utah folk singer Rosalie Sorrels.

He was born in Cleveland in 1935, in a grandly ethnic neighborhood that still knew the clip-clop of horse-drawn milk and rag wagons. He loved its cluttered sidewalks and alleyways, diverse culture, and ample opportunities for mischief.

In 1947, his mother, a onetime labor organizer, moved the family to Utah, where her second husband had found a film-distribution job with Paramount. Phillips adored his stepfather, who soon became an independent movie mogul. His Film Services Inc. introduced Italian Hercules epics, spaghetti Westerns, and kung fu movies to America.

But Phillips disliked the gray-flannel world his stepfather worked in, not to mention the conservative Mormon culture of Salt Lake City. He ran away from home for long stretches, often working on nomadic road crews. It was there he first became aware of folk music.

"I worked with lots of old drunks only fit to shovel gravel, but they all knew songs, and they showed me how to play them. The reason I wound up doing what I do now, I guess, was that the songs these guys sang were so close to their lives, to what they were experiencing in their work and loves and afflictions."

Mostly to have something to share around the campfires, Phillips began making up his own songs, a habit he retained.

During his rambling youth, Phillips also began meeting what he calls his elders, a series of mentor-teachers including Father Baxter Liebler, dubbed "the Padre of the San Juan," who gave up a wealthy eastern parish to work among the Navajo nations; and pacifist-anarchist Ammon Hennacy, who converted Phillips to anarchism by showing him it was not about destroying government, but about creating humane, self-governing communities.

"Ammon taught me that an anarchist is someone who doesn't need a cop to tell him what to do," he said.

He became a radical activist and organizer, supporting himself as a state government archivist. In 1968, he ran for senator on the Peace and Freedom Party ticket, lost, and was unable to get his old job back. He had no idea what to try next.

A few years earlier, dobro player Tut Taylor had heard Phillips's songs while in

Utah for a Mormon convention, and taken them to a Nashville publishing house. Baez recorded "Rock, Salt, and Nails," and Flatt and Scruggs recorded several, including his lonely classic "Starlight on the Rails." In 1970, Sorrels, who had been singing his songs all over the country, urged him to share a gig with her in Saratoga, N.Y.

"Rosalie introduced me at Caffe Lena, and the audience didn't believe her at first," he said. "Turns out a lot of people had become convinced over the years that I was really her alter ego, that there was no such a thing as a Utah Phillips, and that she had written all those songs herself."

He soon disabused them of that notion, though he rather liked the mythic aura of it, and found that audiences relished his smart-alecky wit, political rantings, and homespun balladry. "I was writing and learning songs, working on my act, learning to book gigs," Phillips said. "It took me a year to realize I was not an unemployed organizer; I was a folk singer."

He put his radical background to powerful use, however. He would ask venues to offer potluck suppers before his gigs and invite volunteers and fans, along with members of other folk societies and progressive organizations, to discuss the state of folk music. He made it his mission to collect stories about how various grassroots folk organizations built audiences, found spaces for concerts, created media interest, raised public arts money—and to pass that lore along to other groups he visited.

Phillips's concerts took on the energy of radical town-hall meetings, aided by his brilliantly folksy showmanship. He brought different-colored flannel shirts with him, so he would always stand out against the backdrop, and his own lighting gels, so the audience could always see his face. He labored to make each show its own work of art.

"I always had to know where I was, who I was working with," he said. "When I booked a town, I'd get newspapers sent to me, go to the library and read about what its industries and history were, get place names to hang my stories on. So when I got there, those people really understood I knew where I was and who they were. They all knew this wasn't the same show I'd done the night before; this one was just for them."

Phillips is reaping the rewards of that hard work now. All over the country, tapes of his shows were made and kept by folk societies and fans. His first record with DiFranco came from hundreds of hours of such tapes, as did "The Moscow Hold."

Traveling from town to town, from isolated coffeehouse to ailing folk society, he taught the folk world that it could run things for itself. Along the way, he became, if not a star, certainly a legend, and found a place to pour all the lessons he learned from his elders about community, self-determination, and the abundant, renewable power of a few kindred spirits.

In the opening cut of "The Moscow Hold," Phillips urges the audience to sing along. With a conspiratorial twinkle in his voice, he says, "In a mass-market economy, a revolutionary song is any song you choose to sing for yourself." What a wonderful thing it is to see his own Johnny Appleseed legacy return to him now, in the form of these humbly recorded, superbly performed concert tapes, to support him in his ailing years, and make his star shine even brighter than before.

"I tried to leave behind permanent structures for this music and this community," he said. "And I tried to leave behind an attitude that we're all part of a larger community, and that there's a whole lot of sharing that can go on. What I was looking for was a feeling of fellowship, of loyalty for the people who were keeping these places alive, putting food in my mouth, helping me pay my rent and have this career. So what am I doing for them, besides coming to their town, doing a show and then leaving? What am I leaving behind?"

—August 15, 1999

Paying respects to a legend in song
Rosalie Sorrels, Loudon Wainwright III, Peggy Seeger, Christine Lavin

When legendary folk chanteuse Rosalie Sorrels is asked what advice she would offer a young woman considering a career like hers, she laughs, a dry, wise chuckle that becomes a full-blown belly laugh as she yells: "Go back! It's a trap! It's a trap!"

It is a joke, mostly, but it also reveals much about how the Idaho folk singer, songwriter, and storyteller views her fabled 40-year career as one of folk music's most enduringly popular entertainers. Where many see a commanding performer with a master career plan that has transcended generations and genres, she sees only hard circumstance, to which she reacted as best she could. She views her stardom less as something she fashioned than as something that happened to her while she was struggling to raise five children as a single mother.

At 68, she is in the process of retiring from touring.

"I'm not going to stop singing or writing or anything like that," she says. "I want to stay home more. One of the advantages of becoming venerable is that you get to stay home; another is that you get to stamp your foot and say, `I will have my way.' I've been in show business for over 35 years, and I just don't want to do that anymore. I don't think of what I do as show business, anyway; I never thought of it that way. It's just my life, which I sometimes take onstage."

Fellow folk travelers are gathering to pay tribute to, and play music with, Sorrels.

Edith Piaf had it, Patsy Cline had it, Billie Holiday had it. It's a tone that people can understand, whether they understand the words or not, a feeling coming right from the heart. —Rosalie Sorrels

The breadth of performers is an impressive testament in itself: They range from hip contemporary songwriters Loudon Wainwright III and Christine Lavin to longtime traditional stars Jean Ritchie, Peggy Seeger, Patrick Sky, Mitch Greenhill, and David Bromberg.

Lavin said that Sorrels's intimate songwriting and performing styles became models for the urban songwriters who revitalized folk in the 1980s. Because Sorrels influenced artists who became better known, such as Lavin, Nanci Griffith (whose hit "Ford Econoline" was written about touring with Sorrels), and Mary Chapin Carpenter, Lavin says that many today are unaware of how important she was in shaping the modern folk voice: "I think she's influenced a lot of people who don't even know her name.

"I had never seen a performer who was so comfortable and had such command of a room," Lavin said of first seeing Sorrels in 1975 at Caffe Lena in Saratoga Springs, NY. "Rosalie had these silences in her shows, which I took as a mark of tremendous confidence. She was listening to the audience, making space for them, creating a sense of dialogue. She really casts a spell over a room; it's a very primal thing."

Wainwright also first met Sorrels in Saratoga, where she was, as he put it, "the twisted den mother" to a gaggle of aspiring songwriters who flocked there in the '70s.

"She's influenced everyone she's met," he said. "One of the things that always struck me was her dedication to songwriting. She has had a very dramatic life. You'd often ask how she was doing and hear all these problems she was having with her health or her kids. And then at the end, she'd perk up and say, 'But I wrote two songs last week!'"

The needs of Sorrels's five children always directed her career. She moved places she could stay put with them, where she would essentially become a local performer; first to Berkeley, CA, where she came under the wing of political songwriter Malvina Reynolds, and then to Saratoga, where Lena Spencer offered to share her home.

She now lives in a cabin her father built on Grimes Creek, about 30 miles outside Boise, and hopes to produce a folk festival and concert series there.

It is what she calls a heartfelt tone that first drew her to folk music and that continues to define her craft.

"Edith Piaf had it; Patsy Cline had it; Billie Holiday had it," she says. "It's a tone that people can understand, whether they understand the words or not, a feeling coming right from the heart, very personal. You can hear it in all kinds of music, but more in folk, since people's music is made because they need it, rather than for art's sake or for money's sake. They make it because they have to have it in their lives."

It is precisely that directness and honesty in Sorrels's work, that level of personal authenticity, that has so profoundly influenced other performers and that has kept her in the front ranks of folk stardom since she ventured from her Southwestern home to play at the Newport Folk Festival in the 1960s.

"She sings like somebody sitting on their front porch," says Seeger. "She's a skilled performer without being a capital-P performer. She knows how to get you hooked and keep you there, but by being casual, singing down-home kinds of songs and telling stories from her own life. She's never trying to be something she's not. Who she is is all she needs to be."

—March 22, 2002

Give Yourself to Love: Kate Wolf *remembered*
Kathy Mattea, Utah Phillips, Dave Alvin, Rosalie Sorrels, Nina Gerber

When musicians discuss what they admire about Kate Wolf's songs, it is easy to see why the late California songwriter never became rich and famous. They describe her work with words like "calm," "still," "languid," "centered," and, above all, "kind." These are not words likely to spring to mind while listening to Top 40 radio these days, but they do help explain why, 12 years after her death from cancer at the age of 44, Wolf is a legend in folk and acoustic country music circles. Nanci Griffith has said it was preserving Wolf's legacy, more than any other reason, that inspired her to record her two "Other Voices" tribute albums.

Although she was a fixture on the West Coast folk scene for years, Wolf was just beginning to receive national attention when she died. Now, 15 highly respected folk and country singers and songwriters, including Griffith, Emmylou Harris, Kathy Mattea, Dave Alvin, Utah Phillips, Lucinda Williams, Peter Rowan, Rosalie Sorrels, Greg Brown, Ferron, and Terry Garthwaite, have recorded a beautiful, hypnotically gentle CD of Wolf's songs called "Treasures Left Behind: Remembering Kate Wolf" (Red House). It is a hushed classic, filled with quietly soulful performances, warm melodies, and provocative, insightful lyrics.

"Kate Wolf had a real honesty about what she wrote," said country star Mattea, who sings a beautifully austere cover of Wolf's anthem, "Give Yourself to Love." "My impression is that she was just a person who did what she did; it wasn't about chasing a market or all those other reasons people find to make music these days. Yet her songs are so accessible. There's a real gift to being able to write that simply."

So much of what made Wolf's songs alluring is evident in "Give Yourself to Love." The melody is spacious and welcoming, the words finely carved and heartfelt. But there is a hard edge to the wisdom, too. She does not merely say we must love those close to us, but that love must be a way of life: "Walk these mountains in the rain / Learn to love the wind." As in many of Wolf's best songs, the natural world and the interior emotional world become seamless parts of the same landscape.

Some might be surprised to see raw-boned roots-rocker Dave Alvin, of Blasters fame, on this tender anthology. But his version of Wolf's lonesome "These Times We're Living In" is gritty and dark, highlighting the philosophical toughness that informs even Wolf's most sensitive ballads.

"To me, her songs are similar to Merle Haggard's, in that they seem pretty simple," Alvin said. "I don't mean that in any negative way. They were very deceptively written. Some of them can just fly by you, then once you really listen, you find so much in there. What I liked about 'These Times We're Living In' is that it is just brutally honest, and yet it's still a love song. I strive for that when I write; to say things clearly and directly, and yet have a couple different layers underneath. That's a real balancing act, and she did it so well."

Wolf's songs, however intimate, were always written with clean, graceful melodies others could sing. That helps make this CD such a fluid set, despite the very different artists present. Perhaps as much a factor, however, is the superb production and gorgeously subtle playing of Nina Gerber, Wolf's longtime accompanist and one of the most respected mandolin-guitar players in acoustic music. Both Alvin and Mattea said they signed on as much out of respect for Gerber as for Wolf.

The CD began as an attempt by Gerber to come out from the long shadow Wolf cast over her life. It was hearing her sing at a pizza parlor in Sebastopol, Calif., in 1975 that made Gerber want to be a musician. As she put it, she became nearly a stalker, following Wolf to gigs, taking mandolin lessons from Wolf's husband and accompanist Don Coffin. When that marriage ended, Gerber knew all his parts to Wolf's songs, and became her accompanist from 1978 until her death in 1986.

As Gerber tried to put together a solo record in 1994, Wolf's ghost kept appearing. She thought she should do two of Wolf's songs, since their careers had been so intertwined. She doesn't sing, though, so she mulled over vocalists to invite, and then brooded over what to say about Wolf in the notes.

"At that point, I thought, 'Y'know, I'm making a Kate Wolf album here,' " she said. "I finally realized this was something I had to do for myself, a real piece of grief work."

Asked about Wolf's growing legend as a songwriter, she at first begged off, saying it was still hard for her to separate the Wolf she loved so much and worked with so long from the one the public saw. That is in large part, she said, because it is the real Wolf her fans see reflected in her songs.

"I think there's just a simplicity and honesty and soulfulness to Kate's music that's very accessible to everybody," said Gerber. "It's all about Kate and her life; but at the same time, it's all about us. There's this commonality she could write with that makes it so easy to relate to her music. She just paid attention to everybody she met and every place she went and wrote from those experiences. She wrote other people's stories and her own. But she would also look at the landscape and be able to write a song about the land she was driving across."

Often, simply expressing a mood was Wolf's point, the gray pleasures of idling through a cold, rainy day; the deep, quiet joy of a night spent with friends around a kitchen table.

"Love Still Remains," which Emmylou Harris sings in a husky moan, starkly evokes the pure, primal ache of still loving someone who is lost to you. Wolf does nothing to dilute the raw essence of loneliness: "It rolls like the tumbleweed out on the open plains / Yes, the love I felt for you still remains."

"Kate had a difficult life; some terrible things happened to her," said folk singer-songwriter Phillips, who was Wolf's close friend since they met at a 1975 folk festival. "But she was able to go back into herself and come out with beautiful songs, filled with compassion and forgiveness and understanding, rather than a persistent whine about how it had gone wrong. I always thought that was miraculous. Even when she was talking about herself, she could do it in such a way that people in every audience would think, `That's me; that's what I feel.' "

Phillips sings one of Wolf's most intimate songs, a smartly re-created conversation in which she made collide the chiding phrase "See here, she said" with tender homilies like "You'd better do the things you dream" and "Dreams never lie."

Idaho singer-songwriter Sorrels, a friend of Wolf's since their salad days as aspiring troubadours in the mid-'60s, sings a rivetingly conversational cover of "In China or a Woman's Heart." The deceptively plain-spun ballad uses a woman's humble keepsake as metaphor both for a love incompletely answered and the secret emotional life we all harbor inside. Sorrels is battling cancer herself, midway through chemotherapy that is doubly painful since it's preventing her from playing guitar; her prognosis is excellent.

"Kate was an incredibly kind person," Sorrels said, "and there was a kind and calm atmosphere about all her songs and the way she delivered them. Her music made people feel safe, I think.

"Her songs are so easy to get next to and remember. When you choose to write about something that's incredibly personal, you have to give up some of that for the people who are listening. You have to know that you can make them part of it; then the song becomes everyone's, instead of your own. She had a real gift for that, and I think it had to do with her curiosity about people and her ability to connect with them. She was very thoughtful. I don't mean that in the sense of buying people presents or whatever; she listened."

Asked what songwriters can learn from Wolf's work, Alvin said, "Don't lie. If you're the president, you can lie; if you're in the grocery store with a steak shoved down your pants, you can lie. But songs that lie are horrible. Just capture the honesty of the moment; that's what Kate Wolf's songs do."

Mattea said, "Some songs sound like they have always existed, and someone just found them. `Give Yourself to Love' feels like that to me; it doesn't sound like somebody made it up. Singing it feels so natural, like a well-worn pair of jeans. I think it is such a rare gift to be able to write in a way that makes other people feel in their lives what it is you are writing about in your own.

"You know, no one gives you a Grammy for the most kind song," Mattea continued. "But people do tribute albums to you because you write those kinds of songs. Those are the things that inspire people to want to keep somebody's work alive."

—August 23, 1998

Why won't country radio play Alison Krauss?
Alison Krauss, Brad Paul, country radio music director Ginny Rogers, Billboard Nashville bureau chief Chet Flippo

If that's the price I have to pay
For doing things my own way
Then it's what I'll have to do somehow.
"Find My Way Back to My Heart," by Mark Simos

That refrain, from the new Alison Krauss single, is already being heard as a battle cry in bluegrass, folk, and country music. Last Tuesday, Rounder Records released "So Long So Wrong," the Alison Krauss & Union Station CD that many in the industry see as a real acid test for the ailing country music business, which is experiencing a decline in both record sales and radio listeners. At 25, the gifted singer and fiddler is already among the most respected artists in Nashville and seems to have done everything humanly possible to prove her broad commercial appeal. But will mainstream country radio play her?

"So Long So Wrong" is Krauss's first CD since the stunning breakthrough success of her 1995 collection, "Now That I've Found You." It went double platinum, meaning more than 2 million sales, by far the best-selling CD in the 27-year history of Cambridge-based independent label Rounder Records.

Brad Paul, vice president of marketing for Rounder, has the label poised for its most ambitious marketing campaign ever, with a professional Nashville field staff in place and regional sales representatives throughout the country. But he has no idea if country radio will play Krauss.

"This is kind of the acid test," he said. "She has not taken her success and moved to a major label, and she has not gone in the studio to make a beefed-up fat-drum, electric, pedal-steel-sounding country record. She made the kind of record she wanted to make. So we just don't know if country radio is going to decide whether this is right for their format; whether they're going to take into account her 2 million sales or not."

But record sales were just the beginning of Krauss's very good year. She won Grammys for best female country vocal performance and best country collaboration for her duet with Shenandoah. She also swept the 1995 Country Music Awards, winning in all five categories for which she was nominated, including female vocalist, single, and vocal event of the year.

Even with all that, there is a serious question whether she will be given even a chance on commercial country radio's rigid and rock-bound format. For one thing, she is still on an indie label (her 1995 breakthrough began with "When You Say Nothing at All," a song she recorded for a major-label tribute to Keith Whitley that made commercial radio playlists). More important, she makes music her own way: softly romantic country-pop ballads mixed with pure bluegrass tunes, delivered with acoustic guitars, fiddle, mandolin, and banjo. There are no drums and no electric guitars, anathema to a country format still trying to lure more rock listeners.

To Krauss, the new CD is exciting simply because it's her first effort with the new Union Station lineup, which includes guitarist and Vermont native Dan Tyminski, banjo-guitarist Ron Block, bassist Barry Bales, and mandolinist Adam Steffey. She is renowned in Nashville for having stuck to her bluegrass guns, turning down many major-label offers to stay with Rounder, a label that is utterly committed both to artistic control and acoustic music. She seemed almost insulted to have to explain that she did nothing different in light of her 1995 successes.

"It's not something I had to give a lot of thought to," she said. "We weren't trying to make a point; we just knew we'd never do anything different musically. I mean, if we would've felt like making a whole album with drums and pianos and stuff, we would have. But not because of any success."

"So Long So Wrong" is, in the loveliest sense, just another Alison Krauss & Union Station record. Softly gorgeous ballads alternate with traditional bluegrass barnburners, rip-it-up road songs with devotional romantic anthems. Everyone gets a solo, but when Krauss sings, there is a special magic. She is already one of the finest singers anywhere in American pop; her whispery soprano brims with a delicate control and emotional honesty only the greatest singers ever achieve.

Still, early radio tracking is not encouraging. Local country station WKLB-96.9, the only commercial surviving mainstream country station in Boston, is not currently

I might have a different attitude if I had ever really had to struggle; I understand how people start off not compromising and may end up doing it later. But all I want to do, and all the guys want to do, is make sure we like what we did at the end of the day. And you hope somebody else will like it, too. —Alison Krauss

playing the new single. According to music director Ginny Rogers, they're not sure her soft acoustic sound is right for what she described as their quite conservative format. They did play Krauss's single from the Keith Whitley CD, but according to Rounder's tracking, they played the Grammy-winning "Baby, Now That I've Found You" only once a day for a week before dropping it.

"We didn't feel she fit the mainstream sound of the radio station," Rogers said. "She certainly deserves the acclaim and success she's received; she's incredibly talented. But she's always been a little bit bluegrass, and we're trying to educate the Boston audience about the mainstream country sound."

Billboard's Nashville bureau chief Chet Flippo said that sort of conservatism permeates country radio.

"The thing you have to remember is that these days in commercial country music, every release is a crapshoot," he said. "Nothing's guaranteed, everything's judged release by release rather than artist by artist. There's no more blue-chip artists, apart from maybe somebody like Alan Jackson. The other thing is that, by and large, bluegrass is poison on mainstream country radio."

Krauss's new ballads, such as "Find My Way Back to My Heart" and "Looking in the Eyes of Love," which Rounder is releasing as a single for AAA (adult album alternative) and Americana formats, are bluegrassy only in their soft, acoustic lilt and the spare nuances of her brilliant fiddling. Even the radio industry trade magazine Gavin said of the new CD, "Alison Krauss and Union Station made all the right decisions by releasing an album that will please grandma and her slam-dancing great-grandson." In short, precisely the listeners country radio is losing.

But will it please radio execs? Rogers dismissed the importance of Krauss's 2 million sales, saying she estimates only 10 percent of WKLB's listeners "are motivated enough to go out and buy a CD. That's still 90 percent of my audience that doesn't. And a lot of the people buying her record aren't even country music fans. They're just fans of good music."

Rogers went on to say, "The wonderful thing about Alison is that she's remained true to her art form."

But she also made it clear it is "the wonderful thing about Alison" that is keeping her off WKLB's playlist. She said she liked Krauss personally, and would play her more if listeners called in asking for her. But there's the old cross-fire: How can they request a song they have not heard?

Flippo said, "What radio really looks for is not so much what will draw listeners in, but not playing what will drive them away. That's a terrible way to back into an industry, but that's how their thinking goes now."

As for Krauss, she honestly doesn't understand why people expect her to change her sound to accommodate her success, saying with a laugh, "I mean, I wouldn't have learned to be in a bluegrass band if I was thinking about my career.

"I never expected anything like this; I mean, to get to be able to do this for a living. Everything since that is gravy. I might have a different attitude if I had ever really had to struggle; I understand how people start off not compromising and may end up doing it later. But all I want to do, and all the guys want to do, is make sure we like what we did at the end of the day. And you hope somebody else will like it, too."

—March, 30, 1997

From banjo-picker to music mogul Alison Brown

Whatever your stereotype of a banjo player might be, Alison Brown will dash it. Hillbilly twanger? She graduated from Harvard University and was an investment banker before starting her career as one of the country's most inventive banjo players. She has toured with Alison Krauss and Michelle Schocked, and is the first woman to ever win an instrumentalist of the year award from the International Bluegrass Music Association.

Perhaps you think of banjo pluckers as stuck-in-the-mud folk purists. Brown's sweet, fluid jazz fusions are as sophisticated as they are beguiling; comfortably wearing the influences of Wes Montgomery, Antonio Carlos Jobim, and Joe Pass. She has also invented a groundbreaking nylon-string electric banjo. And if you think banjo players only know one tempo—breakneck—then her quiet, spacious style will cure you of that stereotype, too.

Brown resists notions that she is breaking new ground. To her, it is simply a matter of playing the music she feels.

"Maybe you'd need to be a banjo player to hear the bluegrass in what I do," she said from her Nashville office, "but it really is there. The interesting thing is using banjo picking techniques to play jazz. Even though they may not be bluegrass tunes, the way I'm playing is still because of Earl Scruggs. He invented that three-finger-roll style, which became popular when he started playing with Bill Monroe in 1945. His playing defined bluegrass-style banjo, and it's all over what I do."

The essential contradiction of the banjo has been stumping would-be innovaters for years. While it is a loud, ringing instrument, its metal strings have almost no sustain, forcing players into multiple-note, intricate picking patterns. When Brown developed what she described as a musical crush on gentle jazz guitarist Joe Pass, she ended up inventing a new banjo.

"I wanted an insturment that had a voice like his, that round, expressive sound," she said. "I loved the idea of being able to stay on one note and have that say something. Acoustic banjo is a great sound, and I use it a lot, but it's stiff for some tunes, and requires you to play a lot of notes, because the decay is so fast. It's exciting to have an instrument that is a banjo and plays like one, but being electric with nylon strings, it's more warm and smooth; not so pointed. It's so nice to be able to slide up to a note and just stay there."

On her lilting, sensual, and often playful new Compass CD "Out of the Blue," Brown leads her quartet through alluringly melodic tunes like the brisk, Dave Brubek-inspired "Dante's Paradise" and the be-bop swinging "Four for Launch." Her single-note excursions slip-slide like wet guitar leads, but then explode into lush, chordal banjo runs. In "Return to Pelican Bay," her banjo is wistful, almost regretful, and in the tongue-in-cheek "Rebel's Bolero," she makes grand fun of her own jazzy pretensions; as though struggling to play the sleek Latin melody, only to backslide into old-timey banjo runs.

Still, a banjo is a banjo is a banjo, at least as far as radio is concerned. Commercial country radio all but bans banjo tracks, as do most smooth jazz formats. No amount of instrument-tinkering can solve this dilemma, and when Brown discusses it, the business head of the onetime investment banker takes over.

"There's been so much conglomeration of radio stations, and a lot of them were purchased for much more than they are worth," she said. "I heard recently that some stations are being bought for 20, 25 times their cash flow. So they're carrying enormous debt loads and impossible profit demands. Here's this new corporate owner, who's paid so much more for the station than it generates, so everybody's all in a tizzy trying to figure out ways to increase revenues, pump even more ads into each hour. They have to do it at the expense of the music, which makes them even more afraid of taking any chances with their formats. All I can say is, thank God for public radio."

Wanting to promote good music for its own sake, Brown, along with her producer, bassist, and business partner Garry West, founded Compass Records in 1993. It is already among the most respected acoustic labels in the country, with a stable that includes songwriters Kate Campbell and Pierce Pettis, bassist Victor Wooten, and British rocker Clive Gregson. Most artists start their own labels in hopes of jumping to an established one; but after three CDs on Vanguard, Brown eagerly jumped to her own label. When she discusses Compass, it is clear that her business head and banjo heart have found common ground.

"Compass is an artist-run label in the truest sense," she said. "I mean, we are really running the business, and we are really performing artists. When I was with Vanguard, it was always frustrating to go in the president's office and talk about issues we were dealing with on the road, and this guy had never been on the road. He didn't know first-hand what we were up against and couldn't be much help on certain things. But we're out there the same way our artists are. As a musician, I can understand that your music is a very personal thing. It's a bold step to offer it up to the world at large."

—April 24, 1998

As a musician, I can understand that your music is a very personal thing. It's a bold step to offer it up to the world at large. —Alison Brown

How is an Irish jig like a software program? **Mark Simos**

Waltham is not about to take away Nashville's title as Music City USA, but it can now boast at least one bona-fide country hit maker in Mark Simos.

Alison Krauss & Union Station, among the hottest acts in country music these days, recorded two songs by the 40-year-old fiddler, guitarist and songwriter on their new compact disc on the Rounder label, "So Long, So Wrong." One of the songs, the tenderly philosophical "Find My Way Back to My Heart," was released as a single, and is slowly climbing the charts. The album cracked the top five on Billboard's country album sales charts.

Many saw the song as an anthem for Krauss' commitment to acoustic bluegrass in the face of industry pressure to conform to modern country's rock-heavy sound, with its refrain, "If that's the price I have to pay for doing things my own way/ Then it's what I'll have to do somehow."

Actually, the song was inspired by a painful period in which Simos was making the decisions that led him to move to Watertown in 1993 and make a career of his other passion—software design. In 1995, after years working as a fiddler at folk dances and concerts, and as a guitarist for other fiddlers, he founded Organon Motives, a Belmont-based company that specializes in the new and rather daring area of domain engineering.

It may seem like a long leap from folk fiddler to cutting-edge software designer and consultant, but not for Simos.

"I got into mathematics and computers because I found the same kinds of patterns and structures I loved in fiddle tunes," he said. "My intuitive side and my analytical side have never fought that much, except in the kinds of career labels the world likes to put on these things. To my way of thinking, fiddlers are mathematicians; they're playing this wonderful kind of crystalline math of notes and forms and structures."

Simos was always drawn to the mysterious structures of traditional music, fascinated by the way old tunes change from culture to culture, age to age, without losing their melodic purity. Growing up in Southern California, he was first drawn to American traditional music, but was later lured by the even older Celtic music that so influenced our folk styles. He was in an Irish band, Knock Na Shee, and later toured as guitarist with brilliant Irish fiddler Eileen Ivers, who is now becoming an international star in a hit musical, *Riverdance*.

Simos is a wonderful fiddler himself. His compositions on a self-released instrumental CD, "Race the River Jordan," display his uncanny gift for writing modern tunes within traditional American and Celtic styles. It is this sophisticated understanding of traditional structure and style that make his songs attractive to knowledgeable artists such as Krauss, herself a world-class fiddler, and California bluegrass diva Laurie Lewis, who has also recorded several Simos songs.

"I played Irish and old-timey and all kinds of traditional music," Simos said, "and that affected my songwriting. It gave me this rich set of forms to work with, and they find their way into my songs. I try to craft the melody and chord movement equally with the words; to really weave them all in together."

Simos wrote "Find My Way Back to My Heart" specifically for Krauss, at a time when he was trying to reconcile his music with his growing interest in software design. Writing for other artists was something he could do at home, while also working in the computer field. He'd come to computers as a sideline, but it intrigued him so much that he got a master's degree in computer and information science from the University of Pennsylvania.

Time and again, he said, he saw software problems that reminded him of lessons he had learned about how traditional music evolves. Just as folk artists adapt music to suit their particular community, Simos wants to help develop software that makes it easier for people to design programs suited to their particular needs.

"For me, this was an extension of the question of what it means to have a tradition," he said. "It was like the compulsion some people have to think that every time you're writing a song, you're creating something completely new. Well, you're not; whether you like it or not, all you're doing is recycling a lot of old ideas in some new ways. The same thing happens in the software field.

"Every time somebody sits down to write, say, a new inventory-control program, they act as if they're the first people who have ever had to solve this problem. Whereas there is a whole culture of that particular software, probably hundreds of people who have designed that same program. But there's nothing in the software technology world to allow the creation of a tradition around programs."

Simos said this results in a certain cultural imperialism on the part of the software industry. Consumers are forced to adapt their ways to suit the available software.

Traditional music offers Simos endless examples of how music is designed to be adaptable to real-life needs and situations. For example, he's seen how an Irish jig takes on a slidey, slowed-down gait in the New England contredanse style, in order to accommodate winter dancers in their heavy, clopping boots. Then it quickens and sits bolt upright when played with the blues-influenced pulse of bluegrass—all without losing what Simos smiling calls "its essential jigness."

The same thing can be applied to software design, he said, through a better understanding of what is constant and what can be variable; and by developing a better computer language to communicate those things. That, in a nutshell, is what Simos is helping pioneer in the new field of domain engineering.

"I've taken the kind of thinking I learned from being a musician and tried to turn it into a systemized way of thinking that could be used in software technology," he said. "So learning to write a certain kind of banking application would be like learning a certain tune; once you knew it and understood it, you could play it as a jig or a reel or as a slow air.

"This kind of thing could have a mind-boggling impact on the software industry. What it spends on taking essentially frozen, rigid bits of software and trying to tinker with them—or throwing them out altogether—runs into billions of dollars a year. They're not really designing software to be soft. We keep creating software in these hard, fast images. But software is like music; it's just thoughts."

—June 1, 1997

Jazz adventures in the gentle fields of folk
Wayfaring Strangers: Matt Glaser, Jennifer Kimball, Tony Trischka, Aoife O'Donovan

Fusion can be a dirty word in music these days. Fans of folk, jazz, rock, blues, bluegrass, country, or classical music often balk at hearing foreign strains laid into the music they love. They view such crossovers as attempts to rob the music of what makes it special—to dilute, corrupt, or commercialize it.

So one would think there's something for everybody to hate in the swashbuckling fusions of the Wayfaring Strangers, an ensemble founded by Matt Glaser, chairman of the string department at Berklee College of Music and one of the most influential jazz, swing, old-time and bluegrass fiddlers of his generation. The band also includes clarinet-mandolin master Andy Statman (a major force in the recent klezmer revival), banjo innovator Tony Trischka, smart guitarist John McGann, jazz pianist Bruce Barth, and sublimely elastic bassist Jim Whitney. Its vocalists are Jennifer Kimball, Aoife O'Donovan, and Ruth Ungar, daughter of folk fiddle star Jay Ungar.

Their debut Rounder CD, "Shifting Sands of Time," is a grand success, a bold adventure along the frontiers of American music, and a deeply felt set of timeless songs. There are unexpected notes, but never a false one.

Why does this fusion experiment succeed where so many fail? Glaser believes it is because the fusion was never the point. "The song is the thing here," he said, "always trying to come back to the song. Andy Statman kept me on track with this as well, because he believes melody is dominant, and is always wanting to come back to the emotion of the melody."

Glaser has always sought to mingle the Southern traditional music he loves to play with the jazz and swing at which he also excels. But this project grew out of a deeper need. In 1996, Glaser was diagnosed with melanoma and, though he has since been successfully treated, had to consider that he might be dying. Had he defined himself as an artist? Had he left his mark?

This prompted two apparently contradictory desires. One was to meld his urban, jazz side with his bluegrass and folk side. The other was to explore the brooding emotions beneath the classic spiritual laments that helped him through his brush with mortality—such as "Wayfaring Stranger," "Man of Constant Sorrow," "Motherless Child," and "Rank Stranger." The presence of such powerful songs came to define the project.

"When we first showed up in the studio," Trischka said, "I remember saying, 'Well, Matt, what are we doing?' And him saying, 'I don't know; let's just try it.' And that first day, it really felt like we were feeling our way through alien terrain. But we were also coming to these tunes with great respect; the songs are so rooted and well-anchored and powerful they can withstand whatever you throw at them."

For all its instrumental wayfaring, this is very much a singer's album; a melodic set of traditional songs, country and bluegrass standards by such legends as Bill Monroe and Ola Belle Reed, and two contemporary gems by canny neotraditional songwriter Mark Simos. All the guest vocalists (including Tracy Bonham, Laurie Lewis, Cathie Ryan, and Ry Cavanaugh) are superb.

Bluegrass legend Ralph Stanley sings his version of "Man of Constant Sorrow," popularized in the film *O Brother, Where Art Thou?* Trischka's banjo gently underlays an urbane, loping fusion lick before Stanley sings, his voice wonderfully wild and intense. When Barth's elegant jazz solo takes over, it grows not from Stanley's vocal, but from that banjo lick. This is key to the album's success; the song itself is never disrupted, never bent to the fusions swirling around it.

Young bluegrass star Rhonda Vincent huskily turns the gospel thumper "Rank Strangers" into the lonely soliloquy its lyrics want it to be. Folk-pop singer Lucy Kaplansky sings "Wayfaring Stranger" as if its ancient mood had struck her only yesterday, and Tim O'Brien delivers the Monroe-Hank Williams classic "I'm Blue and I'm Lonesome, Too" the way Williams might have sung it if he had learned it from Ella Fitzgerald.

But the greatest revelation here is the work of local vocalist Jennifer Kimball. She's among the most in-demand backup singers in folk-pop, best known for her '90s tenure with Jonatha Brooke in the Story. Her lead and harmony work is stunningly lovely, fearlessly inventive, and emotionally riveting. On "Motherless Child," she evokes the primal desolation rippling beneath the quiet melody, her whispery soprano dipping to low, naked tones that shimmer like death throes, then soaring to beautiful sustains that ache with despair.

"I'm trying to inhabit a space I haven't heard before," Kimball said of her role as the group's lead vocalist. "I'm hearing the band under Matt's direction, playing these

Wayfaring Strangers

Wayfaring Strangers

very complex, and at the same time kind of spare, chords. But there are all these crazy notes in them, and I'm trying to get at them in a haunting kind of way."

Newest member Aoife O'Donovan, a sophomore at the New England Conservatory majoring in contemporary improvisation, grew up around Celtic music (she's the daughter of WGBH-FM "Celtic Sojourn" host Brian O'Donovan). She found singing with the ensemble a bit daunting, since both Kimball and Trischka were girlhood heroes, but loves its sense of musical derring-do. "With the elements of jazz in there," she said, "you have a lot of room to improvise, even melodically, and that's really cool. In a lot of other traditional settings, singers don't really have the freedom to do what they want with the melody."

For every listener, there will surely be moments in this CD that do not please; just as you are transported to some dark Appalachian glen, a blast of jazzy clarinet whisks you to a table at the Carnegie Deli. Glaser does not want us to think everything here goes together like bread and butter—he almost dares us not to wrinkle our noses occasionally.

But he never invents at the expense of the song, or of the feelings it conveys. And so, in the end, we are gently led to reconsider how compatible these disparate American musics are; with boldly conceived musical virtuosity, but even more by revealing the deep emotions—yearning for home, love of life and fear of death—that bind all true musical expression, just as they bind the human experience itself.

"To me, the blues is the great aquifer that runs underneath all American music," Glaser said. "There's tremendous blues elements in Appalachian music, bluegrass, jazz. But rural music has the power of nature, the mystery of being in the woods late at night, whereas urban music is about the heartbreak of human experience and personal angst. A big part of this project is looking for that place, as Jennifer put it, where Billie Holiday dances with Bill Monroe. They might not go together, but I've always heard some resonance, ever since I was growing up listening to my father's records of Holiday and my records of Ralph Stanley. They just didn't seem so separate to me."

—*November 30, 2001*

Bluegrass cello???
Rushad Eggleston, Darol Anger, Michael Doucet

When three of the world's greatest fiddlers gather for the first time, it's going to be news. When they are as wildly diverse as new age "jazz-grass" player Darol Anger, old-time virtuoso Bruce Molsky, and Cajun master Michael Doucet, of Beausoleil fame, it's going to be big news. But the biggest news is how the title of their new Compass CD and tour was changed from "Fiddlers 3" to "Fiddlers

4." It marks the impressive, potentially star-making debut of Berklee College of Music student and bluegrass cellist Rushad Eggleston, whose first commercial record and first national tour are with Fiddlers 4.

That's right; he plays bluegrass cello.

"I've heard for years about guys trying to play bluegrass cello, and nobody can," says Anger, who also attended Berklee. "I had decided it was basically impossible, like jazz bassoon. But there actually is a jazz bassoon player at Berklee right now, so that should've tipped me off. When I sat down to play with Rushad, he was the equal of any bluegrass fiddler, but on cello. It's impossible, but there you have it, folks."

The idea for the project was sparked when Molsky's manager suggested he tour with a full band. He called Anger for ideas.

"When you think of old-time fiddling, you think of stuff that's broad strokes," says Anger. "Bruce's playing is so incredibly filled with detail and precision, I thought it would be nice to have all fiddles, keep it light, because sometimes when you get other instruments, it obscures those details."

Anger had just played with Beausoleil on its all-star 25th anniversary tour and broached the idea to Doucet, who immediately signed on. A bass or cello might be nice, they thought. Both Anger and Molsky had worked with Eggleston, and they brought him in for what was to be a little supporting work.

Doucet, who is a scholar of all kinds of Louisiana music, says he has seen a few old pictures of cellos in Cajun, jazz, and other vintage string bands, but the only recent example he has seen was a fellow in the '70s who strapped a cello around him like a guitar and played it like a bass. Like Anger and Molsky, he has never heard anyone play like Eggleston.

"There's a lot of intuition going on with us," Doucet says. "You can hear it in our playing. A lot of things don't need to be said, and Rushad is right there. It's really remarkable."

Soon after beginning to record, Eggleston was made a full member of the group. It's easy to see why. So much of the CD's richness and fluidity comes from his cunning countermelodies and bold, quick strokes. His cello is so vivid, whether swaggering merrily, like a drunken bear, on Duke Ellington's "East St. Louis Toodleoo" or pumping dark, threatening drones beneath "Man of Constant Sorrow." Thanks to his rooted, keenly empathetic work, the fiddlers are able to cavort through a dizzying array of styles without surrendering the warm ensemble feel that makes "Fiddlers 4," for all its virtuosity, such a friendly and accessible disc.

The importance of what Eggleston is doing can hardly be overstated. He is inventing a new way of hearing and playing cello. Growing up in Carmel, Calif., he enjoyed the serious challenge of classical cello and the playful joys of bluegrass guitar. Why couldn't he satisfy both cravings on the cello?

At first, he simply tried to play fiddle tunes on the cello, using all his classical technique to reach high notes that, however well played, seemed strained. He wanted the cello to sound like its growly old self while playing bluegrass.

"The first thing I did was to change the register of what I was playing," Eggleston says. "When I moved things down, I didn't have the same open strings as the fiddle, so I had to come up with slightly different ways of playing the melodies. I figured that was OK, because if you listen to any bluegrass, the fiddle and mandolin and banjo all play the melody different ways. I figured, well, I'm going to make the cello valid here, so it can play the melody a different way, too."

He tried to imagine himself not as a gifted Berklee cellist (the first string musician ever offered a full scholarship) but as an old-time Appalachian farmer invited to a front-porch jamboree, and having only a cello to play. He would not try to imitate the others but instinctively build his playing around the cello's richest sound, what Eggleston calls its meatiest tones. The question then became not how to play fiddle tunes on the cello, but how would a cello pick 'n' grin?

"It can get frustrating," Eggleston says, "because if you're a saxophone, fiddle, or mandolin player, you've got tons of models to follow. You can see how they played it and figure out what you want to do. But I'm also pretty happy doing something nobody has done before because it allows me to be really creative—and nobody can tell me what to do. I just try to figure out how the cello can have its own sound, a sound that works in traditional music, without a lot of vibrato and rigid technique. Just a natural, grooving way to play the cello."

—*April 19, 2002*

The cry of the Mammals: trad is rad
Tao Rodriguez-Seeger, Ruth Ungar, Mike Merenda

If folk music had royalty, the Mammals would be heirs apparent.

Two members of the hottest young string band to emerge from the Northeast in years have folk pedigrees. Tao Rodriguez-Seeger, 30, is the grandson of folk's most illustrious and iconoclastic icon, Pete Seeger. Ruth Ungar, 26, is the daughter of uber-fiddler Jay Ungar, of "Ashokan Farewell" fame, and singer Lyn Hardy. Rounding out the rascally trio from upstate New York is songwriter-guitarist-drummer Michael Merenda, 26. He is, by comparison with his bandmates, an upstart—but his background in rock and ska adds greatly to the irreverent hipness that makes this band so much fun.

The band's name was chosen in large part to distance them from any notion of aristocracy. What larger circle could they draw than to call themselves merely mammals?

"I like it because it's so open-ended," says fiddler-singer Ungar. "There's nothing specific; it means nothing as far as what we're going to play. Some people don't like that, but I do; it's about as inclusive as you can get."

Rodriguez-Seeger, a nimble, swashbuckling banjo player, also loves the permission the name implies, to be anything, play anything. He adores the raw grace and homespun aesthetics of traditional music as much as any Seeger, but what he loves most is the freedom he feels within its trusty old melodies.

"The way I like to describe our approach to traditional music is ultimate respect, zero reverence," he says. "We have this passion and respect for where it comes from, why it is the way it is, and why it's survived; but we don't pay any lip service to that `supposed to be played this way' stuff. We can do it; if we're sitting in at an old-time session where everything's being played straight, we can do that and enjoy it. But we can also really take it out there. That's what I love about these guys; they have no fear to take the music somewhere that might make some people feel uncomfortable."

Judging from their high romp of a CD, "Evolver" (Humble Abode Music), about the only thing these three are not willing to do with music is play it badly. They stomp through string-band medleys; bitingly modern folk-pop songs by Merenda, Ungar, and Richard Thompson; and dazzling original instrumentals that play the way great free-verse poetry reads.

At first, they seem almost structureless, just artful noodling. Then they build, congealing around increasingly clear melodic ideas. It is smart fun to have with folk melodicism, but only the savviest musicians need apply.

Rodriguez-Seeger has felt the crushing expectations of being folk royalty more than Ungar. Ungar, in fact, hid her folk roots growing up, often feeling like the only one on the school bus who didn't know the hit songs on the radio. It was in large part meeting Merenda, her personal as well as professional partner, and seeing his newfound passion for folk music, that made her want to resume the fiddle playing she learned as a child.

Rodriguez-Seeger, who spent much of his childhood in Nicaragua, also spent painful years rebelling, never against the man he dotingly calls Grandpa, but against the almost religious reverence with which so many friends and fans treat the Seeger family (and which Pete Seeger himself detests).

After he moved back to the States when he was 16, Grandpa gently led him toward music, first asking him onstage to sing a song in Spanish with him. "But your Spanish stinks, Grandpa," he protested. "Then it'll sound better if you help," the cunning old songleader answered.

Soon they were doing gigs together. One day, Seeger offered his recommendation for the musician's life.

"He said, 'If you're a musician, it means you're going to die unfulfilled,' " Rodriguez-Seeger recalls. "'It means you'll spend the rest of your life on an upward learning curve, because you will never be as good as you can be. Think about that: you will die an apprentice, a student—and there's nothing better than that. To have achieved the best you can ever be, that's a tragedy.' That made a lot of sense to me at twenty."

Merenda is part of a growing number of young people who find mainstream rock and pop hopelessly slathered with corporate influence; in his own search for a more basic, human sound, he discovered traditional music. It is a defining goal for the Mammals to present this music as they believe it exists: not a throwback to bygone days, but a contemporary, living form. That's why Merenda thought up the slogan for their bumper stickers, one that perfectly captures what these rabble-rousers are up to: "Trad Is Rad."

"Rock is in tough shape," he says. "Everyone's racing for the Next Big Sound, splintering into so many little genres trying to break the new sound. What I find more interesting— and more radical—is stripping it down, getting back to basics. What I've discovered is how punk-rock old-time music actually is, how driving and raw. A really honkin' banjo supplies more tension than plugging your Strat into a Big Muff. That's what 'Trad Is Rad' is getting at: coming full circle."

—August 23, 2002

The real story behind "Ashokan Farewell"
Jay Ungar & Molly Mason

At the beginning of Ken Burns's 1990 public television documentary "The Civil War," author Shelby Foote called that war "the crossroads of our being." He was speaking of the impact the Civil War had on the American personality, of course, but he might as easily have been predicting the careers of traditional musicians Jay Ungar and Molly Mason.

Ungar's elegiac fiddle air "Ashokan Farewell" was the theme for that epic series, and went on to be among the best known and most recorded instrumental melodies of recent years. It has had such an impact on the lives of the husband-and-wife fiddle-and-guitar duo that they now refer to their "prewar" and "postwar" careers.

Before their Civil War, for example, they might well have performed at a mid-sized concert space like Lexington's Museum of Our National Heritage. They have been for years among the most respected musicians in American traditional music. But not until their "postwar" career would their show have been billed "The Civil War and Beyond."

Ungar said, "We're still astounded, even now, by how many people are familiar with us through `Ashokan Farewell.' It's amazing how huge a strata of the public it has permeated. It's been recorded by such a range of people, from Charlie Byrd to James Galway to Cleo Laine. As folk musicians, we never expected anything like this."

He said they still get mail every week from all over the world about "Ashokan Farewell," and now also about "The Lovers' Waltz," a similarly evocative Ungar tune that is the title cut of their beautiful, unabashedly romantic new Angel CD, which slow-dances from tender, Ashokan-like airs to the merry yet Victorian-prim "Mountain Home" to the happy hop of "Contradance." Mason accompanies Ungar's brilliantly melodic fiddling with tight guitar and lightly sprinkled piano, and sings a couple of achingly sweet love songs.

They describe their style as classic American, a sound firmly imbedded in folk tradition, but not Southern in root, as so much modern string-band music is. The couple, who live on the edge of the Catskills in West Hurley, N.Y., draw from the deep but relatively obscure wells of northern folk tradition, from the old Yankee and New York styles of contradance fiddling, as well as from 19th-century popular songs and parlor music.

They try to live as traditional musicians in the truest sense. They proudly call themselves "community musicians," and regularly play for local folk dances, weddings, parties, and seasonal celebrations. Despite frequent concert tours and soundtrack work (they've played for five Burns documentaries, including "Lewis

There's a visceral communication going on when you play music at a dance. You put something out, and you immediately feel it coming back. So you put out more, and it comes back as more.

—Jay Ungar

When you play a tune over eight or 10 times the way you do at a dance, you really get to explore it melodically and emotionally. It's like every time through is a new life of the tune, and you say, what mood is it in this time?

—Molly Mason

and Clark," which premieres on PBS next month), they intend to maintain their small-town musical lives.

Ungar said the wild informality of folk dances inspires his playing and composing. It was at the end of one of the more emotionally intense of the fiddle-and-dance camps they host each summer on the banks of the nearby Ashokan Reservoir that Ungar picked up his fiddle, literally in tears, to play his sorrow out. He didn't think he had composed much of a tune until he saw the response when he played "Ashokan Farewell" for friends. Burns heard it on a record by Ungar's old group Fiddle Fever.

"I want to keep both feet planted in the folk-dance tradition, because I think my music is best when it's rooted there," he said. "There's a visceral communication going on when you play music at a dance. You put something out, and you immediately feel it coming back. So you put out more, and it comes back as more. I find that very exciting."

The repetition of the tunes, far from seeming boring or a burden to them, offers creative exploration that helps them understand music in deeper and more intuitive ways than the concert stage offers.

"When you play a tune over eight or 10 times the way you do at a dance," Mason said, "you really get to explore it melodically and emotionally. It's like every time through is a new life of the tune, and you say, what mood is it in this time? That is really so much fun. And it's so valuable in honing your chops for concert work to realize that there are these ongoing lives and moods to music. It's not the same every time."

Ungar said, "I see a lot of people losing the meaning of their lives, feeling the things they do are meaningless except for their economic value. I feel so gratified by being able to play for social events like weddings or dances; to see how music provides a shared expression for the joys, sorrows, and everything else a community experiences in their lives. I think if we only did big concerts, we would rapidly lose our ability to create that in our music. The skills that we have come from our remaining as community musicians, playing at dances, parties, and just around the kitchen table."

—October 24, 1997

The gentle, ancient steps of country dance
The English Country Dance Society

For most Bostonians, the name Storrow conjures images of driving along the Charles River. For a small but growing number of local dancers, however, the name evokes happy images of a much older, much slower form of motion.

In 1915, philanthropist and cultural activist Helen Osborne Storrow helped found the Boston Centre of the English Country Dance Society, and was its president from 1916 until her death in 1944.

Mrs. Storrow would undoubtedly be proud of her center today, as it finds creative new ways to promote the gentle social dancing tradition she worked so hard to preserve. She and her husband, Boston banker James Jackson Storrow, who made a fortune as a founder of General Motors, were the benefactors behind community boating in Boston, and helped create the public park lands along the Charles River, including the Esplanade, which is why the riverside drive bears their name.

In keeping with their founder's legendary largesse, the Boston Centre is recording an ambitious CD series, "The English Country Dance Collection," aimed at helping teachers, students, musicians, and smaller dance societies learn the quiet charms of this quaint and friendly dance tradition.

"We thought that by putting out music that had some real depth of feeling to it, people could see how much country dancing has to offer," said Terry Gaffney, board member and former president who helped launch the project last year.

The center has hosted an English country dance on Wednesdays for nearly 30 years. Last year, it moved from its old Cambridge home to a roomier hall at the Park Avenue Congregational Church in Arlington. At a dance earlier this month, it was easy to see why people still fall in love with the old social dance form.

At first glance, it looks exactly like what it is: a cross between 18th-century court dances and modern square or contra dancing. The dancers form into groups of couples, called lines, and perform a series of moves, called figures or sets, to music that has its roots in a 1651 collection called "The English Dancing Master," published by John Playford. The repertoire has grown to include Celtic and American tunes.

The music, however, is a far cry from the brisk jigs and reels normally heard at Irish set dances or contra dances, the name applied to the New England set-dancing style.

"Contra dance music tends to be basically cheerful, high-energy tunes," said Gaffney, "whereas English country dance tunes have moods ranging from slightly melancholy to tender and affectionate to very lively. And in terms of the dance form, English country dance stresses the connection between dancers, where in contra dancing, a lot of the figures take you away from your partner and then bring you back again."

This particular night, the music was played by Bare Necessities, among the busiest folk dance bands in New England, and something akin to the house band for the English Country Dance Society. Played on violin, viola, piano, and flute, their music combined the prim sweetness of 17th-century chamber music with the wild grace of folk melody. They also perform on the CD collection.

To their sweet-breathed melodies, the dancers did not hop, twirl, and do-si-do so much as walk brisky between and around one another, couples often continuing to hold hands and maintain eye contact through entire figures. Many of the moves resolved in bows or curtsies, always delivered with sly grins and chuckles.

"One of the things that draws people to this kind of dancing is that it has fewer rules," said Bare Necessities pianist Jacqueline Schwab, whose playing has been heard by millions on the television documentaries of Ken Burns. "There isn't really a school of how to play for English country dancing, so we have more freedom to explore melodies, and I think that's the same thing that draws many of the dancers. The style works for people who are complete klutzes, people with disabilities, and it also works for people who are very accomplished dancers."

Schwab often glanced up from her keyboard, not to eye other musicians, but to follow the feet of the dancers, ensuring they were getting through figures in step with the music.

Seventy-one-year-old George Fogg of Boston danced with Jacqueline Silva of Arlington, who has been country dancing less than a year. New dancers are always welcome, but can be hard to spot, as the casual elegance of the moves gives beginners lots of time to catch up. Fogg is a professional country dance instructor, so he whispered and nudged Silva through difficult figures. Among all the dancers, mistakes seemed almost welcome, as they made ideal ice-breakers for betwen-dance banter.

"It's just a lot of fun, nice and social," said Silva, a software developer at Harvard Pilgrim. "You change partners all the time, so it's nice for a single person. You dance with everyone; it's more of a community type of dancing."

Fogg has been involved with the Boston Centre for almost 50 years, and was president in the 1960s. He said interest in country and contra dancing is higher than he can ever recall.

"There are lots of young people getting involved, and older people coming back to it," he said. "I don't know why; maybe people are just getting sick of television. It's a chance for people to get together and socialize that's not threatening. Everybody's welcome, that's the wonderful thing about it."

It is the social ease that drew current president Margaret Keller to country dancing as a little girl in Connecticut. She has come to believe, just as Helen Storrow did, that it is important to create safe places for socializing.

"In our culture, how do you meet people?" she asked. She moved to Boston in 1994 and works as director of principal and major gifts for MIT's Sloan School. "Whether you're single or not, if you want to just go out and be social with people, it's not easy to find places. When I moved here, I immediately had a social circle, because I had been involved in English country dancing elsewhere. I had something I could share with people I didn't know; I didn't feel like a stranger."

The idea behind the CDs was to record an actual country dance band playing as they would for dancers. The hope was that others would be inspired to start their own dances.

The CDs have proven to be a hit. The first printing of volume one, "Favorites of the Boston Centre," sold out in less than three months, enabling them to rush out volume two. Perhaps because the music is casually played, aimed at dancers more than listeners, it makes wonderful mood music. It is at once playful and pretty, like some 17th-century chamber group having a merry night off playing their favorite folk and dance tunes.

"I really believe people are meant to be connected together," said Gaffney, "and English country dancing is really an effective way to make that connection. I think that touches back to the reasons Helen Storrow started the society back in 1915. There was this feeling then that society was changing very quickly and, unless they were careful, they were going to lose a lot of the good things they had grown up with, like community and a sense of connection to one another. It feels kind of like that today, too."

—December 19, 1999

Louisa May Alcott comes to call
Historical recreationist Jan Turnquist

Louisa May Alcott has just had a carriage accident. Nothing serious, but the New England author is led to a room to wait while repairs are made. She is startled to find the room filled with children but seems not to notice they are wearing slacks and jeans, tank-tops and T-shirts. Nor does she notice the television in the corner or the computer atop the teacher's desk.

After all, it is only 1880, and will remain so for the duration of Ms. Kimble's and Mr. McClure's sixth-grade class at the Parker Middle School in Chelmsford.

Alcott is portrayed by Jan Turnquist, who has been doing these "living history" performances for more than 20 years, working through the nonprofit agency Young Audiences, which offers cultural programming to local schools. She also portrays 19th-century author Harriet Beecher Stowe and Phoebe Emerson, who lived through the Revolutionary War. But Alcott is her mainstay, both as actor and in her other job as executive director of Orchard House in Concord, the family home where Alcott's classic novel "Little Women" was written in 1868.

There are a few wrinkled eyebrows and nervous giggles among the children at first, but they are soon drawn into the illusion as Alcott begins to reminisce about her girlhood in Concord, playing pranks on her sisters and wandering the woods with family friend Henry David Thoreau.

To break the ice, Turnquist involves the teachers in the conspiracy of her illusion, asking Stephen McClure if he knows how long it will take to repair her carriage, and Angela Kimble if she has met Ralph Waldo Emerson. Kimble says she has not but enjoys his essays and has seen him lecture once or twice.

"I see these children every day, and I could tell how amazed they were when she was telling them about her life," Kimble said after the performance. "They were just in awe of her. It's such a rare experience for them to be able to see a character living in another time. It gives them an opportunity to experience that time of history first-hand. Once they catch on to the illusion, it actually gives them a chance to ask questions, to interview someone from the past, to really live the history of the time."

And then she paid Turnquist the supreme compliment for any actor: "She wasn't acting like the character, she was the character, and that was the biggest draw for the children."

Indeed, the children were soon peppering Alcott with questions, not just about "Little Women," the 1994 film version of which the class had seen the previous day, but about how her hoop skirt was made and what kind of car, er, carriage she drives. ("Broken, at the moment," Turnquist said dryly.)

Twelve-year-old Emma Easton had loved the movie and sat wide-eyed in the presence of the author. "Which character was your favorite in `Little Women,' except yourself?" she asked, referring to the Jo March character Alcott based upon herself.

When Alcott answered it was Jo's sister Beth, Easton gasped, then whispered urgently, "Me, too!" It was clear she was not connecting with Turnquist, but with Alcott herself.

"It's like a real person coming in and telling you about history," Easton said afterward. "I really liked how she came out of her own time and didn't know anything about now. She would know the clocks but not about cars. It made me think about how different things were then. She's right in front of you and you get to talk to her, instead of just learning from a book or a movie. I thought it was cool that you got to ask questions."

Those off-script moments are the most fun for Turnquist as well. Once the children get involved, each show becomes unique.

"Even the challenges don't bother me, because I incorporate them," she said.

"For example, if an announcement comes on the loudspeaker—'Will Robert Brown please report to the principal's office?'—I just respond as if there's a strange voice coming out of the wall, and it helps the students realize there were no loudspeakers in her day. I come in and act as if I am really Louisa May Alcott, really from the 19th century, and try to act as she would if put in that exact space."

The Parker School performance focused on Alcott's journey of self-discovery, from Thoreau's stirring of her imagination to her realization that her writing should come from within her own life experiences, a then-revolutionary literary style she called "reality writing." Her efforts made her one of America's most beloved and influential novelists.

The day after her Chelmsford appearance, sitting in her office at Orchard House, Turnquist explained the focus was designed for that class. She knows that developing writing skills is a major part of the sixth-grade curriculum, and indeed the Parker class will follow-up the Alcott visit by writing stories from their own lives. For other classes, she might highlight Alcott's Civil War experience as a nurse, or her involvement in 19th-century reform movements, from women's rights to abolition to education reform.

"I think of it like a closet full of clothes," she said. "I have all these stories, anecdotes, memorized passages from her letters, journals and books, all sort of hanging in my mental closet. Then it's like I'm going on a trip, and I pick out the pieces I'll need for that particular program."

Turnquist came to work at Orchard House as a volunteer in 1977 soon after moving to Concord from Wisconsin with her husband, Carl Turnquist, a chemist who now works at Genzyme. She was beginning the family that now includes three children, and wanted to do something with a historical or educational component. Alcott had been among her heroines as a child.

"I loved history and particularly biography as a young girl," she said, "and always seemed to gravitate toward these women of achievement—Louisa, Clara Barton, Harriet Beecher Stowe, Madame Curie. And I especially loved the 19th century.

"I think children today are drawn to Louisa and her stories for the same reasons I was; the fact that she was such a strong, independent character. She was very empathetic but strong, very loyal to her family. She cared so much about what we today call family values, but to her were just the core of who she was."

Her Orchard House job today is consumed by a massive restoration project needed to save the badly sagging structure. An effort is underway to raise well over a million dollars. Turnquist is also negotiating to purchase a small house up the hill from Orchard House where the administrative offices can be moved. She hopes that will resolve the much-publicized lawsuit filed by a neighbor when it was proposed that offices be moved into a house across the street. Orchard House's troubles are coming in large part from the stress that storage files, archives, and office equipment are placing on the old beams—not to mention the 35,000 to 50,000 visitors who troop through it every year.

"I see a real marriage between what I do with my own little show and what I can do to help save the house," Turnquist said. "When people come to Orchard House, they catch the spirit that this was a real person, the Alcotts were a real family, and this is where they lived. And that's the same sense I see come over people at the performances. They begin to see Louisa as a flesh-and-blood person they can talk to, ask questions, that they feel they're really getting to know. The house and the performance are both ways of making history a living thing."

—February 18, 2001

The biography of America's best-known song
A book review of Stuart Murray's
"The Story of Yankee Doodle"

It is impossible to be an American and not know the song "Yankee Doodle." It is played every Fourth of July, a plucky old tune that instantly conjures patriotic images of America's war of independence against Great Britain. But the wonderful story of how this ditty became the nation's first anthem, and the seminal role it played in helping Americans see themselves as citizens of that new nation, is less well known.

In "America's Song: The Story of Yankee Doodle," New York historian and author Stuart Murray has written what amounts to a biography of the tune, from its beginnings as a Dutch harvest song to its maturity as anthem of a new nation. The book is everything one wants a good biography to be, vivid, colorful, brimming with anecdotes and a rich sense of the times and places through which "Yankee Doodle" traveled, changed, and grew.

Despite enduring myths that Murray has a fine time skewering, the song's origins are clearly found in Dutch Colonial America. The Dutch word "jonker" referred to a country squire, "doedel" to a simpleton or fool. Early versions, drawn from a common harvest folk song, were used to lampoon the English farmers whose settlements neighbored, and soon encroached upon, the urban trading hives of Dutch America.

Verses teased the English as country bumpkins: "Jonker Doedel came to town / In his striped trousers / Couldn't see the town be cause / There were so many houses." Other Dutch nouns added clever plays on words, helping the song become a more acute satire as feelings hardened between the Dutch and English.

The Dutch called their English neighbors "Jankes" (Johnnies), pronounced "Yahn-kees." But a slight alteration turned that into "janker," a Dutch epithet for a yelping dog, applied to a noissome, complaining neighbor, which the Dutch increasingly felt the English to be.

"Yankee Doodle" first went to war during conflicts between the British and French in the mid-1700s. By that time widely accepted as a satire of American provincialism, it was taken up by British regulars to mock Colonial militia. When local volunteers wore feathers in their hats, it reminded the British of London fops called "macaronies" because they affected the manners of Italian nobility. So the verse "Yankee Doodle went to town / Riding on a pony / Stuck a feather in his cap / And called it macaroni" ridiculed Colonials for having pretensions of being either gentlemen or real soldiers.

As tensions grew between Colonists and Great Britain, the tune was often played by the British army to taunt Americans. Its constant use had the unintended effect of making the redcoats appear even more like a foreign army of occupation, a separate entity hostile to local militia. It also unintendedly served to remind militia veterans what a fallible, inept force the British army had often been during the French wars.

The Revolutionary War began to the strains of "Yankee Doodle." British troops played it while marching to Concord in April 1775. On the bloody retreat to Boston, it was played back to them by triumphant American militia. Soon after, a British soldier grumbled that " `Yankee Doodle' is now their paean" and that New Englanders now "gloried in being called Yankees."

The song became a powerful force in helping Americans, who had always defined themselves by the colony in which they lived, to now think of themselves as patriots of a nation they were fighting to create. "Yankee" became the nickname for any supporter of the Revolutionary cause, and "Yankee Doodle" was played by American military bands during every campaign of the war. A new refrain was added to suit its new purpose as a cocky, morale-building march: "Yankee Doodle keep it up / Yankee doodle dandy / Mind the music and the step / And with the girls be handy."

Americans came to love the satirical tone of the song, how it described an army of citizens and not professional soldiers, who were overmatched but never outfought, underdogs who would prevail through their native wits, camaraderie, and righteousness of cause. The very fact that it had been used for so long as a British insult became an enormous source of pride and resolve.

In 1781, the Revolutionary War ended at Yorktown, Va., as Lord Cornwallis surrendered to General George Washington. In one final insult, British troops were ordered to keep their eyes fixed on America's French allies. The French Marquis de Lafayette was enraged by this snub of the American army, but knew immediately how to remind the British just who had beaten them and to whom they were now surrendering not only their army, but their colonies. He ordered the Continental Army band to strike up "Yankee Doodle," and British eyes snapped instinctively toward the Americans who played it.

—July 4, 2000

Arthur Rubinstein's grandson finds his home in folk music
David Coffin

It may be the last place you would expect to find a grandson of the great concert pianist Arthur Rubinstein, pumping away on a concertina, belting out a bold ballad about "Captain Kidd" while pint-sized pirates circle him, waving the Jolly Roger and shouting "Arr, matey!"

But David Coffin, grandson of Rubinstein and son of activist pastor William Sloane Coffin, seems as born to the rowdy demands of the halyard shanty as his legendary grandfather was to the concert stage, and his father to the cause of world peace. He is musical director of Boston by Sea, a floating historical pageant of traditional music, theater, and film documentary touring Boston Harbor daily aboard the Boston Harbor Cruises boat Fredrick J. Nolan.

"Maritime traditional music is really where my heart is now," David Coffin said. "I've always lived near the ocean, growing up in New Haven while my father was pastor at Yale, and I've lived on the North Shore since 1987. I just love the heartiness of the songs. The work the sailors did, the energy it took, is so evident in the shanties, which were the work songs they sang while hoisting sails, hauling on lines, hoisting the anchor. You can really feel the work in the songs, the saltiness, what that life was like."

Coffin, 40, is best known to Boston-area audiences as master of ceremonies and featured soloist at the annual Christmas and Spring Revels, leading audiences in choruses of ancient song, riveting them with his thick, sweet baritone and gentle mastery on the recorder, tin whistle, and concertina.

As he does on the Boston by Sea tours, Coffin takes listeners on a robust, sometimes wrenchingly evocative tour of maritime history in his beautiful new CD "Nantucket Sleighride" (Good Dog Records), named for the dangerous way whale boats would be towed behind freshly harpooned whales.

Coffin's road to the rough-hewn joys of maritime music was, as one might expect, a strange one. He still cherishes boyhood memories of hearing Rubinstein practice in his study while he and his siblings splashed in his grandparents' backyard pool, but says his love of music was found elsewhere.

When he was about 4, his parents hired music teacher Grace Feldman, who still teaches at New Haven's Neighborhood Music School, as a live-in nanny. For him, she was a musical Mary Poppins, infecting him with a love for the beauty and the mystery of early music. She would pass notes to him filled with pictures of owls playing viola da gambas and snails playing French horns. She taught him to play the recorder, which led him to a love of medieval, Renaissance, and Baroque music.

"The recorder was pretty much a dead instrument by 1760, so I ended up focusing on early music," he said. "But really, it was just because that's what Grace taught me. She was such a powerful force in my life; if she'd given me a saxophone, I'd probably be playing jazz today."

He would not have been much less likely to find favor in his grandfather's eyes if he had. His voice still wears traces of the bitter disappointment he felt when he asked Rubinstein to help him purchase a good recorder so he could pursue his musical studies. His grandfather turned him down, because he held disdain for early music.

"He didn't want to help me only because he didn't like early music," Coffin said. "Anything before Mozart, sorry, not interested. That's just the way he was. So I can only imagine what he would think about my ending up a folk musician."

And with that, Coffin laughed heartily, just as he did when relating a favorite family story about an encounter between Rubinstein and William Sloane Coffin, then engaged to the pianist's daughter. With his famous acid wit, Rubinstein told the minister he had never expected to have "a Billy Graham in the family." It was meant as a stinging slap to the very progressive, anything-but-fundamentalist preacher, who answered it in brutally equal measure. "And I never imagined I would have a Liberace for a father-in-law," the reverend said coolly.

Pursuing his love of the recorder took Coffin to Sarah Lawrence College in 1978. After two years, he decided, as he put it, to challenge his interest in music, dropping out of school and moving to Stockbridge, Mass., where he worked two years as a musician for the theatrical troupe Shakespeare & Company.

In 1980, Coffin's stepmother, Randi Wilson Coffin, played a Christmas Revels record for him. He was so struck by the ancient folk tune "Abbots Bromley Horn Dance" that he wrote Revels, asking if they needed an itinerant recorder player. He performed that year for the Revels production in Hanover, N.H., and within a few years became a featured soloist in the Cambridge Christmas Revels and Spring Revels. As founder John "Jack" Langstaff retired from performing, Coffin moved into his traditional role as song-leader, a part Revels calls master of ceremonies, but that Coffin respectfully calls "The Part that Jack Built."

His Revels training was evident in everything he did with Boston by Sea, from his gregariously inclusive performance style to the authentic and inviting songs he chose to accompany playwright Jon Lipsky's colorfully realized character sketches. Between set-pieces one hot June Saturday, Coffin darted through the aisles, seeming more like a grandson of Harpo Marx than Arthur Rubinstein, merrily cooling hot patrons with spritzes from a water bottle capped by a fan.

"My ease with an audience all comes through Revels," he said afterwards. "There's no line at the end of the stage between you and the audience, and I don't like there to be that boundary anywhere I perform anymore. I want to work with the audience, not just perform to them. You go to the Wang Center and the idea is to send the audience, to transport you to this other experience. With Revels, we don't want to send you, we want to bring you; we want you to come with us. I wanted the songs for this show to do that, to bring the audience along."

For 10-year-old Joanna Seirup, up from New York for a weekend of sightseeing with her mother, the inclusiveness and authenticity of the music added not only to what she learned, but to how much fun she had learning it.

"I liked the music a lot," she said. "It helped explain what they were telling you. When they told you about something that happened and then sang a song from that time, you could kind of find out how people felt about what happened. It helped you understand it better, kind of made it more real."

Increasingly, that defines Coffin's passion as an artist, to break down barriers between performer and audience, past and present. It is hard not to see the forbidding visage of his legendary grandfather stir in Coffin's memory as he explains his love for the humble old songs he sings so well.

"Folk music is music of the folk, after all; it's such an inclusionary kind of music, not like Brahms or Beethoven, where you really have to hush and you can't sneeze or cough during a performance, and you certainly can't sing along. With Revels and with Boston by Sea, with all this folk music, we just want to make everyone a part of the experience, a part of the history, to come join us and do what we are doing, be who we are being."

—June 25, 2000

The streets are his stage **Eric Royer**

You know it's a tough winter in Boston when the streets grow bare of buskers.

The past few years, it's been so mild that many local buskers, or street entertainers, have been able to ply their trades year-round. But when piles of plowed snow block their favorite performance spots, and bitter winds make fingers too blue to even play the blues, where do Boston's buskers go?

Eric Royer, whose attention-grabbing one-man band show has made him one of the most successful buskers in Boston, has taken advantage of the hard winter to spend more time with his wife, Meredith Sibley, who is expecting their first child in a few months. He does occasional odd jobs and carpentry work and, if the thermometer nudges above 40 degrees, drags his celebrated Guitar Machine to Back Bay or Park Street MBTA stations to entertain crowds with his robust bluegrass tunes.

"The winters haven't been that cold," he said in his small Shawmut Avenue apartment, "but this year, I've really had to slow down. Some street musicians I know have developed problems with their hands from playing too much in the cold. I think I might have messed up my leg from playing through the winter before. When it's cold, you can't relax, so you're fighting yourself and can develop muscle and tendon problems. You get so stiff."

Royer, 35, needs every one of his limbs at full strength to play the unique contraption he calls the Guitar Machine. Crowds gather at first just to see how it all works. He plays banjo and Dobro with his hands while one foot pedal strums a guitar and plucks a bass guitar, and another handles percussion chores by plocking a golf ball against a cowbell. That pedal also operates a hopping puppet named Polly, who dances what might best be described as a Texas one-step.

The gimmick of the Guitar Machine may draw crowds, but it is Royer's vibrant and supple bluegrass music that keeps them hanging around.

It is also making him a rising presence in the Boston-area club and coffeehouse scene, both as solo performer and in the rootsy Resophonics, with local folk stars Sean Staples and Tim Kelly. He also appears with hot young songwriter Alastair Moock's ensemble, Pastures of Plenty.

"When you're doing the streets," Royer said, "it's important to remember that your audience is not there to see you. It's different than playing a club; you have to get them to stop. The Guitar Machine itself attracts attention, and that helps me get them to be an audience. That was somewhat conscious when I designed it—like the puppet. That's just there to get people to look my way. But I don't think of it as a novelty, and the real reason I built it was to create a fuller sound."

As his street-corner fans realize, Royer is dead serious when it comes to the music he plays. On his latest CD, "Barefoot Breakdown," he plays old chestnuts like "Turkey in the Straw" with captivating melodic purity, and delivers daunting classics by folk legends Woody Guthrie and the Stanley Brothers with a youthful freshness. He is a first-rate banjoist and Dobro player, and an inventive songwriter.

"The type of traditional music I'm drawn to is really simple and easy to relate to on a human level," he said. "The lyrics are direct and plain, the chord structures and melodies simple and easy to listen to, like `Turkey in the Straw.' I don't feel melodies like that need to be changed or made modern; I like them just the way they are."

Royer grew up in Haverhill and always liked the sound of acoustic music. Rock'n'roll suited his freewheeling temperament, though, and soon after high school, he was playing Boston rock clubs in the popular grunge-influenced band Junk.

But by then he had also discovered bluegrass, had an acoustic guitar and banjo at home, and was devouring discs by Bill Monroe and the Stanley Brothers.

"Bluegrass seemed more independent to me, not as controlled by the business as pop and mainstream country and other big-business music," he said. "I got the impression that the people were doing what they wanted and were more individual. Even though pop music wants you to think the stars are very individual and unique, I don't think they are. They seem like they're produced much more than bluegrass or folk people are."

The streets were as far away from the music business as Royer could get, and he began busking a little in Boston before he and his wife moved to Tuscon in 1990. He played in some folk-based bands there and got serious about street singing.

But just playing banjo not only failed to draw crowds, it didn't sound good. He wanted the bold guitar strum, slappy bass strides, and backbeat percussion that define bluegrass. That's when he built the prototype of his Guitar Machine.

In 1996, he moved back to Boston, planning to be a carpenter.

One day he took his Guitar Machine to Harvard Square and made more in a few hours than he would have pounding nails all day. He's considered himself a full-time busker ever since.

"I like playing the streets," he said, "especially downtown Boston, because I feel like I'm part of the culture of the area. People are walking back and forth from lunch, shopping, going to work. It's like I'm being part of people's real lives. Before they started recording music, it was all like that; the music was just part of people's everyday lives."

He clearly hates talking about the business of music, but after some prodding said he averages $100 a day busking, not counting profits from the 3,000 CDs he has sold, mostly at T stops and street corners.

Royer has a Web site (www.guitarmachine.com), and feels he should be advancing his career by playing clubs more. But he'd probably make less money than he does busking Park Street or Downtown Crossing.

He said those are his favorite T stops, with Back Bay a close third, since it is just a few blocks from home. The acoustics are all the same: good when there are no trains, horrible when there are. As a result, he prefers the Red Line at Park Street, since there always seems to be a train coming on the Green Line.

Asked if the audiences are different at one place or another, he said Harvard Square crowds are more likely to be aware of bluegrass and folk styles, but that Faneuil Hall tourists are often friendly and agreeably curious.

"Maybe the crowds really aren't that different," he said. "I get the same stupid questions everywhere I go. I think the stupidest is, `Did you build that thing?' It just seems pretty obvious looking at it that I didn't pick it up at Sears.

"But I also get into lots of great conversations with people about folk music and bluegrass. I think a lot of younger kids are interested in the banjo, and may have never heard it before. It's fun to think I might be exposing some people to this music who might otherwise not hear it."

He sighed and reflected on his budding club career.

"I know I should be trying to build a following," he said, "doing all that rock-band stuff, and I tell myself I need to be doing more of that. But then I look out the window, and if it's a nice day, I just go out and play."

—January 28, 2001

A sense of place Kate Campbell, James Keelaghan

James Keelaghan watches the moon rise over the seemingly endless prairie of his native Alberta. Smelling the sweet grass, hearing it sing in the chill wind, he pens a spare ode to the deep pull such land has on people: "Stand at night on the palm of the plains / See the horizon curve / Hear the song of the meadow lark / Across the gathering dark of Sweetgrass Moon."

Two thousand miles to the south and east, Kate Campbell watches lantern lights flicker and spark off the Mississippi River. The constancy of the river, all the more vivid against the fleeting lights on the water, becomes for her a strong image of love's resolve. "You can fall like the rain," she sings in "Lanterns on the Levee," "And I will be a river / Winding, forever, strong and true."

As the contemporary songwriter revival increasingly defines itself as a literary as well as musical renaissance, it grows richer with this sort of regionally vivid verse. Not that this is unique to modern folk music, of course: Everyone knows that Bruce Springsteen buys his gas in New Jersey and that all George Strait's exes live in Texas. But sense of place as a literary device seems stronger, more deeply rooted, in the folk field.

The Louisiana-born, Mississippi-bred Campbell now lives in Nashville. She said, "I've always had this desire to connect my own personal memories and history with an understanding of the culture and history around me, and to put that together in my songwriting. I think of my music more as three-minute short stories than as radio-catchy kinds of songs."

Keelaghan, who now lives in Toronto, said, "No matter how much somebody might want to deny it, I think most songwriters tend to reflect the place they come from in their writing. There's a real sense of the vastness of Canada that is always at the back of our heads and that figures in what we write: this thin line of people stretched across the American border, and behind it wilderness. Especially in the prairies, there's just so much history that's as yet unwritten and unsung."

It is striking how much these quite distinct artists share. Both are in their mid-30s with academic and professional backgrounds in history; she as a college professor, he as a researcher. Both inform their intelligent, keenly visual songs with a deep sense of their region's past and culture. And both mention literary influences in the same breath as musical ones.

Keelaghan cited songwriters Paul Simon and Stan Rogers, but also historical writers Wallace Stegner, Barbara Tuchman and Simon Shama. Campbell mentioned Dolly Parton (beneath the glitter a strong and sadly underrated songwriter), Bobbie Gentry and Guy Clark. But she added that she always keeps collections of Eudora Welty and Flannery O'Connor short stories by her bed.

"That defining sense of place seems to be true more of Southern writers, though it's certainly not limited to them," Campbell said. "The thing is, you've lived here, and there are so many things you can say you love about the South. But in the middle of that is this extreme sense of shame and guilt and always having to deal with that. Our history of race relations is the big one, of course, but also that, until Vietnam, the South was the only region of America that had experienced what it is to lose a war, with all that means. That's all been very detrimental, but it also needed to happen, and we've all grown from that; from slavery through desegregation to today.

"As a songwriter, it's always been part of my quest to discover why there is such a strong need to discover that sense of place: where you fit into your surroundings, what impact that has made on your life and why is that different from the person down the road?"

In "A Cotton Field Away," on her debut disc "Songs from the Levee" (Compass), she powerfully states that confusion as she ponders the still very different realities of Southern blacks and whites. And it pleased her as much as a Billboard bullet that her elegiac ode to farming, "Bury Me in Bluegrass," was just picked Farm Journal's Farm Song of the Year.

Keelaghan has made his mark with sweeping Canadian landscapes and close-up love songs, but also with powerful historical ballads. "On a Recent Future" is his most personal and revealing disc, though still chock full of his populist passions and Canadian as an Alberta sky. When interviewed, he was still reeling from how close the recent referendum on Quebec independence was and very proud of how his country had behaved.

"It says a lot about us that we're able to reexamine who we are as Canadians that way. I sincerely can't think of another country where it could happen this way, and it's something to be eminently proud of. You know, 'Mon Pays,' the unofficial anthem of the separatist Parti Quebecois, written by Quebec folksinger Gilles Vigneneault, begins with the line, "My country is not a country, it is winter." In other words, my country is not a political entity, it is a season, it is a landscape. Well, only a Canadian could write that."

—November 2, 1995

Troubadour to her community Gail Rundlett

photo courtesy Gail Rundlett

In the old days, before music was a business, every community had its own stars. There might be the blacksmith who played fiddle for Saturday night dances, the schoolteacher who knew all the old ballads and local lore, or the elderly woman who taught the children the old nursery songs and games.

Music seems to be viewed mostly as an industry today, and to assume the performers we see on stage are pursuing dreams of stardom. In the quieter corners of our culture, however, the old-fashioned community musician still flourishes, as Gail Rundlett of Waltham proves every day of her hectic, music-filled life.

"As a folk musician, you learn to do a little bit of everything," she said. "Friends are always laughing and saying, 'So, Gail, how many jobs do you have now?' But this kind of life seems natural to me, as much a function of being a working parent as a folk singer."

Still, Rundlett has trouble coming up with an accurate count of her current jobs. She is a regular substitute teacher for the Waltham school system and youth music director at Park Avenue Congregational Church in Arlington. She is also music specialist for Catholic Charities in Waltham and frequently sings at area preschools and elementary schools. She teaches dulcimer, with a student load that ranges from five to 20. She is also a substitute on-air host at folk radio station WUMB-FM.

In addition, Rundlett is a popular coffeehouse performer, known for her warm, pure alto and sweetly melodic dulcimer playing. She has slowed her solo career a bit recently, however, in favor of her increasingly busy female vocal quartet Taproot (formerly Virtual Harmony), which just released its first compact disc, "If You Build It." Rundlett also books the group.

She eased into her favorite rocker in the living room of her Waltham home, arranging a quilt around her knees and glancing at walls festooned with dulcimers and CD racks, trying to imagine why anyone would find her hectic folk-singing lifestyle unusual.

"You don't become a dulcimer-playing folk singer to be a star, you know," she said. "There are all kinds of jokes folk singers tell each other about how hard it is to make money in folk music. But we all have this drive to get the music and the stories out to as many people as we can. Because the songs are about real people, about real-life issues and situations."

As she looks back now, she knows she was always looking for the simple, friendly world of folk music. She grew up in Ohio, part of a musical family: One brother produces musical theater, and another is an accomplished instrumentalist who once worked with the Oak Ridge Boys. Always a gifted singer, it was assumed she would pursue classical training. She disliked what she calls the "pomp and circumstance" of classical music, however, and kept looking for something else.

She found it in 1973, when she attended Eastern Nazarene College in Quincy, and discovered the local folk-music scene. She met Heidi Mueller, now a Seattle-based folk singer, who introduced her to the mountain dulcimer. Rundlett was riveted by the sweet melodic simplicity of the American folk instrument. When she heard local dulcimer virtuoso Lorraine Lee Hammond at a coffeehouse, she asked to take lessons and was soon hooked.

"I love the simplicity of folk music," she said. "Yet it's complex, too, in terms of how many different styles there are and how vast the subject matter of the songs can be. I've always hated gimmicks in music and in songs. I can't tolerate listening to top-40, which is probably to my detriment, but I have a low tolerance for all that production. It's so industry-driven that much of it is meaningless to me. So much of that music is driven by money and ambition. I want to hear the people in the music."

That appetite for reality is abundantly evident in Rundlett's taste in songs, and in Taproot's. The songs on their new CD include fiery, in-your-face populist anthems, gospel-like humanist hymns and witty ditties about such everyday joys as hanging around the house or having a lover who's handy at fixing things. They are songs of, by and for real people, sung with exuberant emotion and lovely, cascading harmonies by Rundlett; Rebecca Brown, late of the Just Peace Singers; Anne Goodwin, best known as part of the local duo, Wild Rose; and Deborah Silverstein, the group's principal songwriter.

Rundlett enjoys performing, but has never wanted to pursue a full-blown concert career. She prefers the intimacy of the coffeehouse stage, where honesty is valued above all else.

"What I love about folk music is that you can be yourself," she said. "I'm pretty much the same person on stage that I am in my kitchen. You have to have that extra gloss and shine in pop and even in classical music. I talk about the same things on stage that I do off it. I mean, people want to be entertained; they don't want to feel like you're just some chatty neighbor up there. But in folk music, they want realness, too."

That gift for realness is the key to her success as a children's performer. She seems particularly proud of her ability to succeed with preschool and elementary-age audiences.

"I can't say I have a natural gift for it," she said with a satisfied smile, "but I can be like a little kid, and I love bringing folk music to them, because I know most of them don't hear it at home. I relate well to kids, I like kids. You have to like children to do this. I've had performers tell me they made a mistake by thinking anybody can do music for kids. It's very hard to keep them entertained. You can't condescend to them; you have to be a real person or they'll just blow you off. They don't have all those social niceties older people get taught so they put up with people who are looking down at them.

"So many times, I've dragged myself into a preschool, full of my own problems from some bad day I'm having, and the kids just pull that out of me. Because you can't perform at kids, you have to perform with them. I have to get over whatever I brought into the room and be real with them. At the end of that hour, I feel so recharged and energized, I can't imagine what I felt so bad about before. It brings me back to center."

Rundlett has two children, Hannah, 10, and Julian, 7. Just last month, she married Dimitri Eleftherakis, formerly a bassist and singer with the bluegrass band, Waystation. They're trying to find time to form a duo, but between Taproot and teaching and children's singing and disc-jockeying, that's on the back-burner for now; just one more musical career to fit in to her dizzyingly busy, song-filled life.

"There's a warmth to folk music that carries over into the people who like it," she said. "That's what keeps me going in the folk world, keeps me involved and active and wanting to do more all the time. There are no stars in this world the way there are in pop, and the people I've seen who try to act like big stars end up not succeeding. Because folk music is not run on stardom and ambition and looking out for yourself. It's just the love of the music that fuels this community."

—*January 18, 1998*

From Club 47 to Club Passim **Betsy Siggins Schmidt**

For Betsy Siggins Schmidt, it all began with a beanie. At 58, she looks back on a rich life of giving to others, and last year came full circle by becoming Club Passim's executive director. By opening new avenues of fund-raising, and even more by helping return it to its roots as a nonprofit member-driven club, she is helping to ensure a tradition she helped create in 1961, when she managed Club 47. It became the most influential of Boston's coffeehouses and launching pad for stars such as Joan Baez, Geoff and Maria Muldaur, Jim Kweskin, and Tom Rush.

"I'm almost grown up to being one of the moms now, where back then I was one of the kids," she said over coffee at the club. "To be here as an adult, or as much a one as I'm ever likely to be, is a nice feeling. And it's still a good fight."

In the 1970s, Club 47's final home at 47 Palmer St. became Passim, which, under the devoted watch of Bob and Rae Ann Donlin, remained among the country's most important folk venues. When folk revived in the early '80s, most of its new stars—Suzanne Vega, Shawn Colvin, Nanci Griffith, John Gorka, and others—honed their craft and found their audience there.

During those years, Siggins Schmidt found other places to turn her genius for caring. In the '70s, she helped legendary folklorist Ralph Rinzler start up the Smithsonian Festival of American Folklife. In the '80s, she was a mover and shaker in the homeless and anti-hunger movements. Through it all, she has taken precious lessons from her salad days at Club 47, lessons about the simple power of an open door.

The beanie that changed her life was given to her in the fall of 1958 at Boston University's freshman orientation. Watching everyone dutifully don the little hats, she refused. There were three hatless young women that day: Siggins Schmidt (then Minot), Debbie Green, and Joan Baez. They drew together in shared revolt.

The trio became inseparable, trawling the dark-lit bohemian coffeehouses of Boston in search of similarly free and un-beanied spirits. What they found was folk music.

"I guess we were beatnik bohemians," Siggins Schmidt said. "Wore a lot of black and the guys all rode motorcycles. A lot of them had trust funds and motorcycles, but the thought was there."

Her childhood prepared her for an unconventional life. Her father, an oceanographer at Woods Hole Oceanagraphic Institution, raised her alone after her mother left. During World War II, they lived in Brooklyn, N.Y., while her father did defense work.

Her father remarried after the war, and they returned to Cape Cod. Her stepmother, Bernice Jackson, who died last month, became a loving and colorful influence. She was a concert pianist. Siggins Schmidt grew accustomed to a life

Mark Spoelstra at Club 47 sometime in the early '60's.

surrounded by music, but when Jackson tried to teach her piano, both decided she was born to be a listener.

"I learned my musical appreciation was better than my musical prowess," she said. "Pop music was so white bread, so color within the lines, and I clearly had a mother who was not conventional and did not color inside the lines. I drew strength from her to believe things outside the norm could be valuable."

In Boston, she was immediately drawn to the raw honesty of American folk music, to the old, traditional masters and to urgent new singers like Baez and Bob Dylan.

"I think what drew me was that folk music seemed like an organized form of creativity everyone could participate in," she said. "People found a commonality in the singer-songwriter, and in the vision of the traditional artist. Watching a room full of Harvard students moved to tears by Dock Boggs, this old Kentucky coal miner, you knew you were onto something."

Club 47 became the hangout of choice for the new folkies.

"They were a nonprofit, music-related community outreach program," she said. "They began mostly as a jazz club, but were very receptive to the folk people. The star quality the club got grew directly out of that sense of mission, that they strove to be as diverse as American music was.

"And they were the most welcoming to young people. You could go in and watch artists actually grow on that stage. I think that's just mesmerizing, and you still find it at Club Passim. If this place has done anything for which it should be totally proud, it is the wish for success that audience and artist, staff and volunteers bring to this room. They want to see people on the stage grow, find their artistic voice, develop it and be successful."

Her first marriage, to Bob Siggins, led her to Washington, D.C., where she worked for the Festival of American Folklife.

In 1974, a new marriage to Columbia law professor (now former Yale president) Benno Schmidt, took her to New York. When that marriage ended in 1980, she found herself more alone and adrift than she had ever been. On her loneliest Thanksgiving, she wandered into a soup kitchen run by Gretchen Buchenholz, a pioneer of the homeless, anti-hunger, and AIDS-relief movements.

"She took one look at me, and barked, `What are you doing? Looking for something to do?' I said `sure' and was immediately put to work. `Now, what are you doing tomorrow?' she said, and gave me the address of a shelter that needed help. I just loved her style. She knew how to make people feel useful, believed that everyone has something to give back. Within two years, I was the one barking, `Get over here and help!' I really got good at it, loved it, learned how to find people's comfort level, and get them involved."

Old lessons from Club 47 quickly resurfaced.

"When I started developing food pantries and soup kitchens for homeless and hungry people and people with AIDS, my ability, without any self-consciousness, to accept street people as just ordinary folks was a direct outgrowth of that Club 47 family."

She moved back to Boston in 1996 and soon found herself involved in Club Passim. She is a cheerful whirlwind there, with a gift for recruiting people to chores at hand in ways that make them feel flattered they were asked.

She recently launched a Celebrity Series, asking high-profile coffeehouse alumni, such as Dar Williams, Tom Rush, Greg Brown, and the Nields, to do special benefit shows for Club Passim members. The shows enhance the value of becoming a supporting member, which works much the way public television and radio membership does.

Beyond the economic stability a member base offers, it reminds people that Club Passim, like Club 47, is a community possession and responsibility. Future stars committed to shows include Vega, Colvin, and her old fellow beanie-resister, Baez.

"In the '60s, we lucked into a party that didn't end for 10 years," Siggins Schmidt said. "Folk music is more elaborate now; it's a business. You can market yourself, be your own entrepeneural folk business, and I find that so exciting."

—January 4, 1998

A hard career's happy ending Chris Smither

The word "career" has different meanings. In the most common usage, it describes a lifetime occupation, a permanent profession. In an older, more obscure definition, it refers to a race course or other swift path. That would seem to better describe what most pop artists experience as a music career these days: fast, risky, and quickly concluded.

For Arlington songwriter Chris Smither, music is finally beginning to feel like a career in the way most people use the word. He has spent his share of years feeling he was on a racetrack without a plug's chance to win, place, or show. He has also felt his life careering helplessly through the pop sky, knowing only that when it landed, it would hurt.

Now, at 54, he does not talk about his superb new Hightone CD "Drive You Home Again" the way most musicians discuss their latest project, using urgent terms like "turning point," "breakthrough," or "new direction." He is deeply proud of it, as anyone with ears would be, but he conveys a sense that he's really gotten the hang of this. Not that he is in a rut, by any means, but that he has found his groove. In fact, what struck him most this time out was the ease with which the songs came.

"Don't get me wrong," he said. "Songwriting is still the hardest thing I've ever tried to do. But beginning with the last record, I just started feeling like there's no uncertainty anymore. I know what I'm doing; I know I'm a songwriter. I'm not pretending anymore. I know how this is done, know when they're good and when they need work. So there was a degree of confidence going in that was never really there before."

It is impossible to hear his songs and not be struck by the degree of craft with which he builds them. His songs draw on simple blues and folk structures, such as stanzas that each begin with a different woman's name, a chorus that echoes the call of a street vendor. But in them, Smither tackles the toughest questions of life, the ones people leading examined lives never stop pondering and know they will never answer. If there is a guiding theme to his songs, it is that the questioning is the answer, or, as he wrote in the title song, "Every step is destination."

"When some people get older, they quit thinking," he said. "You sort of get into a lifestyle that works, and the trouble is you start to think that you've got it figured out. And you don't. To me, the essence of staying interested is in making sure you remember that you haven't gotten it figured out, that constant process of trying to stay in touch with the unutterable, the imponderable, the total mystery of it all. As long as you keep asking those questions, you keep growing."

If Smither speaks with the wizened serenity of a survivor, he's earned his wisdom. His early career resembled Sherman's march through Georgia. Unfortunately, Smither was not Sherman, he was Georgia. Always a stunning guitarist, bluesman, and songwriter (Bonnie Raitt called him "my Eric Clapton" and had a '70s hit with his song "Love Me Like a Man"), his early years were ravaged by alcoholism and brutal disappointment.

His only major-label album fell into the void of one label buying out another and was never released. The shock of that sent him into an alcoholic tailspin. It would be more than 10 years before an uncertain but clearly improved—and sober—Smither would record again in 1985. Much of the reflective power in his songs now comes from that healing.

As a songwriter, he no longer trades in the quick rush of falling in and out of love, but in the long, hard nights of staying there; not in the brooding angst of not knowing, but in the slow, stubborn process of finding out. His songs are ultimately kind and loving, but they are tough.

"The whole point is that with love, and life itself, it's possible to keep them in a constant state of renewal," he said. "Crisis seems inherently more interesting; we're built for it. What I try to point out is that in between crises is where the real stuff is; that's where you really live. How do we make that fun? You don't have to make it exciting; it is exciting. You just have to learn how to look at it and how to talk about these kinds of things in songs."

Smither is among the most consistently successful club and concert attractions on the acoustic circuit these days, but he also knows that the complex songs he's writing, however well crafted, are not the stuff of pop skyrockets. But that's OK ; he knows what happens to skyrockets.

"Love doesn't tie itself up into a cute little bow," he said. "It's the effort that makes it worthwhile. It sounds trite, but it's about caring, thinking about things, not taking things for granted...It's what interests me. But it's hard sometimes to think about writing contemporary pop songs about those kinds of things, because we're so conditioned to think that's not what's going to sell. Those aren't things that are going to resolve themselves in time for the commercial."

"But you know what? For me, the nicest things people say after shows is that I seem like a nice guy. I don't want to seem mean anymore, or depressed and blue. I want to seem like somebody people would like to know. And I actually believe that if they pay attention to my songs, they will have a pretty good idea of what kind of person I am. So when they say that, I know they're really saying it about me."

—April 9, 1999

The harder the knocks, the sweeter the song
Brooks Williams

Ten years ago, nearly everyone in the Boston folk scene was certain Brooks Williams would be a star. The Northampton songwriter was a phenomenal guitarist, equally at home on searing Delta blues or confessional contemporary ballad. He was a provocative, literate, and inviting writer with a knack for reflective songs that seemed at once personal and panoramic. And there was that voice, a pure, warm tenor full of honest satin that gave everything he did an alluring, gentle resonance. His soothing style reminded many of a young, blues-tinted James Taylor. This boy, folkies thought, has pop potential.

Williams went on to build a sturdy folk-size career, but the high-beams of pop stardom never found him. This perplexed critics and disappointed fans. It nearly destroyed Williams.

"For the last 10 years, I've been forced into a corner I never wanted to be in," he said. "I felt like I had to choose between being seen as a guitarist, an interpreter, or a songwriter, and I always felt that was so unfair. The corner I felt most pushed into was the sensitive male singer-songwriter who plays guitar in open tunings. And I really think of myself as a guitarist first, who can write some songs but can also interpret other people's songs, and who really digs playing roots music. It felt like I wasn't getting the roots of what I was doing out; I wasn't getting the blue notes out."

Those blue notes shimmer through Williams's new Signature CD, "Hundred Year Shadow," his most personal and adventurous disc in years. His own songs are as warmly inviting as ever, but also have wonderful edges to them, riding along tight guitar pulses before exploding into the sweet release of sweepingly natural melodic arcs and curves. He also gallivants with the frisky freedom of a sure master, offering exquisitely melodic instrumentals and diverse covers by blues eccentric Ted Hawkins, Irish band Nomos, and the Beatles. The CD sounds like just what it is, a homecoming.

In 1989, Williams released his dazzling debut disc, "North from Statesboro,"

I woke up one night in a hotel room in Manitoba. I was so distraught, and I sat by the window watching the sun come up over the flatland. It was the most beautiful thing I'd ever seen and just acknowledging that was my road back. It said, there's more to life, more to you, than the music business. —Brooks WIlliams showcasing his fiery blues guitar virtuosity, but also his smooth, pop-friendly songwriting. The trouble began when those grand early expectations met the marketing realities of the '90s. A tiny crack in the wall had let a few new folk songwriters into the mainstream pop world.

"After that, I began to get all muddled, to lose track of my roots," he said. "I maybe got a little too excited about the possibilities; that if you had a little bit of a pop thing going, you were going to be the next big thing. I think if you look back at the acoustic records that were coming out in '93, '94, you'll see a lot of people were going for a sound that might appeal to more commercial interests, going for the hit. All of us were a little guilty of that, I think. I was just so excited; everything seemed so possible."

In 1992, he signed a four-record deal with the respected Celtic label Green Linnet, who wanted to enter the songwriter market with Williams as flagship of its new fleet.

The label's interest in that market quickly waned, however, and Williams found himself a flagship without a fleet. Because he had built such a loyal club following, and his records sold so well from the stage, Green Linnet stuck with him, but there was no possibility it would launch him to mainstream pop success. That dream kept eating at him, though, driving him into a dark period he is still not ready to talk about.

"All I can say is I spent a lot of time in the bottle, a lot of time contemplating things that were not healthy," he said. "And then I woke up one night in a hotel room in Manitoba. I was so distraught, and I sat by the window watching the sun come up over the flatland. It was the most beautiful thing I'd ever seen and just acknowledging that was my road back. It said, there's more to life, more to you, than the music business. That was the summer of 1997, and I came home and started working on giving up all the discouragement and enjoying what I had."

What he had was, in fact, considerable. Through all the years he bemoaned his inability to crack the pop stratosphere, he had never stopped working. He was as firmly established on the folk circuit as any of the folk heroes, like Patty Larkin, Bill Morrissey, and Greg Brown, who had inspired him to be a musician. As he worked on his new attitude of contentment, he was approached by the hot new Western Massachussetts label Signature. To Signature, Williams was a star.

"They told me they felt I was a guitarist who could write songs but also knew how to cover other songs and play roots music, and they wanted me to do all that. It was the first time I'd felt my own image of what I do reflected back to me in such a clear way. This record is almost like me coming to my senses, waking up from a nightmare and coming back to a place I had never intended to leave. The only difference is that what has happened in between made me a better guitar player, a more mature writer, a better singer. I never meant to leave the music, but

I know now that I did; that's what I realized making this record. And now I'm back where I started, back where I belong."

—*March 26, 1999*

Keeping the home in homemade music John McGann

Every day, John McGann thanks his lucky stars he is not a star. The Roslindale guitarist and mandolin player is as busy as any globe-trotting superstar, in constant demand as accompanist in bluegrass, Celtic, and modern folk circles. He also runs a thriving business transcribing music for everyone from mandolin superstar David Grisman to hobbyists who want to learn old Leo Kottke tunes.

"Because I have my own business, I get to be a dad," said McGann, waving toward the squealing sounds of his 18-month-old daughter, Hannah. "I get to hang around here, work at my own schedule. I don't do any major touring, so I get to be with my family a lot, and I always have time for my own music."

Not that his is a languid life. In the last month or so, McGann performed with bluegrass legend Tony Trishka and Berklee string department chairman Matt Glaser at Club Passim, with hot songwriting star Jennifer Kimball at the ultra-hip Lizard Lounge, and with septuagenarian Irish accordion master Joe Derrane at a wedding and a couple of local concerts.

He is also working on two instruction books for Mel Bay publishers, the lion of the guitar-book business, and a 140-tune collection of Irish traditional music being compiled at Boston College. As half of the duo Rust Farm, along with Maine songwriter Chris Moore, he just finished their second CD. Their music was featured on the soundtrack of John Sayles' recent film, "Limbo."

Mason Daring, who does the music for all of Sayles' films and whose Daring Records also produced Rust Farm's first CD, said he loved working with McGann. Daring said that, to him, McGann is to the guitar what Nashville giant Mark O'Connor is to the fiddle.

"His playing is very authentic," Daring said from his Marblehead studio, where he is finishing the score for a new Meryl Streep film. "John has tremendous technical skills, tremendous speed and clarity, and yet there's kind of a homespun quality on top of it. So he's swift but folksy. Usually, it's one or the other, but John's that rare player who can sound genuine and like a genius at the same time."

Seamus Connolly is a renowned Irish fiddler and music coordinator of the Boston College Irish studies department. He often uses McGann as accompanist for his concerts, and commissioned him to score a collection of Irish traditional melodies he is compiling for Boston College.

"He's one of the few guitarists I've ever encountered who can play fast reels up to speed," Connolly said. "He's accomplished at accompanying many kinds of music, from specific Irish styles to Scottish tunes and American folk styles. With his understanding of Irish music and his sophisticated knowledge of composition, I knew he'd find the right way to notate the tunes. John hears the subtleties many transcribers miss, knows how important they are, and knows how to notate them."

McGann grew up in New Jersey, and acknowledges he was drawn to the guitar by nothing more exotic than his father's having one and forbidding him to touch it. His secret noodlings, encouraged by his father once they were discovered, led McGann to the great mystery of the guitar, and he is still happily unraveling it. "Every door that opens," he said, "leads you into a new mansion, full of rooms you've never explored."

What fascinated him was not any particular genre, but the way the guitar traveled; what a completely different instrument it was in the hands of country picker Merle Travis than it was in the urbane care of jazz great Tal Farlow.

In 1977, he entered Berklee College of Music, seeing it as the most adventure-friendly of major music schools; a place he could major in dabbling. He was increasingly being drawn to folk styles, particularly bluegrass, but he also discovered he had a knack for transcribing complex, improvised, traditional tunes.

After graduating, he felt obliged to try making a living as a musician, and joined a top-40 lounge band. Asked the group's name, he leaned forward, much the way Marlon Brando did before saying, "The horror, the horror!" at the end of "Apocalypse Now." In that same tone of voice, McGann hissed, "Tiffany!"

"It was squalid, man, really horrendous," he said, "playing six nights a week, five sets a night in places like the Sheraton Tara. I went screaming back to Boston after one tour and decided that, from then on, no matter what, I'm not going to play music I don't like for money."

With that, he began an illustrious piecemeal career, working in locally celebrated groups like the bluegrass-jazz duo Off Center, with Japanese banjoist Hiro Arita, and the smartly rowdy Beacon Hillbillies. He also began playing Irish music on guitar and his newfound love, the mandolin. He sat in at local Irish sessiuns, or informal music gatherings, where he met Connolly.

His next Tiffany-epiphany came when he worked briefly for a huckster who advertised that he could turn people's poems into song hits. McGann wrote music to their humble verse, which was recorded and sent back to clients, along with a hefty bill.

He hated the hustle of it but began looking for honest ways to do similar work. His years learning guitar solos off scratchy old records had given him a sharp ear, not just for the notes but the nuance of instrumental music, and he still enjoyed exercising the composition skills he'd acquired at Berklee.

He began his Original Custom Transcription Service in 1981, and has been as busy as he cares to be ever since. His clients have included such guitar and mandolin heroes as Grisman, Richard Thompson, Clarence "Gatemouth" Brown, Sam Bush, and Tony Rice, but most of his work comes from hobbyists who love music they cannot find in any published music books.

The way it works is that people send him recordings they want scored. He listens, estimates how long the process will take, and offers an appraisal based on an hourly rate.

In 1993, he heard the rustic yet intelligent songs of Chris Moore, and formed Rust Farm with him. McGann regards it as his only serious, permanent ensemble commitment.

With his talents, McGann could probably have become, if not a star, one of those guitar heroes he admires. Any regrets?

"You know, my ambition was much more to try to be a good musician," he said, "to understand as much as I could about how music works and get better at doing things. I'm just not the front-man kind of guy, I guess; I like to be a co-conspirator.

"When I'm trying to play music, I don't want it to be the wonder of me," he continued. "Virtuosity is worthless in itself. Being able to play an instrument with facility is monkeys with typewriters. It's mechanics. So it's amusing to me when I see people in music who have a big head about themselves. Because it's not about them; it's about the music. Just because a person is a great virtuoso does not mean they cannot play great music, but it doesn't mean that they can, either."

—August 15, 1999

Folk humor: finding laughs—and songs—in family
Don White

Don White has made a career out of laughing at Lynn. Or, put more precisely, the Lynn songwriter-comedian has become a star on the national folk circuit by getting audiences to laugh about life and hard times in the working-class neighborhoods where he was raised and still lives.

With the release of his warm, insightful and often hilarious live CD, "Brown Eyes Shine," the 42-year-old White displays a rare gift for allowing audiences to laugh and examine their own lives at the same time. He focuses on his own family life, raising two teenage children and struggling to make ends meet, the mood veering with startling quickness from sharp satire to harrowingly intimate reflection.

Lynn is more of a backdrop to his humor now, but when he was starting out, his signature song was, "I'm from Lynn, What Can I Say?" The laughs were less on the city itself than outsiders' perceptions of it. In one verse, for instance, he extolled the splendors of Lynn's affluent neighbor Nahant, then wondered what curse must have been placed on people there that, whenever they went anywhere, they had to first drive through Lynn.

"Lynn's not funny," White said at the kitchen table of his small West Lynn house. "But I grew up around people who, when they were under pressure, were funny. When somebody's hurting in our family, we tell jokes. Doesn't mean we're disrespectful; it's how we relieve tension. Lynn is a town that presents pressure, and humor is how our family reacts to pressure. So when I look at this town, which I hated, which broke my heart, which I love and which I call home—which I have all these feelings about— I make jokes. It's how I gain perspective."

As "Brown Eyes Shine" opens, it is his 16-year-old daughter Ariel who is presenting the pressure. He tells the audience he has learned to begin every request to her with, "I'm not trying to oppress you, but . . ." When an argument over homework gives him a nosebleed, he troops back to her room and says, "See what you do to me? Every time we argue about your homework, my brain explodes." Utterly unfazed, she replies, "That's cool, dad."

Most of White's humor, and his best songs, connect to real life that vividly. He spent his formative years knocking back and forth between folk coffeehouses and comedy clubs, and learned that just getting a laugh was not enough. There were different kinds of laughs, and he knew which ones he wanted.

"There's the shocked laugh," he said, "when people are nervous. Then there's tricked laughter, when they realize they've been set up. There's a laugh that comes from victim humor, you know, jokes about that idiot in the toll booth, that guy from India who can't make change for me. But I know what the best one sounds like, the one that says, `Oh my God, I can't believe he said that—that's just how my mother is, too.' That's the shared laugh, and I'm always looking for that one."

White's road to a music career, like his road away from and back home to Lynn, was rocky, littered with wasted years and alcohol abuse. He grew up a few blocks from where he lives now, in a typical Irish-American working-class home. His father worked for General Electric, as did the fathers of nearly all his friends.

Already a hard drinker at 19, he and his wife, Terry, could not wait to get out of Lynn. Beginning in 1974, they spent years wandering the country, scurrying briefly back to Lynn, then drifting off again. He imagined himself to be developing a musical career but knows better now.

"You know, I drank and was an idiot," he said. "I had this great big block of time—my whole 20s, basically—where I just sat at some bar pontificating about having a career."

The Whites' love-hate relationship with Lynn led them to take a crack at the rustic idylls of rural Maine. After a few years of that, Lynn started to look a lot better.

"There was tremendous metamorphosis for me after coming back here," he said. "I left Lynn because I thought, who would want to live here? I couldn't wait to get out. So I moved to Maine, thinking my kids would grow up in the country. Then I actually had kids, and it all kind of clicked in to me what home really was. I thought, I really need my mother and father; I need to be in a neighborhood where I know people. I need baby sitters."

"Suddenly I realized that everything I ran away from was what was important to me. I'd had wonderful relationships with my grandparents, and my kids were growing up without really knowing theirs. I needed help; I wasn't a rock. I needed the support of family and friends and help finding a decent job."

In moving back home, White began the slow process of getting serious about his life. Shortly after getting sober in 1989, he got a job for Sentry, now called ADT. He still works there.

"Lynn is unique in some ways," he said. "It's not one of those towns that suddenly turned into malls. My son Lawren had essentially the same paper route my dad had 60 years ago. Even though people criticize Lynn—and it is a tough place—I'm lucky it's my home. I can walk to my mom's house, my brother lives right over there, my sister lives right around the corner up here. I'm always running into people I grew up with. It's still here."

White has his own web site (www.donwhite.net), where he sells his CDs and invites fans to contribute jokes—or hire him for their own parties and special occasions. Half of his work now comes that way, he said proudly.

"I want to design my career to suit my life, not the other way around. The Internet has leveled the playing field. You don't have to sell yourself to a record label in order to sell your records to an audience. You can do it all yourself."

Everything about the settled-in sound of his new CD, the confident, self-effacing humor, the breezy satires and starkly confessional ballads, suggests an artist who knows he's found his niche, who has finally, in every way possible, come home.

"When I look at an audience," he said, "I don't care if they showed up in Volvos or took the bus. I know their lives are hard. Somebody in their family is sick, they hate their job, or one of their kids is on dope. Every one of those people wants some hope, wants to relieve some tension, wants some sense that it can all turn out okay. That's what I'm bringing with me, a sense that you can have some fun with your life, no matter how hard it's been, and that you're better and stronger for going through the hard times."

—June 6, 1999

Art Thieme *comes home*

Chicago in 1960 was an exciting place for a young boy falling in love with folk music, but as Art Thieme strolled the downtown streets, it all started eating at him again. The stuff he was hearing on records and at the coffeehouses was great, but he knew something was missing. He wanted to know where these folk songs came from.

Ever since his girlfriend had dragged him to the Gate of Horn to see "something called an Odetta," Art had been hooked. He remembered listening to country music on the WLS Barn Dance radio show and, as he listened to Odetta, he could tell that those hillbilly songs were somehow connected to the tough field hollers and tender Scottish ballads that Odetta, this sophisticated young black woman, was signing. But how?

photo courtesy Art Thieme

He started going to the hootenannies at the Gate of Horn and the Old Town School of Folk Music. Anybody who was in town was likely to drop by—Bob Gibson, Joan Baez, Peter LaFarge, Earl Robinson, Pete Seeger. He heard more and more songs; there was no end to them. He had devoured the folk music section at Rose Records, where he worked; but he knew there was something missing. These were real songs, about real lives; songs about slavery and tall ships, cowboys and queen's daughters. But the people singing them were mostly young city kids like himself. The more he heard, the more he wanted to know.

Thinking over all this, Art turned the corner and, as he stood in front of Kroch's and Bentano's, billed as "The World's Largest Bookstore," a frigid gust of wind whipped in off the lake, forcing him to turn into the doorway. In the back of the store, holding a huge pile of records, was a fellow Art had seen singing at the hootenannies. He always had a new song, and he seemed to get them from everywhere. His name was Sandy Paton, and he had just been hired by Kroch's to build up a folk record section for them.

"He must know something," Art thought, and wandered in. As he spilled out his frustrations and desires, his fruitless search for the real stuff, Sandy began to smile. It was a warm smile, with just a trace of "spider-to-the-fly" to it; a smile many people over the years would see just before Sandy answered their questions in a way that often changed their lives. Sandy Paton was just beginning a career as one of folk music's real missionaries; he always had time for a young kid who really cared, as Art obviously did.

Sandy answered Art's questions carefully, showing him some of the records he was buying for Kroch's; odd little records on labels Art had never heard of: Topic, Tradition, Folkways. Sandy explained to him about field recordings, how collectors would go to the mountains and prisons and sailing ships where working people made their own music and passed it along from generation to generation. Sandy suggested a few albums, smiled that smile again, and urged Art to come back any time.

Over the next few months, Art spent most of his lunch hours pestering Sandy about this collector or that field recording. He knew he was finally finding the real stuff, songs sung by actual miners and sailors, weavers and cowboys—and he knew it was starting to take over his life.

Art had started playing guitar and banjo, and Sandy urged him to sing more and to look around for songs himself. One day, though Sandy told Art was losing his new teacher. He and his wife Caroline were moving to New England. They wanted to do some of their own collecting.

"Before you go, Sandy," Art said, almost in a whisper—he was blushing furiously. "I've been thinking of becoming a folk singer. How do you do it? Where do you start?"

Sandy gave him that smile again. Twenty-five years later, he still remembers what he told Art. "We'd been doing all this talking about records; talking about folk music in the middle of the world's largest bookstore, for God's sake. I said, 'Take your guitar and get out there; go across country, meet the people, get a sense of them, learn their songs, learn how they live.' I told a lot of kids that back then, but Art's the only one I know who actually did it." He chuckles and says, "I wonder if he's ever forgiven me."

They said goodbye, and would not meet again for 17 years. Sandy and Caroline Paton moved to New England where, within a year, they started Folk Legacy Records. From North Carolina field recordings to younger singers like Bill Staines and Gordon Bok, no record label has most consistently representing what the Patons call "the continuing tradition;" the blending of old and new, authentic and revivalist, which for many defines contemporary folk music.

As for young Art Thieme, he took Sandy's advice. First, he tried a cross-country trip, retracing the Dust Bowl journeys of John Steinbeck and Woody Guthrie. The learning got hard in a hurry.

"A friend and I headed for California to meet the Okies working in the Salinas Valley lettuce fields," Art remembers, his face grim at the memory. "God, we were idealistic. We expected to meet Doc from Steinbeck's 'Cannery Row,' maybe Tom Joad out there organizing the workers. We did find Cannery Row: there was a coffeehouse, six bars, give antique shops, and 200 places selling salt-water taffy. We went down to Salinas, but the only thing that was there from

Woody's days was the incredible poverty. That was everywhere. I realized the America I was looking for was gone, except in the songs."

The trip only deepened Art's desire to look back into those songs.

"When I got back to Chicago, I started digging." Art's memories get softer now, and he begins to smile. "I'd record streetsingers, go to the old churches to hear the hymns, read pioneer journals, go back to the field recordings. I started learning where to look for the history behind the songs; how to connect them to real people. And this wasn't Woody's America or Steinbeck's. It was mine; Illinois, Lake Michigan, Chicago."

Rose Records got smaller and smaller for him. Pop music was so full of what Art calls "me songs." The deeper he got into folk music, and the lives behind them, the harder it got to sell Top-40. One day, he "got disgusted and just walked out." He decided if he believed in folk music so much, he should start singing for a living. It was not an easy transition.

"When I first started performing, I was serious beyond belief," Art recalls, grimacing and chuckling at the same time. "I just used to stand up there and sweat. It was grim."

Seeing Art Thieme perform today, it is hard to picture that. He is one of the most engaging and, to all appearances, natural performers of traditional songs in folk music today. He fills the stage, a big man, 40 years old, with a long graying beard and a physique midwesterners forgivingly call "healthy" ("It is little comfort to me," he often quips, "to know that a Douglas fir with my circumference would be 80 feet tall.")

He might be an intimidating figure were it not for the soft twinkling of his blue eyes, seeming always to be announcing some mischief, and a smile that testifies to his real affection for the songs he sings. And there's that voice, that incredibly gentle, deep voice. "There's a very soothing quality to Art's voice, "Caroline Paton says. "On a sad song, it sounds like a sob; and on a funny song, it sounds like a chuckle. But it's the same thing."

Art tends to string songs together, continuing to pick his guitar or banjo while he sets up the next song or launches into his endless repertoire of folk humor and one-liners: "They say suicide is the sincerest form of self-criticism," or "If we are what we eat, why am I not tall and slim—like a Twinkie?" This style makes every show he does unique and delightfully unpredictable.

"Art is hands-down my favorite folk singer," says Tom Martin-Erickson, co-producer of Wisconsin Public Radio's "Simply Folk" program. "He really is the one who got me excited about folk music. I've seen him more than any other performer, and he always surprises me. He finds songs that really speak to me, and he doesn't let anything get in the way. His humor keeps everything moving, and he's got so many songs. I saw him string together a half a set of insect songs once—and it was great."

Becoming a performer was a very deliberate process for Art; it took a long time. First came the music. He tries to keep an active repertoire of 500 songs.

"I think of a song as a story that just happens to have a tune," he says. "If it's a good tune, all the better. But I'll let a song go if it's got a phrase that doesn't ring true, that is not something someone would really say. That ruins it for me."

Then came the humor. Bruce "Utah" Phillips, the great songwriter and raconteur, once told Art, "You're not just on stage for the time you're making music; you're up there for the whole show. What you say in between songs is just as important as the songs."

From then on, Art says, "I tried to use humor to keep people interested. I want to fill those moments between songs in a way that keeps people in the world I want them in, whether it's for a Robin Hood ballad or a cowboy song. There's a whole wonderful world of folklore and folk humor to help me do that."

Art put himself in front of every audience he could, from the Chicago club scene, where the late shows were described by Chicago Magazine as "most closely resembling the bar scene from 'Star Wars,' to quiet coffeehouses (he played Thursday nights at the No Exit Coffeehouse for 15 years); from protest rallies and folk festivals to churches and grade schools.

"These songs transport me to other times," Art says, his eyes glowing. "It's like sweeping the scum of the present off the top of the pond and letting us look down into the depths of history."

He stops, looks surprised, clears his throat. He prides himself on simplicity, so when the poet in him slips out, he blushes. "Where was I? I try to show that in the schools, and wherever I play for people who may not know this music as well as I do. These songs show us our kinship with other times.

"Whether it's a folk club, a school, or a father-and-son Cub Scout troop, I know I cam make people like these songs if they'll let me."

Art is very serious now, leaning forward, eyes bright. "For whatever reason, these songs have become my cause. I've seen them go from popular entertainment to almost museum pieces. But I don't care. I'm willing to present these songs any way they're accepted. And when people say, 'We didn't know we'd like this so much,' that's when i know I've done my job."

In 1978, with two find Kicking Mule records to his credit, Art was invited to a folk festival in Connecticut. With his passion and puns in full flower, he brought the house down. After his first song, Sandy and Caroline Paton, who were hearing Art for the first time, looked at each other and nodded. When his set was finished, Sandy approached Art, holding out his hand. On his face was smile Art had not seen for 17 years, but that he remembered very well. Uh-oh. What now?

"You should be on Folk Legacy Records, Art," said Sandy.

It was Art's turn to smile now. "I'd love to, Sandy; it's about time."

With the release of his second Folk Legacy album, "The Wilderness Road," Art Thieme is doing the best work of his career. From canal-digging songs and loggers' laments to standards like "Wabash Cannonball" and contemporary ballads like Si Kahn's "Spinning Wheels of Home," Art's easy command rolls the tunes together into one long, sweet song.

Even the humor nestles in gently, seamlessly. "I had a cow, she slobbered bad," he sings in "Down in Arkansas." What other could make that line sound pretty? That he might be the only singer who would want to is not the point. A lifetime of respect for these songs, and for the folk humor he calls "jokelore," is the tie that binds; and it eloquently makes the case for the Patons' "continuing tradition."

Perhaps it is working again with Sandy Paton, feeling his own past brought into the present, that is shining through in his music. As Art Thieme sings his choruses into the Folk Legacy microphones these days, a warm and familiar smile from the man behind the mixing board welcomes him home.

—Autumn, 1986
Originally appeared in Sing Out! the Folk Song Magazine
Used by permission, Sing Out Corporation

me & thee Coffeehouse: *30 years fanning folk's flame*

The secret to the remarkable success of the me & thee Coffeehouse in Marblehead, MA, is embedded in its name. The indefatigable little club begins its 30th consecutive season Friday, a feat nearly unprecedented for any live music venue, much less a nonprofit, volunteer-run folk club in the parish hall of the Unitarian Universalist Church here.

What explains it? It has certainly had its share of major stars appear, including Pete Seeger, Tom Paxton, Suzanne Vega, Shawn Colvin, Nanci Griffith, Dar Williams and Ellis Paul.

But to founder Anthony Silva, who is known to millions as the business editor for WBZ-TV and WBZ radio in Boston, the answer has less to do with who performs than with the community of fans and volunteers who, time and again, have simply refused to let the coffeehouse close. It is to them that the me & thee refers, what Silva calls "the community within."

"There have always been people willing to step up and say we can't let this go," Silva said, "even though there have been lots of storms come to the front doors. The real reason we've lasted is that people keep being drawn to what the entire idea of the coffeehouse community represents, and that is a simpler time, a more personal way to spend an evening. We share some food, some coffee, we sit around a fireplace and listen to music. What could be more simple than that?"

This should not suggest me & thee is not a front-rank venue. According to David Tamulevich, whose Fleming-Tamulevich and Associates is the nation's largest folk music management agency, me & thee is a major player in the modern folk world.

"It is one of the premier coffeehouses in New England," he said, "and one of the better-known folk clubs in the country. One of the real marks of how respected it is is that even established folk stars like John Gorka, Greg Brown and Cheryl Wheeler want to go back there to play."

An evening at me & thee feels more like a long conversation than a concert. Most shows take place in the parish hall, which has been the site of local theater troupes since the Peabody Pew Company in the 1920s. It has a fireplace at the back of the stage, surrounded by bookcases and old pictures. The performer is less than 5 feet from the front tables. And me & thee (the small-case spelling is designed to keep the name from seeming too Biblical, since it is a secular coffeehouse) is known for its leisurely breaks, often lasting up to an hour, during which audience members snack on homemade pastries and visit.

"The ideal me & thee performer," said Silva, "is someone who becomes part of our community for that evening, who is accessible, who comes in and enjoys being with our audience and our staff. The kinds of performers we enjoy having are the ones we could imagine inviting into our homes. And there are lots of them out there, performers who have built careers around places like this and who love to come early and stay late."

At me & thee, the real stars of the show always have been the volunteer staffers, which this year number nearly 70. They are not only the people who cook the food, set up the tables, run the sound system and take the tickets, they are the core of the community that attends the coffeehouse. It always has been central to me & thee's personality—and its success—that a large enough staff be recruited that volunteers know they won't be put to work if they come to a show on a night off.

A number of volunteers gathered around a big table behind the coffeehouse recently to discuss the club's remarkable tenure. They came from Marblehead, Lynn, Swampscott and Salem, and nary a one is in the music business.

Anne Townsend is a child and family counselor, Chris Greene a landscape architect, his wife, Jeb Kahn-Greene, a hospital planner. Ellen Witlinger is a young adult author whose new book, "Hard Love," is based on a song she first heard at the coffeehouse. Pete Rogers is a human resources director, David Pritchard and Kathy Sands-Boehmer are book editors, David Jenkins, an entrepreneurship coach, and his wife, Dianne, an artist.

They were all on hand last year when it looked as if me & thee might not reach its 30th birthday. Asked how close it came to closing, Townsend said, "Three-hundred and twenty-six dollars, that's how close. That's all there was left."

The crisis came largely because two big-name acts canceled, and the crew had to realize the club was more financially dependent on these celebrities than they thought. "We discussed how local we were if that could happen to us," Kahn-Greene said. "Are we just trying to draw the person who's going to drive 25 miles to see one particular performer, or do we want to be a place that's part of the North Shore scene, that people come to because they know what to expect? We don't just want people coming because their favorite artist is here, but because they feel like it's their place."

A Web site (meandthee.org) was started, but the group also started putting up fliers around town, asking local schools for ideas on special nights students might enjoy. The fall lineup is designed to cover the folk waterfront, from hot young stars Lori McKenna and Jess Klein on Friday to Irish music legend Tommy Makem Oct. 15; from major folk stars John Gorka and Patty Larkin to the Dixieland charms of the New Black Eagle Jazz Band and the gentle balladry of Bill Staines and Jeanie Stahl.

Asked their favorite me & thee memories, no one waxed about catching this star or that on the way up. They spoke of moments when performers departed from their planned sets and became even more a part of the 30-year-long conversation that is me & thee. There was the night Sally Rogers played her first set in a full-body pumpkin costume she'd just made for Halloween, and the time Christine Lavin spent the break painting people's fingernails.

They remembered an electrical storm knocking the power out, but Staines singing behind the mikes anyway, joking that he needed them for confidence. And British folk singer David Jones hauling most of the crowd up on stage with him to sing.

Silva recalled 83-year-old Sam Shalfin, who lived next door to the church, coaxed on stage to read his favorite poem, "Gunga Din," and the crowd enthralled by its archaic charms.

"Those are the moments that made it clear that me & thee is not tied to who's the biggest, who's the best, who's going to draw the most," Silva said, "but to the feeling that this place survives because of its own community."

"It was only a few years ago that we were members of the audience," Pritchard said. "But after a while, it was such a friendly place, we wanted to step over to the other side and volunteer. I can't imagine that change happening at the Tweeter Center, you know, going a few times, then being moved to want to work the refreshment stands. But there's something about the social aspect here. The concert and the break start to feel like they're part of the same ambience."

—*September 19, 1999*

The pop world is ignoring folk again: why didn't we notice?
Dar Williams, Jess Klein, Catie Curtis, music managers Ralph Jaccodine and Ron Fierstein, Capitol CEO Roy Lott

Is the singer-songwriter revival over? Beginning in the mid-1980s, a bumper crop of songwriters grew from coffeehouses to national stardom, beginning with Bill Morrissey, Patty Larkin, and Greg Brown, followed by the even greater commercial success of Nanci Griffith, Suzanne Vega, John Gorka, and Shawn Colvin.

The wave only grew in the '90s, with the convincing local climbs of the Story, Ellis Paul, Martin Sexton, and Catie Curtis, and a spate of national folk-pop stars, cresting with Jewel's 1996 break to Madonna-like superstardom and the blockbuster 1997 Lilith Fair tour of women songwriters launched by Sarah McLachlan. Locally, the late '90s saw the astonishingly rapid rise of Dar Williams.

Now, to borrow from Pete Seeger, folkies may well be asking, "Where have all the songwriters gone?" Nationally, the songwriter well seems to have run suddenly dry. The Boston scene, a bellwether for folk appeal since the 1960s, has not produced a genuine national star since Williams, with the possible exception of Jess Klein, whose new Ryko CD, "Draw Them Near," is selling respectably (about 500 a week, according to SoundScan and Ryko) and garnering some national airplay, but has hardly been the breakthrough disc many predicted.

Roy Lott, president and CEO of Capitol Records Group, said, "There was a peak of time during the heat of Lilith, for lack of a better term, when the industry—and by that I mean particularly radio and record companies—were more positive toward the singer-songwriters than they were before or probably are today. There were lots more songwriters being signed during the Lilith thing, both female and male. I guess one way to follow the trends is by who managers and agents are shopping to record companies. Now of course, we're getting everyone shopping us the new Britney Spears and Christina Aguilera."

It is revealing that everyone interviewed—Lott, two managers who represent major-label and indie-label stars, and songwriters Williams, Curtis, and Klein—agreed on two things. One is that major labels have considerably cooled their interest in acoustic-based, lyric-driven songwriters. The other is that the audience for such music is every bit as large, vibrant, and loyal as it was in the '90s, perhaps even more so.

Ron Fierstein, whose AGF management agency helped ignite the songwriter revival by obtaining major-label deals for Suzanne Vega and later Shawn Colvin—and who now also manages Williams and Mary Chapin Carpenter—explains this paradox with what he calls the conglomeration of the music industry, resulting in an inevitable quickening of the profit pulse at major labels. And songwriters, like fine wines, need time to ripen.

"In the early '80s, when I was trying to get Suzanne a record deal," he said, "and even in the late '80s, when I was doing the same for Shawn, you would sit down with a label and talk about a three-album deal, a strategy to break an artist over three albums. I remember specifically with Suzanne, we said let's try to get 100,000 on the first, maybe 250,000 on the second, then go gold and break on the third. That was a real game plan, and the contracts were written accordingly.

"Because all the labels are part of these big corporate entities now, they're not run like the independent entrepreneurial companies they were in the '60s and '70s, when this industry grew up. They are now run like other corporations where the executives are under tremendous pressure to deliver on quarterly numbers, and they have to think short-term, look for product they can get a quick return on. They can't worry about long-term artist development very much, if at all."

As a result, there is also renewed emphasis on hits, labels wanting to see hit potential in an act's first single. This runs counter to the traditional aesthetics of the songwriter, from whom fans expect deeper, more complex musical explorations.

"When I ask at my shows if there are any requests," said Curtis, "I get at least 10 different songs people want to hear. That's really healthy for me, because I'm not constantly thinking about hits, thinking, `Oh, I've got to write another song like that one everyone wants to hear.' "

Boston manager Ralph Jaccodine has guided Ellis Paul to one of the most vibrant grassroots, indie-label careers in modern folk. He also manages local folk-rockers the Push Stars, who have had, at best, a troubled tenure at Capitol. He believes that at heart folk and pop are two distinct musical ecosystems.

"The folk world is more nurturing," he said. "You can take your time, have a real career. Say Ellis plays a coffeehouse on a weekend. That coffeehouse might have one show a month, so they really promote it, have a mailing list, and give it a lot of word-of-mouth in their community, talking Ellis up to their friends and neighbors. The Push Stars will play a club that has music six nights a week, three bands a night. The clubs don't market, they don't care, they treat the artists like animals. And you want to know our nice little secret? The Ellis Pauls and Catie Curtises and Dar Williamses of the world, they're doing great."

To Williams, the road between folk and pop diverges less at a musical crossroads than at a philosophical one.

"I see there are corporate-based careers and audience-based careers," she said. "And I think this is a very strong time for audience-based careers, which get to keep their edges, grow in their art and have strong audiences willing to grow with them. But one of the things that's allowed me to do all those things is that I haven't had to follow a corporate agenda."

Everyone interviewed believes that declining mainstream interest in the songwriter has actually had a positive effect on the genre. Most major labels are trimming rosters across the board, dropping solid songwriting stars such as former Capitol acts Richard Thompson and John Hiatt. The emergence of such commercially potent artists on independent labels—in all music genres—has greatly strengthened the marketing and distribution muscle of the indie industry. Independent labels now account for a startling 16.9 percent of total record sales, surpassing all the major music corporations but the largest, Universal Music Group.

And there are whispers about a new songwriter boom on the horizon. Professionals in both pop and folk are carefully watching Welsh songwriter David Gray, whose smart, elegantly melodic homemade CD, "White Ladder," was picked up by RCA and is climbing the charts. Colvin's new Columbia CD, due next spring, will also be a barometer for the mainstream viability of the genre. Capitol is very excited about their new find, alluring and literate Massachusetts songwriter Amy Correia.

"I want to be a musician and writer for my life," says Klein, explaining why Ryko's three-record deal appealed to her more than major-label interest—which was expressed, but with expectations of quick success. "It was important for me to go somewhere I could develop as an artist, plant seeds for a career that would last and not expect everything to happen overnight. I didn't feel that was quite possible with the majors."

When Curtis was on the EMI subsidiary Guardian, her label representative, who had worked with Barbra Streisand and Liza Minnelli, once watched her schmooze with fans after a show. "I think you need to work on your star attitude," he sniffed. It helped her see that she and the mainstream were not made for each other. She's now on Ryko, having a nice, folk-sized career.

"The industry's job is to look at the math interest of something," Curtis says, "whereas our job is to find our niche audience. So when the mainstream moves on to something else, we have that niche audience to ourselves all the more. We're less at risk of becoming the Starbucks of the folk world; it's easier to maintain our individuality as funky little artists."

Curtis and Williams each fondly described her fans as seekers—thoughtful people interested in leading examined and deeply felt lives. They believe such an audience will always exist, always be willing to look beneath the pop surface for music that moves them. They are also, by nature and preference, a nonmainstream audience—which suits Williams just fine.

"There's sort of this zeitgeist today that the big corporations have taken over, that there's no vibrancy or diversity in music. But I think it's our fault if we think they're winning. Music is more diverse and richer than ever, and audiences are following and supporting those things. I look out at my audiences every night, and I see no dearth of passion for this music from the people who like it. There's always a forest-and-trees effect in music, with Britney Spears, 'N Sync, and the Backstreet Boys being the forest right now. But in a country of 260 million people, the trees are pretty tall and strong."

—November 19, 2000

About the Author: Scott Alarik has written about folk music for the *Boston Globe* since 1986. He is the folk critic for National Public Radio's *Here and Now* news program, a frequent contributor to *Sing Out!*, and was for seven years editor of the *New England Folk Almanac*. He is also a folk singer and songwriter who performs regularly at coffeehouses near his home in Cambridge, Massachusetts.

About the Photographer: Robert Corwin has ranked among folk music's premier photojournalists for over 38 years. His work has been exhibited at the Library of Congress' American Folklife Center, the Newport Folk Festival, the New Orleans Jazz and Heritage Festival, and at galleries and museums throughout North America. His portraits can be seen on CDs by Peter, Paul and Mary, Odetta, and many other folk artists. Also a prolific commercial photographer, his photos were used for the official posters of the 2002 Winter Olympics. Corwin lives in Philadelphia, Pennsylvania.

Also available from Black Wolf Press

ELLIS PAUL'S NOTES FROM THE ROAD

SEE MORE

www.blackwolfpress.com
www.singsongbooks.com
www.robertcorwin.com